INSIGHT GUIDES

The world's largest collection of illustrated travel guides

Malaysia

Updated by Jeremy Cheam & Jessamyn Cheam Gwynne
Senior Executive Editor: Scott Rutherford

Editorial Director: Brian Bell

APA PUBLICATIONS

Part of the Langenscheidt Publishing Group

L

This edition of *Malaysia* represets a milestone in Apa Publications' award-winning *Insight Guide* series. Some 25 years have passed since Apa writers and photographers first ventured forth and discovered the many pleasures of this beautiful land. Since then, the forces of change and progress have left their indelible mark, but the Malaysia of the 1990s retains the same exotic appeal that first attracted modern-day travellers to its tropical shores. Its people, of course, still treat visitors with the same blend of friendly generosity and native charm.

In much the same way that old friends from different countries keep in touch, Apa has revisited Malaysia several times, noting with keen interest the many significant developments that have taken place over the years. The result is this memorable new version of *Insight Guide: Malaysia*. It features new text and photos, putting the country into a modern-day context, yet preserving Apa Publications' formula of presenting the complete picture of a destination.

The series was created back in 1970 by **Hans Höfer**, founder of Apa Publications and still the company's driving force. Each book encourages readers to celebrate the essence of a place rather than to try and tailor it to their expectations, and is edited in the belief that, without insight into a people's character and culture, travel can in fact narrow the mind rather than broaden it.

Höfer

The *Insight Guide* books are all carefully structured: the first section covers a destination's history and culture in a series of magazine-style essays. The main Places section provides a comprehensive run-down on the sights and things worth seeing and doing, with a little bit of practical advice and gossip thrown in for good measure. Finally, a fact-packed listings section contains all the information you'll need on travel, accomodation, shops, restaurants, and opening times. Complementing the text, the remarkable photography sets out to communicate, directly and provocatively, life as it is lived by the locals.

Apa's Singapore-based senior executive editor **Scott Rutherford** gave the overhaul of the book to **Jessamyn Cheam Gwynne**, also based in the Singapore office.

Gwynne, who has lived in the US and UK for 10 years, is by nationality Malaysian. She wrote and compiled several new essays for this new edition, including sections on history, the environment, religion, food, culture, handicrafts and performing arts.

Gwynne

For the field updating, Rutherford turned to Gwynne's brother, **Jeremy Cheam**, who resides in Malaysia's capital, Kuala Lumpur. Educated in England, Cheam travelled extensively throughout Europe and the Americas before finally returning to his native Malaysia to rediscover the wonders of the Orient with fresh insights and

Cheam

perceptions. Through his work as a Kuala Lumpur-based film director, he is able to travel to many neighbouring Asian nations, while his trips by motorcycle almost every Sunday take him the length and breadth of Malaysia. The book's places and travel tips sections were both updated by Cheam.

The essay on Malaysia's architecture was contributed by **Ricky Yeo**, editor of *Interiors Quarterly (IQ)* magazine, one of Singapore's most visually-stunning design magazines.

This new edition of *Insight Guide: Malaysia* has also been brought up to date by contributing updater **Joseph R. Yogerst**. Now based in California, Yogerst edited magazines in San Francisco and London before coming to Asia as the managing editor of *Discovery* magazine in Hong Kong. He has also been a contributing editor to *Conde Nast Traveler* magazine in New York, a special correspondent for the *International Herald Tribune*, and editor of *Sojourn* magazine. An accomplished travel writer, Yogerst has a Lowell Thomas Award from the Society of American Travel Writers as well as a PATA Gold Award for best magazine travel article in 1991.

Yogerst

The task of updating the previous *Malaysia* was accomplished by freelance writer **Susan Amy**, a native of the United Kingdom, who has lived in the South-East Asian region for several years. Having spent several months researching in the rain forest of Sarawak, she has become quite a Malaysia expert. For the book, she travelled to every corner of Malaysia, visiting villages and towns, holiday resorts as well as some of the more remote areas.

The line-up of photographers who helped make the book a visual success includes Kuala Lumpur-based **David Bowden**, as well as **Alain**

Amy

Evrard, **Joseph Lynch** and Singapore stalwarts **Wendy Chan** and **Jill Gocher**. Previous editions of *Insight Guide: Malaysia* were illustrated by veteran Apa contributors **Philip Little, Bill Wassman, Marcus Brooke, Manfred Gottschalk, Ingo Jezierski** and **D & J Heaton**. Also contributing nature and wildlife photos was Singapore-based bird specialist **Morten Strange**.

Most of the original material in the guide was gathered by Höfer, American journalist **Star Black** and veteran adventurer and author **Harold Stephens**. Their collective voice is still very much heard from in this book, as is that of **Sharifah Hamzah**, a Malaysian who conducted a comprehensive historical study of the country.

Finally, thanks go to the people of Malaysia who helped bring about this book and the previous 15 editions with their inimitable hospitality, generous nature and warm smiles.

To these and countless others, *terima kasih banyak*.
— *Apa Publications*

Stephens

CONTENTS

Preceding pages: Petronas Towers, Kuala Lumpur; boy and kite, on the east coast of the peninsula.

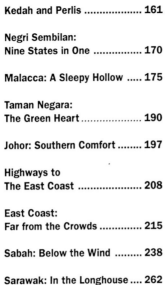

TRAVEL TIPS

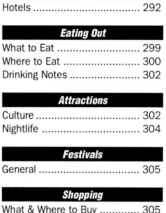

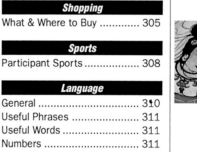

State Legislative Building, Negri Sembilan.

SELAMAT DATANG KE MALAYSIA

"Welcome to Malaysia" is the greeting that welcomes you inside the modern, air-conditioned corridors of Kuala Lumpur's new international airport. It is also a sentiment that will be warmly echoed by the smiling Malay, Indian or Chinese taxi driver who takes you from the airport into the booming capital city of Kuala Lumpur. Even if you enter Malaysia by road and arrive first at a small Malay *kampung* (village), this same friendly greeting will be warmly offered to you.

Over the centuries, Malaysia has been open to millions of visitors from all over the globe, and its people have changed, absorbed and adapted customs and traditions from far-flung countries to suit the Malaysian way of life.

What is the most accurate image of Malaysia? Travel brochures romantically depict a land of beaches with coconut palms and sands as fine as flour, lost idyllic islands and amazing coral reefs. On the other hand, the pages of Somerset Maugham's short stories paint vivid mental pictures of colonial bungalows set in the heart of a tea or rubber plantation, with tea served on the verandah by a young Malay boy, while the Indian *punkah wallah* moves the fan into action to keep the *orang putih* (white man) cool in the heat of the tropics. Another portrayal of Malaysia lies between the covers of naturalist Alfred Russell Wallace's *Malay Archipelago*, allowing us to imagine ancient jungles, screaming with monkeys, brimming with butterflies, and hiding legendary animals such as the most intelligent of primates (next to man), the orang-utan.

These accounts are far from contradictory; indeed Malaysia combines, album-like, every one of these visions... and more.

In Malaysia you will find yourself in many incongruously different scenarios. Your first day in Kuala Lumpur might find you changing money at an automated teller machine in the shadow of the world's tallest building. Or you may be gliding up and down the escalators of a glass-and-steel shopping centre crammed with

Preceding pages: Kuala Lumpur's rising skyline; Penang Bridge; traditional kite; top-spinner, east coast. <u>Left</u>, a night market in Kuala Lumpur.

designer shops, and stopping for some American fast-food. Then, you might be in Chinatown, with its bustling streets and old shophouses. At the market, voices are crying out their wares in a myriad tongues: Malay, Tamil, Hokkien, Cantonese, Punjabi or English – a remnant of the colonial days.

Driving out into the countryside, you will find Malay *kampung* (villages), the focus of a relaxed life containing traditional forms of work and leisure. Apart from the odd Mercedes parked outside the house of a villager who has made good in the city, and the numerous plastic items in daily use, you could well imagine yourself back in the last century. But this is the point: Malaysia binds its past closely with its present in a unique amalgam of cultures and customs.

You might also find yourself in the central jungle of the peninsula, where travel is principally by river, and where indigenous people choose to live a nomadic life on the treasures of the jungle – in spite of material enticements.

Venturing across the sea to the island of Borneo, you might climb Southeast Asia's highest mountain, or stay at a remote longhouse in Sarawak. Surprises and thrills abound throughout Malaysia.

Some of Malaysia's secrets will be unlocked from the pages of this guide; others are waiting for you to discover for yourself. You will find those idyllic beaches and islands, those rubber plantations (with the *punkah wallah* replaced by electric fans and air conditioning) and you will, if you venture out, find yourself in age-old jungles. But no matter how strange the sights are to you, there is an innate sense of being in a land that welcomes you to explore it – Malaysia beckons, as it has done for countless centuries.

The introductory sections of this book include comprehensive history chapters that may answer many of your questions about why Malaysia is as it is; other chapters describe the varied landscapes that make up Malaysia; and you will be introduced to the different racial groups that make up Malaysia's population, with some insight into their culture and customs.

Further into the book, you will be able to explore Malaysia the land, as details are given of some of the country's varied and fascinating destinations. We hope you will enjoy exploring Malaysia with us – "Selamat Datang!"

A young Malaysian patriot.

Gentle, young and growing – Malaysia is all this. But peel away the layer of modern-day life, and the kaleidoscope of Malaysia's history unfolds with a cast of Malays, Portuguese, Dutch, Chinese, Indians, Ibans, English and others. The legacy of the land abounds with ancient temple ruins, impregnable Portuguese fortresses, bejewelled Royal Malay *kris*, indigenous blowpipes and imposing British colonial buildings. The weaving of all this history all started in 35,000 BC.

Prehistoric Malaysia: The beginnings of human habitation in Malaysia are enveloped in shadows as deep as those cast by the equatorial rainforest, pieced together from ancient Indian, Chinese and Arab sources and archaeological discoveries. However, these origins are still rife with theories and speculations.

In Sarawak's Niah Caves, a *Homo sapiens* skull dating back to 35,000 BC has been discovered, providing the earliest evidence of human life in Malaysia. In the Malay peninsula itself, the earliest remains to have been excavated are only about 10,000 years old.

There is evidence that during the period of the Middle Stone Age (about 8,000 to 2,000 BC), Mesolithic people lived in rock shelters and caves in the limestone hills of the Malay peninsula. They used stone implements for cutting and grinding, as well as for hunting wild animals. A typical tool of these people was the hand axe, made by chipping a round pebble until a cutting edge was formed on one side. These people may have been the ancestors of the Negrito aborigines, today known as the Semang and Jakun people.

Around 2500 BC, the Proto-Malays, spreading south from Yunnan in China, made their way to the Malay peninsula and the islands beyond. They were also Stone Age people, but their stone implements were more sophisticated than those of the Negritos. Besides being hunters, they were also cultivators and sailors and thus lived a more settled

life. Eventually they forced the Negritos into the hills and jungles.

Much later, around 300 BC, a new wave of immigrants pushed the Proto-Malays inland. They were the Deutero-Malays and had advanced to using iron weapons and tools. The Deutero-Malays were in fact Proto-Malays who, through intermarriage, had mixed with Chinese from the Chou period, Indians from Bengal, as well as peoples of Arabic and Siamese blood. The Deutero-Malays and people from Java, Sumatra and other parts of Indonesia are the ancestors of today's Malays.

Indian influence: Through trade, the early inhabitants of the Malay peninsula were exposed to older civilisations. Located at the convergence of two major sea routes linking the great markets of India and China, the peninsula was a convenient stopover for Indian ships travelling further east.

The first Indian voyages made to the peninsula were estimated to have occurred less than 2,000 years ago. In order to prepare for the long voyage, some of the ships carried not only a big crew, but also a year's supply of food, including live chickens as well as a vegetable garden in a corner of the vessel.

Along the peninsula's coasts, the ships waited for the monsoon winds to change before continuing their journey. The Indian traders discovered that they could obtain gold, aromatic woods and spices here. They also discovered that by transporting their goods overland, from one side to the other, they could minimise the threat posed by pirates rampaging in the Straits of Malacca.

Soon, many settlements developed along the straits. Through contact with Indian traders, many native inhabitants became Hindus or Buddhists. These new converts built temples, the crumbling remains of which have been discovered in the state of Kedah. Some of the settlements grew to become Indianised kingdoms in which various features of Indian culture were adopted. The local rulers were known as *rajah* and many Brahmin rituals were adopted in the courts. Even today, this early Indian influence can still be seen. Some Malay words are borrowed from Sanskrit, and Malay wedding rites contain numerous Indian customs.

Preceding pages: Sultan Abdul Samad of Selangor and his retinue in 1874. Left, Alfonso de Albuquerque led the Portugese conquest of Malacca in 1511.

The Chinese also had trading contacts in the Malay peninsula as well as in northwest Borneo. In particular, they sought a prized delicacy – birds' nests – used for making soup. Their influence on indigenous culture, however, was minimal.

The founding of Malacca: The Indianised kingdoms of the Malay peninsula were constantly subjected to the dominance of stronger Indianised kingdoms in Southeast Asia. First the kingdom of Funan in Cambodia exerted its influence, followed by the Sumatran power of Sri Vijaya; Borneo, meanwhile, was under the control of the Javanese kingdom of Majapahit. However, a quiet village in the Malay peninsula soon rose to prominence as

good place! Even the mousedeer are full of fight!" Taking a cue from this good omen, Parameswara decided to build a settlement on the site. As he happened to be standing near a *melaka* tree, he decided that the settlement should bear the name of that tree. Under his rule, Melaka (Malacca in English) grew to be a thriving centre.

Parameswara and his followers planted new crops and discovered inland deposits of tin. Gradually, as the community grew, passing ships stopped at Malacca for replenishment. News of this flourishing settlement began to spread and within two years, the population had increased to 2,000.

Meanwhile, the emperor of China was

a major centre of power. The *Sejarah Melayu* or *Malay Annals*, written in the 16th century and comprising legends based on historical events, traces the transformation of a small coastal village into a famous trading centre.

The island of Tumasek (now Singapore), at the tip of the Malay peninsula, was ruled by Iskandar Shah, also called Parameswara. When the Javanese attacked the island, he and his followers were compelled to flee to Muar in the peninsula.

One day, when he was hunting near a fishing village, one of his hounds was kicked by a white mousedeer. The king, always appreciative of spunk, exclaimed, "This is a

expanding his maritime activities. In 1409, he sent his famous admiral, Cheng Ho, to Malacca to proclaim it a city and a kingdom. In turn, he presented Parameswara with Chinese tiles for the roof of his palace. In 1411, the admiral took Parameswara on a visit to China – a trip which confirmed Parameswara's status as an independent king owing fealty to China alone.

Parameswara's readiness to accept China's protection was a clever diplomatic move, for it not only guaranteed protection against the Siamese, but also added prestige and respectability to Malacca.

Not only was Malacca situated at the confluence of major trade routes extending eastward to China and westward to India and Europe, the city was also ideal as a port. The harbour was free of mangrove swamps and deep enough for safe passage; and it was fortunate to have the monsoon winds blowing in the right direction, twice a year. The northeast monsoon brought the Chinese, Siamese, Javanese and Bugis vessels early in the year; in May, Arab and Indian vessels arrived with the southwest winds.

The port was a colourful sight with vessels of various shapes and sizes, from Chinese junks, with eyes painted on the bows in the belief that it would help the vessels to see, to the robust three-masted Bugis schooners.

Straits of Malacca. In Malacca itself, four *shahbandar*, or harbourmasters, were appointed, each representing a group of nations. The duties of a shahbandar included overseeing daily affairs as well as solving disagreements among the sailors and merchants in his group.

The coming of Islam: Towards the end of the 13th century, Muslim traders from India brought Islam to the Malay archipelago. By the 15th century, Malacca had embraced the religion. The rulers took the title of "Sultan" and the Jawi script – the Malay language written in Arabic – evolved. By 1488, the kingdom of Malacca included the west coast of the Malay peninsula, Pahang and much of

The city was an equally exciting bazaar with an exotic range of goods – silks, brocade and porcelain from China, carvings and precious stones from India and Burma, spices and pepper from the East Indies archipelago, and tin, gold and jungle produce from Malacca's hinterland.

Another reason for Malacca's success was its ability to assure the safety of traders. The rulers of Malacca commanded the allegiance of the Orang Laut, or sea gypsies, who managed to curb the pirate menace in the

Left, Malacca was once a bustling trading port. Above, a Dutch bridge over the Malacca River.

the east coast of Sumatra. These subsidiary states eventually embraced Islam, too.

In about 20 years, Malacca had risen from obscurity to become the strongest state in Southeast Asia. Its population at the zenith of its power was 40,000 – mainly Malays, but also including Indian and Chinese settlers. The city was located at the mouth of a river and was divided into two halves. The sultan's palace and the Malay *kampung* were situated south of the river, while on the north bank the houses and stores of the merchants provided the cosmopolitan bustle and activity of the city. The two halves were linked by a bridge over the river. Everyday, the population moved to and fro across the bridge; some enterprising merchants even built their shops on the bridge itself.

The palace was the centre of life. Peasants, traders and noblemen had the right to present their petitions to the sultan in his *balai*, or audience hall, at his palace. The sultan sat on a raised platform, surrounded by richly embroidered cushions, flanked by his ministers, two or three steps below him.

The ruler's power was in theory absolute, and the people believed in the concept of undivided loyalty to the ruler; no one could disobey him even if wronged. There are many tales of Malaccans who would have rather killed their friends or relatives, or

Shapers of Malacca: Parameswara died in 1414, leaving behind him a prosperous trading port. When his grandson died in 1444, there was a power struggle in the court. The Malay chiefs supported the younger heir, as his mother had royal blood, while the elder heir was the son of a common Muslim-Tamil consort. But 17 months after the younger son was installed as ruler, he was killed and replaced in a Muslim-Tamil coup.

Sultan Muzaffar Shah, a fervent Muslim, declared Islam the state religion. He was an able ruler, remembered for his code of laws, and he received undivided loyalty. On one occasion, his bendahara observed the sultan's door being slammed by the wind, and

View of Chinese Mills, Penang, 1817—18
From a lithograph by William Daniell and based on a sketch by Capt. Robert Smith.

suffered in silence, than to have incurred the ruler's displeasure.

Royal power also took the form of other privileges. No commoner could wear yellow clothes, as it was the colour of royalty. White umbrellas were to be used only by rulers, and yellow umbrellas only by princes. Only royalty could wear gold anklets.

In his administration, the ruler was assisted by a *bendahara* (chief minister), a *temenggung* (chief of police), and a *laksamana* (admiral). Below them were the various titled nobles. The royalty, common people and traders abided by this system. Apparently, it worked for Malacca.

wrongly believed that it had been slammed by the displeased sultan. Thinking that he had incurred his ruler's wrath, he went home and committed suicide by taking poison.

In 1456, Tun Perak became the new bendahara and successfully repelled a Siamese invasion. Tun Perak was later to be the brains behind Malacca's expansion, as well as a leading figure in Malaccan politics for 42 years. During the reign of Sultan Mansor Shah, who succeeded Muzaffar Shah, Malacca reached the peak of its glory. Malacca's fame was largely attributed to Tun Perak, who built a formidable fighting force and honoured brave warriors with the title of

Hang, or captain. He also led expeditions and conquered many other states.

One of Tun Perak's fighting men was a young warrior named Hang Tuah. He was so handsome that he turned heads wherever he went. When he joined a Malaccan mission to visit Majapahit in Java, the women there were so struck by his beauty that they composed many songs, like this one:

"Here is betel leaf. Take it to allay the pangs of a whole day's love – but you will still yearn for him!"

Tuah's legendary beauty was matched by his loyalty. A famous episode tells how Tuah killed his best friend to prove his loyalty to the sultan. Mansor Shah had ordered Tuah to be killed, but the sympathetic bendahara imprisoned him instead. Meanwhile, Tuah's friend, Hang Kasturi, had an affair with one of the sultan's concubines; he was discovered and surrounded in the palace, but no one dared go in and attack him. Told that Tuah was still alive, the sultan immediately summoned him to kill Kasturi. In the ensuing duel, Kasturi three times permitted Tuah to free his dagger when it stuck in the wall. But Tuah refused his rival the same privilege, instead stabbing Kasturi in the back. In his dying moment, Kasturi cried, "Does a man who is a man go back on his word like that, Tuah?" To which Tuah coldly replied, "Who need play fair with you, you who have been guilty of treason?" And he stabbed Kasturi again and killed him. Tuah was appointed laksamana, or admiral, for his deed.

Sultan Mansor Shah was an admirer of beautiful women. He married many Javanese and Chinese princesses, and at one time the object of his admiration was the exquisite princess of the mountain of Gunung Ledang. He sent an expedition to scale the mountain, where his men met the princess, who had disguised herself as an old woman. They told her of the sultan's desire to court the princess and she in turn laid down her conditions: bridges of gold and silver from Malacca to Gunung Ledang, seven trays each of mosquitoes' and mites' hearts, vats of areca-nut water and of tears, a cup of the sultan's blood and a cup of his son's blood.

When this message was relayed to the sultan, he answered sadly: "All that she demands we can provide, save only the blood

View of life in early 19th-century Penang.

of our son; that we cannot provide, for our heart would not suffer to take it."

Sultan Mansor Shah was succeeded by Sultan Alauddin Riayat Shah. He was an able ruler who had the habit of walking the streets at night to check the enforcement of law and order. One night, he personally caught two robbers, and reprimanded the red-faced temenggung, or police chief, the next day. His independence made many jealous enemies. When he was only 26, he died after he had apparently been poisoned. In contrast, the next sultan was heavily influenced by his chiefs, which nevertheless numbered his days on the throne.

Invasion of the "Franks": The 15th century was Portugal's age of discovery. The Portuguese were eager to expand to the far corners of the world for a number of reasons – the search for the mythical priest-king Prester John, believed to live in a Christian African kingdom; the crusading spirit against Muslims; and the desire for Asian spices.

Spices were the most important commodity in the trade between Europe and Asia. Portugal wanted to divert the trade route from Muslim traders via a new route around Africa's Cape of Good Hope. Malacca was one of their targets, as it was the collecting point for spices from the Moluccas, the Spice Islands. As the Portuguese writer Barbosa put it, "Whoever is Lord in Melaka has his hand on the throat of Venice."

The Portuguese set sail to Malacca, where they wanted to seek permission to establish a trading post. Unfortunately, it was only to meet the bendahara, who – backed by the Indian Muslim traders – attempted to capture the Portuguese fleet. Warned by a Malaccan woman, the Portuguese – whom the Malays had nicknamed the "Franks" – escaped, leaving 20 of their men behind. They were taken prisoner, which gave the Portuguese a reason to return in force.

In 1511, a large Portuguese fleet, led by Alfonso de Albuquerque, the architect of Portuguese expansion in Asia, invaded Malacca. The Portuguese concentrated their onslaught on the bridge over the river, where the Malaccan defenders put up a courageous resistance. Even Sultan Mahmud and his son were in the thick of battle, riding on caparisoned elephants. Most of the non-indigenous population, however, was either apathetic or supporting the Portuguese.

On 24 August 1511, Malacca was captured. The sultan and his followers fled into the country. Malacca had lost its independence, and under a string of foreign rulers, it never regained its days of glory.

The victor and the vanquished: De Albuquerque set up a Portuguese administration and built a fort. He called it *A Famosa* ("The Famous"), and it was so impregnable that no enemy could penetrate its walls for 130 years. Within the walled area, a medieval Portuguese city developed with a town hall, offices and homes for the Portuguese civil servants. The locals and the other people lived outside the town wall.

The trade that the Portuguese established in Asia was extremely lucrative. For instance, pepper bought in the East could be sold in Portugal for 40 times its original price. Malacca also became the centre for Catholic missionary work, and in 1545 Francis Xavier, the well-known missionary, arrived to spread the Christian gospel.

But Catholicism did not appeal to the local population, and the arrogant Portuguese were not well liked either. They attempted to obtain a monopoly on the spice trade; all ships using the Straits of Malacca had to obtain passes from them, and arbitrary duties were imposed at the port of Malacca. This aroused strong anti-Portuguese feelings. The Europeans found themselves fending off attacks from other Malay states; in many cases, A Famosa proved to be the saving factor.

After his flight from Malacca, Sultan Mahmud settled in Bintang in the Riau Archipelago. He made two unsuccessful attacks on Malacca, and died in 1528. His elder son established himself in Perak, while his younger son started a sultanate in Johor. The new Sultan of Johor continued to harass Malacca. Meanwhile, in North Sumatra, Aceh, an ambitious state, was growing in strength. It launched attacks on Malacca, Johor and other Malay states. This Aceh-Malacca-Johor power struggle for political and economic supremacy dragged on through the 16th century.

Siege of A Famosa: The arrival of the Dutch and the English in the Southeast Asian waters was the result of certain events in Europe. In 1580, Spain had annexed Portugal; in 1594, the trading port of Lisbon was closed to Dutch and English merchants, which compelled the northern Europeans to turn to the East for spices and other goods. Dutch trading companies combined to form the United East India Company in 1602. Although their main interest was focused on the Moluccas, they considered control of Malacca necessary – not only because of the geographical position of the Straits of Malacca, but also as an expression of their antipathy towards the Portuguese.

In 1640, after blockading the port of Malacca and bombarding A Famosa, the Dutch encircled the town. As the siege continued, the Portuguese garrison and the people trapped in the fort ate whatever came into sight – rats, dogs, cats and snakes. It was reported that a mother even ate her dead child. The acute hunger was aggravated by diseases such as malaria, typhoid and cholera. Finally, in 1641, after a seven-month siege, the Dutch forces stormed into A Famosa and fought on to victory.

The Dutch government had decided that Batavia (now Jakarta) should be their capital. Malacca was acquired principally to prevent another power from using it; it was to be just another outpost of the Dutch Empire.

As the only traders then buying spices in the East, the Dutch were able to offer low purchasing prices. To maintain their monopoly, any Indian or English trader who wanted to trade in Southeast Asia had to obtain permits from them. This monopoly made many enemies for the Dutch, and although they held Malacca for 150 years, they left behind little significant influence.

Meanwhile, the other states in the Malay peninsula continued the saga of prosperity and decline. When the Dutch occupied Malacca, many merchants diverted their trade to Johor, and the sultanate there grew stronger. However, after an attack by a Sumatran state in 1673, Johor began to decline. Perak also grew in strength, as it was rich in tin.

Other settlements on the peninsula were founded by immigrants. Menangkabaus from West Sumatra brought a matrilineal social system to Negri Sembilan. The Bugis, who migrated from Celebes in the 17th century and were regionally well-known, possessed exceptional navigational and commercial skills. They infiltrated and occupied positions of power in the Malay states and established an independent state in Selangor.

Italian map of the peninsula, circa 17th century.

salan
LA DI
SALAN

Cornang
Along
Pulo Cara
Pulo Panjag

GOLFO DI SIAM

Claio

Ligor
I. Ligor
Pulo Ubi

Bondelon
Wanting
Singor
Cabo Potane
P. Coffin
Luaro
S.P. Rou
Pinaca

Pendaon
P. Boulon
Keidah

P. Iado

Queda
Vechio
Patane
F. Secco
F. Kedantan
Pulo Ridang

P. Pisang

Torano
P. Serga
Bazuas
Soengei
Boroas
Poncian
Bahan
Kedaor
F. Bossot
F. Dongon

E. Palang

Pulo Capes

E. Lago di Diamanti
dell Olandesi
P. Sambila
Salon
gri
Soengei
Pao
Pontigaran
P. Barbala

ors
I del
Aqui
P. Iara
Feira
Solongor F.
Pulo
Pracelar
Tingaran
Pahang
P. Verella

cly
Parri
Casang
Brama
P. Arà
P. Rachardo
Malacca
Diohor
Passir
Singapora
P. Timon
P. Pisang

Porto Besaar
Behaell.
Utiel I.
I. Pedrus
I. Naos
Tanfon Borro
Quciel Mas
Laut de Mas
P. Laor
P. Tingi

ol. di Loque
ol. di S. Anna
Gol. di
Tempesta
Cinleel
Boere
Pitã
Bancalis
I. Isang
Streitta
Bachia
G. Romania

selan
Cincon
Batahan
Sickerbau
C. Pantou
Sialqua
Carimon
Saban
Streitto di Sincaporea
Bintan

P. Baby
P. Batou
Camper
Domines

ISOLE

Passaman
Acon
Priaman
Catatenga
Pantanvace
Lingen
Velgote
Equino

Drop
Sojo
Fratelli

nda
Padang
Tellekan
Andraqari
Logie
Olandesi
Li
Jutou
Bil.

tona For
na
Manacabo
Saleda
Speriama
Lamby
Baros
Telombuan
Salecar
ISOLA BANCA
Monte
monopili
Gualagrip

Petten I.
I. Cocos
I. Willens
Indrapo
ur
Remtapou
Mochomocho
Lomam
Bantal
La P.ta
Punta
La 2.a Punta
La P.ma Punta

Pietra di Guvin
Palambam
cuca

Nasson I.
Mosquiten I.
I. Tartaruga
I. Cocos
3 Monti
Lamang
Cattoun
Ipoe
Pencolen
Monte Sillebar
F. S. Giouan
orbes

I. Bassa
Fort
Marteboury
Sillebar
Sanjon Tiande
Dampin
Gouan
F. S. Clara
F. Dolce

met Recif
Pisang I.
Pongon
Telluk
Boutou
Sort

ISOLE

Engano I.
Saluamento

The East India Company was an association of merchants who were granted a charter by Queen Elizabeth in 1600 for the monopoly of all English trade in the regions east of the Cape of Good Hope. A very important trading contract that belonged to the company was the export of tea from China to Europe. Not only was this trade a very profitable one, it also provided Great Britain with substantial revenue from tax on tea imports.

The British displayed an active interest in Southeast Asia, primarily to establish a port on the sheltered side of the Bay of Bengal for replenishing supplies and refitting ships along the China trade route.

In 1785, the Sultan of Kedah allowed the company to establish a settlement on the island of Penang. He saw this as a golden opportunity for obtaining protection against his enemy to the north, Siam, in exchange for trading rights granted to the British. Francis Light landed in Penang in 1786, where the Union Jack looked rather odd on the sparsely populated, jungle-smothered island.

Light had promised to assist the Sultan of Kedah against Siam, but it soon became obvious that his company had no intention of fulfilling this vow. The sultan felt that he had been deceived and assembled a fleet to recapture Penang. But Light was swifter, and attacked the sultan's fleet before it even began the offensive. This time, Light made sure that everything was in black and white. A treaty guaranteed the sultan $6,000 a year, while the company got Penang.

Light cleared Penang's jungle and made it into a free port. To the annoyance of the Dutch, ships from throughout Southeast Asia and India began to trade in Penang. The population grew rapidly and Light followed the Malay and Dutch practice of appointing *kapitan* – community leaders with authority to hear all minor crimes committed by members of their representative communities. For major crimes, Light himself tried offenders with his rough-and-ready sense of justice. He died of malaria in 1794.

In 1808, "civilisation" arrived in Penang when the Charter of Justice introduced English law to the settlement. Penang enjoyed prosperous times for a while, but it was too far from the crucial Spice Islands to become really important.

The French Revolution led directly to the British occupation of Malacca. The revolutionary armies of France had overrun the Netherlands, and the Dutch naval bases were due to come under French control. To forestall French use of the bases, Britain and the

Dutch government-in-exile agreed that the British would take over the Dutch possessions during the war and hand them back when the war was over. In 1795, Malacca was transferred to the British

The British were determined that when Malacca was due to be returned to the Dutch, it should be of as little use as possible. The plan was to destroy A Famosa and transfer its population to Penang. For about a year, the historic fort was systematically disassembled. But ironically, the city was never abandoned, and the fort need not have been destroyed at all. The Dutch reoccupied Malacca for only six years, and in 1824, under the Anglo-Dutch Treaty, peacefully ceded it to the British.

The Straits Settlements: The Dutch had returned to Asia when the war with France ended, and reoccupied their former bases, including Malacca. By 1818, they had extended control over parts of the East Indies. This alarmed a number of British officials, one of whom was Stamford Raffles. He convinced the East India Company authorities that another settlement in the Straits of Malacca would establish British supremacy and would also serve as a port of call for British ships en route from India to China.

In 1819, Sir Stamford Raffles landed on the tiny island of Singapore, then populated

They acted as trading centres and protectors of the trade route to China, and had no intention of becoming involved in the Malay states. More territory meant more expenses; hence, the official policy was one of strict nonintervention.

This rule was bent at a few occasions. The Menangkabau people of Naning paid annual tithes to the Dutch but refused to make similar payments to the British. This led to the Naning War, in which armed British troops were sent through thick jungle to capture Naning and make it a district of Malacca. On another occasion, the first governor of the settlements, Robert Fullerton, though lacking authority to make war, sent the Penang

by about 1,000 Malays and Orang Laut. Raffles established a trading post on the island and, in 1824, succeeded in getting the sultan and temenggung of Johor to cede Singapore outright to the British.

With its free port status and its strategic geographic position, Singapore achieved phenomenal success. Ships from India, China and the Malay archipelago filled the port with a wide range of goods. By 1824, the population had increased to 11,000 with a mixture of Malays, Chinese, Indians, Bugis, Arabs, Europeans and Armenians.

In 1826, Singapore and Malacca joined with Penang to form the Straits Settlements.

forces to scare off the Siamese, who were planning an attack on Perak.

White Rajahs of Sarawak: While the Malay peninsula was prospering, the territories on the northern shore of Borneo were undergoing a separate development – Sarawak with its "White Rajah" and Sabah under the British North Borneo Company.

James Brooke was born and raised in India, where his father worked for the East India Company. As a young man, he was an ensign in the Sixth Native Infantry in Bengal, but resigned from service in 1830. When his father died in 1835 and left him a sum of money, Brooke used it to buy a schooner. He named it *The Royalist* and set sail to explore the East. Little did the dashing adventurer realise that he would gain a kingdom.

Sarawak was the westernmost province of the Brunei sultanate. The sultanate's decline in power had brought about greater independence among the Malay chiefs. Brooke landed in Sarawak in 1839 and found the Rajah Muda Hashim, a relative of the Sultan of Brunei, trying to quell a rebellion against the misrule of the governor of Sarawak. A year later, Brooke returned and helped Muda Hashim bring the four-year rebellion to an end. For his contribution, he was awarded control of Sarawak.

In 1841, against a backdrop of Malay guns firing a salute, James Brooke, 38, was installed as the Rajah of Sarawak, beginning over 100 years of rule by the White Rajahs.

With the help of local chiefs, Brooke tried to establish peace and order in Sarawak. He made no attempt to introduce new laws; instead, he based his administration on existing customs and consultation with the chiefs. Brooke was not strong on finances, and his administration was always in the red. But he refused to introduce foreign capital because he believed that "the activities of European government must be directed to the advancement of native interests... rather than... aim at possession only." Under Brooke's rule, the population grew, more territories were brought under Sarawak's control, and peace and order were restored. An 1857 revolt by Chinese gold miners was quickly suppressed. In 1863, the ailing rajah left Sarawak to retire in England, where he died five years later. His dream of a voyage of adventure really had come true.

Brooke's successor was his nephew, Charles Brooke. The second rajah was a better administrator than his uncle. He brought Sarawak out of debt, reduced headhunting, expanded trade, and brought greater prosperity. Whereas James was debonair and charming, Charles was reserved, preferring solitary recreation like tending his private betel nut plantation. The English ladies in Kuching did not fancy his lack of social graces, and he must have created quite a stir when he declared that the most suitable population for Sarawak would be derived from

intermarriage between Europeans and the native races. But he himself married a European woman 20 years his junior.

Meanwhile, sovereignty over North Borneo (present-day Sabah) was obtained in 1877 by Overbeck, the Austrian consul-general in Hong Kong, in partnership with the British company of the Dent Brothers. In 1881, Overbeck withdrew and the remaining partners formed the British North Borneo Company under a royal charter. While the Company agreed to provide facilities for the British navy, it was allowed to "borrow" various senior officers from the Straits Settlements to assist in administration.

The North Borneo Company was not as

successful as the Brookes in fostering recognition of white rule. It encountered recurring resistance, the most significant of which was the Mat Salleh Rebellion of 1895–1905. The introduction of new taxes had created general discontent, and Mat Salleh gathered many supporters in his revolt against the company. Prestige and mystique enveloped Mat Salleh. He carried flags and the umbrella of royalty, and it was said that his mouth could produce flames and his *parang* (cleaver) lightning. In 1900, Mat Salleh was killed, but the rebellion was not quelled until five years later. Today, he is still regarded as one of Sabah's most famous heroes.

Left, British officials strike a pose. **Right**, Sir Hugh Low.

The Pangkor Agreement: The Malay peninsula had always been rich in tin. The ore had been mined and sold in the peninsula for centuries, but after 1861 – with the growth of the canning industry in America – there was an increased demand. Merchants from the Straits Settlements invested money in the new mines in Selangor and Perak, petitioning for British intervention in these states to safeguard their commercial interests.

Selangor and Perak were plagued by unrest. There were power disputes among the Malay chiefs. Chinese miners had formed rival secret societies that constantly fought against one another. This unsettled condition caused the export of tin to drop to a slow

throne and the new Sultan of Perak agreed to accept a British Resident, whose advice had to "be asked and acted upon on all questions other than those touching Malay religion and custom." By August, Clarke had made a similar agreement with Selangor, and British influence began to spread to the Malay states. (Earlier, in 1867, the Straits Settlements had become a Crown Colony under the direct control of London, and were no longer ruled from British India.)

British residents: The government-by-advice procedure in the Malay states was carried out by appointing British "residents" to advise the rulers on how to improve the administration of their states. This control by

trickle. What was even more stressful to the Straits Settlements merchants was that the demand for tin began to exceed its supply.

Meanwhile, officials of the British Colonial Office were fearful that if Britain did not intervene in these states, the merchants who had invested in the mines would obtain assistance from another power, particularly Germany. A new governor, Andrew Clarke, was sent to investigate the situation.

Clarke went one step further. He met the Malay chiefs on his ship, anchored near the beautiful Pangkor Island. In January 1874, both parties signed the Pangkor Agreement. The treaty settled the dispute of the Perak

indirect rule was dependent on how well the resident could exercise his influence.

In Perak, the first resident was J.W.W. Birch. He was intolerant and tactless enough to lecture the sultan in public. He had little regard for local customs and wanted to change immediately anything that displeased him. Birch wanted to abolish debt slavery but failed to see its lack of similarity to the Western concept of slavery. Debt slavery involved a person mortgaging himself in return for financial assistance from his creditors. In bad times, debt slavery was the only way a peasant could raise finances. If he was unable to redeem his debt, he was absorbed into the creditor's household to carry out his orders until the debt was paid off. The locals resented Birch's interference.

There were additional sources of friction. The introduction of a centralised tax-revenue collection system took away the rights of the sultan and his chiefs to collect taxes. Then in 1875, the new governor of the Straits Settlements proposed that British officials should govern directly on behalf of the Sultan of Perak. Birch exerted great pressure on the sultan to have him agree to this proposal.

Birch began to post notices announcing the British government's intention of directly administering Perak. But he was killed while bathing in a floating bathhouse at a Perak village. Those found guilty of conspiracy against Birch were hanged, while several chiefs were exiled for their involvement in the assassination plot.

Perak's third resident was Hugh Low, who made no attempts to interfere with Malay customs and was friendly with the local population. Consequently, he was more successful than Birch. He brought the revenue from the tin mines under his control and constructed roads, a railway and a telegraph line for Perak.

Elsewhere, things were less problematic than in Perak. In Selangor, the resident, Frank Swettenham, was doing well. He spoke good Malay and was quick in winning Sultan Abdul Samad's approval. Swettenham often accompanied the sultan on game-hunting and snipe-shooting expeditions. In 1889, Negri Sembilan also accepted the appointment of a British resident.

In each of these states, indirect British rule was exercised through a state council which discussed the policies to be implemented. The members of the council were the resident, the sultan, major chiefs and one or two Chinese leaders. While the council provided a useful sounding board for public opinion, the resident alone was the real policy maker. He nominated all council members, who met only about seven times each year.

Resistance in Pahang: Reports of "great wealth" in the large eastern state of Pahang whetted the British appetite to gain control. By 1887, Pahang's ruler, Sultan Ahmad, was persuaded to accept a British agent. But the first agent, Hugh Clifford, found the sultan and his chiefs unwilling to relinquish their rights. The atmosphere in Pahang grew tense with the lack of understanding between British and Malays. Rumours began circulating of an impending British attack on the sultan's palace. In 1888, when a British subject was murdered in Pahang, the British enforced a demand that Sultan Ahmad write a letter requesting a British resident.

The Pahang chiefs resented the interference of the resident and their subsequent loss of power and income. In 1891, Dato' Bahaman, an angry and defiant tribal chief, openly declared rebellion against the British. This rebellion became known as the Pahang War,

and proved to be an expensive and arduous affair for the foreigners.

Bahaman's men were acknowledged guerilla fighters, and many stories and legends are told of the rebellion and its leaders. Even now, the Pahang War symbolises the struggle for Malay independence. One of its famous fighters, Mat Kilau, is a hero of Malay nationalism. (In 1969, there was great excitement when an old man in Pahang identified himself as Mat Kilau. The Pahang government conducted an extensive investigation to confirm his claim, but no conclusive evidence was found.) In 1892, a general amnesty was issued. Most of the rebels sur-

Far left, Sultan Abdullah of Perak. **Left**, Sultan Abu Bakar of Johor. **Right**, Sir Frank Swettenham.

rendered while others fled to Terengganu. In 1895, a force led by Clifford chased the rebels north to Kelantan, where they were eventually arrested.

The Federated Malay States: In 1896, the Federated Malay States were created, including Selangor, Perak, Negri Sembilan and Pahang, with its capital at Kuala Lumpur. A resident-general was appointed with jurisdiction over all other residents. To ensure uniformity of the civil service, all laws, except those of a local nature, were drawn up in Kuala Lumpur.

The sultans had agreed to federation under the belief that they would exercise more control over the residents, but they did not regain their lost authority. On the contrary, the resident-general now became the initiator of policies, and greater administrative control was exercised by the resident without any reference to the sultan. In effect, "federation" meant centralised power. The original aim of indirect rule was swallowed up as the states came to be run almost entirely by British officers.

Meanwhile, the northern states of the Malay peninsula recognised the general overlordship of the king of Siam. This suzerainty was demonstrated by the sending of the *Bunga Mas* ("golden flowers") to the Siamese capital. However, the power that Siam had over these states was somewhat vague and was generally interpreted differently from one generation to another.

In 1909, the British made a treaty with Siam whereby Britain gained whatever rights and power Siam possessed in the northern states of Kedah, Perlis, Kelantan and Terengganu. These states became British protectorates, and British advisors with similar status to residents were appointed.

Mad Ridley's miracle crop: At the southern end of the peninsula, Johor was pressed to accept a British advisor in 1914. British control over the Malay peninsula was now complete, although three different groups of states existed – the Straits Settlements, the Federated Malay States and the Unfederated Malay States. Nevertheless, "British Malaya" was born.

In the latter half of the 19th century, new technology brought about an increased use of tin-plate in the West. In response to the demand for tin ore, more mines were opened in Selangor and Perak, leading to an influx of Chinese immigrants to Malaya. By as soon as 1904, Malaya was already producing half of the world's tin.

Even more spectacular was the success story of rubber, which arrived in Malaya as a foreign plant but grew to become the mainstay of its economy. Rubber seeds had been transported from Brazil to London's Kew Gardens for experimentation as an Asian crop. When the seeds germinated, a handful were sent to Malaya. They were immediately planted in Singapore and in the garden of Hugh Low's residency in Kuala Kangsar. From these seedlings developed the millions of rubber trees in Malaysia today.

The development of rubber was slow until H.N. Ridley was appointed to direct the Singapore Botanical Gardens in 1888. Ridley had no doubts about the future of rubber and persuaded coffee estates to experiment with the growing of this new crop. Initially, planters and estate managers sat on the verandahs of their bungalows, nursing their gin-and-tonics, and talked about "Mad Ridley" or "Rubber Ridley" and his enthusiasm for the exploitation of rubber trees. But those who sniggered at him had the tables turned on them when, at the beginning of the 20th century, the increased popularity of the motorcar brought about a high demand for rubber. Many fortunes were made in the great rubber-boom years from 1910 to 1912. By 1920, Malaya was producing 53 percent of the world's rubber.

Indian labour was brought in to work the rubber estates, while many Malays, despite discouragement by the British, became smallholders. The rubber industry went through gluts and slumps, but it survived and remains a thriving industry today.

Revenue from tin and rubber was used to build up the government infrastructure of communications and social amenities. Attention was focused on the mining and estate areas, however, at the expense of the less economically profitable areas.

While the tin and rubber industries were booming, Malay's plural society had developed. In 1931, the population of Malaya, excluding Singapore, was about 4 million. It comprised 49 percent Malays, 34 percent Chinese and smaller groups of Indians, expatriates and other races.

Mad Ridley's rubber trees.

MALAYA, MERDEKA, MALAYSIA

The first sparks of World War II reached Malaya in 1937. In that year, the Japanese launched military attacks on Beijing and Shanghai after having occupied Manchuria six years earlier. By 1941, the Japanese were making no more than slow progress in their conquest of China. This sluggishness was aggravated when the American, British and Dutch governments froze the shipment of all essential raw materials and oil supplies to Japan. To assure its supply, Japan was forced to look to Southeast Asia, which produced these important materials. Already the Japanese occupied Indochina; the threat of a Japanese invasion loomed over Malaya.

Meanwhile, Britain was preoccupied with defending itself against the threat of German invasion and the possible capture of the Suez Canal. It could not do much to protect Malaya. Besides, Britain and the United States had secretly agreed that Europe was to be the area of first defence priority.

On 8 December 1941 (7 December in America), at around one in the morning, Japanese warships began shelling the beaches of Kota Bharu in the northeastern state of Kelantan. The forces landed almost without opposition. At 4.30am bombs were dropped on the sleeping island of Singapore. Within 24 hours, the Japanese had mastery of the air and had seized the British airfields in north Malaya. On 10 December, Japanese bombers sank two British warships off Kuantan, establishing supremacy in Malayan waters.

The Japanese drove relentlessly down the Malay peninsula with their tanks and bicycles. Lt. Col. F. Spencer Chapman, in his book *The Jungle Is Neutral*, wrote that he saw the enemy pouring in and noted:

"The majority of them were on bicycles.... They seemed to have no standard uniform or equipment and were travelling as light as they possibly could. All this was in very marked contrast to our first-line soldiers, who were at this time equipped like Christmas trees... so that they could hardly walk, much less fight."

Left, the Proclamation of Independence. **Right**, an occupation newspaper reports on Tokyo's successes, 1943.

The commonwealth troops defending Malaya were poorly trained in jungle warfare and lacked ammunition. They staggered back from defeat after defeat while the Japanese infiltrated and outflanked the British defensive positions. One by one, they fell to the invaders. By 31 January 1942, the remaining commonwealth troops withdrew across the causeway that linked the Malay peninsula with Singapore.

Singapore was invaded on 8 February and there was fierce fighting. Many civilians

perished in the bomb raids, and the island was also choked by a water shortage. After a week-long siege, on 15 February 1942, the general officer commanding Malaya, Lt.-Gen. A.E. Percival, surrendered Singapore – the "Gibraltar of the East" – to the Japanese.

Troops defending Sarawak, meanwhile, were hopelessly outnumbered, and Kuching was captured by the Japanese on Christmas Day 1941. By 16 January 1942, North Borneo fell. For the next three and a half years of Japanese occupation, natives of these outposts suffered a brutal existence. Some broke down, while others demonstrated bravery and resilience.

Life in "Maraiee": The Japanese pronounced Malay as "Maraiee" and came with promises of a "Co-prosperity Sphere" and an "Asia for Asians". But they ruled with an iron hand and imposed hardship on the population.

The brunt of Japanese brutality was directed against the Chinese. The war in China had made many of them hostile towards the Japanese, who in turn accused them of being British sympathisers. Tens of thousands of Chinese were executed or imprisoned.

Food was extremely scarce. The Japanese occupation currency was useless, and there was spiralling inflation. Troublemakers and suspected criminals were treated harshly and often tortured by the Kempetai, or military

On 6 August 1945, the United States devastated the Japanese city of Hiroshima with an atomic bomb. Three days later, Nagasaki was obliterated. On 14 August, Japan finally surrendered and the war ended in Malaya. In September 1945, British forces landed in Malaya and reestablished their authority as the British Military Administration. The Administration began the gruelling task of restoring the country to normality.

Doomed Malayan Union: In 1945, as the British were reoccupying Malaya, the British cabinet approved a plan to incorporate the Federated and Unfederated Malay States – as well as Penang and Malacca, but excluding Singapore – into a Malayan Union. The

police. Paranoia was rampant. Young women blackened their faces and hands to avoid being ogled by Japanese soldiers, who might drag them away as "comfort women".

The entire European population became prisoners-of-war or civilian interns. Conditions in the prison camps were squalid, and the prisoners were made to do heavy manual work. Those who disobeyed the guards or who were found committing the "heinous" crime of keeping a radio were brutally tortured. Many of them, together with Indian labourers, were sent to construct the infamous railway in Burma, where a great number died from diseases and ill-treatment.

union was intended to embody a unitary state with a central government and a governor. Sovereignty was to be transferred from the sultans to the British Crown. The effect would be tantamount to turning Malaya into a colony. Eager to prove their loyalty to the British, having had it questioned during the Japanese occupation, some sultans agreed to sign the Malayan Union treaty. Those who were reluctant to sign were subjected to British "persuasion".

When the plan was announced, certain ex-Malayan civil servants like Swettenham protested and petitioned Downing Street. Even stronger protests came from the Malays, who took a united stand against this plan. In March 1946, delegates representing 41 Malay associations met in Kuala Lumpur to form a national movement against the Malayan Union. Differences in philosophy were cast aside as the United Malay National Organisation (UMNO) was born. UMNO was inaugurated with Dato' Onn Jaafar as its leader. It declared the treaty signed by the sultans null and void, demanding a repeal of the Union.

The British went on to inaugurate the union in 1946, but opposition was so strong that the plan was never brought into effect. It was finally revoked on 1 February 1948, when the Federation of Malaya was created.

The federation was accepted by all parties

War of Nerves: During the Japanese occupation, guerilla groups of British officers, Malays and Chinese had lived in the jungles and organised resistance forces to harass the Japanese. Chinese Communist guerillas, calling themselves the Malayan Peoples' Anti-Japanese Army (MPAJA), recruited many supporters for a republic in Malaya after the defeat of the Japanese.

The MPAJA was disbanded after the Japanese occupation. The Communists began to infiltrate trade unions, and in 1946 and 1947, they organised strikes to disrupt the economy. Internal problems plagued the Communist Party, however. The Secretary-General, discovered to be a double agent, absconded

because it provided for the sovereignty of the sultans, as indicated by the appointment of a high commissioner instead of a governor; moreover, the states had jurisdiction over a number of important departments.

Meanwhile, in 1946, Sarawak and North Borneo became crown colonies. The cost of post-war reconstruction was beyond the resources of the Brooke government or the British North Borneo Company.

Left, Japanese leaders surrender their swords in 1945. **Above**, Communist caricature (**left**) and British jungle patrols (**right**) were features of the emergency.

with the party's funds. The infamous Chin Peng became the new Communist leader. He reorganised the party and moved all its activities underground. When violence escalated after a spate of murders and attacks on European miners and planters in 1948, the Malayan government proclaimed a state of emergency throughout the country. The tense situation came to be described as the "War of Nerves".

The Communists planned to attack the estates and mines in order to disrupt the economy. They organised themselves into regiments and lived in camps in the jungle. These camps were well-screened from the air, had efficient escape routes, well-organised living quarters and could often accommodate 300 men. Political indoctrination was a major activity.

Communism quelled: During the emergency, high wire fences were built around tin mines and rubber estates to keep out Communist attackers. People who lived in remote villages were in constant fear that the Communists would appear and force them to supply food and money. Travelling was risky as the danger of a Communist ambush lurked behind every roadside bush.

There was not much coordination between the various security forces until the appointment of Lt.-Gen. Sir Harold Briggs as Director of Operations in 1949. Briggs, a veteran of the Western Desert and Burma campaigns, immediately put on his military thinking cap. His war executive committees coordinated emergency operations, and his settlement plan created 500 new villages for Malayan citizens who lived in remote areas beyond government protection.

The latter plan succeeded in removing to safer places the people who were most vulnerable to coercion by the Communists, thereby depriving the insurgents of their crucial sources of supplies and information. As Briggs anticipated, the Communists began to attack the new settlements. But the security forces, now fighting on their own ground, proved to be too strong for them. These forces were soon able to concentrate on jungle operations to destroy the Communists and their camps.

Nationalism and *merdeka*: In 1953, areas from which the Communists had been eliminated were declared "white areas". Their food restrictions and curfews were relaxed, inducing the people to cooperate more fully with the government. By 1954, a large number of the Communist guerillas had been destroyed. Many more surrendered in 1958, and the few remaining guerillas retreated deep into the jungle. The state of emergency officially ended on 31 July 1960.

Merdeka means "freedom" in the Malay language, and stirrings of nationalism had been felt throughout the country soon after World War II. With the Communists virtually wiped out by 1955, Malayans began to clamour for independence.

In 1951, the Malayan Chinese Association formed a political partnership with UMNO. The Malayan-Indian Congress joined in 1954, and the political grouping – called the Alliance – came to represent the interests of the various races in Malaya. It was to play a major role in the path to independence.

The Alliance demanded that elections be held for the Federal Legislative Council. The wish was granted, and in 1955 Malaya's first national election determined 52 of the 98 members of the Council. The Alliance won 80 percent of the votes cast. Tunku Abdul Rahman became the chief minister.

For the first time in memory, Malayans had real influence in the government. Tunku Abdul Rahman, born into a royal family, was a son of the Sultan of Kedah. From 1930 to 1941, he worked as district officer in Kedah and was very popular with the people there. After securing a law degree, he surged along with the tide of Malayan nationalism and entered politics. "Tunku", as he soon became known, took over the leadership of UMNO in 1951.

In 1955, Tunku's government offered amnesty to the Communist terrorists. He met Communist leader Chin Peng for talks to end the emergency. The meeting was unsuccessful, however, and Chin Peng went back into the jungle. Tunku's government also turned its attention to the question of unity in Malaya's multiracial society. A common school syllabus for all language was implemented.

Malayan constitution: In 1956, Tunku led a delegation to London to negotiate for independence. Britain was ready to grant Malaya its freedom, and assigned the Reid Commission to draw up a constitution. The draft document was based on a memorandum submitted by the Alliance, and was accepted by the sultans, the British and Malayan governments.

The Malayan constitution was a federal constitution. While the states retained certain rights and powers, the central government held supreme power in all important matters. The government was set up as a constitutional monarchy. Sultans from the nine ruling families were to elect among themselves the paramount ruler or *Yang diPertuan Agong*, who would reign for five years. The Agong would rule through a Parliament composed of a fully elected house of representatives and a senate of nominated members. Executive power would lie mostly in the hands of the house, while the senate would have the power to delay legislation for one year. Each state would have its own fully-elected state assembly.

At midnight of 30 August 1957, huge crowds gathered at the Selangor Club in Kuala Lumpur to witness an historic occa-

Tunku Abdul Rahman gives the "Merdeka" salute.

sion. The Union Jack was lowered for the last time. Among the crowd, many experienced mixed feelings – a certain sadness about the end of a familiar era, and uncertainty.

The next day, crowds gathered again at the Merdeka Stadium to witness the handing over of the formal instrument of independence to Tunku – Malaya's first prime minister. The nine states and two settlements had become the independent Federation of Malaya. Amidst impassioned shouts of "Merdeka!" that vibrated throughout the stadium, the people felt a new sense of pride and were certain that whatever lay ahead, they were ready for the challenge.

Malaysia... and confrontation: Independence brought with it a new period of vitality and reform. Rural development improved and a national industrial policy was formulated. The Alliance continued to win popular support; in the 1959 federal elections, it took 74 of a possible 104 seats.

In 1961, Tunku proposed a political association – called Malaysia – which would include Malaya, Singapore, North Borneo, Sarawak and Brunei. There was considerable enthusiasm in Singapore; Brunei, however, decided to stay away. A commission of Malayan and British members set up to determine the reaction of the inhabitants of the Borneo territories, discovered that more people were in favour of the idea than against it. Thus, the British and Malayan governments agreed that the new states of Malaysia, minus Brunei, would come into being on 31 August 1963.

Meanwhile, the Indonesian government voiced strong opposition to the Malaysia plan, alleging that the inhabitants of the Borneo territories had not been consulted and that the whole thing was a British plot. In January 1963, Indonesia announced a policy of "confrontation" against Malaya. Many suspected that the real reason behind the antagonism was that Indonesia's President Sukarno's dream of a Greater Indonesia, to include Malaya, Sarawak, North Borneo and Brunei, would be compromised. Meanwhile, the Philippines also opposed the creation of Malaysia, claiming that North Borneo belonged to them.

The confrontation took the form of armed Indonesian invasions across the borders of Sarawak and North Borneo from Indonesian Kalimantan. Indonesia and the Philippines both repudiated a United Nations survey which confirmed that the Borneo territories wanted to be a part Malaysia.

When the Federation of Malaysia was officially inaugurated on 16 September 1963, Indonesia and the Philippines severed diplomatic ties with Malaysia; Indonesia intensified its "Crush Malaysia" campaign. Attacks along the borders of Sarawak and North Borneo (now renamed Sabah) increased, and Indonesian terrorists began landing on the coast of the Malay peninsula to carry out acts of sabotage. But they were quickly killed or captured by the security forces.

In 1966, Sukarno was ousted from power by a new army-dominated administration. This new Indonesian government was not keen on continuing the confrontation, and a peace agreement brought the conflict to an end. The Philippines also dropped its claim on Sabah and recognised Malaysia.

Meanwhile, political differences had surfaced between Malaysia and Singapore. On 9 August 1965, Singapore left the Federation and became an independent nation.

Nationhood: When the decade ended, Malaysia's population stood at 10.4 million – Malays forming 47 percent; Chinese forming 34 percent; Indians, 9 percent; Dayaks, 4 percent; Kadazans, 2 percent; other indigenous groups, 3 percent; and foreign immigrants, 2 percent.

Bringing this "anthropological museum" of people under one national flag was not an easy feat. When the British left Malaysia, economic roles were rigidly defined and unequally divided amongst the ethnic groups. The Malay and the Chinese communities continued to feel threatened by each other – the Chinese resented the Malay's greater political power, while the Malays feared the greater economic strength of the Chinese. The simmering racial tension finally erupted in the wake of the general elections on 13 May 1969. Violent inter-communal riots broke out, mainly in Kuala Lumpur, killing hundreds of people and destroying a considerable amount of property.

The riots occurred after the UMNO-led Alliance government had suffered severe losses at the hands of the predominantly non-Malay opposition parties, which included the Chinese-dominated Democratic Action Party (DAP), calling for racial equality, and the Gerakan (the People's Movement) supported by Chinese and Indians. Gerakan and DAP post-election celebrations provoked counter-demonstrations from the Malays, thus igniting the mayhem – now referred to as the "May 13 incident".

The government suspended the constitution for more than a year, declared a state of emergency, and a Department of National Unity was set up to formulate a national ideology and social programmes. Today, Malaysians live and work by the *Rukunegara* (Articles of Faith of the State), an ideology written in 1970 and aimed at fostering nation-building:

Belief in God
Loyalty to King and Country
Upholding the Constitution
Rule of Law
Good Behaviour and Morality

The May 13 incident represented a watershed in Malaysian politics, as the government was forced to formulate new economic and political strategies to restore long-term national stability. The New Economic Policy (NEP) and the Barisan Nasional (BN) or National Front, came about as a result of the riots, greatly affecting Malaysian history.

The BN was the work of Tun Abdul Razak, successor of Tunku Abdul Rahman who resigned a month after the riots. Tun Razak unified UMNO and the Alliance, incorporating every political party except the DAP and some smaller parties. In 1974, the new Barisan Nasional won a landslide majority, and were to repeat the victory in 1978.

Economic policy: Although the nation's new constitution gave the Malays considerable political and religious power, with a specified number of state leaders to be selected from the Malay race, and with Islam as the state religion, their participation in the country's trade and commerce was virtually nonexistent. The Malays, or Bumiputras (sons of the soil), owned only 2 percent of corporate equity despite making up over half of the country's population. The Chinese had the monopoly in that realm; they practically ran the economy, holding prominent positions as bankers, brokers and businessmen.

To enable the Bumiputras to catch up economically, the New Economic Policy (NEP) was set up in 1970 to encourage a fairer distribution of wealth among the races. This involved setting up corporations and share-ownership schemes to elicit greater Malay participation in diverse areas of the economy. Racial quotas, scholarships and subsidies were introduced to raise the Malay stake in the economy to 30 percent.

The NEP was deemed racist by critics and Malaysia's other ethnic groups, who felt that the pro-Malay constitution which promoted Malay religion and cultural values, and the selection of share-ownership schemes on the basis of racial issues and not on merit, would seriously undermine the economic, political and cultural position of non-Malays in Malaysian society.

However, despite the tensions, the hardy business acumen of the Chinese has kept them prosperous and far from downtrodden. Twenty years later, however, the Bumiputra stake has reached only 20 percent, the majority of which is owned by big Bumiputra investment companies. In 1991, the old policy was replaced by the New Development Policy (NDP), a more liberal strategy which uses incentives rather than quotas, and sets no deadline for the 30 percent Bumiputra ownership target.

Mahathir: In 1981, Malaysia's fourth prime minister, Dato' Seri Dr Mahathir Mohamad, took office. A controversial figure in politics in his younger days, the new prime minister excited Malaysians with his brand of dynamism, pragmatism, forthrightness and genuine concern for the people. Mahathir is often described as the Kemal Ataturk of Malaysia. Whatever his policies, Mahathir's position as prime minister has been, for the last decade of his office, a delicate balancing act, with pressure from the Chinese opposition, followed by the witch hunts of 1987, during which there were many arrests under the Internal Security Act. Pressure is also on the prime minister from the other side – from the Islamic party – to press Malay and specifically Islamic issues to the fore. The recent wave of Islamic revivalism throughout the world has convinced many Malays that a return to a purely Muslim society is the only way to remain true to the faith.

However, Dr Mahathir had demonstrated his strength as a political leader of a multiracial country, and has refused to cede to either side. The present concern in Malaysia is with forging an identity for the Malaysian, re-

gardless of race, based not so much on a merging of cultures, but on an understanding of the different faces of Malaysia and a pride in the country as a whole.

In the global arena, Dr Mahathir has emerged as a champion of both Malaysia and the developing world, with a growing reputation as a regional leader who is not afraid to voice his philosophy and opinions. In 1993, the Australian Prime Minister Paul Keating labelled Dr Mahathir "recalcitrant" for refusing to attend a regional summit. The remark almost resulted in a full-scale trade war, but in the end, an apology was made by Keating. A well-voiced opinion of Dr Mahathir is that the Western media are mis-

Dato' Seri Dr Mahathir Mohamad, Malaysia's fourth and current Prime Minister.

informed and that they project inaccurate pictures of Malaysia.

Economic prosperity: When Malaysia became independent in 1957, the economy was almost completely dependent on tin mining and plantation commodities like rubber and tea. In the harsh reality of the post-colonial world, it quickly became evident that Malaysia would have to develop a much broader economy if it was going to avoid the dubious fate of so many other former colonies. In the early 1970s, the government launched an ambitious crusade to transform Malaysia from its agro-mining foundation to a mixed economy with a strong manufacturing sector.

The economic crusade stumbled at first, because of inexperience and lack of capital. But the government persevered. A key move was a 1986 decision to revise foreign investment laws and strip away much of the government red tape that had prevented multinational companies from gaining a stake in Malaysia. Almost overnight, billions of dollars in foreign investment began rolling in – the economic boom was off and running.

Most of the industrial growth is concentrated in three areas: the Klang Valley, which comprises the federal capital territory and a huge chunk of Selangor state; Penang island and the adjacent mainland city of Butterworth; and Johor state in the far south.

The economies of all three states are growing at more than 10 percent a year, with a continued evolution towards more capital-intensive, high-tech industries. The states have virtually no unemployment and urban wages are about twice as much as the national average. Selangor alone attracts a third of new foreign investment each year, much of it concentrated in booming Shah Alam, where the Proton car factory is situated.

The national car project is often used as a sterling example of what Malaysia has been able to accomplish. A joint venture between Japan's Mitsubishi and Malaysia's Hicom – the national heavy industry conglomerate –

the Proton Saga was the first car made and designed in Southeast Asia. About 65,000 Protons are sold in Malaysia each year, and are exported to more than a dozen countries.

After more than two decades of work, the government can now claim that its crusade to transform the Malaysian economy has been a startling success. In 1970, manufacturing sales accounted for less than 12 percent of Malaysia's total exports. By 1992, the manufacturing share had climbed to nearly 70 percent – a phenomenal turnaround.

Malaysia's ultimate ambition to become a fully-developed nation is enshrined in a new national effort, Wawasan 2020, or Vision 2020. The target is to have real GDP double every 10 years between 1990 and 2020, giving Malaysia a standard of living equal to countries in the West by 2020.

Infrastructure cures: In 1997, Malaysia's economy took a beating, with the ringgit losing considerable value and requiring that other major projects, including an immense dam in eastern Malaysia, be postponed.

Malaysia hosted the Commonwealth Games in 1998, also the deadline for several major infrastructure projects, including the Kuala Lumpur International Airport, south of the city. But KL's traffic congestion has become a prime topic of conversation and a genuine excuse for delays. It is also a significant concern.

With a population of just 20 million, Malaysia is still relatively uncrowded by Asian standards, a distinct advantage over massive nations like Indonesia (200 million) and Thailand (60 million), which have a greater poverty and other social burdens. For instance, Malaysia has a much lower infant mortality rate and much greater proportion of doctors than either Indonesia or Thailand.

At the same time, Dr Mahathir's National Front coalition is firmly entrenched as the dominant political force in Malaysia. Also at UMNO's bow is Datuk Seri Anwar Ibrahim, the youthful heir apparent who was elected Deputy Prime Minister in November 1993. Now seen as the likely successor, especially with enhanced responsibilities starting in 1997, Anwar has excelled in several high-profile tasks. Anwar has also been a strong advocate for development and business.

Left, manufacturing expertise. Right, high technology is high on Malaysia's agenda.

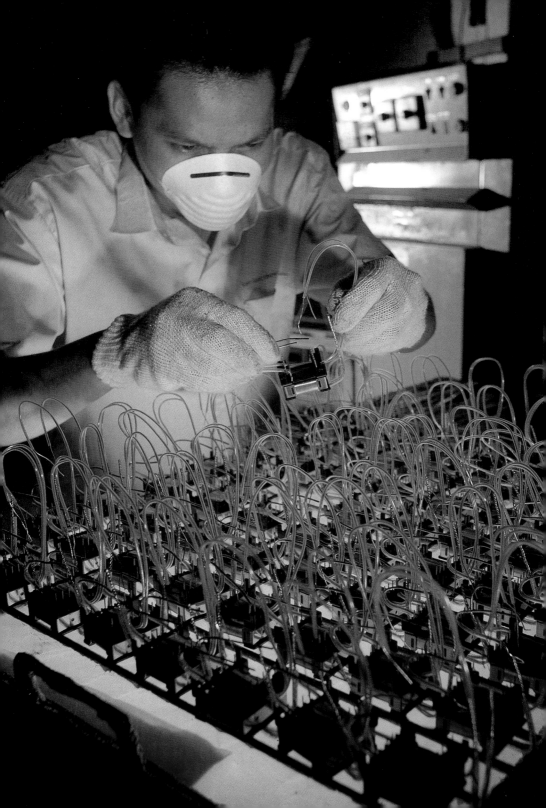

The rain forests in this region are the oldest in the world, making those in Africa and South America seem adolescent in comparison. While creeping ice fronts were swelling and shrinking across the northern hemisphere, the Malayan jungles had lain undisturbed for an estimated 130 million years. Some of the most unique and diverse species of animal and plant life evolved here, and some of the most primitive and remote tribes still inhabit this jungle world, living much like their ancestors did a thousand years ago.

The Malayan jungles, on the peninsula and in particular in Malaysian Borneo, have excited much scientific interest and continue to do so. The jungle holds many secrets which, through today, defy modern technology and remain undiscovered. Optimists believe that the plant life in these jungles may hold cures for many human diseases, but this is still a mystery left to be solved. Much of the flora and fauna of the forests is hard to discover if you are just "passing through", and scientists sometimes spend years searching for rare species of plants and animals.

The diversity in flora and fauna is truly staggering. In Malaysia, there are over 8,000 species of flowering plants, including 2,000 trees, 200 palms and 800 species of orchids, the most exotic of flowers, as well as beautiful highland roses rivalling their English counterparts. The most prominent flower in Malaysia is the elegant hibiscus, the country's national flower. The world's largest flower, the *Rafflesia*, is unique to the region. The entire plant consists of just the flowerhead, which can measure up to 1 metre (3 ft) across and weigh up to 9 kilograms (20 lbs). Being a parasite, it sucks its food from the roots of the *Cissus liana*, and starts life as a red bulb. The *Rafflesia* grows in size and finally bursts open, revealing its pink, red and white interior. If the size of the flower doesn't catch your eye, its odour, often described as that of rotting flesh, will certainly reach you from 50 metres (55 yds) or so away. The *Rafflesia's* glory only lasts a week,

after which it shrivels up into the moist jungle earth from where it was born.

Another world's first is the towering *Tualang* tree, tallest of all tropical trees. It can reach up to 80 metres (260 ft) in height and over 3 metres (10 ft) in girth. The famous pitcher plants can be seen everywhere on the slopes of Mount Kinabalu in Sabah, their honeyed jaws stretched open, waiting for a careless insect to drop in.

Malaysia's jungles also hold thousands of species from the animal kingdom, many unique

to the region, others introduced from mainland Asia. More than 200 species of mammals live here, including tigers, elephants, rhinoceros (though sadly, their numbers are greatly diminishing), black-and-white tapirs, sleek civit cats (*musang*), leopards, honey bears, and two kinds of deer—the *sambar* and the barking deer (*kijang*), with its dog-like call. Malaysia is also home to the region's tiny mousedeer (which is not technically a deer at all), wild forest cattle (*seladang*), the scaly anteater (pangolin), the badger-like *binturong* with its prehensile tail, and many kinds of gibbons and monkeys, including the quaint slow loris with its sad eyes and lethar-

Preceding pages: Rafflesia, world's largest flower. Left, hanging on to the jungles of Malaysia. Right, butterfly rests on a hibiscus.

gic manner. Borneo is also the home of the extraordinary orang-utan ("forest man" in Malay), which are treated like another tribe by the jungle peoples, and the proboscis monkey, the males of the species parading their humorous pendulous noses.

Whether venturing into the jungle or not, you will be sure to see anywhere in Malaysia some of the 450 species of birds, and quite a few of the 150,000 species of insects. Alfred Russell Wallace, who spent more than 10 years in the Malay archipelago, had a particular fondness for insects of all sorts, and often described himself as "trembling with excitement" when he caught a new species of butterfly or beetle.

land dipterocarp forests, which extend up to an altitude of 600 metres (2,000 ft). Trees grow to majestic heights of 60 metres (200 ft) or more, with the first branches 30 metres (100 ft) above ground. This is called the triple canopy forest. Commercially, this region is the most important; from here comes the timber for the sawmills. Timber is becoming Malaysia's main natural export, and efforts are being made to control timber exploitation so that Malaysia's fertile jungle will assure the industry – and ecosystem – a green future.

The next level of forest is mostly oak and chestnut, and above 1,500 metres (5,000 ft), it becomes a kind of never-never land with

Of the over 100 species of butterfly in Malaysia, the king of them is the Rajah Brooke's birdwing – the national butterfly – with its emerald markings on jet-black wings. There are over a hundred more other breathtakingly-coloured butterflies, as well as magnificent moths. They are best seen at butterfly farms all over the country, especially in insect-abundant Cameron Highlands.

Shades of green: More than two-thirds of Malaysia is jungle. The green cover begins at the edge of the sea and climbs to the highest point of land. Along the coastline, there are extensive areas of mud swamps and mangroves. Behind the mangroves are the low-

elfin forests consisting of small gnarled trees, 3–5 metres (10–16 ft) high, covered with folds of hanging mosses and lichen. The highland forests, for the most part, are left untouched and unlogged as catchment areas, ensuring the fertility of the soil.

With conservation gaining importance in Malaysia, the government has set aside tracts of land as national parks or game reserves, where strict hunting laws are enforced. These laws are taken very seriously by both game wardens and even remote tribes in the Borneo jungle, who used to shoot the prized and

Strangling Fig provides sculptural form.

THE GREEN DEBATE

Clumsy, large lorries laden with 15-ton loads of giant logs chained to the back are a common sight on Malaysian country roads. Hundreds of massive but elegantly buoyant logs float down muddy rivers from inland camps in Sabah and Sarawak, to the river mouth, where they are loaded onto ships bound for Japan and Hong Kong. Fresh sawdust is everywhere in peninsular Malaysia's industrial towns.

The felled logs bring in an average of US$4.5 billion each year to Malaysia, the world's largest exporter of tropical timber for the past decade. Despite an all-out US$10 million a year public relations campaign in defence of the anti-logging lobby in the West, Malaysia has been a target for discussion for green critics worldwide. Environmentalists claim that logging in Malaysia has wreaked ecological havoc, has endangered flora and fauna, and has destroyed tribal habitats.

The Earth Summit held in Rio de Janeiro, June 1992, was one such hot global platform of debate. There, Malaysian Prime Minister Dr Mahathir Mohamad, stated that to tell poorer countries to preserve their forests "is the same as telling these countries that they must continue to be poor because their forests and other resources are more precious than the people themselves."

Since then, Malaysia has gone green, not it claims, due to international pressure, but because the country is turning to sustained-yield harvesting to ensure that its forests will remain perpetually profitable. Malaysia is now practising a selective logging system, in which a maximum of 7 to 12 trees are felled per hectare. In addition, Malaysia's furniture-making industry is being aggressively promoted worldwide, to ensure that more money is made from fewer logs.

In answer to allegations of corruption and poorly-enforced laws, Malaysian authorities introduced in 1993, tougher measures against illegal loggers, including heavier fines and longer custodial sentences.

It seems this controversial issue will remain so for some time to come. On one side of the argument, the export of raw logs from Malaysia has been reduced by about half in recent years despite higher world prices for sawn timber. A common reminder by Malaysia for environmentalists is that those who created the greenhouse effect should definitely not be the ones to be pointing fingers.

In addition, logging companies are huge job-providers (an approximate total of 150,000 people are employed by Sarawak's timber industry); and many new laws and stricter punishments have already been introduced to curb illegal logging. Concessionaires, regardless of political position or blueness of-blood, are now all liable for strict fines and sentences. To enforce these laws, forest rangers are empowered to arrest and will have the backup of the police and army.

On the flip side however, it will take the state of Sarawak, (where hundreds of thousands of hectares are cleared each year) several more years to meet international green standards. The process will be difficult, as timber is the state's largest revenue, bringing in about US$1 billion a year, and the industry is more or less in the hands of a small elite of powerful, wealthy men. Hopes are still high for a global environment fund to subsidize the costs of enforcing environment protection, but most feel that chances are unlikely.

In the meantime, the Forest Departments of Malaysia, despite turning to satellites as a method of detection, cannot possibly cope with the dense and vast territory it has to police.

Malaysia's environmental problems at home and abroad will not be resolved too quickly. But to be fair, the country's sustainable forestry programme has made considerable progress, as has the attitude of the nation's leaders. Considering a statement made in defence of Malaysia's logging policy in 1991 by a government minister: "It's not our responsibility to supply the West with oxygen", Malaysia has certainly come quite a way. With luck, what remains of Malaysia's 130 million-year-old forest and inhabitants will be around as witnesses at the finishing line. ∎

sacred rhinoceros hornbill for its "ivory" beak, but now allow it to sit above in the trees while they wait for other game. This state of affairs has come a long way from the days when animals were killed, not just for food, but also for their skins, horns or feathers.

With the growing international consciousness of endangered wildlife and depleting world forests, there is hope that the Malaysian jungle will be allowed to flourish and retain some of its great mysteries.

Ever-green countryside: A smooth, well-maintained highway unrolls through green hills. Rubber trees flash by in never-ending even rows, monstrous tipples of tin mines appear where plantations leave off. Freshly-

ninsula and Borneo were once a single rugged land mass, joined together and running the entire length of the Indonesian and Malayan archipelago. For millennia, the sun, the wind, and torrential rains reduced the mountains to hillocks and outcrops. Precious soils were washed into the sea, and fingers of land became cut off by subsidence and erosion. The meticulous work of nature continues today. The extent and speed of this erosion can best be seen in Malacca. If standing on the ramparts of St John's Fort in Malacca town, you may wonder how the old cannons could have shot so far out to sea. Maps of that early period show that the area, including the present parade ground, was then covered by

planted oil palms stitch the land in a patch-work of deep green against cleared and cultivated red earth. In northern and coastal areas, fields are rich with stalks of golden rice.

As far as the eye can see, the lush green vegetation of the tropics smothers the landscape. Yet, contrary to its looks, Malaysia is not suited to agriculture. Unlike the Nile River Basin or the Ganges Valley, where seasonal rains flooding the land bring new fertile soil, the torrential downpours in Malaysia wash away the thin but valuable top soil. In many places, only red mud remains.

Erosion is one of Malaysia's oldest problems. Geologists believe that the Malay pe-

the sea. Alluvial soils washed down from the hills have reclaimed it in less than 400 years.

Despite the shifting landscape and annual monsoon rain, Malaysia's early settlers were basically food growers. As far back as AD 500, crops such as sugar cane, bananas, pepper and coconuts were grown for export, while rice was introduced to these lands over one thousand years ago. Traditionally, both men and women were involved in the cultivation of this crop – the staple food and prime source of income for the rural Malay. The tempo of *kampung* life has quickened with the introduction of double cropping, using hybrids of rice which reap a second crop each year. Self-sufficiency and reduction of rice imports is high on government objectives, and more fields are yielding to modern rice-growing.

Fortune in a tin pan: Malaysia is not exceedingly rich in mineral deposits, with the exception of tin, and there the country knows no rivals. Tin mining led to new settlements that sprang up from a few prospectors' shacks and became cities as large as Kuala Lumpur. This industry gave the British the revenue to build roads and railways through the jungle terrain, and it also introduced the Chinese to Malayan soil. The all-male mining townships were rough and risky. Malaria and cholera wiped out hundreds of prospectors

Cina, usually a man who commanded some respect amongst his compatriots. This practice continued under British rule.

Rubber, a reckless gamble: What stands out in Malaysia is a plant first grown in Brazil – the rubber tree. This plant, which now takes up more than three-quarters of all the developed land, was originally viewed with great scepticism by the coffee planters.

The man inspired by the rubber tree was H. N. Ridley, director of the botanic gardens in Singapore, where some of the first trees were planted. "Rubber Ridley", as the planters called him, was convinced that his crop had great possibilities, and he journeyed around the country with seeds in his pocket, looking

who sweated in the intense heat. Those who survived did so under a constant threat of tiger attacks, recorded at one time as a daily occurrence. Thousands perished in Chinese secret society feuds. Others made a fortune. For decades, the Chinese held a virtual monopoly on the tin mining industry, and for more than 70 years, Malaysia has been producing over one third of the world's tin.

To maintain a semblance of government in the early mining communities, the Malay chiefs appointed a civil governor or *Kapitan*

Left, a familiar sight in Malaysia – working the rice fields. <u>Above</u>, idyllic cruise.

for anyone he could convince to plant them. Ridley's was a farsighted and lonely crusade, until John Dunlop invented the tyre and Henry Ford put the automobile on the assembly line.

The rubber tapper continues today to set out before dawn to collect the cups of latex that make up nearly half of the world's rubber supply, but he stops short of the old boundaries of the estate to view a field planted with oil palms.

The government encourages farmers to diversify their crops by growing coconut, coffee, tea, fruits, nuts, spices – and oil palm. Palm oil increased in dollars earned in the

THE CITY

Much of present rural Malaysia remains steeped in agriculture. But the once isolated and self-sufficient village is now linked by paved road and public transport to the nearest town, where a farmer can stock up on Malaysian-brewed Guinness Stout and video tapes as well as dried fish and a new sarong.

People from the most isolated longhouse and *kampung* know all about the capital city of Kuala Lumpur with its gleaming skyscrapers and air-conditioned shopping centres, mostly because of the omnipresent television set in both urban condos and jungle huts.

The origins of the large cities and towns are

very different from one another. Some, like Johor, were established by powerful sultans as capitals to their empires. Others were first trading settlements set up by the Portuguese, Dutch or British, eventually becoming centres of administration in British colonial days.

Kuala Lumpur grew from a supplies centre for local tin mining in nearby Ampang, and many other towns emerged during the tin mining boom. Tin trading towns were originally unplanned, enlarging shop by shop as competition increased. Towns such as Kuala Lumpur developed into shockingly filthy, diseased and violent places, plagued by fires, floods and feuds. Chinese secret societies warred over tin holdings; nightfall became a dangerous time. Malacca had its big moment in history when it

became the centre of trade for Asia. Kota Kinabalu was originally a British trading settlement for valuable rhinoceros horns and bird feathers.

In the days of colonialism, British administrative centres became the epitome of bureaucracy, law and order. The centre of town was planned around a *padang* (literally a field, but meaning a stretch of closely-cropped grass), where official ceremonies took place and cricket was played. Around the *padang* would be several administrative buildings, the city hall, a post office perhaps, a law court and often a church.

This arrangement can still be seen in Kuala Lumpur, as well as in many other towns and cities throughout Malaysia. Graceful colonial houses were usually built as far away as possible from the swamps and shanty towns.

Nowadays, Malaysia's colonial buildings nestle between modern office blocks and traditional Chinese shophouses. These shophouses – two-storied terrace houses with shops below – are still the pervasive architecture of Malaysia's urban centres. The business of the day goes on under the shade of the famous "five-foot-ways" – arcades in front of the shop entrances.

Most Malaysian cities retain a distinct Asian flavour. Markets and bazaars crowd the streets, streetsellers calling out their wares in several languages, as Malay love songs and Chinese opera singers wail out from radios. The marketplace is the prime link binding countryside and town, and in small towns of Sabah and Sarawak, the central square becomes a "Borneo Bazaar" every Sunday. Barefoot tribeswomen trudge from the hills carrying baskets of bananas, betel nut and other village and jungle produce.

The Chinese assert the culture of their ancestors by combining pioneering stamina with the romantic memories of ancient Cathay. Signboards spring out from shophouses, painted with elegant calligraphy and sometimes romanized as: "Everlasting Harmony Shoemakers" or "Virtuous Accomplishment Goldsmiths" or "Mercers of the Thousand Prosperities".

In the last two decades, there has been a boom in the building industry, especially true in Kuala Lumpur, which has built one of the most impressive skylines in Asia. Lofty buildings such as the telecommunications tower have already become symbols of 21st-century Malaysia.

Even in modern buildings, arrows on the ceilings indicate the direction of Mecca for the followers of Allah; tucked in corners in 30-storey buildings, small Buddhist shrines smoke with incense and glitter with golden images.

More Malaysians are now moving to planned suburbs equipped with shopping centres, supermarkets and computer-equipped schools. If the proliferation of country clubs, golf courses and swimming pools is any indication, modern suburban living has truly infiltrated Malaysia. ■

late 1970s by 20 percent a year, bringing Malaysia's share up to nearly half the world's palm oil production. With the threat of a US ban on palm oil years ago, Malaysia is now looking more closely at its other industries to bring in the dollars, and to take Malaysia into the 21st century.

Tides upon the sea: Three months in a year, Malay fishing people on Malaysia's east coast store away their fishing nets, dock and repair their boats, move their fishing huts far up the beach, and settle down in the shelter of their wooden houses to wait for the winds to change. During the rains, time is spent following more leisurely pursuits: repairing fishing nets, spinning enormous and heavy tops, or making a trip to the city, or even embarking on a pilgrimage to Mecca if the year's fishing trade has been prosperous. When the winds drop, they will again venture out to sea in search of the wide variety of fish and seafood for the marketplace. This pattern of life has characterized Malaysia's eastern shore for centuries.

Almost completely surrounded by water, Malaysia was where the monsoons met, where the tides of the Indian Ocean and the South China Sea flowed together into the Straits of Malacca. Seafaring merchants, explorers, adventurers and pirates, seeking the wealth of the Malayan and Indonesian archipelago, stopped along these coasts to wait for the winds to change in their favour. Malaysia was the halfway point to this ancient interchange, linking China to India and India to the Moluccas.

It was the Moluccas, a small cluster of islands in the Indonesian archipelago, that set Asian maritime kingdoms against one another, and in Europe sparked off the Age of Discovery in the 16th century, impelling Columbus to cross the Atlantic, and Magellan to circumnavigate the globe. In time, the spice trade to Europe became so lucrative that a vessel loaded with spices from the Far East could make enough profit to pay 10 times over the cost of the voyage, including the value of the ship.

Greatest seaport in the world: "Malacca is the richest seaport with the greatest number of merchants and abundance of shipping that can be found in the whole world," wrote a Portuguese sailor in the 16th century. Business in Malacca was conducted in no less than 84 languages. Small wonder that the Malay language is replete with words adopted from Arabic, Sanskrit, Persian, Portuguese, Dutch and English.

Piracy on the high seas was a widespread, lucrative and once honourable profession, attracting merchants, noblemen, tribes-people and fishermen alike. For centuries, sailors trembled at the thought of passing unarmed through Malaysian waters at night. The most formidable pirate bands were the Lanuns from Mindanao. These men would sometimes recruit Borneo head-hunting warriors, and while the captains pillaged the cargoes, the crew collected war trophies.

Malaysian seas today hold untold riches from ships wrecked by storms or plundered by pirates. Rumours still circulate of hidden treasures buried in caves on islands off the East Coast of the peninsula.

Whether there are treasure troves of sunken boats loaded with gold and silks and buried chests hidden in caves or not, there are certainly other underwater treasures in the beautiful and varied marine life of the Malaysian waters. Much of the coast is surrounded by coral reefs of vivid colours, and creatures both beautiful and curious find their home here. Until recently, the seas were thought of only as a source of food, but today, there is a growing interest in underwater discovery, and the number of scuba-diving and marine clubs is steadily growing.

The east coast has found profitable possibilities for its long stretches of beach and coral islands, as tourists, eager for sunshine and palm-fringed coral sands, flock to coconut-sheltered beach huts and developed holiday resorts all along the coast.

Above water, a steady stream of 200,000-ton oil tankers and cargo vessels, replacing silks and porcelain with oil and tin, sails through the Malacca Straits. This section of water between the Malay peninsula and Indonesia's island of Sumatra still has the same strategic importance that spurred ancient kingdoms to war. Control of the straits remains an international controversy, because both Malaysia and Indonesia claim rights to supervise all traffic sailing within their territorial waters.

The recent increase in offshore oil exploration has greatly enhanced the value of sea territory, and the trading posts established by the British are now the leading commercial centres of the region.

The traveller in Malaysia will encounter warm and engaging people, their lifestyles embedded with rich yet culturally diverse traditions. First there are the Orang Asli, the indigenous people of Malaysia who have managed to retain some of their centuries-old roots. Those who followed, the Malays, built upon traditions of the soil and ocean, but embraced influences from elsewhere as well. And because of its rich resources and strategic location, Malaysia attracted still others, the culturally-rich Indians, Chinese, and Europeans.

Orang Asli: Who are the Orang Asli? The question is not so simply answered. The Malay term means "original people" and covers three more or less distinct groups and a score or more of separate tribes. Orang Asli has become a convenient term for explaining those groups of people who do not belong to the three predominant races found on peninsular Malaysia.

Undoubtedly, one group of people, the Negritos, are the oldest inhabitants of the Malaysian peninsula. Other groups only arrived here as recently as 100 years ago. Inaccurate as the term is, it is also to some extent harmful, for Orang Asli has come to denote amongst other Malaysians a "primitive" or "backward" people, a generalisation which cannot possibly be backed up. The Orang Asli can only perhaps be grouped together in the sense that, economically and educationally, they are less advanced than Malaysia's dominant groups.

The British were perhaps the first to group the Orang Asli together, using the term *sakai* or debt-slave to define them. Their origins still remain something of a mystery. What is known is that the main groups vary from one another racially, culturally, linguistically and economically.

Of the estimated 60,000 Orang Asli, 60 percent are jungle dwellers, while the other 40 percent are coastal peoples, many of them fishermen. The largest group are the Senoi

Preceding pages: Sarawak snapshots on a longhouse wall. **Left,** Muslim schoolgirls with warm Malaysian smiles. **Right,** an Orang Asli family.

(embracing the Temiar, Semai, Semok, Beri, Che Wong, Jah Hut and Mah Meri tribes). The second largest are the Proto-Malays or Orang Melayu Asli (including Temuan, Semelai, Temok, Jakun, Orang Laut, Orang Kanak and Orang Selitar. The smallest and oldest in number of all are the Negrito (including the Kensiu, Kintak, Jahai, Lanoh, Madrik and Batek). Reading this, the names will not mean much, but travelling around the peninsula, you will hear the various tribal names mentioned, rather than Orang Asli.

Negritos: The features of the Orang Asli are strikingly different from tribe to tribe. In general, as their name suggests, the Negritos are mostly dark-skinned and frizzy-haired, and their features, though unique, remind one of the peoples of Papua New Guinea or East Africa.

Their true origin is unknown. It is thought that they arrived in Malaya 8,000 years ago. Nowadays, the Negritos mostly inhabit the northeast and northwest, and are the only truly nomadic tribes of the Orang Asli. Practising little or no cultivation, the Negrito tribes pride themselves on their mobility, and possessions are thought only to be a hindrance to their lifestyle. Although some Negritos have left the protection of the forest and sought a modern education, the majority of the tribes have spurned the specially-built government villages.

The Negritos do not have a written language, but they demonstrate their sharp intelligence by being competent linguists, often speaking up to a dozen tribal dialects, as well as Malay and Thai.

They are an extremely shy people, and if frightened, are more likely to flee than fight. Social order is more or less unspoken and relaxed, with the oldest or the most suitable senior man being the chief. Respect for all living things dictates their code of behav-

ago. Most of the tribes are shifting cultivators, moving from a settlement when the land is exhausted. Their land is marked, and within their *saka*, or territory, they will return to abandoned villages once the soils have become more fertile. Many Semai in the Cameron Highlands have become wage-earners, working on the highland tea estates. Others have headed for the bright city lights, obtaining jobs as varied as government employees and taxi drivers.

Proto-Malays: This last group of Orang Asli were the latest group to arrive, no earlier than 4,000 years ago. The Proto-Malays are perhaps the least connected, however, and many of the tribes arrived from the Indonesian

iour. Fear of the spirits of dead ancestors and hunted animals is still strong among them, and it is still an unwritten law that all animals caught or hunted in the jungle should suffer little or no pain.

Senoi: Some of the darker Senoi people could be mistaken for Negritos, while some of the fairest, walking down the street in Kuala Lumpur in jeans and a T-shirt, look exactly like Malays. In general, however, the faces of the Senoi reflect a different ancestry.

The Senoi are thought to have common ancestors with the hill peoples of northern Cambodia and Vietnam, arriving in present Malaysia between 6,000 and 8,000 years

island of Sumatra only a few generations ago. The Johor Orang Laut were still in the islands south of Singapore a century ago. Many of this group also have a distinct resemblance to the Malays, not surprising, as modern Malays have a common ancestry with many of them. Others have decidedly Polynesian features.

Malays: The Malays, long linked to the land as *Bumiputra*, or Sons or Princes of the Soil, are renowned for being generous and hospitable with an easy smile and a well-developed sense of humour – traits perhaps of a people who have had the good fortune to live peacefully in a land abundant year-round with food. As far back as AD 500, Malays had so much in excess that they were growing crops for export, including sugar cane, bananas, pepper and coconut.

Back then, the *Rakyat*, or common people, lived to serve their ruler, who was invariably as far away from a village as a one-month river trip. Few of the power struggles among the ruling class penetrated the ruling *kampung*. With ample food and a warm climate, life in the isolated villages remained the same for centuries.

Rural Malays today still cherish the simplicity of the uncluttered, outdoor life, nurturing a provincial conformity laid down centuries ago. Malay kampung remain peace-

that are now an everyday part of kampung family life. Photographs of the King and the Prime Minister hang prominently on living room walls next to traditional batik, woven and other works of Malay art.

Kampung youth and children may favour cool shorts, and blue jeans may have established its usual cult popularity, but the daily dress code is still the comfortable cotton *sarung*. Rolled expertly at the waist, and topped off with a batik or T-shirt, this airy garment is especially indispensable among older Malays. Most men wear the sarung long at mid-calf, or hiked up between the legs and adeptly tucked at the waist if a shorter style is needed. The adaptable sarung

ful enclaves, with wooden houses propped up on stilts above a neatly-swept courtyard, shaded by coconut palms, banana and papaya trees. Chickens still wander freely in between and under houses, and crowing roosters are heard every dawn. Monkeys are still trained to harvest coconuts from tall trees. The aroma of curry and salted fish wafts from the kitchens at the back of each house.

The village mosque wakes up several times a day to call the faithful to prayer, often interrupting evening television programmes

Left, inside an Orang Asli home. Above, relaxing on the Penang Bridge.

can also double as a wrap-around towel after bathing, or unravelled, as a blanket at night, or even worn as a modest swimsuit. On special occasions, the traditional and comfortable *baju kurung* is worn by women, while men don their *baju melayu* and *songkok*. But these occasions are exceptions for kampung dwellers, as is travel. The ultimate in travel is a prestigious journey to Mecca, but other than the great pilgrimage, few kampung dwellers wander far.

The inherent talents of the Malays, however, find outlets far from the countryside. Malay businessmen and civil servants in the cities dress Western style, drive cars, speak

English fluently, and are armed with the prestigious cellular phone. Urban youths pick up the latest in street fashion from the US and display their new togs in city shopping centres. Despite a ban on men with long hair appearing on national television, many young men sport a popular straggly hairstyle. Also trendy is hard rock and heavy metal music, hence the cultish popularity of bands such as Guns and Roses, and of course the electric guitar. The amplified sounds of the instrument can even be heard blaring from isolated kampung houses.

Though the rift between the farm and the city generally widens as years go by, it does not threaten the strong unity the Malays

their *baju* and tudung only their hands and face. Despite this seemingly strict dress code and traditional Islamic laws (which, for example, allows polygymy), Muslim women in Malaysia are given an increasing amount of employment and property rights, and run businesses and have high-profile jobs.

Although there is little difference in status between men and women, some class differences remain between the nobility and the commoners. While they may have much less power than previously, sultans still occupy an important position in Malay ceremonies and official occasions, especially in their own states. There are 11 sultans in Malaysia (with the heads of Penang and Sarawak be-

derive from a common faith. The laws of Islam immediately set a Malay apart from fellow Malaysians. Pork, a food relished by the Chinese, is forbidden to the Muslim Malays. Intermarriage between races is uncommon, though Muslim foreigners are accepted, keeping the Malay-Muslim cultural identity distinctly separate.

Muslim women, especially, stand out from other ethnic Malaysians mainly because of their dress codes. Recently, an increasing number of Malay women (and foreign Muslims) have chosen to wear the veil, or *tudung*, an garment of modesty. Even school girls are seen playing in school, exposing from under

ing governors) and a king is elected from amongst them every five years. The official residence is the *Istana*, or the palace, in Kuala Lumpur, although all sultans have their own palaces in the capital and only use the Istana for official functions.

In the considerably less palatial home of the average Malay family, traditional customs are observed daily. The most noticeable is cleanliness of even the most modest kampung dwelling, as cleanliness is next to godliness for the Malays. It is said that the brighter the house, the more blessings God will bestow. Kampung houses are kept spotless and a basin of water is placed at the bottom of the entrance stairs for the washing of feet before entering. As in practically all Asian cultures, to tread into someone's home wearing shoes is absolutely unthinkable.

Indians: Indians began visiting Malaysia 2,000 years ago following rumours of fortune in a land their ancestors knew as Suvarnadvipa, the fabled "golden peninsula". Tamil blood even flows through the royal lineage dating back to 13th century Melaka, where the first sultanate grew up. But it was not until the 19th century that Indians arrived and stayed in large numbers, employed mainly as rubber tappers or other plantation labourers. Most came from south India, and approximately 80 percent were Tamil and

Four out of five Indians, mostly Tamils, are still manual labourers on plantations or in cities, a situation that has been explained as a legacy of colonial Malaysia. However, as the nation gains in economic prosperity, northern Indians are well-represented among successful professionals, and economic programmes have been initiated to raise the Indian share of Malaysia's wealth.

Indian Muslims are also a significant part of the Indian community. When they arrived in Malaysia, many opened restaurants, textile shops and other successful businesses, and some of them married Malay women.

The greatest cultural influence was brought over by the southern Indians, leaving a rich

Hindu, with small numbers of Sikh, Bengali, Keralan, Telugu and Parsi. Malaysian Indians still maintain strong home ties with their former villages, sometimes even taking wives from there and bringing them to live in Malaysia.

Today, Indians (mostly concentrated in the states of Selangor, Perak and Penang) make up less than 10 percent of the population of Malaysia, yet they own less than one percent of the country's corporate wealth.

Left, *songket* weaver, and Malay friendliness in a smile. **Above**, newsstand vendors in downtown urban areas are a common sight.

and colourful stamp on Malaysian life. Bright silk saris, Tamil movies on television with their formulaic song-and-dance scenes, Indian weekly magazines, and the indomitable prevalence of the Hindu faith that continues to absorb change have all become part of Malaysia. The Indians also introduced their hearty foods, adopted enthusiastically by everyone. The most interesting is the banana-leaf curry, now an indispensable local meal. Rice, vegetables, curried fish and meats are eaten off a banana leaf, using the fingers of only the right hand (the left hand is used for purposes of personal hygiene and thus considered unclean).

Chinese: The Chinese population makes up 35 percent of the country's total, yet their presence in and control of major industries such as rubber, tin and import and export companies would seem to make their numbers far greater. They can be found in any trading centre, from Kuala Lumpur to the smallest isolated shop far up the Rejang River in Sarawak. In 1794, Sir Francis Light, founder of Georgetown, Penang, wrote, "The Chinese constitute the most valuable part of our inhabitants:... they possess the different trades of carpenters, masons, smiths, traders, shopkeepers and planters; they employ small vessels. They are the only people from whom a revenue may be raised without expense and corruption amongst officials was widespread and the country was overrun by flood, famine and rebellion. An edict was issued making it virtually impossible for Chinese to travel abroad, but some, mostly out of necessity or encouraged by reports of wealth and employment in the Nanyang, risked their lives and escaped. These peoples were mostly from the coastal areas of Amoy and Canton, and included dialect groups such as Hokkien, Teochew, Cantonese, Hakka and Hainanese.

Tough jobs in the Nanyang: These later Chinese immigrants were organized under clan associations (*kongsi*) and secret societies, which often engaged in rival warfare. The new settlers took on many of the toughest

extraordinary effort by the government."

It was for both fortune and adventure that the Chinese first headed for *Nanyang*, the South Seas. From the 13th century onwards, the Chinese were frequent traders throughout the Indonesian and Malay archipelago. The famous Cheng Ho, admiral of the Ming Emperor Yongle's navy, first visited Malacca in 1403, and many Chinese traders afterwards followed his example and set up warehouses there.

However, the majority of the Chinese arrived in the 19th century during the Manchu dynasty. Problems were rife in China at that time: the class structure was disintegrating, jobs in tin mining, road and railway construction; but they also played as hard as they worked, and opium and gambling were the popular pastimes.

Mainland China remains important to the Chinese. Until recently, Malaysian Chinese were forbidden by the Malaysian government to return to communist China, but the older generations regularly sent financial help to relatives there, while others saved their money to return and die on their mother soil. China provides the tradition for the Chinese Malaysian community; it is the focal point for family ancestry and worship, and its customs continue through language and religion. Younger generations are more caught up in modern Malaysian and Western lifestyles, and express more nationalistic feelings than their elders. Rather than integrating with Malay culture, the Chinese community has put its own traditional stamp on the land. All Chinese must learn Malay, but at home, Mandarin and local dialects are often spoken.

There is a strong belief in self-help and industriousness among the Chinese, but close family and clan ties are also priorities. The Chinese in Malaysia are defined by their history of hardship and pioneering, as well as the three important Chinese ethical strands: Confucianism, Taoism and Buddhism. Even if converted to Islam or Christianity, this

time in the year that all Chinese businesses close for at least one day.

Everywhere, Chinese of all backgrounds start the new year by spring cleaning (to sweep out the previous year's bad luck), donning brand new clothes and shoes, and travelling great distances to attend the extended-family reunion dinner on the festival's eve. *Nian gao* (year cakes) are on sale as well as oranges and tangerines, symbols of gold that are presented as gifts when visiting homes. Younger or unmarried members of the family receive *hong bao,* small red-and-gold packets containing a token gift of money. Street calligraphers paint lucky gold characters, the astrological animal of

background is deep-rooted and many of the associated festivals are regularly celebrated.

The festival with the biggest bang (literally, thanks to Chinese fireworks), is the Chinese Lunar New Year. Occurring usually in late January or early February, the festival lasts not for just one day, but for a fun-filled, colourful fifteen. Unlike the Muslim Hari Raya Puasa or the Hindu Deepavali, the Chinese New Year is celebrated by Chinese of denominations other than Tao Buddhist and even non-Chinese. This is also the only

the year, or auspicious New Year greetings on red paper to be displayed on doors and walls in homes and businesses.

Much of the New Year's fortnight is spent visiting relatives and friends, with the younger generations visiting the homes of their elders. The highlight of these visits is a large trayful of festive cakes and tidbits, and if time permits, a good friendly game of *mahjong*.

During the rest of the year, Chinese belief in symbolism is equally prevalent. Jade is worn by the majority of Malaysian Chinese for aesthetic reasons as well as for its evil-warding powers. *Feng shui* (literally, "wind, water") is the Chinese belief system based on

Left, multi-ethnic camaraderie. **Above**, exhilarating dragon-boat races.

KAMPUNG PASTIMES

Every Malaysian is a *kampung* kid at heart; so opines Lat, Malaysia's favourite cartoonist who has a series of books contrasting the easy, down-to-earth kampung lifestyle with the cellular-phone and pager-punctuated life of the modern yuppie. Despite the city-dweller's perfectly groomed image and array of electronic devices, every holiday in Malaysia results in airports and highways jammed with city residents returning to their villages – *balek kampung*. Their kampung are their roots, where they slept on the coolest mats, ate the freshest foods from the land, and played the most economical yet heartwarmingly nostalgic pastimes.

Top-spinning: Throughout most of the country, top-spinning is a teenage pastime, but in the Malay kampung of the northeast coast, a champion spinner is the village hero. Record times for spinning are about two hours. Requiring great strength to spin, tops vary from a simple wooden cylinder to fantastic streamlined discs with spindles trimmed with inlaid gold, and large ones can be as big as dinner plates. With the harvest completed and all the rice stored, farmers traditionally settled down to watch and bet on the top local team. Contests feature either the endurance spinners or the strikers who spin down 7-kilogram (15-lb) fighting tops faster than a speeding bullet. Attackers need both skill and muscle, as the defending team contrives spinning formations to eliminate the attacker's top.

Kite-flying: Another traditional entertainment most popular in Malaysia's northeastern states, kite-flying was enjoyed in 15th-century Malaysia. Today, great pride is still taken in the design and the hand-crafting of each aerodynamic piece of art. The paper *wau* (kite) comes in creative and unique shapes, such as the crescent-shaped *wau bulan* (moon kite), with a wingspan and length of up to 3 metres (10 ft); the batik-covered *wau cantik*; and the *wau kuching* (cat kite), now the logo for Malaysian Airlines. Bow-shaped bamboo pieces are often attached underneath a kite to produce a melodic humming sound (*degung*). Contests of all levels were and are still held for serious kite-flyers to vie for height, manoeuvring skills, design, ability to stay airborne, and quality of sound. Today, international kite festivals are held in Malaysia, drawing cosmopolitan participants from both European and Asian countries.

Sepak takraw: This traditional *kampung* game has as its focus a ball about the size of a large grapefruit, made of woven rattan strips, and weighing 170 grams (less than half a pound). The aim of the game is to keep the ball in the air as long as possible by passing it from one player to another, using all parts of the feet, thighs, knees, shoulders, or any other part of the body except for the forearms and the hands. Scores are given for the number of kicks made before the ball falls.

Like volleyball in many aspects, the game requires acrobatic flexibility and practised skills, and is exhilarating to watch.

Congkak is a game requiring more wits than physical skill. Comparable to backgammon or checkers, *congak* substitutes the board and plastic chips with a wooden boat-shaped "board" and marbles or seeds. The congak board has two rows of holes in which the marbles are placed, and the object of the game is to have the most marbles to finish.

Marbles are also a favourite game in itself, especially among kampung children. However, the best childhood memories come from games provided by nature.

The pea-sized, red saga seeds from the large saga tree, for example, are used in a game of accuracy much like marbles. The game of pick-up-sticks is played with coconut twigs or satay skewers; little cloth pyramids are filled with raw rice and expertly flipped and caught in a favourite girl's game of "five stones".

Colourful chicken feathers are stuck into a flat rubber disc, and this *catek*, resembling a shuttlecock, is kept in the air while being nimbly kicked using only the instep of one's foot. Even conker-like rubber seeds are the centre of numerous, imaginative kampung games, which are all still fresh in the minds of almost every Malaysian. Just go ahead and ask. ∎

geomantic omens. The number 8 is extremely coveted for house numbers and car license plates, as its sounds like the Cantonese character for "prosper"; meanwhile, the number 4 is carefully avoided, as it sounds like "death".

Peranakans: The colourful *Peranakan* culture was first established when Chinese trade missions established a port in Malacca in the early 1400s. Inter-cultural relationships and marriages were naturally forged between traders and local Malay women, as well as between Malacca's sultans and the Chinese Ming emperors. In 1460, Sultan Mansor Shah married Ming Princess Hang Li Poh, who brought with her 500 "youths of noble birth", and many handmaidens to be settled

Malay dress such as the *sarung kebaya*, a unique bi-cultural cuisine, and a spoken language of mixed Malay, Chinese and some English colloquialisms.

Peranakan culture reached its height in the 19th century, and though Malacca was the Peranakan centre, large communities also flourished in Penang and Singapore. The women were well-known for their delicate clothing, intricate silver jewellery and accessories, glass beadwork, and prized delicate china known as Nonya ware – typically decorated Chinese porcelain with peony-flower and phoenix motifs in pinks, greens and other pastels. For centuries, the Peranakans nurtured a sophisticated and in-

around Bukit Cina (Chinese Hill).

Subsequent generations of Chinese-Malays were known as Straits Chinese, or Peranakans, which in Malay means "born here". When the Dutch colonists moved out in the early 1800s, more Chinese immigrants moved in, thus diluting Malay blood in the Peranakans, so that later generations were almost completely Chinese. However, this did not alter the Straits Chinese identity – combining the best of Malay and Chinese cultures. This colourful balance encompassed

Above, Peranakan culture in Malacca. **Right**, the traditional Chinese Lion Dance.

fluential society well-known for their business acumen. The cliquey upper-class Peranakans assimilated easily into British colonial society after the Straits Settlement was formed in 1826. Today's Peranakans are proud of their heritage – generally one of wealth – and consider themselves apart from the other Chinese.

Eurasians: When the sultanate of Malacca fell to Portuguese invaders in 1511, the new rulers sought to establish control by encouraging Portuguese soldiers to marry local women. The Portuguese men were instructed to treat local folk as equals and it is said that some displayed this by escorting local women to their seats in church as though they were noble Portuguese ladies.

As can be expected, a strong Eurasian community grew up with loyalty to Portugal through its ties of blood and the Catholic religion. After 400 years, the Portuguese Eurasians in Malacca, as well as in other towns in Malaysia, bear such names as Sequiera, Aranjo, Pinto, Dias, D'Silva and D'Souza, and still cherish the traditions of their European lineage. They are proudly protective of their unique Eurasian cuisine, and continue to speak Cristao, a medieval dialect once spoken in southeastern Portugal, but now used only in Malaysia. Descendants of cross-cultural marriages in the interior along the jungle rivers, although some live near the coastal regions, while others with formal education have found work in towns, commercial centres and national industries throughout Malaysia.

In Sabah, the largest group comprises the Dusun or Kadazan tribes, followed by the Murut (hill people, and the last of the tribes to renounce head-hunting), the Bajau (Muslims and famous cowboys and seafarers of Sabah), the Rungu (with their beautiful coiled armbands and black costumes), and Bisaya, Suluk, Lundayeh and Kedayan in smaller numbers. In Sarawak there is an even greater diversity of peoples and languages: the Dayak include Ibans, who make up the majority of

19th and 20th centuries are equally proud of their English or Dutch heritage.

Eurasians are just one more thread of the multiethnic, interwoven culture shown on the faces of Malaysia's people – not all Malay, but all Malaysian.

SABAH and SARAWAK

The two easternmost states of Sabah and Sarawak, situated in the north of the island of Borneo, have the most diverse racial groups of all Malaysia. Most of them are of Mongoloid extract and moved here from Kalimantan (Indonesian Borneo). They generally live in the Sarawak population, and the Bidayuh or land Dayaks. The Melanau are also a large community and then there are many tribes lumped together under the name of Orang Ulu. This term, meaning "interior people", has become somewhat derogatory in the sense that it denotes a primitive and ignorant people and most tribes prefer to be known by their own names. The Orang Ulu group includes the nomadic Punan and Penan, the highly structured Kayan and Kenyah communities, and the Kajang, Kelabit, Lun Bawang and Bisaya. Even these names house several different tribes who have their own special names.

The majority of the indigenous tribes have traditions and ways of living in common, but each group has some unique belief or activity that sets it apart from the rest.

A house for all: Most of the peoples of Sabah and Sarawak live in longhouses, large buildings that house the entire community under one roof, and may contain up to 60 families or more.

The Malaysian government is attempting to move longhouse communities into villages with separate houses, but with much resistance from the longhouse dwellers. Living in the longhouse is naturally very communal, and social organisation range from the very stratified to egalitarian. Each

A notched pole is the traditional mode of entry to the longhouse, as it could be drawn up at night to prevent intruders from entering; permanent ladders are now also used.

There are four main areas in a longhouse: the much-used *ruai*, or communal verandah, which takes up about half the space of the longhouse; the *bilik*, or family apartments, whose doors open onto the *ruai*; the *tanju* or outer verandah, attached to the *ruai* and used for drying rice and sometimes for ceremonial occasions; the *sadau* or attic, which is used for storing grains, weaving baskets and cloth, and as an extra bedroom.

As the longhouse usually faces the river, it is open to river travellers who may stop for a

longhouse has a headman, traditionally an inherited position but nowadays elected by the people. His job is mostly to settle disputes and arrange ceremonies.

All longhouses are situated next to rivers or streams, which are used for washing, fishing, and waste disposal. Waterways are also their main form of transport and contact with other longhouse communities. The longhouse is raised on stilts for security and airiness, and to avoid river flooding during the monsoon season.

Left, Kadazan traditional costumes. Above, Iban in traditional dress.

night's rest before continuing their journey, and also to Chinese traders who barter commercial goods for the much sought-after baskets and beadwork of the resident longhouse women.

Most tribes, and especially the Iban, are extremely hospitable and guests are welcomed with a glass of strong *tuak* (rice wine) before being offered a bed. It is customary for visitors to bring gifts of food, money or clothes to pay for their stay, but they are more than repaid in kind. Staying at a longhouse is a casual affair – it is really just a matter of arriving there and asking to see the village headman for permission to stay.

There may be a time, however, when a special sign is placed at the entrance of a longhouse or even down on the path by the river. This is a longhouse taboo and is marked by a stick with green leaves, a piece of white cloth or areca blossoms placed on the top. This signifies that some bad luck or unfortunate event such as death, a curse or a crop failure has befallen the longhouse, and visitors may not stay as guests until the sign has been removed.

For a death, this taboo can last from two weeks to three months. A hat placed outside a bilik door signifies that just that household has a taboo due to death, and visitors may still stay in any other bilik.

Most longhouses are self-sufficient in food. Rice and fruit trees are cultivated around the longhouse land, as well as cash crops such as rubber, cocoa and sago for sale at markets downriver. Fishing, hunting and the building of boats and canoes are also undertaken.

Myths and traditions: Borneo has been known as a land of headhunters, a term which seems to conjure up a cruel and aggressive people. Contrary to this misconception, the people of Sarawak are gentle, law-abiding people and in the days of head-hunting, taking the heads of one's enemies only occurred when the community was suffering some plague. The heads of enemies were thought to bring protection from danger and sickness. Taking a head was also a way of proving one's manhood. Only the heads of warriors were coveted, and the women and children of the enemy eventually became integrated into the victor's community. Today head-hunting is outlawed, and the skulls to be seen hanging in longhouses are those that have been inherited by families.

Tattoos are another cultural tradition in Borneo, and men and women receive many. Both for protection and decoration, each tattoo is arranged and designed to suit the wearer. Many tribes also place long weights or simple wooden plugs in the ears of children in order to stretch the earlobe. Only women, however, wear the heaviest ones so that their lobes may eventually stretch down to their chest. Such lobes are still considered a sign of great beauty by traditional tribes people, although many young women are now snipping and stitching their long lobes for more modern "normal" lengths.

Omens are of particular importance to Borneo tribes, and some Dayak groups' entire rice cultivation rests on whether a certain bird should call, heralding a good harvest, or dreading an unlucky bird adding its voice, forewarning of crop failure. Amongst the protective cover of the jungle, many of these age-old traditions continue, although now wristwatches adorn Iban men along with tattoos, and Guinness Stout may be offered as an alternative to rice wine.

With the migration of the younger members of the communities to towns, however, it may not be long before this traditional way of life dies out forever. Many of the young do return to the longhouse, but numbers are dropping as opportunities elsewhere increase.

The nomadic Penan and Punan people are mostly unaffected by these changes. Government attempts to make them settle permanently in one place have largely failed, as their love of freedom and inherent self-possession lead these tribes to pursue their traditional ways of life. While other tribes prefer to remain in the proximity of their longhouses and to travel by river, the nomads have an uncanny knowledge of the jungle and its inhabitants. Extensive logging threatens this lifestyle, but they are committed to protecting the jungle.

Left, ready for Malaysia's National Day. Right, young woman during National Day celebrations.

SPICE AND ALL THINGS NICE

Malaysia has been blessed with constant, paradisiacal weather and a lush landscape: tropical jungles, verdant rice paddies, endless coconut groves bending to meet teeming coral reefs submerged in emerald seas. These gifts of nature and the ethnic complexity of Malaysia's population provide the country with ample cornucopian flavours to titillate the palates of gourmets and gourmands alike. This wonderfully sinful, hedonistic encounter extends not only to multicultural tastes, aromas, colours and textures, but to the vast spectrum of dining experiences as well. Eating establishments range from dusty roadside stalls and noisy Chinese coffee shops, to air-conditioned plush restaurants and fast-food joints. The choices are infinite.

Kampung feasts: For centuries, Malays lived peacefully in *kampung* (villages) close to rivers and coasts, enjoying the natural abundance of food. Traditional meals consisted of rice, fish, vegetables, and chilli sauces (*sambal*). Fresh herbs and coconut milk added much fragrance and richness.

However, because travel across the jungle-covered peninsula was limited till this century, regional styles of cooking prevailed. The northern states of Kedah, Kelantan Perlis and Terengganu have incorporated sour tamarind (*asam*), limes and fiery chillies in their cuisine because of the influence of neighbouring Thailand. One of the best known northern dishes is *nasi ulam*, a dish consisting of rice, finely sliced raw herbs and vegetables, a spicy chilli-coconut sauce, grilled fish and other cooked dishes on the side.

Indonesian influences are also evident in various Malaysian states. In Johor in the far south, Javanese food was assimilated into Malay cooking over the past two centuries. In the central state of Negri Sembilan, Menangkabau settlers from West Sumatra brought with them their rich, spicy dishes cooked in coconut milk. A perfect example is *rendang* – a semi-dry coconut-based curry which needs hours of gentle simmering, melding beef, mutton, or chicken with a multitude of fresh herbs like lemon grass,

Selling fresh local produce with a smile at a Kota Bahru market.

turmeric and ginger, and spices such as coriander, nutmeg, cloves and cinnamon. The result: a melt-in-your-mouth dish with just a hint of sweetness and plenty of richness.

Despite differing regional styles, Malay food in general is heavily seasoned with pan-Asian spices: cumin, coriander, pepper, cardamom, star anise, and fenugreek for starters. Even soy sauce (*kicap*) is liberally used. Chillies of all sorts are an everyday pick-me-up, either in dishes or as a blended *sambal* side-dish.

The key to almost any Malay dish however, is the *rempah* – a pounded paste of fresh seasonings which include onions, garlic, chillies, fresh turmeric, and the delicate galangal rhizome (*lengkua*). The rempah is cooked in hot oil in a *kuali* (Chinese wok), patiently stirred to prevent sticking and to release a tantalizing blend of aromas. It is said that this process is the make or break of the whole dish. A subtle seafood flavour is often added in the form of dried shrimps, dried anchovies (*ikan bilis*) or a pungent, pinkish grey shrimp paste (*belacan*).

Mouthwatering as they may sound, these Malay recipes are lost without the simple, indispensable staple: rice (*nasi*). To have curry without rice can be likened to having a sandwich without bread. Rice dishes take many forms: *nasi minyak* (enhanced with spices like cardamon and cinnamon), *nasi tomato* (delicately red and universally appealing), *nasi goreng* (stir-fried with meat, eggs and chillies), and entire meals consisting of rice and side dishes: *nasi padang* (of Indonesian influence), *nasi kandar* (famous in Penang), and *nasi dagang* and nasi ulam (in Kelantan and Terrenganu). Some Malay dishes demanding to be tried are:

Satay: Possibly the world's most popular Malay food. Marinated bite-sized pieces of beef, mutton or chicken (and pork, sold by Chinese) are skewered on thin, bamboo sticks, and barbecued over a charcoal fire. The sizzling satay is served with a thick, spicy peanut gravy, chunks of raw onion and cucumber, and *ketupat*, pressed squares of rice. Leave the remaining bamboo sticks on the table, as the "bill" is settled by counting the total number of sticks left. For offalphiles and the adventurous, there are satay variations of tripe, pig intestines, or crispy chicken skin – although these are now increasingly rare. The best satay is reputed to be in Kajang, in Selangor, but very good satays can be found in almost any town in Malaysia.

Nasi lemak: More of a meal than just a dish, nasi lemak is usually eaten as a substantial breakfast. The name means "rich rice" – a savoury rice cooked not in water, but gently steamed in coconut milk till every drop of the liquid richness has been absorbed. The rice is then served with a fiery sambal (a cooked blend of chillies, onions and belacan), cucumber for coolness, small crispy fried fish, and a fried egg or omelette. Depending on

from coconut milk, glutinous rice or rice flour, eggs, and brown palm sugar (*gula melaka*). Classic desserts are: *cendol* (green jelly-like strips in coconut milk and *gula melaka*, topped with shaved ice), and *ice kacang* (fruit, red beans and jelly buried under a mountainous heap of shaved ice generously drizzled with coloured syrups and canned evaporated milk).

To be completely immersed in the whole Malay culinary experience, it is imperative to try at least once the traditional Malay way of eating, still practised in the average Malay home: with your fingers. It may look simple, but it is a skill to be mastered. Using only the tips of the fingers on the right hand (the left

your appetite and where you eat it, nasi lemak can also be served with a rendang and other curries.

Noodles: Chinese immigrants have introduced noodles to Malay cuisine and are now indispensable: *mee* (a spaghetti-like yellow wheat noodle), *kway teow* (flat strips of smooth rice noodle), and *mee hoon* (thin rice vermicelli); all can either be stir-fried (*goreng*), served in a light soup, or in speciality dishes such as *mee siam* (mee hoon in a red, spicy, *asam* soup), and *mee rebus* (mee in a thick, brown spicy gravy).

Desserts: Malay cakes (*kueh*) are a colourful and decadent assortment, mostly made

hand is considered unclean and never used), any Malay can pick, tear, and scoop with complete deftness. Increasingly, however, outside the home many Malays use a spoon in the right hand, which is brought to the mouth, and a fork in the left, used mainly for manoeuvring food onto the spoon.

Chinese food: Chinese immigrants to Malaysia brought with them the cooking styles of their mainland regions. Cantonese, Hokkien, Teochew, Hakka, and Hainanese are the predominant strains found throughout Malaysian cuisine.

Symbolism plays an important part in Chinese cuisine. Parts of the animal are supposed to strengthen the corresponding part in the human body.

Hence, eating pig's brain soup will increase concentration and alertness, braised beef tendons or chicken feet will boost tired legs or heal strained muscles, and similar connections are made for liver, kidney and other offal dishes.

Symbolic meaning also comes from the (usually Cantonese) names of foods. For example, a seaweed that looks exactly like black hair is called *fatt choy*, meaning hair vegetable, but which is phonetically identical to the Chinese characters meaning to prosper. This weed is usually stewed with dried oysters (*hou si*), which sounds like

sauces and sambals. This penchant for hot stuff is evident in Malaysian Chinese homes where curries are commonplace and varieties are boundless. Curries of chicken or pork with chunks of potato are the most popular, while vegetable, salted fish and fish head curries (using only large, meaty fish heads) are other favourites on the spicy list.

For milder tastes, the selection at hawker stalls and Chinese coffee shops on practically every street corner in every town present a mind-boggling selection.

Wantan mee: Thin, fresh egg noodles either served in a broth or tossed in an oil-and-soy-sauce dressing; topped with roast pork slices and prawn and pork dumplings.

"good business". Not surprisingly, this dish is a standard inclusion on annual Chinese New Year menus, as are prawns (*ha*), which symbolize happiness.

Although many authentic mainland dishes still remain intact, some so-called Chinese food in Malaysia would baffle any mainland Chinese, just as "chop suey" and "egg rolls" astound many non-American Chinese.

To start with, Malaysian Chinese food is almost always consumed with chilli of some kind: pickled green slices, or pungent chilli

Left, satay, succulent skewers of meat. **Above**, rich and spicy *mee rebu*.

Ipoh kway teow: As the name suggests, this soupy dish gained fame in the town of Ipoh, in Perak. Smooth, translucent strips of rice noodles are served in a tasty prawn and pork broth, garnished with crisp bean sprouts, shredded chicken and prawns. Ipoh boasts the most delicate *kway teow* and fattest bean sprouts, supposedly because of the soft water which runs down from the surrounding limestone hills.

Char kway teow: Another classic Malaysian Chinese noodle dish of flat rice noodles, garlic, prawns, cockles, bean sprouts, eggs, chilli paste, and lashings of thick, dark soy sauce for a hint of sweetness.

Chicken rice: There are several variations, but the most popular is Hainanese chicken rice. Whole chickens are gently simmered in chicken stock, so that each slice served is moist and tender. Of equal importance is the rice, which has been cooked in chicken stock instead of water. A garlic, ginger and chilli sauce, cucumber slices and coriander leaves are standard garnishes.

Balls, and more balls: Innocent meaty morsels, they are made of different pureed meats and usually served in a clear soup, or in noodle dishes; beef balls, pork balls, and fish balls are the most common.

A note for the confused: the names of Chinese food often vary because the

ally comprises different fried or baked breads, rice, and a vast range of soft, cooked vegetables and bean curries (*dhal*). For sheer entertainment value, however, Buddhist vegetarian food wins hands down. The meatless menu is fascinatingly creative: mock duck, mock abalone, mock prawns, mock oyster sauce, even mock fried fish with crispy skin, all prepared in mild or spicy sauces. Although the "meats" are all made of soy protein and wheat gluten, the variety of resulting textures is truly impressive.

Indian food: Although the Indian population makes up only about 10 percent of all Malaysians, Indian stalls and restaurants proliferate everywhere. The majority of Indians

romanization of Chinese words depends on the dialect in which it is pronounced. Hence, flat rice noodles could be called *kway teow* by a Hokkien, while it is *hor fun* in Cantonese, or *guo tiao* in Mandarin.

Restaurant Chinese food in Malaysia is considerably more traditional and less novel. Dainty Cantonese dim sum, spicy Sichuan food, crispy Peking duck, luxurious shark's fin and any other unadulterated Chinese classics are available and of a high standard.

Vegetarian food: Delicious meat-free fare can be enjoyed by even the most ardent meat-lover at many Buddhist or Indian vegetarian restaurants. The Indian variety usu-

are Tamils from the south Indian state of Tamil Nadu, whose food is coconut-based, hot and spicy, and served with rice – a logical favourite with Malays. There are also northern Indian restaurants, dishing up milder fare with delicious breads, while other stalls and restaurants are run by Indian Muslims, strictly observing Muslim dietary laws.

Eating at one of the many "banana leaf curry" restaurants in Malaysia, you will experience one of the heartiest and most colourful culinary spreads around. The banana leaf itself is not eaten, but acts as a natural, disposable green plate from which spicy dry mutton, fried fish, chicken curry, red curry curried crabs, and a variety of spiced vegetables and pickles are eaten. The meal is often accompanied by fresh yoghurt to cool the palate, and cups of thin, spicy soup (*rasam*) to aid digestion. The entire meal is strongly but perfectly seasoned with the dried spices used by Indians for thousands of years: chillies, cardamom, cloves, cumin, fenugreek, cinnamon, fennel and mustard seeds, to name just some. Fresh lime juice is almost always available to top it all off.

Despite this complexity of Indian spices, many Malaysians would stand firm on the claim that India's greatest culinary contribution to Malaysia is the multi-layered, featherlight *roti canai* (flattened bread) – a flaky

curries for lunch or dinner. When roti canai dough is stuffed with minced beef, mutton or chicken, with diced onions and sometimes egg before frying, it is transformed into *murtabak*. Served with simple accompaniments like curry gravy and sliced pickled onions, the meaty murtabak is actually a meal in itself.

When visiting Indian hawker stalls, take note of these Malaysian Indian creations: Indian *mee goreng* (fried yellow noodles), similar to the Malay mee goreng, but with slightly different spices; and Indian *rojak*, deep-fried fritters dipped in a sweet, hot sauce – noticeably different from the Chinese and Malay salad-like rojaks.

fried bread made of wheat flour, *ghee* (clarified butter) and touch of milk for lightness. A stretchy dough is kneaded, rolled into balls, then dramatically tossed repeatedly into the air (*à la* pizza); the resulting dough is paper thin, and is folded and fried to give a crisp, flaky pancake. A popular breakfast item, canai can also be eaten at any time of the day. For breakfast, it is usually served with a small dish of curry gravy for dipping, and with more substantial meat and vegetable

Left, succulent chickens are a Malaysian favourite. **Above**, dining *au naturel* on Indian banana leaf curry.

Peranakan food: A lovingly-prepared, bicultural cuisine that is unique to Malaysia and its island neighbour Singapore. It is a food of love, conceived by the interracial marriage of early Chinese immigrants and native Malays, resulting in a Peranakan, or Straits-born Chinese culture. These Nonya women combined the best of both cuisines, producing delectable dishes for their Baba men. Nonya food subtly merges typical Chinese ingredients such as pork, soy sauce and preserved soya beans with Malay spices, standard rempah ingredients and the ever-present coconut milk or tamarind. Being non-Muslim, Nonya pork dishes were everyday fare. Some favourites: *babi asam* (a tamarind-based pork curry), and pork satay, with pineapple-enhanced peanut sauce.

Another non-Malay meat is duck, popular in Nonya kitchens. This poultry is braised whole, or made into a curry or sour soup (*itek sio*). Chicken is also commonly used, transformed into varied dishes such as chicken *kapitan* (chicken cooked in spicy coconut milk) and *encik kabin* (fried chicken with a tangy dip).

Much like Malay cuisine, Nonya food evolved differently in different parts of the peninsula. *Laksa*, a classic Nonya dish, comes in two varieties: *laksa lemak* (also called curry laksa) consists of noodles, prawns and

please their would-be Baba husbands. Under the watchful eye of elder Nonya women, the girls would practise pounding rempah in the correct manner, and slice and chop everything to the desired measurement. Nothing in traditional Nonya cooking is large or clumsy; every bite has to equal in size, approximately 2 centimetres (1 inch) in length. Garnishes are prepared with equal care, and vegetables such as cucumber almost always have their peels and seeds removed even if edible, then pared into thin, curly strips.

Eurasian food: This is Malaysia's other ethnically-complex cuisine. The mecca of Eurasian food is undoubtedly Malacca, which fell to Portuguese invaders in 1511. Although

other toppings bathed in a lemak (rich) spicy coconut soup; it is prepared by Malacca Nonya cooks.

Then there is *asam laksa*, a famous speciality of Penang Nonyas. This variety, with clear Thai influences comprises noodles in a clear, fish-based soup, topped with raw cucumber and onion rings, pineapple chunks and mint sprigs.

Not only is the taste of Nonya food impressive, it is also painstakingly prepared. Despite the many attending servants of old-style Peranakan homes, young Nonya women traditionally spent hours in the kitchen mastering the precise culinary skills that would

Portuguese rule ended 350 years ago, a century of mixed marriages resulted in modern-day descendants who are Catholic Malaysians, with Portuguese, Malay, Javanese and Indian ancestry. Children of mixed marriages during the 19th and 20th centuries, with one parent commonly being English or Dutch, are also part of Malaysian Eurasians, and share a possessive passion for the multi-ethnicity of East-meets-West food.

The Eurasian cuisine is typically multicultural: Malay herbs spice up Chinese cuts of pork, further enhanced by Indian mustard seeds and chillies. A famous dish is Devil Curry, a fire-and-brimstone name for a spicy dish based on a Goanese Vindaloo, further pepped up with vinegar and chillies. Similarly, English dishes such as stews and roasts are transformed for the better with a simple addition of soy or oyster sauce, sliced green chillies, or sour tamarind juice.

Undoubtedly, though, the highlight of any Eurasian kitchen wafts through the air in the form of warm, buttery, baking aromas. Eurasian cakes are sinfully delectable – rich fruit cakes, and the infamous *sugee* cake: a rich yellow cake made with heaps of only the best churned butter (traditionally imported in a can), sugar, vanilla, and a mixture of wheat flour and gritty sugee flour (Indian semolina flour). The result is a decadent tea treat favoured highly by most Eurasians.

Related to Eurasian cooking is colonial food – British dishes that were originally cooked by hired Chinese help (almost always Hainanese Chinese). These cooks apparently slipped Chinese seasonings such as soy sauce, oyster sauce, and corn starch into sedate the English food, resulting in tastier roasts, and famous chicken and pork chops slathered with peas, onions and a gravy seasoned with garlic and soy sauce. The altered dishes met little protest and have remained till today. A few older colonial cooks are still plying their fare, in older hotels and locally-run Western restaurants across Malaysia.

Food from the jungle: Void of European influence is the food of Bornean Malaysia, namely the foods of Sabah and Sarawak. Traditional Borneo food is hard to find these days, mainly available only in the longhouses and remote villages. Rice is the main staple, although traditional tribes still adhere to diets based on boiled sago palm and tapioca root. Raw meats and fish are preserved by smoking or left to cure in bamboo jars of salt. Fresh jungle vegetables like bamboo shoots and fern tips are regular accompaniments, as are lashings of lime and chilli.

Nowadays, what is typical food in Borneo is in fact a Chinese- and Malay-influenced cuisine. From the Chinese immigrants this century, Borneo food has adopted soy sauce, stir-frying and other cooking methods; from the Malays, chillies, dried shrimp, and prawn paste (belacan). Using these ingredients, vegetables, jungle animals such as wild boar,

Many Malaysians claim that dining *al fresco* at a hawker stall is unbeatable.

and seafood from the coast and rivers are deliciously braised and stir-fried. Stranger jungle fare can be found even on the peninsula. For those with adventurous spirits and strong stomachs, jungle-food restaurants can be found in many states.

Johor, for example, (see Travel Tips restaurant listings), boasts popular Chinese restaurants serving bullfrogs, wild-boar, snake, monitor lizard, flying fox (a kind of bat), civit cat and a host of seasonal "chef specials", which should be tasted before being identified if they are to be enjoyed. Although the types of meats used may turn Western stomachs, the quality of cooking is usually deliciously outstanding and imaginative.

Thirst-quenchers: A wide choice of fresh fruit juices are available in every coffee shop and restaurant; guava, starfruit, watermelon, pineapple, sugar cane and young coconut juices are especially refreshing.

Or try the homey tastes of Milo (malted chocolate), cloudy and sweet barley water, sweetened soya-bean milk, black Chinese herbal tea, or good, old-fashioned Indonesian coffee or Cameron Highlands tea, all of which come either hot or iced. For a more lingering effect, Anchor, Tiger and Carlsberg beers, and locally-brewed Guinness Stout, are Malaysian male favourites, as are their blatantly seductive, "sex-sells" advertising posters and calendars, plastered on every coffee shop wall. Don't be surprised if ice is served with your beer – locals like their brews very well chilled, albeit a little watered-down.

Ordering a simple tea or coffee in Malaysia may be a little trickier than expected. The beverages are always served with generous lashings of sweetened condensed milk – this is *teh* (tea) or *kopi* (coffee); black with sugar is *teh-O* or *kopi-O* ("O" is a transliteration of the Hokkien Chinese word for "black"); with just milk (here, usually evaporated) and no sugar is *teh* or *kopi kosong* (*kosong* meaning "empty" in Malay); without milk or sugar is *teh-* or *kopi-O kosong*. One of the most entertaining facets of tea-drinking is the *teh tarik* (pulled tea) man, who runs the *mamak* (Indian) drinks stall. This performance artist displays the refined art of the tea-cooling ritual – the liquid is thrown from one cup to another in each hand, over a distance of about 1 metre (3 feet). The tea served is frothy and perfectly cooled – a perfect drink for any Malaysian meal.

The Malay house is a fine example of the indigenous architectural idiom that has emerged from Malaysia. It is also a unique solution for life in this tropical climate. This building type is characterised by its thatched roof and raised-above-ground stilts, a functional feature which provides cross-ventilation and which leaves the house high and dry during the all-too-common monsoon floods.

If there should be an image that captures the essence of Malaysia's cultural, traditional and historical heritage, a picture post-

card of the traditional Malay house would do justice. The various architectural styles are influenced both by Menangkabau forms, with its sweeping, curved "horns" or "wings", (most pronounced in Negri Sembilan), and Thai-Khmer design. Differences are most evident in the shape of the roof. The *bumbung panjang* (long roof) design is the oldest and most common, with its graceful long gable roof thatched with *attap* (nipah palm leaves).

Towards the north, Thai influences are more evident in *kampung* dwellings. There are fewer windows, and walls are wood-panelled and decorated with relief carvings.

The oldest Malay houses on the peninsula date back to the 19th century. These are designed in the *rumah berpanggung* style, built on stilts, with an A-shaped roof.

From the intimate scale of the kampung to the country's political and economic seat in Kuala Lumpur, the architectural scenario changes likewise. The twin 88-storey Petronas Tower, also known as the Kuala Lumpur City Centre, is a 1.1-million-square-metre (11.8 million sq ft) development in the hub of the city, currently the tallest buildings in the world. Its architect, Cesar Pelli from New York, has considered Islamic geometric principles and has incorporated them into the building's design.

One such modern building that has applied Islamic motif with success is the Dayabumi complex. This 35-storey office tower makes creative use of grille that is cast in an Islamic pattern, which also functions as an efficient sun-shading contraption. At night, the tower glows with elegance, delivering a subtle message of nationalistic confidence.

The use of Islamic idiom in architecture in forging a national identity is not new. In fact, it began in the late 19th century, and it is interesting to note that it was the British colonialists who left behind this legacy. When the Sultan Abdul Samad building was erected by the British in 1896, a crucial precedence was set for a newfangled genre of architecture. Elements sourced from the Moorish, Gothic and even the Renaissance were melded together to create a unique design language.

The Kuala Lumpur Railway Station, designed by A.B. Hubback in 1900, is another distinguished monument that abides by the Islamic theme. Majestic towers and minarets soar skywards, making a striking contribution to the lofty landscape of Kuala Lumpur.

A noteworthy building type was developed by the Peranakans, the first ethnic Chinese to settle in the Straits Settlements, and who adopted the Malay language and ways of life.

An insight into the rich tapestry of their heritage can be found in the sprawling, pastel-painted mansions in Penang, and the eclectic long and narrow, five-foot-way terrace houses in Malacca, built around a central courtyard, and dominated by an interior of dark wood furniture inlaid with marble and mother-of-pearl. Perhaps leaving an even greater indelible mark upon Malaysia's chequered colonial history were the Portuguese, Dutch and British settlers. The Portuguese made their presence felt in Malacca in the early 16th century. They built the A Famosa fortress in 1510, which is by far the most significant relic in the Malay peninsula.

More than a century later, Malacca came under the Dutch rule. The governor built the *Stadhuys* (Town Hall), which became the

In Malaysia's eastern states of Sabah, the longhouse typifies the indigenous residential building type. An elongated gallery runs through the length of the rectangular timber-and-thatch structure, raised safely above the ground on stilts. Access into the interiors is by ladders at both ends of the longhouse.

This house can sometimes support an entire village of people, with each family allocated a section of living quarters. No nails are used in the construction of the longhouse, only ropes are used to secure the timber

administrative seat of the Dutch. The red building still stands today in the heart of Malacca town, and is a popular background for many holiday snapshots.

The British rule in the late 18th century saw a concerted buildup of colonial administrative buildings. In the hill stations of Cameron Highlands, where the misty and chilly climes are similar to England, Tudor-style cottages complete with chimneys, fire places and rose bushes became retreats for the expatriate community.

Left, modern Islamic architecture. **Above**, traditional Malay wooden house.

together. Attap is used for roofing and split bamboo covers the floor. The longhouse, therefore, might be regarded as an ecological house, even long before being friendly to the environment became fashionable.

Longhouses and Malay houses are just a part of the varied, multicultural building landscape that characterises Malaysia. However, like other parts of the world, the country moves inexorably forward into the 21st century. In the last few years, Malaysia has been buoyant with considerable economic success and this paves the way for concrete-and-brick, glass-and-steel residential and commercial architecture to proliferate.

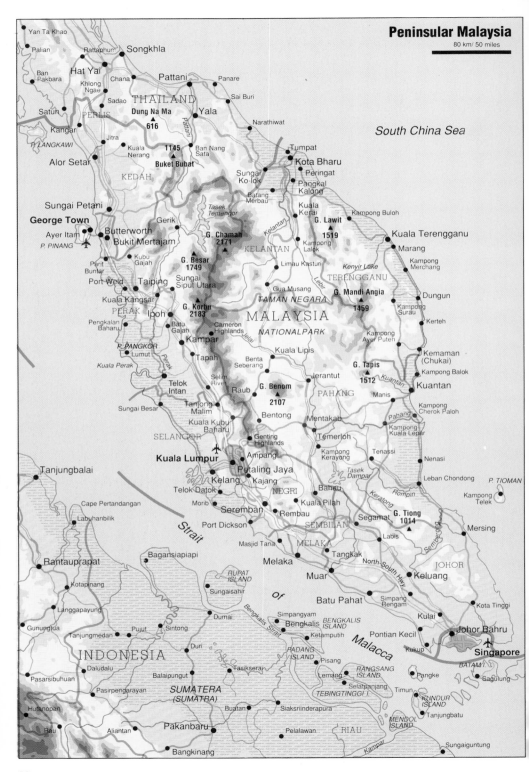

Peninsular Malaysia

80 km/ 50 miles

Yan Ta Khao
Palian
Rattaphun
Ban Pakbara
Hat Yai
Songkhla
Chana
Khlong Ngae
Pattani
Panare
THAILAND
Sadao
Sai Buri
Satun
PERLIS
Yala
Dung Na Ma
616
Narathiwat
South China Sea
P. LANGKAWI
Kangar
Jitra
Kuala Nerang
1145
Ban Nang Sata
Alor Setar
KEDAH
Buket Bubat
Tumpat
Kota Bharu
Peringat
Sungai Petani
Gerik
Sungai Ko-lok
Pangkal Kalong
Kampong Buloh
George Town
Butterworth
Tasek Temengor
Batang Merbau
Kuala Kerai
Ayer Itam
Bukit Mertajam
G. Chamah
2171
Kelantan
G. Lawit
1519
Kuala Terengganu
P. PINANG
Kubu Gajah
KELANTAN
Kampong Lalok
Marang
Parit Buntar
G. Besar
1749
Limau Kasturi
Kampong Merchang
Port Weld
Taiping
Sungai Siput Utara
Kenyir Lake
TERENGGANU
Kuala Kangsar
PERAK
G. Korbu
2183
Cameron Highlands
Gua Musang
G. Mandi Angin
1459
Dungun
Pengkalan Baharu
Ipoh
Batu Gajah
MALAYSIA
Kampong Surau
Kerteh
P. PANGKOR
Lumut
Kampar
NATIONAL PARK
TAMAN NEGARA
Kampong Ayer Puteh
Kuala Perak
Tapah
Benta Seberang
Kuala Lipis
Kemaman (Chukai)
Telok Intan
Selim River
Raub
Jerantut
G. Tapis
1512
Kampong Balok
Sungai Besar
Tanjong Malim
G. Benom
2107
PAHANG
Kuantan
Kuala Kubu Baharu
Bentong
Mentakab
Manis
Kampong Cherok Paloh
SELANGOR
Genting Highlands
Temerloh
Pahang
Kampong Kuala Lepar
Kuala Lumpur
Ampang
Kampong Kerayong
Tenassi
Nenasi
Tanjungbalai
Petaling Jaya
Tasek Dampar
Leban Chondong
P. TIOMAN
Kelang
Kajang
NEGRI
Bahau
Rompin
Kampong Telek
Telok Datok
Morib
Kuala Pilah
Keratong
Cape Pertandangan
Seremban
Rembau
Segamat
G. Tiong
1014
Mersing
Labuhanbilik
Port Dickson
SEMBILAN
Labis
Masjid Tana
MELAKA
JOHOR
Bantauprapat
Bagansiapiapi
Melaka
Tangkak
North-South Hwy
Keluang
RUPAT ISLAND
Muar
Batu Pahat
Simpang Rengam
Kota Tinggi
Kotapinang
Sungaisahir
Langgapayung
Dumai
Simpangyam
Bengkalis
BENGKALIS ISLAND
Kulai
Gunungtua
Tanjungmedan
Pujut
Sintong
Duri
Ketamputih
Pontian Kecil
Johor Bahru
Pasarsibuhuan
Daludalu
Balaipungut
Tasikserai
PADANG ISLAND
Pisang
Kukup
Singapore
Pasirpengarayan
INDONESIA
SUMATERA (SUMATRA)
Buatan
Siaksriinderapura
RANGSANG ISLAND
Lemang
Selatpanjang
Timun
Pangke
BATAM I.
Sagulung
Hutanopan
Bau
Aliantan
Pakanbaru
Pelalawan
TEBINGTINGGI I.
KUNDUR ISLAND
Tanjungbatu
Bangkinang
RIAU
MENDOL ISLAND
Sungaiguntung
Kampar

Strait

of

Malacca

The tourist brochures claim that "Malaysia... has it all." And so it does. Picturesque fishing villages, cosy hill resorts, unexplored tropical forests and miles of empty white sand beaches. Mix into these scenes the cultural pastiche that is the Malaysian people, and the result is an irresistible combination of rural charm, intriguing lifestyles and a hint of adventure that's guaranteed to give expectant visitors a glimpse of the closest thing to paradise.

And that's just the tip of the coconut tree. Malaysia's multitudinous attractions also include traditional arts and crafts, colourful religious festivals and copious amounts of comestibles to pacify even the most epicurean tastes. In fact, sampling mouthwatering Malaysian food comes close to being a religious experience in itself.

Situated smack in the middle of Southeast Asia, with a total land area of 342,000 square kilometres (132,000 sq mi), Malaysia is about the size of Japan, but with only a fraction of the population (about 18 million compared to Japan's 124 million). Peninsular Malaysia accounts for 40 percent of the land area, and 86 percent of the population. The East Malaysian states of Sabah and Sarawak are separated from the peninsula by 640 kilometres (400 mi) of the South China Sea, but each of the 13 states has a charm and character of its own. Malay and indigenous tribes make up over half the population while Chinese, Indians and others also come under the broad spectrum that is covered by the term "Malaysian".

Since independence in 1957, Malaysia has faced a series of economic and political pitfalls. Each time it has emerged with the same clear-eyed determination to succeed. Perhaps the biggest achievement is a complete transformation of the Malaysian economy from almost total dependence on raw commodities like rubber and tin, to a broad manufacturing base that has made Malaysia one of the emerging "Little Dragons" of Southeast Asia.

Despite these sweeping changes, the inevitable outcome of living in an age of rapid development and high technology, Malaysia is still very much a land of *kampung* (villages), jungles, beaches and rice fields, made that much more appealing by a friendly, deeply religious and uniquely diverse group of peoples. Malaysia does have it all.

Preceding pages: the Niah Caves contain traces of prehistoric people; business is booming in Kuala Lumpur.

KUALA LUMPUR: BOOMING CAPITAL

A mining outpost 100 years ago, a big city today, **Kuala Lumpur** is the capital of Malaysia, with a population of 1.5 million. To the newcomer, Kuala Lumpur – or "KL" as it is popularly known – is a fascinating mixture of old and new, increasingly so with the recent completion of the world's tallest buildings in downtown KL. Mosques of Moorish design, elaborate Chinese temples and crowded shophouses, Hindu temples with towering gates and Indian restaurants, and regal remnants of the shipshape British order – all set the colourful scene of multiracial activity.

On the green of the Padang (now officially named Dataran Merdeka), a cricket match is in progress with British, Chinese, Sikh and Malay players. Clinics in town prescribe colourful Western medicines or earthy Chinese remedies; shop signs form a chequered pattern of Chinese, Arabic and Roman scripts. There are stately mansions of eclectic style, traditional mosques and temples are squeezed between modern office blocks, and supermarkets vie with well-stocked shops selling everything from hairspray to incense sticks. KL's restaurants and open-air stalls offer food for every palate.

Bare beginnings: Various stories tell of how Kuala Lumpur got its name. The best one is the simplest: the miners and traders who first came in search of tin poled up the river to where the Klang and Gombak rivers converge. The Gombak estuary was the highest point upstream that the miners could land their supplies for prospecting tin in Ampang, a few kilometres further inland. The first party of 87 men to do so, however, fared badly, and within a month 70 had died from fever. Nonetheless, others soon arrived and persevered, building shelters and opening trading posts. They named the settlement Kuala Lumpur, which means Muddy Estuary in Malay. By the 1860s, the miners' landing place had become a flourishing village. Kuala Lumpur was founded in turbulent times, when fierce rivalries over mining claims and water rights led to civil wars. Gang clashes, feuds and murders went hand in hand with an ever-present threat of devastating fires and pestilence.

Essentially a rambunctious pioneer mining settlement, KL was predominantly Chinese, with its brothels, gambling booths and opium dens. It was put under the leadership of Yap Ah Loy, the *Kapitan China* or Chinese headman, who was supposed to keep some semblance of order in this wild, all-male settlement. He played a major role during the civil wars and continued to direct the affairs of the town till his death in 1885.

The Kapitan warred against crime, built a prison and quelled revolts. Under his guidance KL was rebuilt, but the damage done during the civil wars was more than skin-deep, so that by the time of Yap Ah Loy's death, the town was nothing but a jungle outpost of wooden huts along narrow lanes.

Then Frank Swettenham, the British resident of Selangor, made his entry and moved his administration to KL. The settlement began to assume its modern shape as Swettenham encouraged local businessmen to build brick kilns; street by street, the old town was pulled down and reconstructed with wider thoroughfares and stone and brick structures. A rail line from Kuala Lumpur to Klang, connecting the capital to the sea, was opened in 1886.

Kuala Lumpur's development was rapid from this time onwards. With its establishment as the state capital of Selangor, more and more people from surrounding villages moved there. It quickly grew in size and population to become an administrative centre and the hub of all business and trade. By the end of the century, it was the colonial capital of the then newly-created Federated Malay States, and graduated in 1946 to become the headquarters of the Federation of Malaya.

After independence in 1957, the pace of KL's progress became even more rapid. Kuala Lumpur came of age in

Petronas Towers, world's tallest buildings.

1974, when it was formally detached from the state of Selangor and made into a unit of its own called the Federal Territory. Today, it is the seat of government for all Malaysia, with its own administration headed by a minister of cabinet rank. Over the past 15 years, the skyline of the city has changed out of all recognition as new high-rise buildings continue their upward thrust.

A tour on wheels: In order to get a sense of the different faces of KL, it is a good idea to start your visit with one of the tours offered by local travel companies, often running from major hotels. Or make up your own tour by hiring a taxi for the day (negotiate the price before setting off). This will give you a chance to see some of the fascinating sites which are more spread out, so that you can save your feet for a stroll around the vibrant streets of Chinatown.

You might do well to start at **Jalan Benteng**. Although there is very little to see nowadays, this is the site of the first KL settlement, next to the confluence of the Gombak and Klang rivers. From here, the tin mining supplies were unloaded and taken to Ampang. Behind Jalan Benteng lies the area that was originally Yap Ah Loy's empire, now the business centre with towering glass and steel blocks, and blending into this area are the old streets of Chinatown.

If you cross the rivers, you will come to the old centre for British colonial rule, with its Moorish administrative buildings, still important today. The Old City Hall and a British colonial club face the **Padang**, also known as **Dataran Merdeka**. A similar stretch of green can be found in most towns influenced by British rule, notable examples including Singapore and Ipoh.

It was here that the strangest of all British games, cricket, was played, and the crack of bat against ball can still be heard today. The Padang was the centre for the British community, and games could be watched from the verandahs of the British Selangor Club on one side of the green. Other games such as hockey, football, rugby and tennis were also played here, although nowadays these

The Padang's expanse fronts the Selangor Club.

are more likely to take place in KL's modern stadiums. The Padang saw the British flag lowered for the last time on 31 August 1957 and the new Malaysian flag replacing it. The Padang is still used as a venue for national events, and parades on National Day start here. After nightfall, a different kind of parade takes place here, as local transsexuals and transvestites take over the green. In 1989, the Padang was dug up to make way for an underground carpark to help alleviate KL's parking problems.

The imposing **Sultan Abdul Samad Building** casts its shadow on the Padang. The core of colonial KL, this building was once the colonial secretariat headquarters, and now houses the **Supreme Court**. It was the first building to be built in a North Indian-cum-Moorish style, a trend brought to Malaysia by two architects, A.C. Norman and A.B. Hubbock. Both men had spent some time in India, and deemed that an architectural style featuring Moorish, Indian and Arabic motifs would best suit a predominantly Muslim country, apparently ignoring the fact that the Malays already had a very highly developed and practical building style of their own.

The Supreme Court was once the most photographed building in the city, with its 40-metre-high (130 ft) clock tower, the Big Ben of Malaysia, topped with a golden dome and flanked on either side by two dome-topped towers. (The Petronas Towers, looming into the clouds, now draw the most cameras.)

On state occasions, coloured bulbs light up the arches of the Supreme Court. Its foundation stone was laid in 1898. Sir Charles Mitchell, the governor of the Straits Settlements at the time, thought the building a ridiculous extravagance, and was heard to say: "The tin won't last forever, you know."

He was right, of course, but tin was later replaced by other natural resources, and later manufacturing, forming the backbone of Malaysia's economy.

One end of the building houses **Infokraf**, or the Handicraft and Information Centre, which features exhibitions of local art as well as an art gallery.

The Sultan Abdul Samad Building houses the Supreme Court.

A white man's club: On another side of the Padang is the **Selangor Club**, built in 1884 in mock-Tudor style, with a more recent extension which blends in well with the older and smaller building. The club was sometimes known as the "Spotted Dog", a derisive allusion to the club's emblem of a running leopard. It was once the watering hole for colonial officers and a white man's club. Today, its members represent the changing faces of Malaysia, and senior government administrators and prosperous businessmen prop up the long bar where the British once sat over their *setengah* (literally half, meaning half a peck of liquor). A.C. Norman was responsible for the building of the Club, and if you look closely, you may find several Malay architectural styles incorporated into the building's design.

The third side of the Padang faces **St Mary's Church**, also built in 1894 by A.C. Norman as well. Colonial families once trooped across the Padang on Sundays in their Sunday best, retreating to the church's cool interior to listen to the magnificent pipe organ built by Henry Willis, a renowned British organ maker during the 19th century.

Minarets of Islam: The Church has somewhat taken a back seat since Malaysia was declared a Muslim state. Until the opening of the National Mosque after independence, the **Jame Mosque** was the principal Muslim centre for prayer in the city. Lying behind the Padang, on the tongue of land at the meeting of the Gombak and Klang rivers, this serene and elegant mosque was designed by A.B. Hubbock, and adapted from a Moghul mosque in North India. Its onion domes and minarets rest on the level of the palm trees in the surrounding gardens, and its pink and white walls are especially spectacular at sunrise and sunset. It is accessible from Jalan Tun Perak, from which visitors enter the grounds of the mosque through the *sahn* or walled courtyard.

Open to visitors, shoes must be removed before entering and women should be well dressed. At sunset a mirrored glass skyscraper nearby gives **Answering the calls to prayers.**

a mystical reflection of the mosque, combining old and new Kuala Lumpur.

There are other buildings in the area around the Padang built in Moorish style, and which have influenced more recent edifices since. Along the same riverside, but further down from the Padang and connected to the Central Market and business district by a pedestrian bridge, is the towering white **Dayabumi Complex**. Fragile Islamic arches raise this 30-floor skyscraper, reputedly once the most expensive building in Malaysia, and built entirely from imported materials. It was completed in 1985 and is fully computerised. It houses government offices.

Below are shops and restaurants and the equally impressive **General Post Office**. On Saturdays, there are excursions to the top of the Dayabumi building which start from the fountain between the Dayabumi and the General Post Office. It is an excellent way to get a bird's eye perspective of Kuala Lumpur and its surroundings, and it inspired one artist so much that he painted his version of the view on the wall at the top of the building.

Beyond these modern buildings on Jalan Hashamuddin lies the **Kuala Lumpur Railway Station**. To arrive by rail in Kuala Lumpur is a fantastic experience as turrets, spires, minarets and Arabic arches greet the eye in every direction. Inside, the design is that of many large Victorian railway stations in England. This was so much the case that construction was held up because the roof design did not meet the then-British standards, which stipulated that the station roof must be able to support one metre of snow! The station was completed in 1911 and its platforms have been crowded ever since.

Within the railway station there is a post office, a selection of restaurants and a hotel. The wonderfully old-fashioned **Station Hotel** underwent renovation in recent years, although it still retains an air of faded grandeur. The original lift is still in operation for a leisurely ride upwards, the lobby and restaurant downstairs have lofty ceilings with spinning fans, and the bed-

rooms are enormous, with large balconies and huge attached bathrooms with Victorian bathtubs. Opposite the station is the **Malaya Railway Administration Building**, with the same Moorish design. Along from this giant building is the old colonial Majestic Hotel, which formerly provided lodgings for important British officers and their families. It has now been converted into the **National Art Gallery**, which exhibits permanent pieces, as well as temporary exhibitions, in rooms that were once the lobby and restaurant of the old hotel.

Next to the gallery is the **Balai Kuala Lumpur**, a tourist information centre, open Monday to Friday from 8.30am to 4.45pm, and from 8.30am to 1pm on Saturdays, closed on Sundays. It has few brochures but the staff are helpful and will be able to give you directions. Upstairs is the **Sang Kanchil craft shop**, which has a representative selection of handicrafts, carpets, pots and clothes for sale.

Just up the road from this Victorian enclave is the ultramodern **National**

Kuala Lumpur's classic railway station.

Mosque or **Masjid Negara**. Completed in 1965, the jagged 18-point star roof and the 70-metre-tall (240-ft) minaret catch the eye. The 18 points of the star represent the thirteen states of Malaysia and the five pillars of Islam. This was one of the country's first post-independence constructions and is one of the largest mosques in the region. Its Grand Hall – busiest on Fridays – can accommodate 8,000 worshippers.

On the roof there are 48 smaller domes, their design and number inspired by the great mosque in Mecca. It is an impressive building with cool marbled halls, long galleries, and reflecting pools in the courtyard. The minaret rises from the centre of one of these pools. The mosque is set in 5 hectares (13 acres) of gardens. One area of these gardens is reserved for the tombs of Malaysia's most celebrated dignitaries; the former prime minister and other pioneers of independence are already at rest there. Decorous clothing and behaviour is recommended, with shoes removed before entering. Scarves and covering robes are available for women, who should also use the separate entrance.

A garden retreat: Downtown KL is crowded with buildings, both old and new, and you may begin to wonder if there are any green spaces in the city apart from the Padang. A recent upsurge of interest in the greening of KL now allows it to boast 30 public greens, from roundabouts planted with bougainvillea to spacious parks.

The best-known and most popular of these parks are the **Lake Gardens,** or **Taman Tasik Perdana**. Seventy hectares (170 acres) of undulating green with magnificent trees and flowering plants prove that the jungle can be tamed. The park owes its existence to A.R. Venning, a British official who managed to persuade Swettenham in 1888 that Kuala Lumpur needed a public park. The largest lake, **Tasik Perdana**, once known as Sydney Lake, has boats for hire by the hour. The gardens are popular with locals and visitors alike; they are especially crowded at weekends when in the early morning or evening, joggers puff their way around the humid paths, families have a lavish picnic, lovers seek more secluded spots, and old Chinese men go through their *tai c'hi* routine. The park is open from 10am–6pm. (Mondays to Saturdays) and from 8am–6pm on Sundays and public holidays.

Within and around the park are several interesting buildings. Seventy-six metres (250 ft) above the lake stands the gleaming white **Parliament House**, a mixture of modern architecture and traditional motifs. The building consists of an 18-storey tower and a transcepted chamber, housing government offices, committee rooms, a banquet hall, restaurants, bars and a library. In use since 1962, the building is also open to visitors, but respectable attire and appointments are necessary.

On a smaller hill but in an imposing position stands the **National Monument**, erected to commemorate those who died in the struggle against the Communist insurgency in the 1950s. The galleries at the base of the statue record the names of all the units who

National Mosque.

fought, including British, Australian, Fijian, Maori and Malay troops. The statue itself may seem surprisingly familiar to some visitors, as it is a model of the famous Iwo Jima Memorial in Washington DC. This statue caught the eye of the late Tunku Abdul Rahman, Malaysia's first Prime Minister, while on a visit to the United States. Felix de Weldon cast the Malaysian model in bronze in Italy, and the statue now has a purely Malaysian symbolism.

The topmost figure holds the Malaysian flag and symbolises unity and strength; two men on either side of him denote strength and vigilance; a man comforting a wounded comrade on the centre front of the group stands for the suffering and sacrifices made by soldiers of all ranks. The base of the statue is moated by a pool with a cascading fountain and pewter water lilies, pewter being one of Malaysia's prized metals. A small bridge over the moat gives access to the monument.

Not too far away is the **Cenotaph**, erected by the British to commemorate the soldiers who died in World Wars I and II. It originally stood near the railway station.

Also in the gardens is the **Lake Club** – founded by breakaways from the Selangor Club in the early 1900s – and the **Carcosa Seri Negara**, a pair of magnificent colonial mansions that have been transformed into a super-luxury hotel. Carcosa (built in 1896) was once the official residence of the British governor of Malaya; Seri Negara was a guest house for visiting foreign dignitaries. Among the famous people who have stayed here are Queen Elizabeth and Prince Philip. More recent additions to the Lake Gardens include orchid and hibiscus enclosures, bird and deer parks, and **Butterfly World**, with more than 6,000 beautiful winged creatures flitting around in a natural habitat.

Another interesting edifice is the **Tun Abdul Razak Memorial**, the official residence of the late Tun Abdul Razak, the second Prime Minister of Malaysia. Known locally as Sri Taman, the house is now open to visitors, and exhibits

The National Monument commemorates victory over the Communists.

documents and possessions belonging to the late Tun Abdul Razak, who was best remembered for his rural developments and his sense of social justice. On the edge of the gardens, sitting on an incline on Jalan Damansara and facing Jalan Travers, is the **National Museum**. The museum was initially built on the site of the old Selangor museum, but was destroyed during World War II. The new museum opened in 1963. It sports a huge Menangkabau roof and front walls covered with Italian mosaic flanking the main entrance. The museum is well worth whiling away a few hours, especially for its social and cultural sections. These include an extensive section on the Nonyas and Babas, the unique culture born of a fusion between Chinese and Malay traditions.

There is also a complete reconstruction of a Malay *kampung* (village) and, on the other end of the social scale, a courtly scene complete with antique attire and gold and silk adornments. Also represented are Malay pastimes and sports, and there is a detailed history of shadow puppets, with displays from Turkey, India, Indonesia, Thailand and Malaysia. The Orang Asli cultures and societies are well documented, and displays inform on wildlife and natural resources, with a diagrammatic representation of an open-cast mine. Other interesting exhibits include the skull of an elephant which is reputed to have derailed a train! There is also an *amok* catcher, a frightening device once used to catch and render harmless a person who has "run amok".

In the basement is an extensive reference library with original manuscripts and charts, accessible to the public with permission from the curator. The museum is open daily from 9am–6pm, except Fridays, when it is closed between noon and 2.45pm.

The **Museum of Asian Arts** is 4 kilometres (2.5 mi) down the road from the National Museum, heading away from the city. The museum is in the grounds of the University of Malaysia, itself worth a visit if you are interested in doing research on any aspect of the **Flower shop in downtown KL.**

country. The museum has more than 2,000 items of Chinese, Japanese, Indian, Persian and Southeast Asian origin on display. The museum is open during office hours, on weekdays only.

Tai c'hi **on the hill:** Still on your tour on wheels, cross the river to Jalan Kinabalu which leads to Jalan Stadium, where Kuala Lumpur's three main stadiums dominate Cangkat Stadium, or Stadium Hill. The **National Stadium (Stadium Negara)**, with its enormous unsupported roof, looks more like a spaceship from *Close Encounters*.

Chin Woo Stadium, the oldest of the three, has a swimming pool; the grandest of all is the **Stadium Merdeka** (Independence Stadium), a huge arena with a capacity of 50,000 spectators, and built in time to mark the nation's independence in 1957. The formal handing over of power from the Queen's representative to the nation's first Prime Minister took place here in the presence of the nine rulers of the peninsular Malay States. Today the stadium continues to function as the venue for national occasions, ranging from annual international Koran-reading competitions to military tattoos and football cup finals. Soccer enthusiasts take the opportunity to watch a football match by floodlight, for, sensibly enough, Malaysians like to play after the sun has set.

In the early morning, at Cangkat Stadium, you can catch sight of many exponents of *tai c'hi*, a graceful and dignified Chinese martial art. Most of the performers are elderly citizens, oblivious to the sound of the city starting up the morning rush to the office.

Prisons, palaces and temples: The **Pudu Prison** on Jalan Pudu has its name in the Guinness Book of Records for having the longest wall painting done by one man. This man was a prisoner who, every day from 8am–6pm, painted a mural on the outer walls of the prison, depicting rural and jungle scenes. After completing two walls, the painter stopped as he had finished serving his sentence. Enjoy the mural while you can; Pudu prison is earmarked for redevelopment within the next few years.

Early morning exercise at Merdeka Square.

Also in this part of southern Kuala Lumpur is the **National Palace**, the official residence of the king. The palace began life as the town house of a wealthy Chinese *towkay* and was sold and converted into a palace for the sultans of Selangor in 1926. Its design, with its white walls and large balconies, is colonial, but on the roof a golden dome surrounded by a crown proclaim otherwise. Yellow is the colour for royalty, and only kings may walk on the welcoming yellow carpet while politicians and visiting dignitaries tread on red. Royal garden parties, investitures and receptions are held here, but normally the king lives in his own palace, every sultan having his own "mini" palace in the capital. Each sultan is given a turn as king for a five-year period, and election is by rotation and consensus.

Beyond the National Palace and further south along Jalan Lepangan Terbang is a small road which climbs a steep hill (Jalan Kerayong). Follow it and you will find yourself near the Chinese cemeteries, and with a command-ing view over the city. On this hill stands the largest and newest Buddhist temple in KL, which was completed in 1985. This is the **Yuen Tung Tze Temple** and was built by several Chinese multimillionaires who, it is said, each donated one pillar of the temple – count the pillars! Although it is known that the cost of building the temple was phenomenal, the exact figure remains a firm secret.

The building is a complete community centre, with a large conference hall on the ground floor for meetings and weddings, a restaurant in the basement, and youth and women's clubs and offices on the first floor.

The temple itself, with its many large and small roofs, sits right at the top. There is even a small garden inside the temple, which is perfect viewed from any angle. The building is an incongruous mixture, gaudy yet impressive, mystical yet decidedly worldly.

Towers and mansions: The city's newest landmark is currently the world's tallest building, or, rather, pair of build-

Sikh fortune teller awaits a customer.

ings: the **Petronas Towers**, whose identical twin towers, linked midway up by a skywalk, reach an auspicious 88 stories above the traffic-congested streets. Competing for lofty attention is the **Menara Kuala Lumpur**, a 421-metre (1,380-ft) telecom-and-tourism tower completed in 1995, and one of the highest structures in the world. Consider a ride to the observation deck on top.

Historic **Jalan Ampang** presents a much different aspect of urban architecture – a row of old tin miners' mansions that have been well preserved despite the tropical weather. The tin empire gave mine-owners the money to build lavish mansions, and these were generally built along Jalan Ampang itself. They were all large and flamboyant, and served as signs of how well the owner was doing in the mines. Many have since fallen into disrepair and have been pulled down, making space for the modern version of the mansion: the skyscraper and office block. Some remain, quietly being taken over by the jungle that was once a well-kept garden; yet others have been preserved and give a glimpse back into the tin boom days when elegant ladies and gentlemen peopled the rooms, danced on the verandahs and walked in the gardens.

The best preserved of these mansions is **Dewan Tunku Abdul Rahman**, built in 1935 by a wealthy Chinese tin mogul and rubber planter named Eu Tong Sen. When the Japanese invaded Malaya in 1941, the house served as the "war office" for the British Army. Ironically, following the British surrender to the invading troops, the mansion was taken over by the Japanese and housed the headquarters of the Imperial Army until the end of the war. When Malaysia gained its independence in 1959, the mansion served as a temporary Parliament. The building witnessed not only the early struggles of a nascent nation, but was also the scene of installation ceremonies for Malaysia's kings. Over the years, the building has served as the National Art Gallery and also as the National Welfare Department, its role in the nation's history constantly chang-

Just outside Kuala Lumpur at dusk.

ing, but perennially prominent. In the late 1980s it was refurbished and commissioned as the **Malaysian Tourist Information Complex (MATIC)** – a one-stop visitor centre with booking desks and information counters, as well as a souvenir shop, Malay-style restaurant and a venue for demonstrations of traditional Malaysian games and crafts. Many of the other mansions that are still standing now house embassies and consulates, so much so that Jalan Ampang has come to be known among locals as Ambassador's Row.

Another grand mansion you may enter to get the feeling of the old grandeur of Jalan Ampang is **Bok House**, which now holds the restaurant, Le Coq d'Or. The house retains much of its original flavour, with porticoed verandahs, Italian marble floors and 18th-century paintings. Its past is fascinating.

Chua Cheng Bok was a poor young man who lived in Kuala Lumpur in the last century. He ran a bicycle repair shop, and was desperately in love with the daughter of a wealthy mine owner whose house stood proudly on Jalan Ampang. The mine owner forbade the couple to marry, and so Chua put all his energies into his work, bitterly disappointed and longing for revenge. From a bicycle repair shop to a garage to tin-mine holdings, Chua's fortune grew, until at last he was able to build his own mansion right next door to his enemy's, overshadowing it in size and grandeur. Bok's house still stands, while the arrogant tin miner's house next door has long since disappeared.

In his will Chua decreed that Bok House should never be sold nor its design or decor changed; thanks to him, we can continue to imagine the days of fine living and experience for ourselves the romance of Chua's Malaysia.

Also along Jalan Ampang is the **Khoon Yam Buddhist Temple**, the oldest Chinese temple in KL, although extensive renovations have been made to the original. At the junction with Circular Road (Jalan Pekeleling) are several shopping centres and the **Ampang Park**, with a boating lake and

Busy night market in Chinatown's Jalan Petaling.

cloud-flecked mountains as a backdrop to your trip on the lake.

KL's Chinatown: Your feet (or the trishaw) are still the best means of discovering the heart of the old city. There is indeed much to be missed by driving, as the old shophouse interiors conceal many fascinating sights.

Chinatown lies within the boundaries of Jalan Sultan, Jalan Bandar (now known as Jalan Tun HS Lee, once the old High Street) and along Jalan Petaling. For the inveterate shopper and connoisseur of exotic oddities, Chinatown is a paradise. Chinese apothecaries display their herbs and medicines in porcelain pots, or beneath glass counters, mixed with more familiar western brands. There are jewellers and goldsmiths, casket and basket makers, dry goods shops, pet shops, optical houses, coffin makers, frame makers and haberdashers. Along the five-foot ways, there are shoe repairers, fortune tellers, Chinese sign painters, leather workers and Indian flower sellers. Look out for a small crowd gathered in one spot and you may find a medicine man trying to sell his wares, or a snake charmer coaxing onlookers to part with their dollars.

Jalan Petaling changes its appearance constantly. In the early morning, Chinese housewives visit the market stalls for fresh produce, and Chinese bakeries emit delicious aromas of traditional dumplings and sweet breads filled with red-bean paste and chicken curry. As the city wakes up, traffic pours down the street, flashy Mercedes fighting for space between bicycles and trishaws.

To get away from the crowds, move into the cooler interior of the **Chan See Shu Yuen Clanhouse and Temple**, built in 1906. Inside are elaborate ceramic glazed tiles and ornamentation, and intricate wall paintings; amongst these you may find a small cat chasing a beautiful butterfly.

Outside, the business of the day is underway. Shops selling pots, shoes (made to order), coffins, wedding clothes, spectacles, tinware, jewellery and medicines open up their shutters. A temple shop makes and sells paper models of servants, mansions, limousines,

wads of money, all to be burnt and sent to the departed for their success in the after life. Drop in at Yoke Woo Thin's, a busy Chinese restaurant further down the street, that sells delicious *dim sum* from 6am. Or there is the Seng Kee restaurant, reputedly the oldest in Chinatown, which makes its own moon-cakes for the autumnal Moon Festival. There are Chinese medicinal drinks stalls, where you can sit and sample bittersweet drinks to cure all ailments. Here, you will also find a shop which makes flags to order.

At 5pm every evening, the mood of Jalan Petaling changes again, as many of the shops replace their shutters. A section of the street closes to traffic to make way for a night market, which is erected with lightning speed. Here you can find all the "genuine" copies of brand name watches and tee-shirts. Swarthy Nepalese display an exotic selection of jewellery, gems, silverware and fabrics, "fresh" from Nepal. Antiques and toys, household goods and incense sticks jostle together in this ani-

Pottery with local motifs.

mated scene. It is said that it is still possible to barter here – try your luck! Exotic meats such as crocodile, cat and dog are for sale, or sit down for a Chinese seafood meal or a beer at one of the tables that spill out from restaurants onto the street. Music is supplied by a nearby Cantonese cassette stall.

Jalan Bandar (look out for its new name, Jalan Tun HS Lee) also holds treasures. At one end sits the old **Victorian Institution**, built in 1893 in an incongruous English cottage style, which has now become a drama hall. More shophouses, selling clocks old and new, cane goods, Chinese crockery and spectacles, line the street. Many have been restored in an effort to preserve some of the old KL from the onslaught of the new.

On Jalan Bandar is the **Kwoong Siew Association Temple**, and, quite suddenly in this very Chinese quarter, you catch sight of the **Sri Mahamariamman Hindu Temple**, its towering gate an explosion of colourful gods entangled in an arresting design. It was built in 1873, and occupies an important place in Hindu religious life, as it is from here that the Thaipusam pilgrimage to the Batu Caves, just outside KL, begins. Outside, women and children sell strings of fragrant jasmine, and a man in a *dhoti* keeps watch by a shoe stall for those wishing to enter the temple courtyard. Devotees emerge from prayer, their foreheads smeared with sacred white ash.

In **Jalan Sultan**, look for the pet shops, alive with singing birds in cages. Lap dogs, kittens, rabbits, and guinea pigs are to be found inside, as well as more unusual pets such as monkeys, mongeese and snakes. Watch out for the large turtle making its way across the shop floor! Not all these animals will end up as pets – some are destined to furbish a lavish wedding table or a showy business banquet.

The **Central Market** stands where the original one, according to Swettenham "a very insecure shed", once housed market sellers from out of town, displaying fruit and vegetables, as well as household products and handicrafts. The present building, completed in 1936, initially served as a produce market, was recently spruced up with its art-deco features and high ceilings renovated and repainted in pastel pinks and baby blues, and has now become a handicraft centre. Inside, there is a good selection of handicrafts at fairly reasonable prices, though bargaining is still usually advisable.

Besides housing various shops, stalls and restaurants, the Central Market also has a programme of live shows. Pick up a brochure here or at the tourist office, and you may be lucky enough to catch a music, dance or shadow puppet performance. At the end of Central Market is the business centre. This juxtaposition of the old and the new creates interesting alleyways. There is a shophouse with a tree growing out of its walls on one side, small food stalls in the middle and the stark wall of a highrise building on the other.

A short alley opposite the Central Market in Jalan Hang Kasturi leads to the oldest temple in Kuala Lumpur, the **Temple of Szu Yeh** (Hsien Szu Yeh

Sri Mahamariamman Temple.

Miao). Duck your head so as not to bang into the low-hanging awning poles and walk past the alley's food stalls to arrive at the temple gate.

The temple itself is rather small and dark, its ceiling blackened by a century of incense smoke curling up from the altars below. Fine examples of wood carvings illustrate scenes from the Buddhist canon. A framed photograph of Yap Ah Loy sits on a side altar, looking more like a kindly and gracious saint than the tough and exacting leader he really was.

Temples were among the first permanent buildings on which successful Chinese pioneers lavished their wealth. When Kuala Lumpur was being rebuilt in the 1880s, much money was spent on such buildings. Built in 1884 by Yap, the **Temple of Sen Ta** became the centre of a major Chinese cult which was to last for years. The cult of Sen Ta and those of many other Chinese deities were marked by processions through the town every year, on some occasions with great wealth and splendour.

Saris, batik and steaks: Besides Chinatown, there are several other districts in which it is pleasant to stroll and enjoy the sights. Northwards from the Padang lies another area of interesting shops. The main road here is **Jalan Tuanku Abdul Rahman**, named after the country's first Prime Minister following independence. To the locals this road is often referred to as **Batu Road**. The street leads off the Padang and all along it lie shops, both old and new, as well as modern department stores, cheap hotels and many *kedai makan*, or eating stalls, some of which the food should definitely be sampled.

The **Coliseum Cinema**, built in the 1920s and one of KL's first, lies halfway down this road, and the **Coliseum Cafe and Hotel** next door is the most famous bar and restaurant in town for its past history. The Coliseum has been serving customers for more than 60 years, and behind its plain facade, it is reputed that the town's best steaks at the most reasonable prices are offered here. For decades, it was the favourite water-

Central Market.

ing hole for planters, miners, government officials and soldiers; today, the bar is still patronised by a medley of their modern-day counterparts. The decor has not changed much either, and the Chinese waiters' service is of a bygone colonial era.

For six days a week, Batu Road is crowded with traffic, but every Saturday night it becomes a pedestrian mall. In place of the taxis, minibuses, cars and motorbikes are stalls offering, sometimes for half the price (or even less), goods to be had from Batu Road's shops by day.

Off Batu Road where the Padang ends is **Jalan Melayu**, which was the site of one of the original kampung lying on the outskirts of the city, now closely embedded in it. This area is principally interesting for its Indian shops selling silks, saris and handmade jewellery. After 6 every evening, portable kitchens with tables and chairs take over the street, offering food which is as spicy as you can stand it.

Eating *al fresco* is definitely more enjoyable than dining in a large restaurant, where the atmosphere can be contrived and overly-adequate air conditioning can make one long for winter clothing. Food stalls set up under the stars are common all over the city, but the most famous are still the ones here along the riverbank.

Beyond Jalan Melayu is **Jalan Masjid India**, whose mosque sits on the spot where one of the town's first mosques used to be. The road leads to what was formerly the red-light district, but which now boasts shops, restaurants, business premises and moderately-priced hotels.

Where Batu Road crosses Jalan Dang Wangi, the street broadens and leads to **Chow Kit**, an area filled with cheap hotels catering to those with modest means. Here many "ladies of easy virtue" seek their livelihood. At night, this is the place for one of the most colourful and lively night markets, and is said to be the cheapest. Stalls by the roadside serve Malaysian delicacies; in season, the pungent smell of durian pervades the air. Above the roar of the traffic, the

<u>Left</u>, modern batik painting. <u>Right</u>, cultural show.

108

night air is rent with the raucous sound of pop music. In the heart of all this activity stands the **Chow Kit Market**, reputedly the best and cheapest food market in town. Struggle through the Sunday morning shopping brigade to witness how Malaysian housewives choose their household goods, and to capture the aroma and atmosphere of Malaysian marketing.

On the right off Batu Road on the way to Chow Kit, **Wisma Loke** poses as another reminder of KL's past. Cheow Ah Yeok, a contemporary of Yap Ah Loy and a Chinese mine owner who made his fortune, built this charming Chinese townhouse with classical Greco-Roman arches and pillars, balustrades of glazed jade-coloured porcelain from China, Malaccan tiles and a "moongate" within. After Cheow's death, the house was bought by Loke Yew, who had landed penniless in Singapore at the age of 13 and went on to become one of the most colourful of Malaysia's millionaires. The first house in Kuala Lumpur to be lit by electricity,

the mansion became the showpiece of the community.

The other end of Chow Kit has now been renamed **Jalan Putra**, and has become an important national centre, with several attractive modern buildings. The **Putra World Trade Centre** with 40-odd storeys was built at an infamous cost, and houses government offices as well as the head office for the **Malaysia Tourism Promotion Board** (MTPB) on the 24th to 27th floors.

Nestled in its shadow is the **Putra Concert Hall** and conference complex. With its Menangkabau roof, the concert hall looks like an outsized traditional ceremonial hall. Next door is the **Pan Pacific Hotel** with elevators riding on the outside of the building, affording an interesting view of Chow Kit, Jalan Raja Laut and the city beyond. This set of buildings itself can be seen from many other points of the city including the ring-road, which brushes close to the Pan Pacific Hotel's front steps.

Across the road is **The Mall Shopping Centre**. Here are modern shops

Puppets depicting Malaysian folklore.

with Western goods and brand names. But if this kind of shopping does not interest you, perhaps the more traditional **Kampung Bahru**, with its exclusively Malay shops and stalls, will.

Saturday's Sunday Market: In 1889, 90 hectares (220 acres) of land were set aside at the request of the Sultan of Selangor for a Malay agricultural settlement to meet the needs of Malays in that area. This marked the origin of **Kampung Bahru** (literally the new village), a large Malay enclave set back behind Chow Kit. To enter the "village" is to leave the sounds and smells of a bustling city for a rural world of quiet grass-lined roads and dignified wooden Malay homes shaded by fruit trees. Although this image is perceptibly eroding as the more affluent brick structures replace their wooden counterparts, the feeling of no longer being in a big city remains.

Sheltered under the blocks of flats found here, the **Pasar Minggu (Sunday Market)** springs to life, not on a Sunday, as you might think, but on a Saturday night, lasting into the early hours of Sunday morning. It is well worth a visit for an exclusively Malay market. *Songkok* (fez or cap), prayer books, hand-printed batik, and all kinds of handicrafts are on sale at the various stalls. Ashtrays, vases, jewellery boxes, flowerpots made from shells, traditional earthenware pots (*labu*), Kelantan silverware and the richly embroidered *songket* from Terengganu are common merchandise here. All around are *sarong*-clad men, wearing their white skull caps, token of their having performed their pilgrimage to Mecca.

The ever-present satay and other choice dishes of the Malay kitchens are sold at many of the stalls found here or in most of the air-conditioned restaurants. Right in the centre of all this is a permanent stage on which Malay pop songs are crooned.

KL's Golden Triangle: The fulcrum of modern consumer life in Malaysia is the intersection of **Jalan Sultan Ismail** and **Jalan Bukit Bintang**, an area of expensive shops, high-class restaurants, international hotels and sophisticated nightlife, often called the **Golden Triangle**. You will find a number of large shopping malls in this area: **Sungai Wang Plaza** and the adjacent **Bukit Bintang Plaza** offer more than 500 shops, including some of the best bookstores in KL; **Imbi Plaza** concentrates on computers and software; **KL Plaza** has fashion accessory shops and electronic outlets; flashy green **Lot 10** has European designer boutiques and Isetan.

Northeast of Kuala Lumpur Plaza, along **Jalan Raja Chulan**, is the handicraft village of **Karyaneka**. The country's 13 states are represented by 13 identical kampung houses in which exhibits of each state's famed artistry are to be found.

Handwoven textiles, woodwork, batik, basketwork, silver and pewter goods, shellwork and pottery are on display; and there are demonstrations of cloth weaving, batik printing and silver and copper tooling.

There is also a large showroom, where some of the handicrafts exhibited are on sale; unfortunately, some of the finest and most unusual handicrafts are not.

Left, the mall – a popular KL hangout. **Right**, colour, grace and the Dayabumi.

SELANGOR:
THE HEARTLAND

One of the first things you notice on leaving Kuala Lumpur are the *pintu gerbang* or ceremonial arches over the road announcing that you are departing the Federal Territory and entering the state of **Selangor**. Even more of these arches are erected to celebrate National Day. The most famous arch, with its pleasing Moorish architecture, is called the **Kota Darul Ehsan** – Land of Good Will – which spans the Federal Highway that sweeps south from Kuala Lumpur to Subang International Airport, then down into the Klang Valley.

Petaling Jaya, a sprawling satellite town, is immediately beyond this arch. "PJ" has grown in the last 40 years from a squatter settlement into a self-contained urban centre, whose tree-lined avenues now house more than half a million people. Petaling Jaya is a major educational centre, home to the **University of Malaya** and the **International Islamic University**. It is also a plush suburb where many higher-salaried Malaysians and expatriates reside. To accommodate their leisure and pleasure needs, an active nightlife and a busy shopping area has developed.

The town boasts several popular parks, including the **Taman Jaya** lake garden, as well as good sports facilities. Dominating the scene is **Menara MPPJ**, the Petaling Jaya Municipal Council Building, its 27 storeys overlooking the growing city. PJ's affluence has spread to nearby **Subang**, where a major shopping centre called **Subang Parade** attracts shoppers from all over the metropolitan area.

Historic Klang Valley: Once it leaves Petaling Jaya, the Federal Highway – the country's oldest motorway – cleaves its way through the **Klang Valley**, birthplace of modern Malaysia and the industrial heartland of the Malaysian economy. The highway shuttles past **Subang International Airport** on the right and the new township of Subang Jaya on the left before entering **Shah Alam**, the capital of Selangor and another rapidly growing city.

Shah Alam has several claims to fame. The city is a thriving centre of heavy industry, including Proton, the national car project. A joint venture between Mitsubishi of Japan and the Malaysian government, Proton now exports to more than a dozen foreign countries. The city is also known for the **Shah Alam Racing Circuit**, which stages major international competitions like the annual Malaysian Motorbike Grand Prix.

As the newest state capital, Shah Alam is still in the midst of a construction boom that, in less than 20 years, has transformed this once sleepy market town into a bustling modern city. High-rise government offices like the **Sultan Salahuddin Abdul Aziz Shah Building** surround a man-made lake in the middle of the city. The Sultan of Selangor resides in a lavish palace called **Istana Bukit Kayangan**. But the city's most eye-catching building is the **Selangor State Mosque**. It features some of the largest domes and tallest minarets in the

Left, limestone interior of the Batu Caves. Right, Royal Selangor pewter.

Islamic world. Set in lush gardens, the dominant colours of the mosque are silver and blue, reflected in the giant aluminium dome.

At the western end of the Federal Highway, the city of **Klang** conceals a colourful and violent past. Given its commanding position near the mouth of the Klang River, it was soon obvious that whoever possessed the town controlled the lucrative tin trade. Klang became a centre of fighting during the Selangor Civil War of the 1870s. Raja Mahdi, one of the chief protagonists, built his fort on the hill where the municipal offices now stand. Another landmark is an old warehouse called the **Gedong Raja Abdullah**, built in 1857 by Raja Abdullah, one of Mahdi's principal opponents in the civil war. The warehouse exemplifies traditional Malay workmanship and has been converted into a museum bringing Klang's exciting past to life. Klang is also famous for *bak kut teh* (pork rib soup).

The highway runs another 8 kilometres (5 mi) before arriving at **Port Klang**, once called Port Swettenham. Motorists usually don't stop here. But if they do, it is because of the wonderful seafood restaurants by the quayside. Port Klang is the major seaport for Kuala Lumpur and the Klang Valley, as well as one of the fastest growing container ports in Southeast Asia.

Port Klang is a springboard for trips to the various islands in the Klang River delta. A sampan ride to **Pulau Ketam** (Crab Island) takes only two hours. The largest island is **Carey Island**, famous for its Orang Asli community. The Mah-Meri tribe is well-known for their beautiful wood carvings inspired by mystical dreams, but visits to their communities must first be arranged with the Orang Asli office in Shah Alam.

Morib Beach is situated 44 kilometres (27 mi) south of Port Klang. It is not one of Malaysia's most beautiful beaches, but it is a popular weekend getaway for Klang Valley residents and one of the most historic beaches in Malaysia – the Allied forces landed here in September 1945, ending the

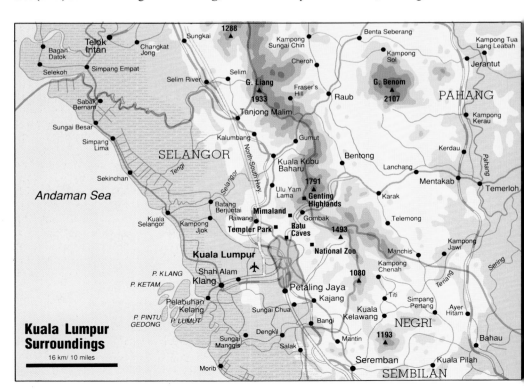

Kuala Lumpur Surroundings

16 km/ 10 miles

Japanese occupation of the peninsula. Just before Morib, a side road winds its ways to **Jugra**. On the hill overlooking this village and the estuary are the graves of Selangor royalty and noblemen; the ruins of some old government buildings can be seen below. Nearby, standing alone in the *padi* fields, are the abandoned palace, built by a Selangor sultan in the 1800s, and an equally elaborate mosque where the sultan used to pray.

Hilly landscapes: Geography gives **Kuala Selangor** a spectacular setting; history gives it a sense of mystery. The town lies 45 kilometres (30 mi) north of Klang on the coast road. Two small hills dominate the landscape, guarding either side of the Selangor River.

Bukit Melawati is the site of **Fort Altingberg**, where Selangor's Bugis rulers made their base in the 18th century. The fort's cannon still points out to sea, an impotent warning to traders and seafarers. A lighthouse and wooden rest house also crown the hill. Inside the fort are seven wells and the **Batu Hampar**, once an execution block for traitors. A mausoleum of Bugis sultans lies nearby. A new visitor centre has historical and natural history exhibits.

A short trail leads down the hill to the **Kuala Selangor Nature Park**, a joint development of the highly respected Malayan Nature Society and the state government. Over 130 species of bird have been sighted in the park, and an estimated 100,000 waterbirds pass through during their annual migrations. Artificial ponds have been constructed to attract the birds, as well as nature trails and observation blinds for humans. The primary mammal here is the silver leaf monkey, now a protected species.

There are several interesting villages around Kuala Selangor, mostly Chinese fishing villages where salted fish and fishballs are prepared. It is possible to take an evening trip up the Selangor River to witness a spectacular sight near the village of **Kampung Kuantan**. Along the riverbank here, hundreds of *klip-klap* (fireflies) alight on the branches of the overhanging trees, looking like multicoloured Christmas decorations. During the day, coconut processing can be observed in this village.

For the return trip to Kuala Lumpur, visitors who like to travel along narrow twisting lanes can take the route which goes through Batang Berjuntai and Rawang. A kilometre or two from **Batang Berjuntai**, on the left-hand side through the surrounding trees, is a large wooden bungalow with a sweeping *attap* roof, a typical planter's home from the turn of the century. It now belongs to SOCFIN, an organisation that was the pioneer of oil palm cultivation in Malaysia. The house is also associated with one of the country's pioneer rubber planters, Henri Fauconnier, whose book *The Soul of Malaya* is a "must read" for anyone who visits Malaysia. Past Batang Berjuntai, the road becomes remote as it snakes its way around the contours of thickly wooded hills.

The side road from Kuala Selangor joins the North-South Highway at **Rawang**, providing an easy 20-minute drive back into Kuala Lumpur or a longer haul to the northern states of Perak, Penang and Kedah.

Putting for par at the Saujana Golf Club.

Much of the land around Kuala Lumpur, particularly in the south, is scarred by the mining of tin, which gave the state its initial fortune. A few kilometres from **Sungai Besi**, just south of KL, a little platform by the roadside provides a vantage point for looking out over what is claimed to be the largest open-cast tin mine in the world. The Hong Fatt mine has been producing tin since the 19th century, and its resources are obviously still not exhausted.

About 26 kilometres (16 mi) south of Kuala Lumpur, on the old highway, is a small town called **Kajang**. If you are hungry, and even if you are not, stop awhile, as Kajang boasts the best satay – or rather, sauce – in Malaysia.

Digital future: This southeast corner of Selangor will take on immense importance in years to come as the site of the **Multimedia Super Corridor** (MSC), Malaysia's gamble to catapult it into the technological age as a major player. Extending south 50 kilometres from Kuala Lumpur, the 15-kilometre-wide MSC is a high-tech, information-technology investment of epic scale. Linked by one of the world's fastest fibre-optic networks and a new rapid transit line, the MSC is intended to give Malaysia a technological edge over its Asian competitors by nurturing both local and foreign IT development.

At the southern end of the MSC is the **Kuala Lumpur International Airport** at Sepang, opened in 1998. In between the airport and KL, and anchoring the MSC, is **Putrajaya**, a new city being built to house the national government. The Prime Minister's office will relocate there sometime in the next few years, followed later by the remainder of the government.

A limestone cathedral: Thirteen kilometres (8 mi) north of Kuala Lumpur, via Jalan Kuching and the old trunk road, a bold limestone outcrop lies across the scarred landscape of old tin mines. Within are the famous **Batu Caves**.

During the Japanese Occupation half a century ago, the Batu Caves were still sufficiently remote to serve as an anti-Japanese Communist guerilla hideout. For centuries, however, it was ob-scured by the jungle, and known only to forest inhabitants who lived nearby. In 1878, William Hornaday, an American naturalist, was on a hunting expedition when he smelt the pungent odour of bat guano. His Malay guides led him to the caves. The existence of the caves was soon public knowledge, and they became a popular destination for picnics by the town *tuan* (travelling by elephant) and their elegant *mem*.

Years later, the local Hindu population, with their predilection for sacred caves, began making pilgrimages there to celebrate the Thaipusam festival. As a sign of repentance for past sins and to demonstrate their vows of reformation, devotees often carry *kavadi* burdens, from a simple milk jug carried on the head to the wooden frames decorated with flowers and fruit and supported by long thin spikes pinned into the carrier's body. Worshippers had to scale the steep jagged cliffs to the Hindu shrine in the topmost grotto. Today, the way to the top is paved with 272 concrete steps and is surrounded by hanging ferns and tropi-

Worshippers flock to Batu Caves for the Thaipusam Festival.

cal flowers. The sight is never so spectacular as at the time of Thaipusam.

Apart from the main cavern – known as the **Cathedral Cave** – there are about 20 known caves, only some of which are open to the public, as there is a danger of collapse and falling rocks. Most interesting are those situated along the south face, which bear such names as Hermit's Hole, Priest's Hole, Fairy Grotto and Quarry Cave. But the main Cathedral Cave is definitely the most breathtaking. Under a huge vault pierced by stalactites that point downwards for 6 metres (20 ft) spreads an empty hollow. Eerie shafts of light streak down from gaps in the ceiling high above.

Nearby are the **Dark Caves**, now closed to the public, as limestone quarrying has made them unsafe for regular visits. However, the Malaya Nature Society conducts tours here (contact their head office in KL) of varying degrees of adventurousness. Bats, white cave racer snakes, scorpions and monkeys can be seen here. The society also conducts some rock climbing expeditions. These caves have an elevator, though occasionally closed, which runs parallel to the main steps. A small cave at the base of the outcrop houses a small museum, displaying figures of some of the Hindu gods. Amongst the sprawling tourist shops down below, good Indian vegetarian food can be found.

Tamed jungles: There are several interesting nature parks beyond Batu Caves. Another 11 kilometres (7 mi) north via the old trunk road (Route 1) is **Templer Park**. It was founded by the once British High Commissioner, Sir Gerald Templer, a man very fond of the great Malaysian outdoors. A 1,200-hectare (3,000 acre) tract of jungle was set aside, offering jungle paths, natural swimming lagoons and waterfalls. To the north of the park are the dramatic limestone formations, Bukit Takun and Anak Takun, the latter with some interesting caves to explore.

A few kilometres west of Batu Caves is the **Forest Research Institute and Museum** (FRIM) at Kepong, covering an area of 600 hectares (1,500 acres) of natural forest, experimental plantations and arboreta. FRIM also has a herbarium, a museum and a library on forestry. Laboratories studying chemicals, insects and timber may be visited. There are camping grounds for those wishing to stay overnight, but you must get prior permission from the institute and bring your own equipment and food.

The pride of the Malaysian forest is seen in more orderly surroundings such as the green captivity of the **National Zoo and Aquarium**, 13 kilometres (8 mi) from central KL by way of Jalan Genting Kelang. The attractive 20-hectare (55-acre) grounds hold a good cross-section of Malaysia's wildlife. Plumed birds, pythons, wild buffalo (*seladang*), tapir, crocodiles and, of course, tigers are on view in concrete enclosures or fenced pastures, only paces away from their jungle habitats.

The heart of tin country: Old Pahang Road and the Karak Highway lead northeast to the Genting Highlands, where many urban dwellers head on weekends. There are a number of interesting stops along the way.

Pain is transcended by Hindus fulfilling their vows to the son of Siva.

Ten kilometres (6 mi) from Kuala Lumpur is a suburb called **Setapak**, home of the famous **Royal Selangor Pewter Factory**, where most of Malaysia's pewter products are made from a combination of antimony, copper and refined tin. You can see demonstrations of pewter being made and purchase various pewter items at the factory shop. Further north is the old tin-mining centre of **Gombak**, where you can tour the **Gombak Traditional House** (also called Pa Ali's House), a traditional Sumatran-style building built by an expert brought over from the birthplace of the Menangkabau culture.

In the hills north of Gombak is **Mimaland**, an artificial playground fashioned in an elevated hollow enclosed by jungle hills. Recreational facilities include fishing and boating, swimming and jungle trekking. There is also a natural swimming pool, a children's amusement centre with its own model dinosaurs, a small zoo and even a mini rubber plantation.

Accommodation is available in the form of chalets, a motel by the lake and native-style *bagan* raised on stilts. The park is best visited during the week, as it can get very crowded on weekends. Another 1 kilometre (0.5 mi) along Old Pahang Road is the **Orang Asli Museum**, well worth a visit. Exhibits include various aspects and artifacts of aboriginal life.

Wooing Lady Luck: From a distance, the **Genting Highlands**, shrouded in mists that blanket jungle-covered hills high above Kuala Lumpur, stand aloof – here is a mystical palace of pleasure perched on top of the Barisan Titiwangsa mountain range that runs down the centre of the peninsula.

This all-modern and civilised hill station houses Malaysia's only casino, where Western gambling games are played among traditional Chinese games like *tai sai*. Neckties are compulsory, or you can opt for traditional Malaysian dress. A sign over the door of the casino is a warning from the sultans of Selangor and Pahang that Muslims are forbidden to enter and try their luck here. At weekends, gambling continues around the clock, but during the week the casino closes its doors between 4am and 10am.

Set in a lush countryside, Genting has several modern hotels. There is also an artificial lake, a golf course and a family theme park, which features roller-coasters, boat rides, monorail and the largest video/virtual reality arcade in Malaysia. Save your jungle shoes for the other hill stations.

Situated at 1,500 metres (5,000 ft), **Fraser's Hill** was initially created by the British as a cool retreat in the mountains. The resort takes its name from Louis James Fraser, an elusive English adventurer, who had long disappeared when the hill station was built in 1910. Stories circulated that he held a gambling and opium den here, but not much else is known of him. Fraser's Hill is a relaxing retreat for business executives seeking respite.

Scattered over seven hills that make up the resort, a series of English greystone bungalows were built, surrounded by neat English gardens blooming with roses and hollyhocks. More modern facilities have been added, including a 109-room hotel which unfortunately fails to blend with the landscape. Economical and old-fashioned accommodation is offered in the form of bungalows and a youth hostel. Fraser's Hill is for those who like to relax in the countryside, walk along jungle paths or swim in the pool of the **Jerlau Waterfall**. There is also a 9-hole golf course, tennis courts, playgrounds and pony rides for the slightly more active.

Unfortunately, for those without private transport, Fraser's Hill is rather difficult to reach. Start with a one-hour bus journey from Kuala Lumpur (100 kilometres 60 mi to the south) to Kuala Kubu Bahru, from where you have to board a second bus which takes another one and a half hours to get to the top. The last 8 kilometres (5 mi) is up a narrow road, on which a one-way traffic system is in place.

It was along the winding road from Kuala Kubu Bahru that Sir Henry Gurney, the once British High Commissioner, was ambushed and killed by Communist guerillas in 1951.

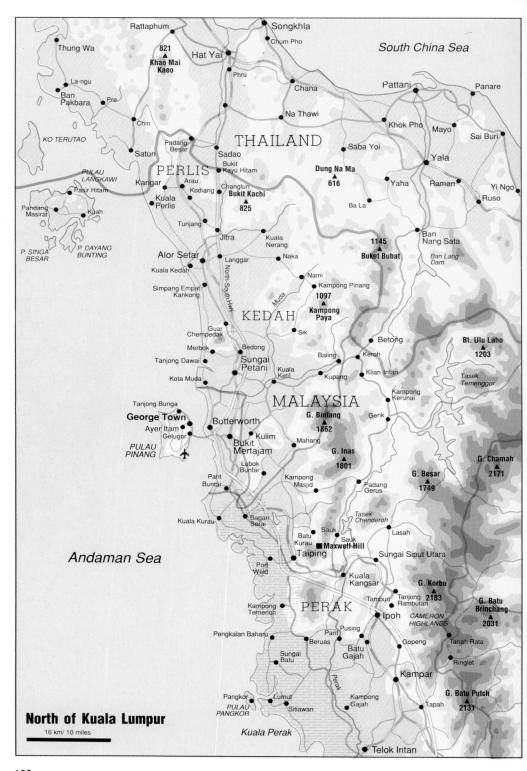

North of Kuala Lumpur

16 km/ 10 miles

PERAK:
THE SILVER STATE

Perak is the Malay word for silver, but the "silver" of the state of **Perak** is actually tin, which has made it into one of the richest states of the Malaysian Federation. One of the oldest in the peninsula, Perak is the only state whose royal house can claim direct descent from the sultans of Malacca. The current ruler is the heir of a line founded in 1528 by Sultan Muzaffar Shah, who was the eldest son of Malacca's last Malay monarch.

The history of the state revolves closely around its abundant tin supply, but until the 19th century its civilisation was concentrated along the banks of the Perak River, where state rulers made their capitals. With the discovery of tin, the wealth of the trade became of interest to these rulers who attempted to control it from their bases, as the tin was brought downstream from the mines further inland. However, they had to contend with greedy outsiders – the Achenese from Sumatra, the Bugis from Selangor, the Thais from the north, as well as the Dutch and the Portuguese from Europe. The Dutch built forts at the mouth of the Perak River and on the strategic island of Pangkor in order to take a hold on the tin trade.

The tin revolution of the 19th century, however, transformed the face and the politics of the state. Mining on a large scale for the first time shifted the centre of power from the Perak River Valley to the tin-rich areas of Larut and Kinta. During the 1840s, newly discovered deposits in Larut made its Malay territorial chief the wealthiest and the most powerful man in the state. It also turned Larut into an arena for the struggles of rival Chinese tin miners until their activities, affecting the welfare of the Straits Settlements, led the British to intervene. Within a decade of British intervention, the main interest in tin mining had shifted to the Kinta Valley, which contains the richest tin deposits in the world. Since the turn of this century, Kinta has been the leading district in Perak, and Ipoh, the most prosperous of all its settlements.

Town that tin built: The tin centre of the world is **Ipoh**, which lies astride the modern North-South Highway and rail line about midway between Kuala Lumpur and Penang. Like Kuala Lumpur, Ipoh started as a landing stage at the point beyond which the river was no longer navigable, and sprang up almost overnight into another Chinese miner's settlement, on the ancestral land of the Dato' Panglima Kinta, the local Malay territorial chief.

By the 1890s, brick buildings were replacing the fire-prone wooden shacks of the miners' town, and by the 1900s, it was *de facto* the principal town in the state, although the state capital remained at Taiping until 1937. By this time, Ipoh had emerged as the best-planned town in the peninsula, as can be witnessed today from its broad, regularly laid-out streets. It is now Malaysia's second-largest city, with a population fast approaching half a million.

Perak Tong cave temple.

Apart from its excellent amenities, good accommodation and its convenience as a centre from which to explore other parts of the state, Ipoh doesn't hold too much to detain the tourist. The old part of the town lies on the west side of the Kinta Valley, and it is here that the official buildings are to be found. The railway station and the municipal colonial buildings surrounding the **Padang** have a stately, dignified air.

The immense **State Mosque** rises within close proximity to the **Clock Tower**, another colonial legacy built long ago to commemorate the assassination of James Birch, Perak's first British resident.

The Padang – surrounded by the **Royal Ipoh Club**, court houses, municipal library and the stately **St Michael's School** – is the epitome of every Malaysian town with a colonial past and the scene of important matches, school athletic meets, parades and public rallies. The **Railway Station**, with its graceful arches, silver dome and interminable colonnade bears a striking resemblance to the one in Kuala Lumpur and is known locally as the "Taj Mahal".

On the eastern side of the river is the new section of Ipoh, dominated by the **Majlis Perhadanan Ipoh** (MPI) or Ipoh Municipal Council, which has great plans for the city's future, including making it worthy of the name "City of Bougainvilleas"! Other attractions in Ipoh are the **D.R. Seenivasagam Park**, with its roller-skating rink, and the DBI **Swimming Complex**, with the first wave pool in Malaysia.

The **Geology Museum** is worth a visit to study Perak's rock structures. Opened in 1957 on Jalan Sultan Azlan Shah (Tiger Lane), the museum has over 600 examples of minerals, an exhibition on tin ore, including one of the best examples of cassiterite in the world, and a fine collection of precious stones.

Just off Gopeng Road, the **Perak Turf Club** is set against a magnificent backdrop of craggy limestone outcrops and the more distant hills of the Main Range. Nearby are the orderly **Japanese Gardens** and the well-tended **Polo Ground**.

Temples embedded in the rockface are common around Ipoh.

Further east is a town called **Tambun**, where you can join the North-South Highway. North of town along Route 13 is the **Tambun Hot Springs**, as well as the **National Stud Farm**, where thoroughbred race horses are raised, and the Tanjong Rambutan Waterfall.

Temples in the rock face: The limestone formations of the **Kinta Valley** lend mystery as well as beauty to the surroundings of Ipoh city. Many of them are riddled with caves, which in their time served both as homes for ancient peoples as well as convenient hideouts for bandits.

In 1959, a British Gurkha army officer, leading a patrol hunting for Communist guerillas, came across the only rock paintings ever to have been found in peninsular Malaysia. They are on a cliff face barely 275 metres (300 ft) from the main road to Tambun and are easily accessible with the help of a guide. While perhaps not as impressive as the paintings found in European caves, they are reckoned at being at least 2,000 years old and are of great importance and value to Malaysia's early history. More recently, unfortunately, aspiring rock artists have used the cave walls as an emotional outlet, adding their own rebellious designs to the originals.

The limestone caves around Ipoh, so reminiscent of similar features in southern China, are of great fascination for both Buddhist and Hindu worshippers. Odd-looking white buildings, some with red-tiled pagoda roofs, are seen spread out flat against the rock, close to the road. These are in fact the entrances to caves, which have been converted into temples. One of the largest shrines is the **Perak Tong**, 6 kilometres north (4 mi) from town on Jalan Kuala Kangsar, the old trunk road. Traditional Chinese paintings adorn the walls and retell traditional folk tales and legends. Built in 1926 by a Buddhist priest from China, the temple has more than 40 Buddha statues, the central one being the largest Buddha in Malaysia, sitting at 13 metres (40 ft) high.

Beyond the main altar are more Buddhas and a painting of Kuan Yin, God-

dess of Mercy. In semidarkness you can then climb a stairway (ask the caretaker for the key) to the upper reaches of the cave. After an arduous climb of 385 steps, follow a thin shaft of light to where the cave opens out to reveal the surrounding countryside. Here again Kuan Yin, now seated on an elephant, gazes out over the scene.

South of Ipoh, near the intersection of Jalan Gopeng and Jalan Raja Musa Mahadi, is **Sam Poh Tong**. The largest of the rock temples, its origin dates back to the 1890s, when Ipoh was emerging as Perak's largest town. A monk passing through found the cave and decided to make it his abode and place for meditation. He remained in the cave for 20 years until his death. Other monks followed his example. The present temple facade dates back to the 1950s, and today the cave houses a temple where a group of monks and nuns live, having dedicated their lives to the Buddha. Buddha statues are dotted everywhere in between the stalagmites and stalactites. A stiff climb of 246 steps leads to an open cave with an excellent panorama of Ipoh and surroundings.

Hollowed out in the centre of the outcrop is an almost perfect circle of perpendicular cliff 70 metres (230 ft) high, where an old dilapidated stone house stands. Thousands of small turtles, symbols of longevity, swim in a garden pool in front of it, waiting to be fed by visitors to the temple. Apparently, the privacy of this inner chamber has lured other people besides the clergy: on walls in the cliff face is enough modern romantic graffiti to fill a book.

Underground riches: The Kinta Valley, whose tin production a few years ago was half that of the rest of Malaysia combined and 17 percent that of the world's total, stretches funnel-shaped for 70 kilometres (45 mi) from Sungai Siput in the north of Ipoh to Kampur in the south. The speedy North-South Highway cuts straight across these hills, joining Ipoh with the Perak River Valley and Kuala Kangsar. What was once a vast expanse of forest crossed by sluggish jungle streams and swamps has

Buddhist statues crowd a shrine in Sam Poh Tong.

over the past 100 years been virtually denuded of all its trees, its swamps drained and even the course of the Kinta River straightened out. The land now lies flat and open, offering vistas of deserted mining pools over the bleached scars of tin tailings; dotted here and there are the wooden *palong* (boxes) of the Chinese mines; and floating majestically in pools of their own making are the huge tin dredges.

Mining townships, occupying land once roamed by wild herds of elephants, scatter themselves over the face of this valley. Some, like Ipoh, rose with the tin industry, but when the local tin deposits were exhausted, they declined and shrivelled into villages or even became ghost towns, like Papan, Tronoh and Pusing. Some, such as Batu Gajah and Gopeng, were once greater and more prosperous than Ipoh itself.

Kampar, a very Chinese town at the foot of the Bujang Melaka on the main trunk road south of Ipoh, prides itself as being the largest of these towns, while **Gopeng** has its long-gone prosperity wanly reflected in its large wooden market, the Chinese theatre and the dignified rows of shophouses. Just south of Gopeng, a narrow side road to the right branches off to Kota Bharu, a little village on the railway. It then leads on to **Makam Teja**, the tomb of Bendahara Alang Iskandar, one of the great state officers of 19th-century Perak and a direct ancestor of the present ruler. As is often the case with the graves of distinguished Malays, the site has become a shrine (*keramat*) visited by humble folk in search of blessings or special favours. It has also become a tradition that a newly installed Sultan of Perak must pay his respects at this shrine.

A pioneer's castle: Between Gopeng and Ipoh, another branch road follows the Sungai Raya, a tributary of the Kinta, across the valley to Batu Gajah. Suddenly about 5 kilometres (3 mi) before you get there, a bend in the road reveals a large ruin on the other side of the river – **Kellie's Castle**. Until recently this building was overgrown with wild fig and banyan trees, spreading over and

Kellie's
Castle.

into it, but an effort has been made to rescue this interesting structure from the encroaching foliage. It stands on the land of what was once the estate of a William Kellie-Smith, a rubber plantation owner who made his fortune in Malaya. The house was in fact his second home, and was never entirely finished, as Smith died while on a visit to his native Scotland. The house was meant to be a reminder of his own Scottish castle far away, and its fine architecture and orange-coloured bricks, lying in ruins and all but forgotten, give it the air of something from a fairy tale.

Smith was an interesting man who was evidently popular with his Indian workers. A Hindu shrine stands nearby, erected for the plantation workers during a time of sickness. Amongst the figures of animals and gods stands a man in a white suit and topee, presumably Smith himself. A walk around the ruin is to step back into the prosperous days of colonial life. A bridge has now been built across the river, providing access from the main road. Tours can

also be arranged from Ipoh. **Batu Gajah** itself is a small town once destined for greater things: it was designed as the administrative centre for the Kinta Valley in the early days of British rule, before circumstances placed Ipoh to the fore. The evidence of what it might have been is found in the palatial government offices on top of the hill overlooking the town. Batu Gajah now hopes to attract visitors with its modern park for children, modelled along the lines of a Malaysian Disneyland.

The heart of Perak: A 20-minute drive from Batu Gajah brings you to **Parit**, which is in the heart of the historic Perak River Valley. For centuries the Perak River provided the only means of access to the state's interior and was therefore the main area of Malay settlement and the scene of some of the most dramatic events in Perak's history. Now good roads run along either side of its banks through villages which were once the homes of Perak's greatest heroes. At various places along the way are the simple tombs of Perak's sultans, all carefully marked and cared for by the local villagers.

Across the river at Kampung Gajah is **Pasir Salak**, where British resident James Birch was assassinated in 1874. Birch was killed, while out bathing in the Perak River, by a group led by Dato' Maharaja Lela. The latter was later executed for his part in the assassination plot and a stone slab declaring "let this place be desolate for ever" was placed just outside the village mosque. The slab has now been removed to the state museum at Taiping, but an obelisk commemorating Birch still remains at Pasir Salak. A state memorial is also planned in honour of Lela. Around the village of Pasir Salak are many attractive *kutai* houses of very fine workmanship.

The road on the left bank from Pasir Salak eventually crosses the Kinta River, near its confluence with the Perak River, continuing across the broad rice fields of Sungai Manik into Teluk Intan. **Teluk Intan,** formerly known as Teluk Anson, is the chief town of Lower Perak and the market for the local produce, particularly pineapples. Its main claim to fame **Characteristic limestone hills of Perak.**

128

is the century-old clock tower, with its distinct tilt and which was originally used for water storage. Teluk Intan was earmarked as the main outlet for tin of the Kinta Valley, which was why the railroad was extended to it. But the North-South Highway, built for the benefit of Penang and Port Klang, has passed Teluk Intan by and reduced it to a backwater.

Island of princesses and pirates: Pangkor lies off the coast of Perak, and is the most popular beach resort in the state. To get there, you need to take the road from Ipoh to Sitiawan and Lumut. The broad Perak River is crossed at **Bota Kanan**, where there is a hatchery for river terrapins. After the town of **Sitiawan**, head for the coast at **Lumut**, the principal base for the Malaysian Navy. Their offices, ships and apartments can be seen from Pangkor just across the bay.

Many locals don't even make the crossing to Pangkor, but instead make for **Teluk Batik**, a pleasant beach resort 6.5 kilometres (4 mi) from Lumut. Others go to the **Wilderness Adventure Camp**, south of Lumut, where activities are arranged to exercise the body and to teach adults and children alike about life in the forest. The Pesta Laut or Sea Festival is held in Lumut in August every other year, and sea-sport competitions, funfairs and food outlets attract the crowds. Pangkor can also be crowded during this time and any of the Malaysian school holidays; so if you like the beach to yourself, make sure you choose the right month.

Pulau Pangkor is one of the few places on the west coast to offer palm-fringed beaches that reflect those lone stretches of sand on the east coast. Unfortunately, the sea on this side of the peninsula is never as crystal clear as it can be on the other coast.

Legend tells that once a Sumatran warrior fell in love with a beautiful princess, and to win her favour he sailed north to distinguish himself in battle. When he failed to return after many months, the princess set out to find him. She searched high and low, and upon reaching Pulau Pangkor learned the tragic news that he had died in battle and

was buried there. The villagers led her to the grave, whereupon, distraught and heartbroken, she climbed a cliff and flung herself onto the rocks below. **Pantai Puteri Dewi** (The Beach of the Beautiful Princess) is named after her.

Ferries run to several parts of the island all day until early evening. The ferry slides down the Dindings River, with mangroves on one side and a huge navy base on the other, out of the kilometre-wide channel into the Malacca Straits and the island of Pangkor lies directly ahead. The trip takes about 35 minutes.

The eastern side of Pangkor has changed little over the years. Until tourism arrived, the island's economy depended on the sea, and its two main *kampung* (**Sungai Pinang Kecil** and **Sungai Pinang Besar**) are fishing villages with narrow streets which extend on stilts far out over the water. Pangkor Village, further south, has not changed much either.

On the road south of the village are the remains of a Dutch fort built over

Fishing boat off Pangkor Island.

300 years ago in an attempt to control Perak's tin trade. It was also a stronghold against the many pirates of the Malacca Straits. The fort was abandoned after it was attacked by a local warrior, Panglima Kulub, and although later regained, it was by then no longer of any great importance. If the fort looks remarkably well-preserved, it is because the national museum undertook its reconstruction in 1973. Chiselled on a boulder close to the fort is the Dutch East India coat-of-arms. Later adventurers have since added their own messages! In the vicinity of the fort there is said to be a famous snake man, who, for a small fee, will demonstrate his fearlessness for poisonous snakes.

The name of Pangkor is as familiar to every Malaysian schoolchild as that of Gettysburg to an American teenager, for it was on board a warship anchored off the island that the historic Treaty of Pangkor was signed in January 1874, granting the British entry into the Malay states of the peninsula for the first time. Before this event took place, the island had long been notorious as a pirate base and stronghold.

The western side of the island is primarily a beach resort. It is a short taxi ride or walk of twenty minutes from the main village to **Pasir Bogak**, where most of the tourist accommodation is to be found. Pasir Bogak is by no means the prettiest beach on the island, but luckily far more beautiful beaches are easily accessible by the small road which encircles the island. Rent a bicycle or motorcycle and pedal round. Sometimes the road dwindles into nothing more than a sandy track, and cycling can be difficult but rewarding.

The accommodation at Pasir Bogak is sadly rather run-down but the area makes a good base from which to explore the island. The main road from the village runs directly to the Sea View Hotel and the Beach Huts Hotel; both have boats that can take you out to nearby islands. Along the side road that follows the west coast is a string of tidy little A-frame hut resorts. These are cheap and a good place for relaxation. The owners are friendly and will make you feel most welcome. Continuing past Sam Khoo's Mini Camp – small huts much favoured for their low prices by impecunious Malaysian students – the road climbs up a hill to allow lovely views of both sea and jungle. Birds and butterflies abound here. The road slopes down again onto a string of deserted beaches, which very often you can have completely to yourself, but for a few villagers passing by.

Teluk Ketapong Beach, which sometimes has turtles coming ashore to lay eggs, is followed by the beautiful **Teluk Nipah Beach** and finally the loveliest of all, **Coral Bay**. Coral Bay is off the road and is reached by following the beach. Here the water is deliciously warm and very clear, even during the monsoon. Save for a set of small beach huts behind Teluk Nipah, where a Malay family will take care of your needs, there is no accommodation all along these beaches.

Moving back towards civilisation, the road now cuts inland at a narrow point of the island and comes out at **Oyster Bay**, where there is a small jetty. This jetty is the entry point for visitors patronising the posh Pan Pacific Resort on the Beach of the Beautiful Princess, or more popularly called **Golden Sands Beach**. The resort has chalets which incorporate traditional building styles spread along the beach, and a swimming pool right next to the beach. The beach is pleasant and all water sports can be arranged here. Included in the grounds is a 9-hole golf course. But if you want to be alone, Coral Bay is a 40-minute walk back along the road.

For the energetic, the road now moves along the eastern side of the island and a tough walk up the hills surrounding Bukit Pangkor will bring you out at the coast near a fishing village, Kampung Sungai Pinang Kecil.

Off the coast of Pasir Bogak is Pangkor's other big hotel, the luxurious Pangkor Laut Resort, on a small island of the same name. Owned and operated by the same people who have a large stake in the Eastern & Oriental deluxe express train, the resort features a wonderful beach on **Emerald Bay**. Even if you don't wish to stay here, day trips can be arranged to the island. Boats also carry passengers directly from Lumut to Pangkor Laut.

Accommodation in Lumut comes in the form of the Orient Star Hotel or the Lumut Country Resort. The government rest house in Lumut has a mini museum with an excellent collection of seashells, corals, ancient weapons and other items of historical interest.

Golden dome, royal town: About 35 kilometres (20 mi) north of Ipoh on the North-South Highway – which crosses the Perak River over the graceful 50-year-old Iskandar Bridge – lies the attractive town of **Kuala Kangsar**. The Government Rest House here overlooks the river and is worth a night's stay, both for its own quiet beauty and as a convenient centre for exploring the countryside. Kuala Kangsar, the residence of the Sultan of Perak, is a royal town and is famous for three other things besides – possessing one of the first rubber trees to be planted in the country; its spectacular golden-domed mosque; and for its Malay College, the earliest of residential schools in Malaysia.

A plaque on **Government Hill** near the Old Residency (where the British Resident lived but which is now occupied by a girls' school) marks one of the few surviving original rubber trees, originating in Brazil, then cultivated in Kew Gardens, London, and finally sent to Singapore for experimental purposes in the late 1870s. The seeds flourished but it was almost another generation before British planters took the cue and began to plant rubber seriously. Another of these pioneer trees is situated near the agricultural office in town.

The road which winds along the riverside past the Old Residency and the Rest House ends up on **Bukit Chandan**, where the huge golden dome of the **Ubadiah Mosque** gleams. This must be one of the most photographed Muslim buildings in the country, and justly so, if just for its striking and symmetrical domes and minarets. The construction of the mosque began in the reign of Sultan Idris Murshidul Adzam Shah,

Rock depicts the coat of arms of the Dutch East India Company.

but was interrupted a number of times, including once when two elephants belonging to Sultan Idris ran over the imported marble floor, and again during World War I.

Beyond the mosque, which was finally completed in 1919, the road arrives at the compound of the sultan's palace, the **Istana Iskandariah**. Conspicuously placed on a hill overlooking the river valley, the stone vulgarity of the palace is clearly shown up against the much smaller but more dignified and graceful **Istana Kenangan**. Its name means the Palace of Memory and it was previously known as Istana Lembah. Built as a temporary residence while the Istana Iskandariah was under construction, the Istana Kenangan is an extraordinary architectural achievement, being built without a single nail or any architectural plans.

The Palace has now become a royal museum and contains an interesting collection of mementos and photographs connected with the Perak royal family.

The **Malay College** is near the main part of town, set back in its own spacious grounds. Founded in 1904 as a residential school for the sons of the rajah and of the Malay aristocracy, its doors are now open to all Malay boys of talent. A good cross-section of Malaysia's establishment today received their education under this roof.

A short trip in a sampan across the river at Kuala Kangsar takes you to **Sayong** on the opposite bank, also once the home of sultans. A walk of 3 or 4 kilometres – get a guide in town to show the way – brings you to the place where Sayong pottery is made, in particular, the grey-black *labu*, water pitchers distinguished by their broad bases and tall narrow spouts. Other kinds of pottery are available for sale at low "warehouse" prices as well: ornamental tortoises, elephants, birds, practical ashtrays, vases and bowls.

Uncrowned king: From the highlands of the interior, the waters of the Perak River, the second-largest river in the peninsula, pour southwards. Formerly it flooded the towns and villages along

Outcrops and hidden valleys.

its banks every year. Nowadays, however, the river's flow is controlled by Malaysia's largest dam, which lies deep in the jungle 150 kilometres (95 mi) upstream from Kuala Kangsar on a tributary called the Temenggor River.

The region in which the dam is built is known as **Upper Perak**, a district which is still largely covered by mountainous jungles and which has only in modern times formed part of the state of Perak proper. In the 19th century, Upper Perak belonged to the Malay principality of Reman, whose territory extended into southern Thailand and whose rulers paid homage to Bangkok. In 1909, Reman was formally transferred by treaty to Perak and the story goes that Perak gained a few extra square miles territory as a result of what Hubert Berkeley did: the British district officer at Gerik, with his men, moved the jungle boundary stones outwards in the dead of night to increase the size of the land.

For the next few years, Upper Perak continued to be so remote from the rest of the country that Berkeley, who was its district officer for almost 20 years, ruled like an uncrowned king. Many are the stories told about him by the district's old folk; he identified with the local people and by the time he retired he had become a living legend.

On the map, a solitary road winds from Kuala Kangsar into this domain until it reaches the Thai border at Keroh before swinging back into Kedah. The scenery is picturesque and becomes increasingly wilder.

Not far from Kuala Kangsar, it crosses **Tasek Chenderoh**, an artificial lake formed by the dam of the same name built across the Perak River. At Kota Tampan, near Lenggong, the road passes caves once occupied by prehistoric people, who left behind their tools and utensils as evidence. As it continues northwards, the land becomes wilder and more lonely, with only occasional clearings in the hillside jungle for patches of tobacco and Orang Asli crops.

Gerik is a self-contained colony in this jungle wilderness, important not only as an administrative centre but also

Paddling on the calm waters of Tasek Chenderoh.

as the starting point of the East-West Highway on its way to Kelantan and the East Coast. There is a government rest house and some other smaller hotels in town. On the way to the East Coast, the road crosses the spectacular **Temenggor Dam**, where the waters are enclosed by the wild hills; dead and dying trees are blackened by the water and shrouded in mist, adding to the feeling of eerie mystery. At **Banding**, on the shores of the Temenggor, is an isolated retreat for fishing enthusiasts.

From Gerik, the road makes its way to Keroh in the west, through Orang Asli villages and impressive scenery, eventually climbing past the open-cast tin mine that sprawls across the slopes of the hills above **Klian Intan**. This mine was sending tin to Malacca in the days of the sultanate, but its resources might have been long exhausted if mining had not been inhibited by the fear of offending the jealous spirits of the hill.

After Klian Intan comes **Keroh**, the small and pleasant frontier town about 5 kilometres (3 mi) from the Thai border

with a government rest house, as well as customs and immigration offices if you wish to enter Thailand from this unusual entry point.

Town of everlasting peace: A narrow pass at Bukit Berapit separates Kuala Kangsar and the Perak River Valley from the plains of Larut and Matang and the north. Both road and rail go through this gap, first passing the impressive rock of **Gunung Pondok**, which stands like a sentinel to moving traffic. While the railroad burrows through the hillside, the highway runs above, and as it goes down the other side it crosses a cold, fresh mountain stream which is a favourite spot for picnickers.

From there, it is a quick 20-minute drive to **Taiping** ("peace" in Chinese), the chief town of Larut and Matang, and for 50 years the capital of Perak state. Taiping has the heaviest rainfall in the peninsula and the peace referred to in its name was first acquired at the end of the bloody struggles between rival Chinese mining factions in Larut, when the Treaty of Pangkor was signed. The town seems to have been left undisturbed ever since.

In the 1890s, long before the word ecology was in use, an abandoned tin mine on the edge of the town was landscaped to create the beautiful **Lake Gardens**. The creation of these gardens owed much to the generosity of the *Kapitan Cina* of Perak at that time, Chung Keng Kwee, on whose concession the gardens lay. Situated in the gardens is a nine-hole golf course and a rustic zoo that covers an area of about 50 hectares (125 acres).

The Government Rest House in Taman Tasik is built in the Menangkabau style but supported by a row of classical Doric columns, demonstrating the Malaysian genius for marrying different traditions. More architectural gems include the colonial town hall and the government offices standing not far away in a corner of the gardens. At the foot of the hills is an extensive war cemetery. Also in the gardens is a prison, used by the Japanese during the war, later a rehabilitation centre for Communists during the emergency.

The **State Museum**, the oldest in the

Towering trunks of the lowland forest.

country, is housed in a venerable Victorian building, placed, perhaps not so appropriately, opposite the prison. The museum has a wide variety of displays, many of which were gathered at the beginning of the century, and are now no longer obtainable anywhere else. Taiping was also the starting point for Malaysia's first railway, which went as far as Port Weld, but the trains no longer run here. The **Ling Nam Temple** in Taiping is the oldest Chinese temple in Perak and there is a model of a boat within, dedicated to the Chinese emperor who built the first canal in China.

Privacy in a rose garden: Rising above the town, and largely responsible for Taiping's reputation as the wettest place in the peninsula, towers **Maxwell Hill**, now called Bukit Larut. On the slopes of this 1,020-metre (3,350-ft) hill is Malaysia's oldest British hill station: there are no golf courses, fancy restaurants or swimming pools, but limited jungle walks and a badminton court. However, the cool air and moist clouds hanging low over the jungles below, the ever-changing view as the clouds wash off the Straits of Malacca from Penang to Pangkor, and the comfortable bungalows with their English names and fireplaces give Maxwell Hill the simplicity of a natural hideaway that sets one's heart and mind delightfully at ease.

The first road to the top of the hill was constructed after World War II with the "help" of Japanese prisoners-of-war and was completed in 1948. Before that anyone who wished to reach the top but did not fancy hiking had the choice of going by pony or on a sedan chair. In the early years, the trail was lined with porters carrying heavy loads of fragrant tea down the hill. Now tea growing is no longer practised here and only a handful of Indian labourers remain to keep the all-powerful jungle at bay and the gardens neatly manicured.

Although the road is paved today, access is prohibited to private vehicles. Government-owned Land Rovers, which operate from the far end of the Lake Gardens in Taiping, serve as mountain taxis departing every hour between

A tree-lined Taiping street.

dawn and dusk. The one-lane road is steep and narrow; at sharp bends the jungle suddenly parts to reveal the green land below divided into a pattern of roads and fields. The air turns brisk and the sun becomes lost in a bow of mist and clouds.

At the **Tea Gardens House**, traffic halts until the Land Rovers coming down the hill have passed. The 12 kilometre (7.5 mi) journey takes 40 minutes. Land Rovers will deliver a traveller to the front step of his bungalow and leave one to the privacy of this delightful retreat. If feeling energetic, at the foot of the hill, a stone's throw away from the Land Rover station, there is a large freshwater swimming pool, fed constantly by a waterfall.

Back on the coast: Going west from Taiping, Route 74 passes through **Matang**, the old fort of Nagah Ibrahim, named after the Malay territorial chief of Larut who became rich through the tin trade, but who was unable to control the turbulent Chinese factions producing the wealth. Later it was used as the first teacher-training college in the Malay States. Further west is **Port Weld** (Kuala Sepetang), terminus of Malaysia's first railroad. Opened in 1885, the line ran between the coast and Taiping, but is no longer used.

From **Simpang**, the old trunk road heads north through pleasant *padi* country, crossing through towns with fanciful names like Bagan Serai (Lemon Grass Quay), where the rice-growing Krian district begins; Parit Buntar (The Bulging Dyke) and Nibong Tebal (The Stout Nibong Palm). Another half hour and you are on the shore facing Penang.

Nestled among the mangrove swamps south of Bagan Serai is the **Kuala Gula Bird Sanctuary**. Over 100 species of bird, some of them rare and thus protected, have been sighted in this area. Amongst the mammals to be found there are the smooth otter, the dusky-leaf monkey, the long-tailed macaque and the ridge-back dolphin. The months between August and December are the best time for watching the thousands of birds which flock to this place. Informa- **Cameron Highlands.**

tion on the park can be obtained from the Wildlife Department in Batu Gajah.

Deer parks and waterfalls: In the south of Perak, close to **Tapah** and on the way to the Cameron Highlands, are a number of small parks of interest to the nature lover. Situated in Sungkai – about 80 kilometres (50 mi) south on the North-South Highway – is **Sungkai Deer Farm**. The park provides space for around one hundred deer to wander freely on the 100 hectare (250 acre) breeding and conservation site. There is also a bird sanctuary.

Closer to Tapah is the **Kuala Woh Jungle Park**. Facilities are available here for picnickers, fishermen and walkers, and there are a number of waterfalls to visit. Other cascades in this area include the **Lata Iskandar** waterfalls on the way up to the Cameron Highlands.

Cameron Highlands: Although not part of Perak but of Pahang, the **Cameron Highlands** can only be reached through Perak. The road to the Highlands branches off the main trunk highway 60 kilometres (40 mi) south of Ipoh at

Tapah. It shoots off toward the hills and for 90 kilometres (60 mi) winds and twists its way to the top. As cool air funnels down the mountain pass, the temperature drops. Palms and banana trees give way to deep jungle growth. Coniferous trees appear, thick ferns line the road and clusters of bamboo add the touch of a Chinese scroll painting. Orang Asli wearing loin cloths and carrying blowpipes amble along the road.

The Cameron Highlands are actually spread out over three districts. For the newcomer it can be a little confusing, and at first somewhat disappointing, especially when after 45 kilometres (30 mi), you arrive at **Ringlet**, the first district and a rather ugly little settlement. Better to push on! Four kilometres (2.5 mi) later comes the pretty **Sultan Abu Bakar Lake**, an artificial body of water formed by the damming of the Bertam River, and extensively covered with lush green plants. Perched on a bluff above the lake is The Lakehouse, a Tudor-style hotel with sweeping views of the surrounding valley.

Malaysia's hill resorts are richly endowed by nature.

Fifteen kilometres (9 mi) further on lies **Tanah Rata**, the principal township in the Highlands. The scenery becomes superb – cool and clean air, streams, lakes and a view of rolling green mountains which fade into distant greys on the horizon.

The scenery has not always been so charming. Steep, hostile, seemingly impenetrable and infested with spirits and demons, the Cameron Highlands were unknown even to the Malays until 1885, when William Cameron, a government surveyor on a mapping expedition, reported finding a hidden surprise, "a fine plateau with gentle slopes shut in by the mountains."

Tea planters hastily claimed the plateau, and the Chinese, discovering that the high altitude was ideal for growing vegetables, began farming the valley floors. To carry produce to market, they built a road. A wealthy rubber planter came looking for a place of leisure and built a weekend house for his family.

Cameron Highlands has not stopped growing ever since, and tea and vegetables continue to be cultivated.

It seems somewhat incongruous to arrive from the tropical lowlands at Tanah Rata, where the single street is lined with shops and restaurants, many of which advertise "Cream Tea" and "English Breakfast". But strawberries and strawberry jam are part of life in the Camerons. Among the Chinese hotels are several very good Indian restaurants, serving simple snacks and meals that agree very well with the climate here. Shops sell mounted butterflies and scorpions for tourists alongside more practical household goods.

At the end of this street is a small park. Adjacent is the Government Rest House, a quiet setting with pretty gardens that is an absolute haven of peace. It is possible to arrange a visit to the Agricultural Research Institute, and also to the **Blue Valley Tea Estate**, where tours take visitors around the various processes involved in making tea.

Everywhere among the Camerons' many tea-shops and restaurants, the tea seems to taste fresher and its perfume sweeter somehow than when drunk in the lowlands. Tanah Rata has become a popular destination for Malaysian college students and diplomats alike. Local boy scouts with knapsacks on their backs thumb rides up the winding hills, while expatriates from Singapore lounge on colonial verandahs, munching fresh strawberries and cream.

Ye Olde Smokehouse near Brinchang has these delicacies on its tea menu. Sitting there beside a roaring fire, it wouldn't be difficult to imagine that one was in England, so perfect a copy it is of an English inn. The Smokehouse is situated between Brinchang and Tanah Rata, and behind it is the Highlands' 18-hole golf course with a cosy pavilion equipped with a bar and a restaurant. If golf is your reason for being here, then you can stay at the nearby Merlin Inn or Strawberry Park Resort. There is cheaper accommodation in Brinchang, the third district of the Camerons.

In Tanah Rata, buy a map from one of the shops and decide on your walking capabilities. The map gives advice on which trails are family strolls and which are tough hikes.

These trails lead to tea plantations, waterfalls, Orang Asli settlements and, for the energetic, to the summits of the surrounding mountains, with **Gunung Brinchang** as the ultimate goal. It is the Highlands' highest mountain reaching 2,000 metres (6,500 ft), and on especially clear days, Ipoh and other west coast towns, as well as the Malacca Straits, are visible.

The jungles of the Highlands are deceptively dense. Information booklets cautiously advise visitors hiking into the interior to tell someone which way they are going and to stick to the paths, standard precautions anywhere.

Probably the most famous person to have gone missing here was the Thai-silk entrepreneur, Jim Thompson. The American-born Thompson was on holiday in the Cameron Highlands in 1967 when he announced his intention to go for an evening stroll.

He never came back, and his strange disappearance without a trace has invited many explanations for the continuing mystery.

Ubadiah Mosque.

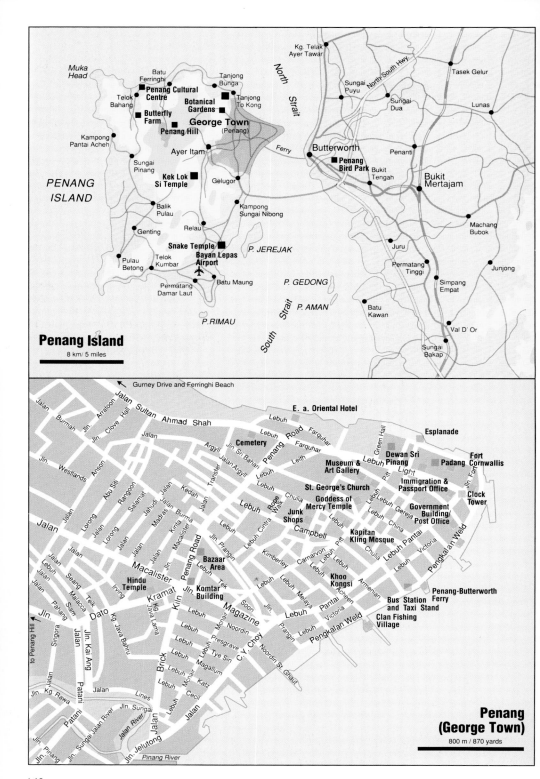

Penang Island

8 km/ 5 miles

Muka Head

Telok Bahang

Batu Ferringhi

Penang Cultural Centre

Tanjong Bunga

Tanjong To Kong

Botanical Gardens

Butterfly Farm

George Town (Penang)

Penang Hill

Kampong Pantai Acheh

Sungai Pinang

Ayer Itam

PENANG ISLAND

Kek Lok Si Temple

Gelugor

Balik Pulau

Relau

Kampong Sungai Nibong

Genting

Snake Temple

Bayan Lepas Airport

Telok Kumbar

Pulau Betong

Permatang Damar Laut

Batu Maung

P. JEREJAK

P. GEDONG

P. AMAN

P. RIMAU

South Strait

North Strait

Ferry

Kg. Telak Ayer Tawar

North South Hwy.

Tasek Gelur

Sungai Puyu

Sungai Dua

Lunas

Butterworth

Penang Bird Park

Penanti

Bukit Tengah

Bukit Mertajam

Machang Bubok

Juru

Permatang Tinggi

Junjong

Simpang Empat

Batu Kawan

Val D' Or

Sungai Bakap

Penang (George Town)

800 m / 870 yards

to Penang Hill

Gurney Drive and Ferringhi Beach

Jalan Burmah

Jln. Aratoon

Jalan Sultan Ahmad Shah

Jln. Clove Hall

Jalan

E. a. Oriental Hotel

Lebuh

Penang Road

Lebuh Farquhar

Farquhar

Green Hall

Esplanade

Cemetery

Jalan Sri Bahari

Argyll

Jalan Argyll

Leith

Lebuh

Lebuh

Chulia

Museum & Art Gallery

Light

Dewan Sri Pinang

Padang

Fort Cornwallis

Pitt

Immigration & Passport Office

Jln. Fort

St. George's Church

Goddess of Mercy Temple

Junk Shops

Lebuh Gereja

Clock Tower

Government Building/ Post Office

Jalan Westlands

Jln. Anson

Abu Siti

Rangoon

Salamat

Jalan

Lorong

Jahudi

Jalan

Madras

Jalan Burma

Kinta

Macalister

Jln. Prangin

Lebuh

Cintra

Campbell

Lebuh China

Kapitan Kling Mosque

Chulia

Lebuh Pantai

Jalan

Jalan

Kedah

Penang Road

Bazaar Area

Kimberley

Carnarvon

Lebuh

Pitt

Victoria

Pengkalan Weld

Macalister

Hindu Temple

Teik

Irving

Kramat

Jln. Tek

Komtar Building

Soon

Jln.

Khoo Kongsi

Acheen

Armenian

Penang-Butterworth Ferry

Dato

Kg. Java Lama

Kg. Java Bahru

Kiln

Magazine

Mcnair

Noordin

Lebuh Melaya

Lebuh Pantai

Victoria

Bus Station and Taxi Stand

Clan Fishing Village

Jln. Kai Ang

Brick

Presgrave

Lebuh Tye Sin

C. Y. Choy

Noordin St. Ghaut

Prangin

Pengkalan Weld

Patani

Lebuh Magallum

Lines

Lebuh Cecil

Jalan

Jln. Sungai

Jalan River

Jalan Jelutong

Pinang River

PENANG:
PEARL OF THE ORIENT

Penang is one of the most famous islands in Asia and perhaps the best-known tourist destination in Malaysia – a place of mysterious temples and palm-shrouded beaches that has been attracting curious visitors for several hundred years. Since 1985, it has been joined to the mainland by the Penang Bridge, which has become a modern symbol of the island. It costs more than the ferry, but the 7-kilometre (4.5-mi) drive affords exhilarating views of the harbour, and you have the satisfaction of knowing that you have just driven over one of the longer bridges in the world.

Although once under the dominion of the Sultan of Kedah, Penang has always been on its own. Until the British came, it was largely deserted despite its strategic position. To encourage trade and commerce, the British made the island state a free port; no taxes were levied on either imports or exports. This strategy worked and in eight years the population increased to 8,000, comprising many immigrant races – Chinese, Indians and Bugis, among others.

In the beginning: The story of how Penang fell into British hands and developed into Malaysia's leading entrepot does little credit to the British themselves. Penang was acquired on the initiative of an English trader and adventurer named Francis Light, who had been living in the area for 15 years. Light spoke fluent Thai and Malay and was a familiar figure in the Kedah court. He fully envisaged the advantages that the possession of Penang would hold for the British, who were then represented by Britain's East India Company. The company had an increasingly urgent need for a station on the eastern side of the Bay of Bengal, in order to secure naval domination of the bay from the French.

The base would serve to replenish company ships on their long haul to China in the flourishing tea and opium trade, and as a headquarters from which to further British interests in Southeast Asian waters. In the 1780s, when the rulers of Kedah sorely needed help against the imminent threats of a Thai invasion from the north and Bugis attacks from the south, Light persuaded them to trade Penang for British protection. The Kedah Malays agreed, and in 1786, an East India Company settlement was established on Penang.

The company confirmed its approval of Light's action in acquiring the island, but refused to honour the commitment to protect the Sultan of Kedah against his enemies. The angry Sultan tried to recapture Penang but was easily defeated and, as a result, Kedah had to surrender more land to the British – this time, the land between the Muda and Krian rivers opposite Penang island, which was named Seberang Prai by the Malays. The British called it Province Wellesley, after the governor-general in India at the time.

Today, Seberang Prai and Penang constitute the State of Penang, which is headed by a governor, who is appointed

142

by the Malaysian king. Throughout history Penang has changed names like the seasons. Early Malays called it Pulau Ka Satu, or Single Island. Later it appeared on sailing charts as Pulau Pinang, or Island of the Betel Nut Tree. The British renamed it Prince of Wales' Island, and finally, with Malaysia's independence, it reverted to Penang. Penang is nowadays sometimes spelled Pinang.

There are still many nicknames attached to it – Pearl of the Orient, Gateway to the East, Isle of Temples. Place and street names are again undergoing a change in Penang Island as colonial names are being exchanged for more representative Malay ones. To add to this confusion, the locals themselves have their own names for certain streets.

King George's town: Like most cities of Asia that juxtapose the glass and concrete of the new with the tile and teak of the old, Penang has several dimensions. A newcomer can arrive by ferry, be transported by trishaw to a Chinese hotel on Lebuh Kimberley or Lebuh Chulia in the heart of Chinatown, eat at the small food stalls, walk the waterfront and visit the villages set on stilts, and after two weeks leave Penang not knowing there is a tourist complex. On the other hand, another visitor may have cocktails served at the poolside overlooking the sea and later dine in a revolving restaurant, 16 storeys above the flickering lights of the city, and never really know that an exciting, vibrant Chinatown exists.

Georgetown, named by the British after King George III of Great Britain but referred to by the Malays as Tanjong (or Headland), is unmistakeably a Chinese town, from crowded streets with Chinese characters spelling out mystic logos, to the thriving port from which Malaysia's exports find their way to the world's markets.

Georgetown has one of the most unusual waterfronts in Asia. Visitors arriving by ferry usually do a double take when they first see it. The area is what locals call the **Clan Piers**. It consists of villages built on stilts over the sea. The people who live there are either boat-

Georgetown from above, with the mainland in the distance.

men or fishermen and each group belongs to a clan. On Lim's Pier only members of the Lim family can live, while Chew's Pier is the sole property of the Chew clan.

The houses extend far out to sea, and at low tide the fishermen's boats rest high on the mud-banks. On tiny docks that consist of no more than a few narrow planks on the sand and a shed, labourers unload heavy burlap sacks stuffed with cargo brought in by the lightermen. No one minds if a visitor strolls along the often shaky wooden piers, provided he is not a Chew in Lim's territory.

As predominantly as the port is Chinese, the countryside is Malay. Outside the city, the hustle and bustle of commerce is left behind; the noise and crowd are swapped for an agrarian, quiet and thinly populated world.

Penang is also Indian. With the British came the *sepoy* (Indian natives employed as soldiers by a European power), Indian merchants, and also Indian convicts, who built the first roads and filled in the swamps on which the town now stands. Not all of them stayed, but they left behind their stamp. The spicy scent of curry dominates the older section of Georgetown; a taxi driver speaks Tamil as well as Malay, English and some Hokkien. A Hindu temple stands on top of Penang Hill and a Hindu shrine rises next to a Buddhist image on a promontory in the south.

Traces of old Penang: Probably the most costly cannon ball in history was shot at **Kedah Point**, near Fort Cornwallis. The site, which Francis Light had chosen for his settlement, was thick with jungle and the task of clearing the undergrowth proved arduous for the sepoys, who complained of hardship. So Light loaded a cannon with silver dollars and fired it into the jungle. This was enough inducement to get all to work to retrieve the coins; before long the land was cleared and the first camp established.

Originally, **Fort Cornwallis** was a wooden structure. Between 1808 and 1810, it was rebuilt with convict labour. Today, the old fort still stands, but its

Municipal building evokes memories of colonial splendour.

precincts have been converted into a public park and playground. Its ramparts are still guarded by old cannons, the most venerable and famous of which is Seri Rambai, known to many Penang residents as "the travelling cannon". The cannon has certainly travelled. Cast in Holland, it was presented by the Dutch to the Sultan of Johor in 1606. Seven years later, in a devastating raid on Johor, it was captured by the Achenese and taken to Aceh, where it remained for almost 200 years. The cannon was then sent to Kuala Selangor by the Achenese in search of a Bugis alliance. After the British bombarded Kuala Selangor in 1871, the cannon was brought here to Penang.

For several years, it was left lying in the sea off the Esplanade until it was hauled out and placed at its present location. Like most ancient cannons, Seri Rambai is attributed with magical powers; it is believed that women desiring children will have their wish fulfilled if they place flowers in the cannon's barrel and offer prayers.

Heart of history: Next to Fort Cornwallis lie the Padang (town green) and the **Esplanade** (Jalan Tun Syed Sheh Barakbah), which is the heart of old historical Georgetown. Handsome 19th-century colonial government offices stand at one end of the Padang; at the other, near the entrance to Fort Cornwallis, traffic circles the **Clock Tower**, presented to Penang by a rich Chinese *towkay* named Cheah Chin Gok in commemoration of Her Majesty Queen Victoria's Diamond Jubilee.

The dignified and well-designed **St George's Church**, built in 1818 on nearby Lebuh Farquhar, draws much attention as the oldest Anglican church in Southeast Asia. Francis Light lies buried in the adjoining, frangipani-shaded cemetery, along with a host of other notables of old Penang, many of whom succumbed early in life to the rigours of the climate and dangers of life in the tropics.

In **Penang Museum**, on the other side of the street, visitors can peer into a Chinese bridal chamber created in the

Feet fit for a food stop.

lavish style of the 19th century, when Malaysian-Chinese girls took great pride in the quality of beadwork on their slippers. One room, dedicated to a glimpse of yesteryear, is hung with old paintings and etchings from the days when Fort Cornwallis was the centre of town. Another is an opulent showcase of bejewelled *kris*, the dagger-like weapons Malays used for protection and for prestige. The **Penang Art Gallery** upstairs displays batik paintings, oils, graphics and Chinese ink drawings. Most of the techniques are new, but the solemn, moody sea scenes and village portraits recapture a way of life that is little changed from the pioneer days.

Georgetown streets: On arrival, visitors are usually intrigued by the narrow, congested streets of Georgetown and its pulsating waterfront. It is here, on the waterfront, that Penang is commercially linked to the rest of the world by the flotilla of freighters and steamers anchored in the harbour, which cause the ferryboats from Butterworth to zigzag a 4-kilometre (2.5-mi) course to reach the landing at Weld Quay.

Penang is a Far East warehouse for everything imaginable, from electronic gadgets to plastic toys. There are silks from Thailand and India, fabrics from England, cameras from Germany and Japan, textiles from America, and from Malaysia, brocade and sarongs. **Jalan Pinang** is the main shopping bazaar. Shops open in the early morning and do not close until the bars are empty and the late moviegoers have cleared the streets.

Lebuh Campbell, just off Jalan Pinang, is the main "Chinese" shopping centre where Nepalese street vendors sell nylon shirts, fake alligator-skin shoes, laughing jack-in-the-boxes, and precious stones, guaranteed to cut glass.

Perhaps the most exciting shopping in Penang is in the many junk shops along **Rope Walk**. Here, shoppers must literally climb over mounds of discarded gear. Those who do not mind getting their hands dirty are certain to discover a dusty thing or two. One London boutique saleswoman found a luxurious Chinese emperor's robe salvaged from the local opera stage.

Disappearing markets: One typical Malaysian institution is the *pasar minggu* or *pasar malam* (weekly market or night market). These are temporary markets which spring up in the street or an open space in the evenings or on the weekends. How and where they appear varies from place to place: in Penang, they are called pasar malam and move from location to location every two weeks. One Italian tourist returned to Penang after visiting the south for a week and was greatly disappointed to find that the market had apparently closed down. Only by chance did she learn that it had been moved somewhere else. The areas, wherever they might be, are well lighted and the bargains range from tiny trinkets to cheap Kelantan batik sarongs and plastic sandals and slippers. People-watching here is especially enjoyable.

In Georgetown, walking is a delight and distances pass unnoticed. Taxis are plentiful and inexpensive but they are not allowed to "cruise" for customers. The easiest and most enjoyable way to

Shopping cart with a difference.

get around is by trishaw. That way, the city passes by in a kaleidoscope of changing colours, the way it should be in Georgetown. Even a trishaw ride in the monsoon rain can be enjoyable. The driver zips his passengers into a plastic covering, and pedals slowly through the misty streets. At night, there is a special romance about riding in a trishaw when the driver lights small lamps that adorn both fenders. The tiny lights flicker in the inky darkness like fireflies in the jungle night.

Night-time niceties: The streets of Georgetown are made for nightlife. The Chinese, in particular, never seem to go to bed. Their open-front restaurants are noisy gathering places where waiters shout your order to someone in a back room. A jukebox, if there is one, is turned on full volume. Hawker stalls on Gurney Drive and the Esplanade do a thriving business, while brightly lit stores cater to late-night shoppers. At the fashionable hotels, latecomers wait in line at the discotheques. There are roof top restaurants where diners look down over the city lights, hills and harbour, and dark cellar cabarets with no view at all.

Those who prefer to seek entertainment in bars can find a few around Georgetown and on the northern outskirts of the city. Some small and friendly establishments keep a "family album" of snapshots showing just about every traveller who has walked in and bought a drink. They provide jukeboxes for dancing, game machines for entertainment and barmaids for conversation. Others are more consciously sophisticated, like the 1885 Room in the **Eastern & Oriental Hotel**. The leader of the band and the pianist as well, Albert Yeoh, has been playing for varied audiences at the E&O (once sister to the Raffles Hotel in Singapore) for over 40 years. He once remarked that nowadays people prefer to sit and drink while they listen to the band, whereas previously his audience was always keen to get up and dance.

Penang is undoubtedly a place that makes evening walks fond memories. One does not have to look for excite-

Despite the Penang Bridge, traditionalists still take the ferry.

ment on the streets of Georgetown. If you take a room in a Chinese hotel, you will understand why. Early morning might begin with a funeral procession through the streets: there are drums and gongs and mourners. In the afternoon, a lion dance might pass by – a noisy affair with more drums and gongs, followed by mobs of youngsters. Come evening and it could be a Chinese opera, where people sit and watch heavily painted faces pantomime classical tales of old, or a rock band playing pop tunes on the Esplanade. You can never tell what you might find – a bargain or a baritone.

Georgetown is still a city with few skyscrapers. **Komtar**, Penang's civic centre, is one and it has the most fashionable office block and the most sophisticated shopping plaza in the city. The lower storeys are taken up by shops, a couple of cinemas, restaurants, and right down below, a bus station. Its probing circular tower forms a landmark clearly visible from the mainland.

Dainty doorways: It is not just the shops and junk stores that make wandering through the streets of Georgetown a delight. Narrow alleyways off bustling roads lead to quiet rows of Chinese homes, whose carved lintels and doorways bedazzle passers-by. The small family temple erected on **Gat Lebuh Gereja** (Church Street) by millionaire Chung Keng Kwee is a good example. Inside the temple, a lifelike bronze statue of Chung in the robes of a Chinese mandarin stands resplendent. Chung made his fortune from the tin mines in Larut and is remembered as one of the leaders of the Chinese factions in the Larut Wars of the 1860s.

Chinese immigrants arriving in Malaysia a hundred years ago fell under the protection and control of one of the clan associations, whose functions were not unlike those of medieval European guilds – to promote the interests of their members and to provide help to those of their number who were in distress. The ancestral halls of these clan associations – such as the Khoo, Ong, Tan and Chung – are called *kongsi* and are scattered all over town.

The Eastern & Oriental in colonial days.

The most impressive is the clan hall built by the Khoo Kongsi. The **Leong San Tong Khoo Kongsi**, at the junction of Lebuh Pitt and Lebuh Acheh, comprises two buildings standing on opposite sides; one is the ancestral temple itself, while the other serves as a stage for plays and operas on various appropriate occasions.

Dragons on the roof tops: The Khoo Kongsi is so elaborate that it almost exceeds celestial proprieties. The clan house was designed to capture the splendour of an imperial palace with a seven-tiered pavilion, wondrous dragon pillars and hand-painted walls engraved with the Khoo rose emblem. The original design was so ambitious that conservative Khoo clansmen cautioned against it, lest the emperor of China be offended. Construction began in 1894 and it took eight years to complete.

However, on the first night after the building was finished, the roof mysteriously caught fire. Clan members interpreted this as a sign that even the deities considered the Khoo Kongsi too pala-

tial for a clan house. The Khoos rebuilt it on a smaller scale and the result was one of perfection.

Entering its courtyard is like being guided out of time to a heavenly abode where dragons dance on roof tops and fairies play lutes among the clouds. Sagging eaves are transformed into enamel mosaics of celestial kingdoms. Gilded beams become curvilinear gardens where saintly immortals dwell. The outer walls are a pageant of legendary episodes, carved, painted and polished by experts from Cathay. Giant guardian gods on the main doors prevent the intrusion of evil spirits, while stone lions chiselled from green granite help keep guard. Behind the altar's facade of glistening gold leaf and red lacquer stand statues of the gods of longevity, wealth, prosperity and happiness. On either side of the central shrine are ancestral halls honouring the patron saints of the clan. Surrounding their images are *sinchoo*, wooden tablets remembering deceased clansmen. Gold plaques on the walls are inscribed with the names of members who have earned a high academic degree or who have attained a position of leadership, such as justice of the peace.

Goddess of Mercy: Of all the Chinese temples, Penang's oldest is the **Kuan Yin Temple** in Lebuh Pitt, which is also the most humble and the most crowded. The temple belongs to the people in the street – the noodle hawkers, trishaw riders, housewives doing the daily marketing, old shopkeepers counting abacus figures, workers building cupboards, repairing bicycles or selling sundries. A Buddhist deity who refused to enter Nirvana as long as there was injustice on earth, Kuan Yin (Quanyin) typically personifies mercy.

She is ever-present on Chinese altars, whether the worshippers be Taoist, Buddhist or Confucian. Throughout the day, people visit her temple to burden her with problems they cannot solve or to thank her for the blessings which ended their worries. The clicking of divining sticks ricochets throughout the halls as devotees ask her advice for the coming week. Men and women of Georgetown know that Kuan Yin will reply. She is

Rooftop patterns in Chinatown.

perhaps the most beloved divinity of all the Chinese altars in Penang. The worshipping of Kuan Yin is a meeting-ground between traditional Chinese belief and Buddhism.

Kuan Yin's temple has a well-worn look. The halls are heavily laden with scented smoke. The floors are littered with joss-stick wrappers and discarded shopping bags. The altar looks like a banquet table, with roasted chickens, sweet cakes, oranges, pineapples and cookies neatly placed as humble offerings to the goddess.

On the eve of the Chinese New Year, when good luck is in highest demand, Kuan Yin's temple seemingly catches fire. Hundreds converge at her altars to burn joss sticks, light red candles, and invoke her name. Smoke billows from furnaces set up in the courtyard, as paper joss money is sent to Kuan Yin via the fire. Businessmen and beggars alike jam the front gates, carrying a stream of glowing joss sticks. An apparition appears amid the smoke – a human face transfigured by goggles and a kerchief over the nose. Looking like a space-age bandit or an air-pollution survivor behind a makeshift gas mask, it is actually the boy hired by the temple to collect the plethora of burning joss sticks and dump them in the furnace outside.

Set nearby, in direct contrast, is the Indian-Muslim-styled **Kapitan Kling Mosque**; built in 1800, it is the state's oldest mosque.

Penang Buddhism: The eve of Chinese New Year at the **Penang Buddhist Association** on Jalan Anson is a more formal affair compared to the mad rush of devotions at other temples. Women arrive in traditional *samfoo* or store-bought Western dresses, conscientiously fashionable. A teenage girl patiently leads her dignified grandfather across the wide marble floor, where a seated congregation chants praises to Lord Buddha.

The association organisers busily arrange patterns of bright flowers, fruits and coloured cakes on a large, shiny table carved out of blackwood imported from Canton. Enthroned on the high

Kapitan Kling Mosque.

altars are six white marble statues of Lord Buddha and his disciples. Crystal chandeliers from Czechoslovakia hang overhead, and the walls are decorated with paintings depicting Buddha's path to enlightenment.

As temple bells ting, the chanting rises to usher in the new year, to celebrate an eternal rebirth for all generations. Outside the front door, beggars sit quietly chatting amongst themselves. They know benevolence is a precept of the Chinese New Year and they receive it passively.

Ordinarily, the large, luminous hallway that dominates the Chinese Buddhist Association is the most serene sanctuary in Penang. The building, completed in 1929, reflects the desire of a Buddhist priest who wanted to indoctrinate his followers with orthodox rites and ceremonies. Joss-stick hawkers or paper-money burners are not found here. Prayers are considered the essence of Buddhist worship, and the Penang Buddhist Association cherishes the simplicity inherent in its Buddhist faith.

The variety of Buddhist worship in Penang is so striking as to make sightseeing a new experience in every temple. One can enter the gigantic meditation hall at **Wat Chayamangkalaram** and find a workman polishing the left cheek of the 32-metre (105 ft) long Reclining Buddha, the third-largest statue of its kind in the world. Wat Chayamangkalaram, on Jalan Burma, is a Thai Buddhist monastery. Gigantic *naga* serpents, mystical creatures that link earth to heaven, form the balustrades at the entrance of the meditation hall. Fierce-visaged giants tower over the doorways in the role of otherworldly bodyguards, who leave little to the imagination. Monks with shaven heads and saffron robes soundlessly tread over lotus blossoms patterned on the tiled floor. All around the monumental image of slumber are smaller statues of lesser Buddhas with donation boxes on their pedestals. Inscribed on one box are the words: "To devotees who worship this god, your wish will come true, what you wish will come to you."

Wat Chayamang-kalaram.

Another form of Buddhist worship can be seen in the Burmese temple on the other side of the road. A Buddha with a haughty, yet serene expression is worshipped here. Another shrine is surrounded with a moat over which "heavenly" bridges fly. On either side is a Buddha, one refusing tempting fruits cradled in vast shells offered by a goofy-toothed man, who looks the picture of worldly indulgence. The other is accosted by two young women, and though the Buddha seems to be casting them aside, he almost looks as if he is secretly enjoying the temptation. Little shops in the shaded walkways sell little pink and green lotus flower-shaped candles to worshippers, who leave the lighted candles reverently in front of the shrines.

Inspired by a vision: High above the bustle of Georgetown on a hilltop at **Ayer Hitam**, which is about 6 kilometres (4 mi) from the Buddhist Association, looms the **Kek Lok Si** or **Temple of Paradise**. This temple, the largest Buddhist temple in Malaysia and one of the largest in the region, owes its existence to Beow Lean, a Chinese Buddhist priest from Fujian province in China who first arrived in Penang in 1887. Soon after his arrival, he was appointed resident priest of the Kuan Yin Temple in Lebuh Pitt, and so impressed was he by the religious fervour of Penang's Buddhists that he decided to found a monastery to propagate the religion. He chose this site at Ayer Hitam, whose hills reminded him of his home in Fujian.

Work on the temple started in 1890, with its main buildings completed by 1904. The great pagoda tower, however, was not finished until 1930. It is dedicated to all manifestations of the Buddha, hence appropriately named the Pagoda of a Million Buddhas, renowned for the three architectural styles it contains – a Chinese base, a Thai middle section and a Burmese top.

When completed, Kek Lok Si became an instant tourist attraction as well as a centre for Buddhist devotion. The tourism aspect dominates, however; visitors walk through arcades of souvenir stalls to the top of the pagoda and pay

Burning joss at Kek Lok Si.

"voluntary" contributions for the privilege of ascending the tower.

On Sundays, Kek Lok Si witnesses a holiday parade as Chinese families spend their free afternoons strolling among the opulent gardens on the threshold of paradise. The spiritually-oriented playground has an informal give-and-take atmosphere, free from the solemnity of secluded shrines.

Kek Lok Si is split into three tiers spread over a rocky incline. The three "Halls of the Great" honour Kuan Yin, goddess of mercy; Bee Lay Hood, the Laughing Buddha; and Gautama Buddha, founder of the faith. It is here that the monks pass their hour in prayer. The Tower of Sacred Books on the topmost tier houses a library of Buddhist scriptures and *sutra*, many of which were presented by the Kuang Hsu Emperor of China. An edict from the same emperor, cemented into a wall of this block, grants imperial approval to the establishment of the temple.

Rooms with a view: In the northern direction, Jalan Ayer Hitam leads to yet another hill – the **Penang Hill**. Despite the first impression one might have of Georgetown as a busy place, it is a town of leisure beneath its facade. People who live here enjoy their city and island. They frequent the parks and gardens, take trips around the island and visit the many temples. Penang Hill is one of their favourite spots. As far back as 1897, people were struck by the scenic beauty and "the desirability of Penang Hill as a health resort".

There was only one problem: getting there. Someone finally came up with the idea of building a railway to the summit. After years of labour, the line was completed. Two passenger cars mounted on tracks were attached to a thick cable, which passed through pulleys. Steam power was ruled out in favour of a Pelton wheel, propelled by water power. "An ingenious method" was the remark at the time. Everyone awaited the day when the rail cars would start rolling. But when that day finally arrived, the water wheels failed to even spin.

In the next 25 years science pro-

Ornate entrance to a Georgetown house.

152

gressed. After studying the funicular railway system in Switzerland, Penang residents opened the present line in 1923 and it has been in operation ever since. The ride to the summit is one of the highlights of a visit to the island. As the cars rumble slowly up the steep incline, a panorama of sea and islands, mountains and tropical valleys continuously unfolds. From each small substation along the way, paths disappear into the cool forest or gardens of private bungalows on the terraced slopes. One of the most pleasant experiences a visitor can have is to spend a day or two staying at the Bellevue Hotel at the summit. The 500 people who live on the hill have built a small Hindu temple and a mosque. The funicular railway operates from 6.30am–9pm daily.

Apart from funicular railcars, Penang has much to offer in the way of recreation. Georgetown is Asia's Monte Carlo where, once a year, racing cars from all over Southeast Asia whip around the winding roads and along the sea front to compete in the Malaysian Grand Prix.

The Kek Lok Si Temple, and the funicular railway at Penang Hill.

Horse racing is also extremely popular and races are held five times a year at the Penang Turf Club. There is also an 18-hole golf course.

Penang has also its share of the latest Chinese language films. Anyone who has not seen a Chinese swordsman of old on the silver screen, wreaking vengeance against great odds and usually winning, might find it an enjoyable and memorable experience.

Bliss below the waterfall: "Another very important consideration in a place proposed for a Colony is fresh water," wrote Lt. Popham of the Royal Navy. "No country can be better supplied with this valuable article than Prince of Wales' Island. Water descends from the hills and is collected into several small rivulets, the two principal of which empty themselves into the harbour, the one near, the other 5 kilometres (2 mi) from the town; and in the latter of these the ships' casks may be filled in the long-boats at low water."

After nearly 200 years, the freshwater springs in the hills above Georgetown

continue to lure visitors up from the lowlands. Although they are labelled Waterfall Gardens, situated about 3 kilometres (2 mi) due northeast from Penang Hill, they are actually Penang's **Botanical Gardens**, in the grounds of which grow some of Malaysia's most beautiful tropical plants. Monkeys inhabit the trees and delight visitors when they come down to the lawns to be fed, especially in the early mornings or late afternoons. The waterfalls start over a hundred metres above the gardens and come tumbling down through the green, where there are footpaths and small wooden bridges, much like a Japanese garden. On holidays, families round up distant relatives for a picnic lunch by the stream, while barefoot children romp on the rocks or play follow-the-tourist. Benches are scattered throughout the gardens and provide pleasant resting spots in the shade. And, like other similar places in the world, lovers come to take advantage of blissful nature.

One of the most scenic spots on the island is **Ayer Hitam Dam**, with an 18-hectare (45 acre) lake reflecting the lush green foliage of the surrounding jungle. A 3-kilometre (2-mi) road from Kek Lok Si Temple winds its way up to the dam. The air becomes increasingly cool, especially in the evening when the breezes blow across the lake.

Beyond the dam, atop a hill and reached by a long flight of steps, is the Indian shrine of **Nattukotai Chettiar**. As in Kuala Lumpur, the awe-inspiring festival of Thaipusam is held here. There are those who claim that the Thaipusam festival in Penang is even more dramatic and interesting than the one in Kuala Lumpur. Certainly, it does not suffer in comparison.

Round-the-island trip: Beyond the outskirts of Georgetown, another Penang begins. By starting at the waterfront in the morning, the visitor can head south, follow the winding and sometimes mountainous road for 74 kilometres (46 mi) and by the evening return to the same spot from which one started. One can visit a temple where poisonous **Chinese** snakes hang from the rafters, watch **opera.**

tropical fish swim in an aquarium, see an alleged footprint of a heroic Chinese admiral, swim in a pool beneath a waterfall, meet Malay fishermen in remote villages, have lunch in a polished teak restaurant and lounge away the afternoon on a soft, white beach.

Travellers have a variety of ways to make a round-the-island tour. Hotels and tourist offices can arrange for group tours in air-conditioned buses with guides. Private chauffeured cars with or without guides can be hired through the tourist office. There are also rent-a-car services. Or make the trip by public bus: for less than a dollar it will take you anywhere. The only difficulty is that unless you want to hike, you cannot leave the main road.

On the outskirts of town are the mills and factories, and the Malay countryside. The roads are well marked with kilometre-stones indicating the distances from Georgetown. A road map is helpful but not essential. You cannot really get lost. There are a number of side roads, some worth exploring, but most

of them end in remote villages on the coast. Where there is little traffic, the fishermen have the habit of drying their *ikan bilis* (small fish) on the pavement. Often there may be a half-kilometre stretch of fish drying, with slightly more than tyre room left on the road.

"Not worry, no bite," a Chinese lad insists as he probes at a small tree. Interwoven amongst the branches slithers an impressive one-metre-long (3-ft), green and yellow viper. The jaws open and red fangs hiss. "See," the boy repeats, "no bite."

The viper lives in the famous **Temple of Azure Cloud**, more popularly known as the Snake Temple. The road south from the aquarium passes the **Science University of Malaysia** (Universiti Sains Malaysia) and the 14-kilometre stone marks the serpents' shrine. When you climb the steps to the ornate temple, you may think there is nothing unusual about it. Even when you see a few snakes curled up, it does not seem too extraordinary – until you begin to notice that the poisonous pit vipers are every-

Malay kampung house.

where: on altars, shrines, incense burners, candlesticks, vases, tables, underfoot and overhead. There is even a "maternity" tree where smaller vipers slither along the branches. In an adjoining room a photographer stands by to take your photo, if you care to pose with a snake or two curled around your arms and neck. These vipers, the photographer guarantees, have no poison fangs.

The snakes are venerated because of their kinship to the mythical dragons of Chinese folklore. It is claimed that, during the day, burning incense in the temple keeps them doped. At night, they let themselves down from the ceiling and branches to suck the chicken eggs left for them by worshippers.

Sacred footprints: Having no luck with lotteries? Do you suffer from poor health, or need success over business rivals? Or is it one of the opposite sex you wish to seduce? If so, you might try joining the multitude of believers who pay their respects at a small shrine on a rocky promontory at **Batu Maung**, a fishing village on the southeast tip of the island about 3 kilometres (2 mi) from the Bayan Lepas Airport. The shrine marks the sacred footprint of Admiral Cheng Ho, the Chinese "Columbus of Malaysia". Villagers believe that Cheng Ho called at this spot on one of his seven voyages to Southeast Asia. On Langkawi Island, 96 kilometres (60 mi) to the north, is a similar footprint. The two are believed to be a pair and anyone who lights joss sticks and places them in the urns beside the footprint will have good luck and great fortune.

When it is high tide at Batu Maung, fishing boats are run up on the beach, left high and dry when the waters recede. Ships' joiners take advantage of nature's drydock to repair vessels before the next tide ends their work day. These skilled carpenters use tools that should be museum pieces, as ancient as the result of a thousand years of handed-down experience.

It was in vessels such as these that their distant ancestors explored and traded in the islands of the Malay archipelago. They have perhaps turned from

Young temple visitor, and giant joss.

traders to fishermen but their art remains the same.

Malay kampung: Several small roads in the south branch off to the coast. Usually they are the commercial link between a fishing village and the trunk road. It was in small villages such as these that the few Malays lived during the time when Francis Light established the first settlement.

Malaysian architecture in cities and towns changes constantly with the times, but the *kampung* houses look much the same as they did a hundred years ago. Malays take pride in their homes and their interiors can often be glimpsed from the road. The furnishings are simple and each house will have a framed photograph of the King and Queen. Houses are elevated, making the lifestyle within cool, dry and clean. Fruit trees grow in the neatly swept courtyards, bearing rambutans, mangosteens, bananas and papayas.

Each house has an outside basin for washing the feet before climbing the stairs. Malays always leave their shoes outside to keep the interior of their houses clean. Cleanliness is one of the prime virtues laid down in the Koran and most women dutifully sweep their homes several times a day.

To the north: The road skirts around the southern end of the island and turns north. The scenery changes from flat rice land to rolling hills. Cultivation gives way to dense, damp jungles. The road twists upward, and where the foliage clears, there are striking views of the island dropping to the sea far below. Here, spice plantations of pepper, clove and nutmeg lured Arab, Spanish, Portuguese and other Western traders to this part of the world long ago. At **Titi Kerawang**, there are waterfalls and a serene view of the Indian Ocean. The natural freshwater pool that is filled from the waterfalls is suitable for bathing, though a big water pipeline mars the scenery.

The road reaches the southern end of the island at **Teluk Kumbar**, where it again swings eastward to run along the coast, which has become the preserve of

Hotel pool at Batu Ferringhi.

hotels and sun worshippers. As it does so, it leaves behind the rugged jungled promontory of **Muka Head**, which has a lonely lighthouse at its tip. Muka Head is part of a forest reserve and there are no roads to its quiet isolated coves; however, hired boats at Teluk Kumbar take visitors out to any one of them to spend the day or to camp for the night. The small forest station near Teluk Kumbar itself is set in a well-laid out arboretum.

The road to Penang's north coast follows the curve of the land, twisting up and around a hill or skirting the fringe of the sea. Rocky headlands jutting out into the sea divide the shoreline into small bays and coves, each with a different character and charm. Although the waters are not as clear as on the East Coast, the beaches are still popular for swimming and sunbathing.

Most activities are centred around **Batu Ferringhi**, one of the most popular beach resorts in Southeast Asia. The large luxury hotels of Rasa Sayang, Mutiara, Golden Sands and the Holiday Inn are found here. Their facilities include waterskiing, sailing, windsurfing, water scooters, and horseback riding. Smaller and older, but comfortable and reasonably priced, are the Palm Beach and Lone Pine. Small inns and motels, as well as many villagers in this area, also offer accommodation.

At the north end of Batu Ferringhi beach is **Yahong Art Gallery**, a storehouse of some of the finest arts, crafts and antiques of Malaysia and China. It is also the home of Mr Chuah Thean Teng, Malaysia's foremost batik artist, whose work has won international recognition at a number of one-man exhibitions in the major capitals of the world.

Six kilometres (4 mi) further along the north coast is the fine **Teluk Bahang** beach. Near the centre of town is the **Penang Cultural Centre**, which features arts and crafts, music and dance, and traditional architecture from all around Malaysia. Besides an exhibition gallery and restaurant, the complex also sports a Malay kampung and Dayak longhouse imported from Borneo.

Another good place to shop is **Craft Batik**, which is situated at the southern end of Teluk Bahang village, on the road to Sungai Penang. The showroom features batik clothes, paintings and other handicrafts, and you can duck behind the scenes to see how the block printing and painting are carried out. Further along the same road is the **Penang Butterfly Farm**, where some of the loveliest butterflies and most awe-inspiring insects of Malaysia are bred and displayed – alive, and not pinned down! A couple of minutes down the road is a 100 hectare (250 acre) **Forest Recreation Park** for trekking and picnicking.

Microchips and jungle gardens: The mainland section of Penang state is nearly twice as large as the island, a thriving industrial area built around **Butterworth** that has become one of the world's leading producers of microchips, disk drives and other computer parts. Both sides of the North-South Highway and the approach to the Penang Bridge are covered with sprawling high-tech factories.

High-tech industry aside, the mainland has also staked a claim to the local tourist market with a number of recent attractions. **Penang Bird Park** is probably the best, a lush garden with over 200 species of tropical birds from around the world housed in specially designed homes, including a huge walk-in aviary and geodesic domes. The Bird Park is located in **Seberang Jaya**, a suburb just east of Butterworth.

To get a taste of the "real" jungle, head for **Bukit Mertajam Recreational Park**, about 18 kilometres (11 mi) from the mainland end of the Penang Bridge. Ferns, orchids and rain forest trees thrive in the 37-hectare (91 acre) reserve, which has numerous walking trails and rest huts. Near the park entrance is the stark white **St Anne's Church**, a 19th-century colonial relic that has been well preserved over the years. A candlelight procession takes place each year on the Feast of St Anne's. An old clock tower marks the centre of **Bukit Mertajam** town. Six kilometres (4 mi) north of town is the **Mengkuang Lake**, the largest in Penang state, with picnic areas and jungle walking trails.

Golden sunset at Batu Ferringhi.

158

KEDAH AND PERLIS

One of the best views in Penang is from the Esplanade, looking across the water over to the mainland, where **Gunung Jerai**, or Kedah Peak, rises majestically – a bluish-grey mass which, at 1,200 metres (3,950 ft), is the highest point in the northwest of the peninsula. This same peak, standing prominently above the flatland surrounding it, was the first sight the land-hungry sailors from across the Bay of Bengal had of Malaysia. It is hardly surprising that Kedah Peak served as a lodestar to early merchant voyagers, and that the peninsula's first centre of civilisation should spring up at the foot of its slopes.

But Kedah's position at the crossroads of Southeast Asian trade also exposed it to constant danger. In its early years, the state was subject to the control of the great trading empire of Funan, based in Vietnam, and then of the Sri Vijaya empire, established near Palembang in southern Sumatra. Later, Kedah fell under the shadow of the Malaccan sultanate and in the years that followed had to fight for survival against the Portuguese, the Thais, the Bugis, the Burmese and the Dutch.

Up until the beginning of the 19th century, Kedah's rulers were remarkably successful in preserving their independence, but having put their faith in British power (and lost Penang in the process), they fell to the Thais. Kedah spent the next 20 years under the direct rule of Bangkok. The price it had to pay to regain its autonomy from the Thais was the loss of Perlis, which became a separate principality under Thai protection in 1842. From that time until 1909, both Kedah and Perlis were vassals of Bangkok; then in 1909, the two states were transferred to British suzerainty. They accepted British control but were more successful in maintaining their own way of life than most other peninsular states during the British period.

The inhabitants of Kedah and Perlis are mainly Malays, and the Malay character of the state is immediately evident.

Ancient temples: Running up from Butterworth, the North-South Highway crosses the Muda River, marking the entrance into Kedah. Penang island appears as a low hump to the rear and the mass of Kedah Peak looms in front. **Sungai Petani**, Kedah's second-largest town, is 15 kilometres (9 mi) away, from where the road runs northwards. At **Bedong**, another few kilometres north, turning left leads to Merbok and the Bujang Valley.

The whole area between the Bujang Valley and the Muda River seems to have its roots in being the outpost of the Pallava culture of South India. It is littered with the remains of ancient Malaysia – buried temples, ancient inscriptions in Sanskrit (the sacred language of Hinduism), numerous examples of porcelain from China, Indian beads, and glassware from the Middle East. These remains paint a picture of the ancient civilisation which once flourished here, to the delight of archaeologists who, for over a hundred years now, have been uncovering them from the edges of vil-

Left, heading home with the nets after a day at sea. *Right*, waiting for the school bus.

lages, sides of rivers and at the foot of jungled hills.

To get an idea of what has been found, leave the North-South Highway behind and take the old coast route from Bedong. At the foot of Kedah Peak is a village called Merbok, where the **Temple of the Hill of Chiselled Stone** (Candi Bukit Batu Pahat) stands beside a rushing mountain stream. The *candi* is the largest and best preserved temple among all those found in the area, and fittingly, the Museum Department has established an **Archaeological Museum** nearby, which contains the most important finds. Other relics can be found in the state museum at Alor Setar. Because of the historical importance of the whole Merbok-Muda area, it has been designated as a national park.

Beyond Merbok, the road winds picturesquely on and eventually turns south to **Tanjung Dawai**, a postcard fishing village on the Muda Estuary, where the day's catch is laid out on concrete slabs to dry in the sun. A ferry (but not for cars) crosses the estuary to **Pantai Merdeka**, a popular beach for bathers. The beach can also be reached direct from Penang by road.

To get onto **Kedah Peak**, the young and energetic climb the mountain track; the older and wiser take the narrow road which winds up from its junction with the main highway near Guar Chempedak. The only place to stay at the summit of the peak is Gunung Jerai Chalet.

The rice capital: Leaving the peak behind, get back on the North-South Highway at Gurun and head north to the state capital of **Alor Setar**, about 40 kilometres (25 mi) farther on. The country through which the highway passes is flat, offering vistas over broad, green (or fallow, depending on the season) rice fields which stretch as far as the eye can see, merging with the misty cloud-flecked hills of the Main Range in the distant background. The flatness of the landscape is only interrupted here and there by clumps of bamboo and coconut palm trees sheltering a rural village or a small homestead.

If you take the old main road to Alor Setar, you will find that it is accompanied all the way from Kedah Peak by a 19th-century irrigation canal built by Wan Mat Saman, the state *menteri besar* (chief minister) of the day, in order to boost rice production.

Kedah's rice output has quadrupled in recent years as a result of the construction of a dam on the upper reaches of the Muda River, and by the development of a vast irrigation scheme. Known as the Muda Irrigation Project, it is one of the few schemes financed by the World Bank which has fulfilled the aims of its sponsors and provided adequate returns. This jolted Alor Setar out of its centuries of small-town existence.

In the heart of Alor Setar is the traditional **Padang**, somewhat marred by a modern and monstrous fountain. Nothing can obscure the grace and beauty of the **Zahir Mosque**, built in 1912 and one of the largest mosques in Malaysia. The charming and unique Thai-style **Balai Besar** (Great Hall), built in 1898, occupies another corner of the Padang. Balai Besar was used as an audience hall by Kedah's sultans of old when they appeared in public to receive petitions and hear grievances. Today, it is still the place where His Royal Highness the Sultan of Kedah observes ceremonial, festive and other occasions.

Opposite, the **Balai Nobat** houses the instruments (*nobat*) of Kedah's royal orchestra. Only four such orchestras exist in Malaysia today – the other three are to be found in Terengganu, Selangor and Johor – and Kedah's orchestra is reputed to be the oldest.

According to tradition, the drums of the Kedah nobat were a gift from Malacca's last sultan. The nobat is an important part of the regalia of state: no Kedah sultan is considered a legitimate ruler if he has not been installed to the accompaniment of the nobat. The Kedah nobat is also played on other state occasions when the sultan is present, and may be heard daily during the Muslim fasting month, when it is played for five minutes before the end of the day's fast from the Balai Nobat.

The privilege of being a member of the royal orchestra, by the way, is hereditary and has been handed down through the generations. Special permission to see the nobat may be obtained through the offices of the state secretariat in the modern government building nearby.

The **State Museum**, across the street from the municipal stadium and Merdeka Park, displays an interesting collection of items connected with Kedah's past as well as exhibits from the Bujang Valley. A few kilometres farther on, at **Anak Bukit**, lies the sultan's modern *istana* (palace), the grounds of which are open to the public on weekends.

Side trips: The small fishing village of **Kuala Kedah**, 12 kilometres (8 mi) from Alor Setar, has one of the best preserved Malay forts in the country and is renowned for its excellent seafood. Fish and shellfish are obtainable "on board" two boat-like restaurants set out on the sea. As you eat steamed crabs with hot chilli sauce, fried squids, and *otak-otak* (a spicy fish and coconut concoction of Thai origin steamed in banana leaf), watch the sun set over Pulau Langkawi 50 kilometres (30 mi) away,

and savour the taste and scent of the fresh salt air.

The fort is on the other side of the river, easily reached by an inexpensive sampan trip. At about noon on a calm November Sunday in 1821, "a large fleet of prows full of Siamese was observed standing into the Quedah river". The Siamese landed on the pretext of collecting rice supplies and then, without warning, turned on the Malay dignitaries assembled to greet them. Although the flower of Kedah's aristocracy had been killed or taken prisoner within the hour, the fort held out for another six days before it too fell. This disaster marked the beginning of 20 years of subjugation to direct Siamese rule. The fort was built in the 1770s to meet the attack which came in 1821. Today it stands, partially restored, with its handsome main gateway bearing witness to strong Western influence on its design.

From Alor Setar, other roads branch inland to remote and less-frequented parts of the state. Along the road to Kuala Nerang at **Langgar**, Kedah's

The Crown of Kedah monument in the town centre.

rulers lie buried in stately mausoleums. **Kuala Nerang** is a small market town prettily set at the confluence of two streams. Many of its inhabitants are of Thai descent.

Another road branching off from Pokok Sena runs to Nami, Sik and eventually, to Baling, passing through wild hilly country with occasional patches of settlement. **Nami** is the scene of the *mak yong* performances, a traditional Thai-Malay dance-drama which is only seen elsewhere in Kelantan. **Baling** is famous as the place where talks took place in 1955 between Tunku Abdul Rahman, the prime minister at the time, and Chin Peng, the leader of the Malayan Communist Party, in an attempt to find a peaceful solution to the Communist insurrection. The talks failed, but Communism petered out. The massive limestone hill which looms over the town is a landmark for kilometres around. From Baling, the road climbs up to Keroh and the Thai border, and from Keroh down to Gerik and the East-West Highway or to the Perak River Valley. Another road runs from Baling to Sungai Petani and Penang.

Along the border: Malaysia's smallest state, **Perlis** is really an extension of the Kedah plain and of Kedah itself. The boundary between the two states is invisible except for the large posted signs. However, there is a change in the scenery; the flat rice fields give way to stark, solitary limestone outcrops which stand like sentinels marking subterranean caves. Spectacular and mysterious, these caverns hand out secrets to those who care to explore them. Many were the homes of ancient people.

Perlis has two main towns – Arau and Kangsar. **Arau** is a royal town, seat of the Perlis Rajah, and it has an attractive centre although it is of little interest to the tourist. Fifty kilometres (30 mi) to the north is **Padang Besar**, where the Malaysian and Thai railway systems meet and which has a market very popular with Malaysians during the weekends. The road to Padang Besar also leads to **Kaki Bukit** – literally "the foot of the hill" – where an interesting tunnel

Kuala Perlis is the jumping-off point for Pulau Langkawi.

through the hill illuminated by electric light leads to a tin mine on the other side. Another road connects Kaki Bukit with Wang Kelian and Setul (Satun), across the Thai border.

Labyrinths and legends: Tucked into the northwest corner of the peninsula and nestled on the Thai-Malaysian sea-border are the **Langkawi Islands**, all 99 of them. Unlike the other islands of the west coast, the vast majority of the 30,000 people who live here are Malay. Of the 99 islands, only three are populated, and two of these very sparsely. In recent years, the government has concentrated on promoting Langkawi as a tourist destination and on making this island more appealing and accessible: an airport was built, regular ferry services were organised and Langkawi was given duty-free status in 1987. There has not been the great rush that the government hoped for and, even in season, Langkawi is a quiet and relatively unspoilt island as yet. Ferries run from **Kuala Perlis**, a small port an hour's drive from Alor Setar. The crossing

takes just over two hours. Flights can be made from Penang, Kuala Lumpur, Alor Setar and Singapore.

When the islands are first seen from the ferry, they appear as one, spread out along the horizon in a jagged and uncertain silhouette. But as the ferry gets closer, the view changes. The various outlines of hills and bays separate themselves into a maze of islands, amongst which are secret channels, narrows, inlets and bays. Shadowed cliffs, topped by dense virgin jungle, reach up to 600 metres (1,950 ft) and drop abruptly into the sea.

In the inlets, fishermen catch small *garoupa*, which they take to fish farms to be fattened for the market. This indeed does seem the perfect setting for the many legends that surround the island. It is also obvious why pirates and buccaneers who preyed upon the trading ships in the Malacca Straits used these islands as a place of refuge.

The ferry passes the Langkawi Island Resort, an imposing building built in a neo-traditional style, situated at the water's edge 800 metres (850 yds) from the main quay of the main village, **Kuah**. This small village has been transformed by the island's duty-free status, and nearly every shop in town is crowded with bottles of liquor, boxes of tobacco and electronic items. Not all items are a bargain, compared to prices in Penang or Singapore, but the shopper may like to spend some time browsing in these shops. There are also one or two local craft shops, with hand-painted fabrics, shellwork and Langkawi stones with miniature paintings on them.

A few years ago, Kuah was the only area on the island where visitors could find accommodation; there are several small hotels in town, as well as a government rest house and the Langkawi Island Resort at the other end of the scale. Nowadays, however, visitors can choose from a variety of hotels, beach chalets and huts situated at pretty beaches around the island.

Coves, corals and caves: Ornithologists and lepidopterists will delight in these islands, which have species of butterflies not found anywhere else in Malay-

Resort facilities are readily available on Langkawi.

sia. For others, the main joys are the relatively uncrowded beaches and the pretty little islands that lie offshore. The main island boasts some beautiful coves rich in corals and marine life.

Most of the accommodation on the beach can be found at **Pantai Cenang**, in the southwest of the island and an hour's bus ride from Kuah.

The huge Pelangi Beach Resort was built here in early 1988, and its attractive two-storey buildings are built in a traditional style. Small jeeps and bicycles with little carts attached drive between these chalets, delivering passengers and their luggage, sundowner drinks on your verandah facing the sea, and fresh supplies of toiletries and towels. Although service is much the same as found at many international hotels, the unique layout and its pretty setting make this a luxurious as well as a relaxed place to stay.

More modest accommodation is found further south along the beach, where many of the huts and chalets are very pleasant and the staff friendly. Some of the nicest chalets are at **Semarak**, which is located at what is perhaps the prettiest part of the beach.

To the west, past the airport, **Pantai Kok** offers a small assortment of beachfront chalets and small hotels like the Burau Bay Resort. Other accommodation can be found along the north coast at Teluk Datai – location of the luxury Datai Langkawi Resort – and at **Tanjung Rhu**, a delightful stretch of beach protected by huge offshore rocks. From Tanjung Rhu, fishing boats can be hired to go round the cape to the grey limestone cliffs beyond.

There, a legendary sight called **Gua Cerita** (Cave of Legends) is inscribed with writings from the Koran. To reach its entrance, one must climb precariously up a rickety bamboo ladder hung from stalactites.

After choosing a place to stay and taking a dip in the lovely waters surrounding Langkawi Island, you may like to go on a round-the-island tour, taking in the landmarks and the legends attached to them.

Waiting for a bite, left, and for the tide to roll in, right.

A tour of legends: Hotels and shops in town rent bicycles and motorbikes. For a really reliable and versatile vehicle, none is better than the four-wheel-drive jeep hired out by the Pelangi Beach Resort (for hotel guests only), which will allow you to negotiate some of the rough roads inland. Start from Pantai Cenang with your jeep or motorcycle, and take the new road that passes the airport and leads through **Kuala Teriang** and around the wooded headland to Pantai Kok and its lovely beach. Stop for a swim and turn your eyes inland to catch your breath over the glorious mountains, swathed in clouds, their black jagged peaks cut out against the sky.

Your next destination will lead you into this range as you turn off for **Telaga Tujuh** (seven pools) on the northwest road. The rough road finishes at a *warong* (roadside cafe) where you can park your vehicle. A short walk uphill will bring you to a view of the pools that tumble one into the other down the mountainside. Legend has it that the mountain fairies come here to bathe and wash their long hair with tree roots and sweet plants. You will not meet any of them, however, as at the sight of a human they will vanish, leaving behind them a fragrant and lingering perfume.

The road now proceeds northeast, with mountains to the left and rice fields to the right. After passing the turn-off to **Pantai Datai**, drive eastward until the road meets the coast at **Pasir Hitam**, or Black Sand Beach. The smooth, fine sand here is streaked with black lines, giving the beach its name. Next you reach Tanjung Rhu. The small town here looks more developed than Kuah itself, partly because here is the jetty where large boats used to arrive from Penang. A road travels north to Pantai Rhu and Gua Cerita.

After turning back along this road, you will meet the main road again. Turn left and after a kilometre or so, a small fenced-off area with a few huts will announce that you have arrived at **Telaga Air Hangat** (Hot Water Pools). The springs are not especially attractive – just three small pools (the size of large

washing-up bowls) set in concrete. However, the area will soon be developed into a major international spa featuring four separate health villages with traditional Japanese, American, Malaysian and Indian themes.

There is also a marvellous legend attached to Telaga Air Hangat. Two rich families once lived on Langkawi; the son of one fell in love with the daughter of the other, but her parents did not approve of the match, and refused the union. The son was furious, and the disagreement between the families developed into a full-blown feud. It erupted into a free-for-all fight with all the family members taking part. In the ensuing fight, pots and pans were thrown wildly.

The gravy pot with its contents landed at Kuah (meaning gravy), the jugs of boiling water formed the present Telaga Air Hangat and the water remaining poured into the ground at **Kisap** (meaning "to seep"). It is said that the fighting raged on until the two fathers were suddenly and miraculously transformed into two mountain peaks.

Continue along this road to Kuah and a small track to the right about 5 kilometres (3 mi) from Tanjung Rhu leads to **Durian Perangin** waterfalls. The track is deeply rutted and passable only by four-wheel-drive or with difficulty by motorbike. A trek up the side of the waterfall through the undergrowth is well worthwhile to see the pool at the top. Dense jungle lies all around and civilisation seems far away.

You will by now most probably have worked up a healthy appetite. Drive on southwards to Kuah and stop at the restaurant on the seafront, which serves excellent seafood.

To complete the tour of the island, take the road leading westwards from Kuah. A turning to the right 10 kilometres (6 mi) or so from Kuah takes you to **Mahsuri's Tomb**. This famous lady who, it is said, lived about 200 years ago was wrongfully accused of adultery with a man she had shown kindness to. Derembang was a weary traveller who welcomed her help with much gratitude and respect. But the chief's wife became jealous of Mahsuri, and after a short battle Mahsuri was condemned to death. A soldier was ordered to plunge a *kris* (dagger) into her heart, and as he did so, white blood spurted out from the wound. As she lay dying, Mahsuri raised her arms to the sky and laid a curse on the island that would last for seven generations. Until today, it is said that Langkawi lay desolate and deserted during this time. Mahsuri is now a local heroine, and her tomb has become a shrine. Gleaming white walls and resting huts enclose the tomb.

Another result of Mahsuri's curse can be seen at **Padang Mat Sirat** (Field of Burnt Rice), further inland in the rice-growing area where monsoon rains occasionally upturn strata of black earth. These darkened grains are said to remain from the time when villagers preferred to burn their rice fields rather than let their precious harvest fall into Siamese hands.

An intriguing legend is connected to one of the islands that lies off the shores of the main island. **Dayang Bunting**, the second-largest island of the group, has a lake set in dense jungle and separated from the sea by a narrow strip of land. The freshwater lake is known as the **Lake of the Pregnant Maiden**. The maiden was a Kedah princess who had been forbidden to marry her Malay prince lover. After drinking water from the lake, Telani the maiden became pregnant, and on discovering this, the King became angry and banished her to the deserted island. In her sorrow, Telani drowned herself in the lake and she became *Sang Kelembai*, a rock by the lake. Her child who had fallen into the lake was transformed into a white crocodile. The lake has now become a famous place where barren women from all over the country come to drink the water, and many pilgrims even claim to have conceived after the visit.

Boats from Tanjung Rhu, Pantai Cenang and Kuah will take you on a tour to this island, and also to other islands, such as the pretty **Pulau Bumbon**. Fishing, snorkeling and scuba-diving amongst the coral-filled waters can also be done by hired boat. Inquire in Kuah, the Island Resort or on Pantai Cenang. **West coast beach.**

168

Negri Sembilan: Nine States in One

The North-South Highway slashes across **Negri Sembilan** on its way from Kuala Lumpur to Johor, dissecting countless rubber estates and palm oil plantations. Few visitors bother to leave the highway, which means that Negri Sembilan is one of the least explored states in Malaysia.

Negri Sembilan means "Nine States" in Malay. The name alludes to the loose federation of Malay chiefs who ruled these lands before they were united under British administration. Much of the countryside – small wooden homes with batik on the clotheslines and papaya trees in the front yard – is reminiscent of the quiet Malay villages that were sprinkled over Negri Sembilan centuries ago.

The state owes its existence to Malacca, which thrived as a trading port at the beginning of the 15th century. As Malacca rose and developed, Menangkabau settlers from Sumatra moved across the Straits of Malacca and made their homes in the fertile valleys and hills behind the port. They brought with them their unique traditions, including the matrilineal system, the social order in which inheritance follows the female line; their laws and political organisation; and their style of architecture. The small principalities they founded formed the nucleus of the Nine States.

Negri Sembilan is, in fact, a federation within the Federation of Malaysia; some of the original nine states have disappeared, however, and its present ruler is not a sultan but a *Yang Tuan Besar* (translated as "He Who is Greatest"). The first Yang Tuan was elected in the 1770s and his successors faced the usual problems caused by the great tin rush of the 19th century – over-mighty subjects and civil wars, which eventually resulted in British protection.

Under the new dispensation, Seremban, the principal town of Sungai Ujong (the largest of the nine states), was made the administrative capital,

Promontory at Port Dickson juts into the Malacca Straits.

while the Yang Tuan continued to reside at Sri Menanti, a safe 26 kilometres (16 mi) away.

True to the past: The North-South Highway runs south from Kuala Lumpur, through the scenic **Langat Valley**, where the National University of Malaysia is situated, to a small city called **Seremban**, the state capital of Negri Sembilan. Seremban is typical of the Malayan-Chinese towns that sprang out of the tin mining boom a hundred years ago.

The town's Chinese core is represented by the regular lines of crossed streets, laid out in the commercial and shopping district. Characteristic rows of two-storey Chinese shophouses line up here, although their even lines are being increasingly punctuated by taller modern buildings in between. Above the din of trishaw bells and bargain sessions, government clerks mill over their paperwork in colonial buildings set on the hills behind the town. The state council and municipal offices feature late 19th-century architecture in the neoclassical colonial style at its best.

They overlook the attractive **Lake Gardens**, formed by a narrow valley running down to the main town. And true to Negri Sembilan's past, the impressive state mosque rises nearby on nine pillars, symbolising nine states.

Seremban is in Menangkabau country, settled by West Sumatran Malays. Menangkabau means "buffalo horns", which is seen in the sweeping, peaked roofs of many of the town's houses.

The **Cultural Handicraft Complex** (Taman Seni Budaya) in Seremban provides a grandiose example of the Menangkabau architectural style, including distinctive overlapping peaked roofs that are said to reflect the shape of water buffalo horns. The centre displays handicrafts and stages frequent demonstrations by prominent artists. Cultural shows and traditional Malay games are also featured.

Within the cultural park boundaries is the **State Museum**. The main building is a 19th-century Menangkabau palace, once the residence of a Malay princess who lived at Kampung Ampang Tinggi.

ce cream
reak on the
each.

It was dismantled at its original site and brought piece by piece to Seremban, where it was reconstructed. The museum features a fine display of ceremonial *kris* daggers, a collection of Bugis and Menangkabau swords, various royal ornaments, as well as fine examples of local woodcarving.

Another example of modern Menangkabau architecture is the **State Secretariat Building** in Jalan Dato Abdul Kadir. Nearby is something completely different, the Edwardian-style **State Library**. Designed by an English architect and completed in 1911, the library features stout columns, arches and towers, a striking reminder of Malaysia's colonial past.

Seremban makes a good centre from which to explore the surrounding countryside. Low rolling hills tuck away small villages, set amidst orchards and rice fields. These towns bear romantic names redolent of Menangkabau history – Johol, Kuala Pilah, Jelebu, Inas, Terachi and Rembau – but there is nothing spectacular about them apart from the quiet charm of their location. For a sultry dip, head for **Pedas Hot Springs**, located just outside Pedas Village in the Rembau district, which is 30 kilometres (180 mi) southeast of Seremban.

Carpentry without nails: A welcome neighbour to Seremban, 50 kilometres (30 mi) east, the town of **Sri Menanti** boasts the **Istana Lama** (Old Palace). The palace, built in the 1890s, was the creation of two well-known master craftsmen of the day. Not a single nail was used in its construction. Made of timber throughout, its 21-metre-tall (70 ft) tower used to house the private apartment of the Yang Tuan Besar as well as the royal archives and treasury. It ceased to be a royal residence in 1931, when a new stone palace was completed, and today it serves as a museum.

The next town, east of Sri Menanta, is **Kuala Pilah**, which retains much of its Old Malaya atmosphere. Shophouses line the main street and there is an interesting Chinese temple, just north of town, called **Rumah Berhala Sim Tong**. Kuala Pilah is also known for its tasty Menangkabau food.

The tall, irregularly-shaped stones lining the wayside prove another attraction for visitors. Local villagers regard these stones with veneration and often use them as shrines (*keramat*), referring to them as "living stones" because they believe that the stones actually grow – although there has been no evidence of growth in recent years. Also believed to mark the graves of forgotten leaders of the distant past, the stones usually appear in pairs with a distinct north-south orientation. Thirty groups of such stones have been located in the Kuala Pilah district.

Pengkalan Kempas, a small village on the road between Port Dickson and Malacca, owns the most enigmatic of these stones. Popularly known as The Sword, The Spoon and The Rudder (on account of their respective shapes), the three stones are elaborately carved to spell their Hindu origin, although one has "Allah" inscribed on it.

They lie next to the tomb of Sheikh Ahmad Majnun, another mystery in its own right. The Sheikh died a hero's death in 1467, so says the inscription, during his fight to save "the princess". Time has erased what actually happened from the memories of the local folk, although they continue to pay homage to the dead man.

The place's creepiness heightens with the "ordeal" stone, which has a hole big enough for a man's hand. The story tells that it will tighten around the fist of any liar brave enough to make the test.

By the blue lagoon: Thirty kilometres (20 mi) south of Seremban lies **Port Dickson**. At the end of the 19th century, this relaxing coastal town was planned as a new outlet for the tin mines of Sungai Ujong, and as a health resort where tired expatriate officials could recuperate from the rigours of their work. Today, Port Dickson is a popular weekend rendezvous for Malaysians.

Don't expect a bustling port; Port Dickson isn't much more than a one-street town. The 16 kilometres (10 mi) of beach to the south, which terminate at the old Rachado Lighthouse, is something else indeed.

That first view of the lonely sea, seen

through the coconut trees, is a silent spectacle. The sea is deep blue and seems to merge with the sky in the horizon afar. The drive southward along the uncluttered coast is so exhilarating that it is easy to be tempted to park and dive into the inviting water.

The **Yacht Club**, 7 kilometres (4 mi) out of town, encourages travellers to use its facilities, but you must be introduced by a member, and its four pleasant bedrooms cannot be booked in advance. There is a swimming pool and four good, hard tennis courts. The boats are not for rental to nonmembers.

Boats can be hired 12 kilometres (8 mi) further down the coast at **Kampung Telok Kemang**, where there is a cluster of seaside hotels and restaurants, including the luxury Ming Court Beach Hotel. Further south is the turnoff to **Blue Lagoon**, with a white sand beach backed by casuarina trees. Clown fish, stick fish and live coral compensate for the murky lagoon waters.

Nature and history: Behind the lagoon is majestic **Cape Rachado** (Tanjong Tuan), which juts into the Straits of Malacca like an ancient sunken ship. The cape actually belongs to the state of Malacca and much of it is given over to a nature reserve with monkeys and many different species of bird. Most people come to visit the **Old Lighthouse**, a British colonial structure built on the site of an earlier Portuguese light.

The lighthouse was built to guide sailing ships toward the historical port of Malacca, then the most important trading station in Southeast Asia. Although the lighthouse is closed to the public, a smile and a nice word will generally gain entry. Or, obtain a pass from the Malacca Tourist Office, 90 kilometres (60 mi) away. The lighthouse keeper takes you up a narrow spiral stairway to the light chamber above. The sudden view is striking. After the visit, an exciting jungle walk down to the beach can be made from the lighthouse gate.

From Port Dickson, a 90-minute drive takes you to Malacca, where the past of the southwest coast is very much alive.

MALACCA:
A SLEEPY HOLLOW

History is everywhere in Malacca; peeping out from odd corners, hinting truths from epitaphs, yet never really telling it. It is a town with a glorious past; about four centuries ago, a Portuguese chronicler and frequent visitor said, "Whosoever holds Malacca has Venice by the throat." Even though present-day Malacca no longer holds the key to the trade by which Venice kept "the gorgeous East in fee", it still occupies the foremost place in the hearts of Malaysians.

Despite its power and glory, the history of Malacca is brief. It had hardly been in existence for more than a hundred years before it was attacked and conquered by the Portuguese. Until a Malay prince from Sumatra chanced upon the scene, Malacca was a small, unknown settlement of sea gypsies, scraping a living as fishermen and subsistence farmers.

In the 1400s, Parameswara arrived, a prince fleeing from his own invaded domain of Tumasek. He proclaimed himself ruler of Malacca and proceeded to mould the obscure fishing village into a powerful centre of trade. By the end of the 15th century, Malacca had become the centre of a great trading empire and held an undisputed claim over the entire southern portion of the Malay peninsula, as well as the shores of East Sumatra opposite.

It became a rendezvous for every seafaring nation – Persians, Arabs, Tamils, Malabarese and Bengalis from the west; Javanese, Sundanese and Sulus from the archipelago; Chinese, Thais, Burmese, Chams as well as Khmers ventured to the harbour town in search of profit through trade, piracy or plunder. Each in turn left something of their own culture behind to be forged and blended into a new and unique mix.

Baba and **Nonya**: The small colony of Chinese merchants, in particular, stayed behind to found the *Baba* and *Nonya* community, which has become one of the most striking and colourful Chinese

fraternities in Malaysia today. The *Baba* (or Straits Chinese) are descendants of the Chinese pioneers who accepted the practical realities around them, but whose ideas of social relationships and religious aspirations are still derived from the traditions of their forefathers in the villages of Fujian. The women may have worshipped at a Malay *keramat* (shrine) once in a while, but that is not so much an indication of their respect for the Muslim religion as an expression of the Chinese desire to keep on the right side of all spirits of whatever origin. The Malays, for their part, seem to have been equally unaffected by the Chinese outlook on social and spiritual matters.

It was also through Malacca that the Islamic faith came to Malaysia. Malays have been Muslims since the second half of the 15th century, when rich Moorish merchants from Pasai in Sumatra settled in Malacca. From here Islam spread throughout the peninsula, and eventually to many of its neighbouring islands.

Monsoon-driven trade: Geography was responsible for Malacca's multicultural history. Located at the mouth of the Malacca River, astride the maritime route linking the Indian Ocean with the South China Sea, Malacca stood where the monsoon winds met. As tillers of the soil depended upon monsoons to bring them rain, so trusting sailors relied upon the winds to move their ships. Sturdy junks from the ports of China and Japan came with the riches of the East in their holds – silk, porcelain and silver – and let themselves be driven up the Straits of Malacca by the northeast monsoon.

So did the traders from the islands of the archipelago, arriving with various forms of crafts, camphor, nutmeg and cloves, mace and sandalwood. At the port, their cargoes were unloaded and new precious wares from India and the Middle West were loaded on – cloth, carpets, glassware, iron and jewellery. When the winds changed, the southwest monsoon assisted the same vessels to return to their home ports.

It was the rich port of Malacca – the key to controlling the spice trade – that caused some of the early East-West power struggles. Malacca's golden age was during the Malay sultanate of Malacca, and these great days effectively came to an end when it fell in 1511 to the Portuguese. Malacca remained their fortress for more than 100 years, before they themselves were ousted by the Dutch. After 150 years of occupation, the Dutch in turn ceded the land to the British. The place-name Malacca has been "Malayanised" and is now spelt Melaka. Most tourist brochures retain the other spelling to avoid confusion.

Walking through history: The story of Malacca, and all Malaysia in a sense, need not come from a textbook. A 1-kilometre walk or a leisurely trishaw ride through the town reveals the past. Trishaws are an excellent means of getting around in Malacca. The drivers know the sights and many of them speak understandable English, in which case they make fine guides. You might not only learn that the Portuguese came "a much long time ago" but also that along

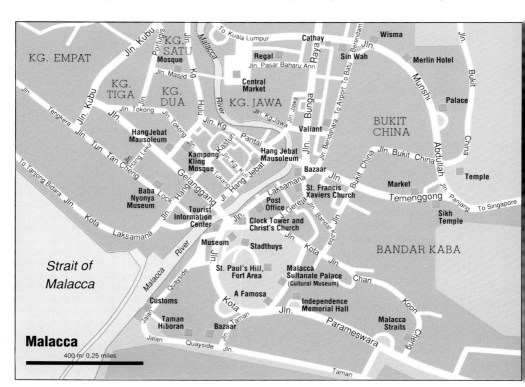

Malacca

400 m / 0.25 miles

the seafront there is a great soup stall that sells some of the best *mee hoon* (thin rice noodles) in Malaysia.

The visitor to Malacca may find it difficult to visualize life behind the medieval fortress 400 years ago. But, as one walks the narrow streets, visits old temples and mosques, lingers among ancient ruins and epitaphs, Malacca's history begins to fall into place.

It is easy to get around, and although there are many things to see, Malacca can, except for the expert, readily be toured in one day. However, those who wish to linger awhile and absorb the atmosphere of the "sleepy hollow" – as the inhabitants of Malacca love to call it – will find that they can intermingle their sightseeing with sunning and swimming 8 kilometres (5 mi) to the north, on the main road to Port Dickson.

Off the coast is a group of small islands. On weekends, there are regular boats from Umbai to the largest island, Pulau Besar, which has sandy beaches, clear water and seafront chalets. Legend has it that should you eat pork within 48 hours of visiting the island, your boat will sink.

Reflections of a river: The best place to begin your visit is right in the centre of the town, near the bridge built on the site where the Portuguese made their final successful assault on the town. The Malacca River itself contains a history lesson. Time seems to have passed by this part of the town. Great, ancient junks, high bows and raised poop decks – reminiscent of their distant cousins that once brought Admiral Cheng Ho's dragon court entourage to Malacca centuries ago – float side by side against the wooden pilings of the dock. Their exotic cargoes of spices, silks and camphor have been forsaken, for these battered, unkempt vessels now carry bulky sacks of charcoal that fire the kitchens of Malacca. The labourers, balancing on the narrow planks that join ship to dock, strain under the heavy loads, and like the sturdy junks they unload, they are part of Malacca's timeless past.

From here river trips can be arranged up river and to the Portuguese settle-

Malacca River.

ment. But you will not get to travel with the local fishermen, who, it is said, are extremely superstitious. They will not allow any woman on board their vessels, never speak vulgar words at sea, and will not even call each other by names, for fear that the gods will become jealous of their good catch and send them misfortunes.

Yet once the Malacca River was different. When the Portuguese colony was at its zenith, the river was a deep, bustling waterway jammed with ships of a dozen nations. Great sailing vessels, loaded onto the scuppers, vied with each other to manoeuvre up the river to dock at the quay, while countless smaller vessels, anchored in the roads, depended upon flat-bottomed scows to load and unload their valuable wares. Ship chandlers did a thriving business selling stores to captains, and there is a story that the town was so vast that it took a cat a year to make the circuit by walking over the tiled roofs. The storytellers might exaggerate but we do know that when the Portuguese captured Malacca, de Albuquerque sailed his warships up the estuary to besiege the town.

Architecture from Holland: As you cross the Malacca River bridge onto the east riverbank, you will stand face to face with a neat, little square with a clock tower, surrounded by salmon-coloured government buildings and a towered church, and you almost expect to see tulips growing in the gardens or a passing cyclist wearing up-pointed clogs. The square obviously was built by the Dutch, and architecture is Holland's main contribution to Malacca.

The large building facing the square is the old Dutch **Stadthuys** (Town Hall). A broad flight of stone steps fronts this building, constructed of incredibly thick walls and massive hardwood doors supported by studded, wrought-iron hinges. For more than 300 years after its completion, the Stadthuys served as government offices until the administration finally shifted out in 1980. Today, it houses the well laid-out **Malacca Museum**, and within its galleries, the history of Malacca unreels in a fascinating way. The exhibits trace the city's past

times from the ancient Malay kingdom, through Portuguese and Dutch rule and British occupation to its present status as a state in Malaysia. No other town in the peninsula evokes the past as strongly as Malacca, once one of the greatest seaports of Asia.

The museum also contains a unique collection of old coins, stamps, a rickshaw, Portuguese costumes from the 16th century, Dutch weapons, British cannons, gold and silver filigree jewellery and framed, sepia-toned photographs of sailing ships anchored in the Malacca River, as well as old Malay *kris* and shields. (Members of the court elite carried a jewel-studded golden dagger called the kris, a weapon which has come to symbolise Malay royalty.)

The Stadthuys itself is an antiquity. Erected in 1650, it is the oldest known Dutch building still standing in the Far East. On the embankment near the entrance to the Stadthuys is an ancient memorial whose significance has been lost in time. It stands in the shape of a much-weathered stone fish with an elephant's head. This relic is Hindu legacy from the period predating the glorious Malaccan sultanate. The historical General Post Office in the Stadthuys square is also of Dutch origin.

Water fountain and mousedeer: On the eastern side of the flower-filled square is the fabled **Christ Church** with its bright red facade. As if to guarantee that the 150 years of Dutch occupation should not be forgotten, the pink bricks were shipped all the way from Holland. Malaccan masons then faced them with local red laterite. The church is full of old, engraved tombstones, many telling a grim tale about the hardships the early European settlers faced. The immense rafters within the nave were each carved from a single tree and date back to the church's foundation. The original solid, heavy wooden pews for Sunday worshippers still remain in use, and above the altar a wooden crucifix hangs from the iron hoops fastened to the wall.

There is a story that when the church was first in use, it had no pulpit. The pastor would sit in a chair that had ropes running to the hoops. When the time came for him to deliver his sermon, his sextons would winch him halfway up the wall. Thus, he gave his sermon every Sunday without fail.

Outside the church, the famous century-old tower, with the same pink brick as the rest of the square, provides a landmark. It was presented to the town by the wealthy Tan family. The small water fountain nearby was built to commemorate the Diamond Jubilee of Queen Victoria. Four white mousedeer (*pelandok* in Malay) surround the fountain to remind passers-by of how Parameswara came to select Malacca as the site for his new capital.

Hill of memories: Behind the Stadthuys and Christ Church rises another Malacca relic – **St Paul's Hill**, the scene of many of the more important moments of local history. At the summit lie the ruins of **St Paul's Church**. A Portuguese *fidalgo* built the chapel in 1521 in order to fulfil a vow he made on escaping death in the South China Sea. It was later taken over by the Jesuits who completed the building and painted it white so that it could serve as a guidepost for ships out on the Straits. St Francis Xavier conducted mass in the church during his several visits to Malacca. After his death near Canton, his body was interred in St Paul's for several months before being taken to Goa in India.

The Dutch discontinued services in St Paul's Church when their own Christ Church was built. However, they used the burial ground around St Paul's to lay their own noble citizens to rest. Lining the inside walls of the old church are engraved tombstones, worn down over the centuries.

Early morning or late afternoon is the best time to climb St Paul's Hill to the church. The characteristic beauty of St Paul's lies in the fact that the church is now a ruin. No restoration could make it more attractive.

The slopes of St Paul's Hill balance another historical relic – the ruins of the **A Famosa fortress**. Under the Portuguese, Malacca was to see colossal changes. At first, when the town fell, Sultan Mahmud withdrew to Muar with

Dutch influence, Christ Church.

the hope that the invaders would plunder the city and move on.

However, the Portuguese had other ideas; they were determined to make it one of the mightiest strongholds in the Orient. De Albuquerque immediately ordered the construction of a formidable fortress. Hundreds of slaves and captives were put to work. Stones from demolished mosques and elaborate tombs were used to build the thick-walled fortress, which de Albuquerque called *A Famosa*. Once completed, with cannons on the walls and soldiers standing guard, it filled the townspeople with both fear and respect.

A Famosa was later enlarged to enclose the entire hill, including the European settlement. The city walls encircled a castle, two magnificent palaces, a hall for the Portuguese Council of State and five churches. The fortress withstood attacks for 150 years, until it was finally breached in 1641 by the Dutch.

The Dutch arrived in 1641 as conquerors, having driven out the Portuguese after a siege that lasted eight months. They did not find a rich and prosperous port of the fabulous East, as they had expected. The city for which they had struggled so hard to conquer lay in near total ruins.

The industrious and fastidious Dutch lost no time putting things in order. As soon as they were in control, they began to rebuild the city with a Dutch flavour. The walls of the fortress were repaired and the bastions renamed. A moat was dug around the fortress and a drawbridge built. Protective ramparts were laid round the suburbs and heavy brass cannons mounted on all the walls. In a short time Malacca became again a well-defended port.

Unfortunately, when the British first occupied Malacca at the beginning of the 19th century, they decided to blow up the fortifications. The walls and gates were badly damaged and all that was left of A Famosa was the Porta de Santiago – a gate without a wall.

Bullock carts and light shows: The broad expanse of the **Padang** lies on reclaimed land at the foot of the St Paul's Hill.

St. Paul's Church.

Malaccan bullock carts with swayback roofs make their way around the big open green (RM1 per person) and there are usually trishaw drivers hanging around Porta de Santiago (negotiate your own fare). There is also a thriving street market with Malaysian arts and crafts, and the big grandstand at the Padang is the scene of a nightly sound-and-light show that recounts the fascinating history of Malacca.

The Padang has a special significance for modern Malaysians, because it was here that Tunku Abdul Rahman, the country's first prime minister, announced Malaya's independence upon his return from negotiations with the British in London. A small obelisk records the event.

The struggle for independence is more substantially commemorated by the imposing **Proclamation of Independence Memorial Building**, which contains materials connected with the campaign for independence, including historic documents, films and artifacts like the car that Tunku rode in on his return from the successful London negotiations. The building is not new; it was built in 1911 as the Malacca Club, where British officials and planters took their ease.

Nearby is the new **Malacca Cultural Museum**, an elaborate reconstruction of the sultan's palace described in the *Sejarah Melayu* (*Malay Annals*). Inside are displays on various aspects of Malaccan royal culture, including clothing, weapons and furniture. Around the west side of St Paul's Hill are several other museums. The **Muzium Rakyat (People's Museum)** contains items relating to Malaysian economic and social progress, including exhibits on agriculture, industry and tourism.

A small park called **Taman Bunga** sits in front of the museum, with several transport relics including an old railway car and a propeller aeroplane. Directly in front of the plane is a small obelisk that commemorates British soldiers killed in the Naning War, an almost farcical affair in the early 1830s when it took two military expeditions over two years to subdue Penghulu Dol Said, the

Peranakan heritage on display at a local museum.

defiant territory chief of the petty principality of Naning.

Sitting between the park and the river is the city's newest tourist attraction, the long-awaited **Malacca Maritime Museum**, built in the shape of a Portuguese caravel. Although the pickings are slim at present, the museum will eventually contain porcelain, weapons and other artifacts gleaned from shipwrecks in the Straits of Malacca.

Across Jalan Merdeka on the western side of the Padang is an American-style shopping mall called the **Mahkota Parade**, where many of Malacca's students hang out after school. Besides pleasant air conditioning and fast-food outlets, the mall features several antique and handicraft shops, a supermarket and cinema.

Further down Jalan Merdeka is **St John's Fort**. After a short climb to the top of the hill where the concrete fort stands, you can enjoy a panoramic view of Malacca. Apart from the absence of cannons, the fort is much like the Dutch had left it when the British took over after Malacca was exchanged for Bencoolen in Sumatra. Fearing that Malacca might fall into enemy hands, the British had all the strongholds, except for St John's Fort and Santiago Gate, destroyed.

A Chinese princess and a magic well: On a hill at the back of the town, Chinese tombs have been left unattended by relatives for generations. Hills are auspicious burial grounds, according to Chinese geomancy, for the mass of land blocks the winds of evil and offers the spirits of the ancestors a good view over their descendants. On **Bukit Cina (China Hill)** most names and dates have been eroded by the rains. What remains is an old, half-forgotten cemetery and the story of a Ming princess.

In ancient times, Malaya and China carried on a diplomatic war of wits which grew to be legendary. Around 1460, when Sultan Mansor Shah ruled Malacca, a Chinese ship sailed into port with special orders from the Son of Heaven. The entire interior of the ship was delicately pinned with gold needles,

Locals of Portuguese descent often speak an antiquated dialect.

and the message sent to the sultan read: "For every gold needle, I have a subject; if you could count their number, then you would know my power."

The sultan was impressed, but not dismayed. He sent back a ship stuffed with bags of sago and the message: "If you can count the grains of sago on this ship you will have guessed the number of my subjects correctly, and you will know my power." The Chinese emperor was so intrigued that he sent his daughter Hang Li Poh, to marry the sultan. She arrived with no less than 500 ladies-in-waiting, all of great beauty. The sultan gave them "the hill without the town" as a private residence and promised that the land they occupied would never be taken away from them. To this day, Bukit China belongs to Malacca's Chinese community. Several of the graves there date back to the Ming dynasty; they are among the oldest Chinese relics in Malaysia.

Princess Hang Li Poh's followers built a well at the foot of the hill, whose waters soon became as legendary as her marriage contract. The Chinese say that after Admiral Cheng Ho drank from the well, its water attained an extraordinary purity. It never dried up, even during the most severe drought, and many believed that if a visitor drank from it he would return to Malacca before he died.

Now the **Perigi Rajah (Sultan's Well)** is protected by wire mesh. It has not dried up and its purity has entered history. Young Malaccan students of Chinese descent come to see the landmark and perhaps snap some pictures, but few tread the paths up the hill where their forefathers lie buried. Malacca is changing, leaving its secrets behind.

Catholic crowds and high-rise buildings: Throw a stone in a northwest direction from this spot and it will probably land on Jalan Bendahara, where **St Peter's Church** is. When the Portuguese garrison was forced into submission, the Dutch gave safe conduct to the soldiers and amnesty to the Portuguese descendants, many of whom chose to remain behind rather than take up a new life in Goa. The church was built in 1710 by

Colourful tiles characterize typical Malaccan designs.

Colourful tiles characterize typical Malaccan designs.

the Portuguese Eurasians of Malacca and they named it after St Peter. Unlike its richly decorated counterparts in Goa, it is simple and relatively unimpressive. Good Friday, Easter and Christmas are still celebrated here, but throughout the year, except for an occasional wedding or a funeral, not much goes on.

Good Friday services at St Peter's Church are the most elaborate in Malaysia. Thousands of people – Chinese, Eurasian and Indian – crowd the church to attend the services and take part in a candlelight procession. A life-sized statue of Christ, crowned with thorns and draped in deep purple robes with gold embroidery, is solemnly borne above the devout Catholic congregation. The churchyard becomes a sea of flames ushered in by the mournful sound of hymns. On Easter weekends, Malaccan Chinese and Portuguese Eurasian Catholics living all around the country try to return to their home town. To attend the ceremonies at St Peter's which they had known so well as children, is an annual must.

Despite the solemnity of a staunch Catholic mass, the crowds that gather outside the church after the service meet friends and cast flirtatious eyes as if it were carnival time in spring. Children, looking most reverent and pure in their Sunday clothes, romp around the lawns or negotiate coins with the Indian peanut seller. Everyone laughs with ease, including the priest and the young girls selling religious literature, which appropriately includes a biography of St Francis Xavier.

The busy intersection of Jalan Bendahara and Jalan Munshi Abdullah is the fulcrum of Malacca's modern downtown district, with lots of hotels, shops and offices. Rising above the intersection is the **Malacca Renaissance Hotel**, the highest building in town, with a lofty rooftop swimming pool and outdoor cafe that affords fine views of the colourful old town nearby.

At the western end of Jalan Bendahara, on the fringe of the old town, is **St Xavier's Church**, with its twin Gothic towers. Built in 1849 by a French priest on the site of a former Portuguese chapel,

the church is dedicated to the 16th-century missionary St Francis Xavier.

350-year-old heritage: The legacy the Portuguese left behind is far greater than their ruins. Proud descendants of Portuguese soldiers bearing such names as Sequiera, Aranjo, Dias, D'Silva and D'Souza cherish the traditions of their European lineage.

"I gave to each man his horse, a house, and land," wrote de Albuquerque in 1604 when he reported with pride to Portugal that 200 mixed marriages had taken place. On direct orders from the king, de Albuquerque encouraged men of the garrison to marry local women, whom he called "his daughters." Such intermarriages flourished and women were even sent out from Portugal to marry local men. The Portuguese were instructed to treat local people as equals, and it is said that de Albuquerque even courteously escorted local women to their seats in church as though they were noble Portuguese ladies.

As can be expected, a strong Eurasian community grew up with loyalty to Portugal through its blood ties and religion.

After 400 years, the Portuguese Eurasians in Malacca, as well as in other towns of Malaysia, continue to speak Cristao, a medieval dialect once spoken in southeastern Portugal. When asked how closely the language spoken conforms to that in his homeland, Father Manuel Pintado, a local parish priest, notes: "It is pure 16th-century Portuguese. Remarkable, but it is spoken nowhere else."

Today, the descendants of the early Portuguese live in a community called the **Portuguese Settlement**, 3 kilometres (2 mi) from the centre of Malacca, near the beach. There are about 500 Eurasians, mostly fishermen. However, there are no cobblestone streets, white stucco walls or red tiled roofs as one might find in towns in Portugal. Instead, the dwellings resemble Malay kampung houses with wooden walls and tin roofs. All painted in pastel blues and greens, they are small, unpretentious and identical to one another.

Pass through the Portuguese Settlement quickly and you will be disappointed – there isn't much to see. Instead, linger and meet the people. Young boys still sing beautiful ballads in Portuguese and their sisters show you a dance which their grandmother learnt from her grandmother. An old man at a fruit stall tells you about a secluded tunnel from St John's Fort to St Paul's Hill, in which the Portuguese had hidden all their treasures before the Dutch overran Malacca. Some of the best places to meet locals are the open-air cafes around **Medan Portugis (Portuguese Square)**, which serve up spicy seafood dishes and cold beer.

The Festa de San Pedro, held each year in June, is a happy time for these remarkable people. At this time, the fishermen elaborately decorate their boats with bunting and sacred texts. A mass is usually conducted in the open and after the boats have been blessed by the parish priest, the evening is spent in merrymaking.

Another unusual custom called Intrudu (Introductions) is celebrated on the Sunday preceding Ash Wednesday, when the residents wear fancy costumes and throw water over one another. Even those at home are not spared. The merrymakers make a point of visiting and drenching them with water as soon as they open their doors. To show there are no hard feelings they are invited in for refreshments. Later in the day men dress up as ladies and the ladies dress as men, and go around selling cakes and fruits.

Antique streets: The main centre of Malacca's shopping and business activities is where it has always been, on the western bank of the **Malacca River**, away from the hills and the forts. On this side of the riverbank, visitors find themselves in a maze of ancient and narrow streets. **Jalan Tun Tan Cheng Lock** – called Heeren Street by the Dutch – is named after a leading Baba who was also an architect. His family house and the palatial townhouses of several other prominent Chinese families line both sides of the street, flaunting Peranakan hand-painted tiles and finely carved wooden doors.

At No. 50 is the fascinating **Baba**

Baba architecture: Tun Tan Cheng Lock house.

Nonya Heritage Museum, where you can actually explore the interior of a typical Peranakan house, decorated in the rich style of the 19th century, a style variously called Chinese Baroque or Chinese Palladian. The decor is a gorgeous blend of Chinese, Malay and European styles, the heavy wooden furniture inlaid with mother-of-pearl, the staircases covered in gold-leaf gilding. The family which owns the house gives guided tours and can tell fascinating stories about some of the architecture and curios.

Some of these treasures spill out into the antique shops on **Jonker Street** (Jalan Hang Jebat), one of the most interesting streets in Malaysia, as well as Malacca's main tourist drag. The street contains every imaginable trade: spirits importers, hairdressing salons, wooden shoe stores, coffin makers, apothecaries with Chinese herbs on display, sign printers, an acupuncture clinic, several furniture factories, a dental hospital, temples squeezed between commercial enterprises, and dozens of antique shops. At No. 17 Jonker Street is the Jonker Melaka Cafe, a combination craft shop and restaurant that has been restored to pristine Peranakan condition. Duck in for lunch or a cool drink – the menu features Nonya delights like chicken curry, black-nut soup and spicy grilled fish.

The myriad antique shops along Jonker Street mirror Malacca's past. Heavy brass irons with receptacles for hot coals, wooden bullock carts, ornate oil lamps, Peranakan-style furniture inlaid with mother of pearl, opium beds and altar stands, Victorian clocks and early gramophones, brass urns and marble statues, silver trinkets and Chinese wedding beds, as well as rare stamps and coins and Malay *kris* (daggers). The shopkeeper points to a carved, wooden jewellery box.

"I saved it for a prime minister," he tells you, "but I don't know when he'll be back." You study the box with an unconvinced look on your face. "No matter," he continues, "I like you. You can have it."

Tourists are not the only ones who flock to Malacca.

Where the faithful flock: The streets crisscross one another to form suitable sites for three of the oldest places of worship in Malaysia; while the Cheng Hoon Teng Temple in Jalan Tokong pays tribute to the Chinese faith and Kampung Kling Mosque, in the same street, was according to the Muslim creed, the Sri Poyyatha Vinayagar Moorthi Temple in Jalan Tukang Mas flies the Hindu flag.

Out of the three, the prestigious **Cheng Hoon Teng**, or Temple of Bright Clouds, is the oldest Chinese temple in Malaysia, being founded in 1645. It was originally built by a fugitive from the Manchu conquest, and was later restored and embellished by local Chinese leaders. The temple is dedicated to three deities: the main altar being given to Kuan Yin, the goddess of Mercy; Kwan Ti (also known as Kwan Kung), the god of War who triples up as the god of Wealth and the patron saint of Tradesmen; and Machoe Poh, the Queen of Heaven.

The building is a beautiful example of Chinese architecture. The carved roof, ridges and eaves are elegantly decorated with exquisite Chinese mythical figures, animals, birds and flowers, all made of coloured glass and porcelain that glitter and sparkle in the sun. Step through the massive hardwood gates, and you feel you are stepping back in time by centuries.

Amongst the wood carvings and lacquerwork within, all brought from China, is an inscription cut in stone, commemorating Admiral Cheng Ho's visit to the town in 1406. An illustrious envoy of the Ming emperor, and also an adventurer as famous in his own right as Columbus, Admiral Cheng Ho was also the city's earliest Chinese pioneer.

Monks in yellow robes move silently among the gilded pillars while Chinese worshippers with lowered heads walk from image to image, holding smouldering joss sticks reverently in their hands. The golden lions standing guard at the entrance have had the yellow worn off their heads by the countless devotees who, in passing, have rubbed them for good luck.

A creative touch to this bullock cart.

The **Sri Poyyatha Vinayagar Moorthi Temple** was built by the Hindu community of Malacca in the 1780s. It is dedicated to the god Vinayagar, to whom is ascribed the power to remove all obstacles for businessmen who want to get rich, and for couples who want to be married to one another.

Kampung Kling Mosque is the town's oldest mosque and sports a typical Sumatran design. The mosque, with its three- or four-tiered minarets, is characteristic of the Malaccan territory. Another good example is provided by the mosque in the suburb of Tranquerah. The cemetery encloses the tomb of Sultan Husain of Johor, who ceded Singapore to Sir Stamford Raffles in 1819.

Surrounding suburbs: It is a delight to drive at leisure through the suburbs of Malacca town. Beyond and behind it, rice fields stretch into the low hills which continue down to the southernmost spurs of the **Main Range**. Since long settled, this area is interlaced with numerous side roads, cutting through groves of rubber and fruit trees and past peaceful villages and compact market towns. Traditional Malay houses, with curving gables, carved eaves, wide-fronted verandahs and tiled entrance steps, are commonplace all the way from Tanjong Kling in the north to Merlimau in the south, where there is one particularly fine example to explore.

Tanjung Kling, about 10 kilometres (6 mi) from Malacca, has a beach resort and several cheap beach huts. Although some luxury resort-style condominiums are in the works, the sea here is not very clean, however, and is sometimes infested with jellyfish. Shah's Beach Motel has its own swimming pool for those who wish to swim.

Fifteen kilometres (9 mi) from town in the same direction is **Hang Tuah's Mausoleum**. Hang Tuah was a famous Malay warrior during the reign of Sultan Mansor Shah, and south of town is a well, believed to be the abode of his soul. His soul is said to have been changed into a crocodile, but only holy people will ever catch a glimpse of it. The waters of the well, situated at **Kampung Duyong**, are reputed to have medicinal values, and bring good luck to those who drink from it.

Still travelling towards Negri Sembilan, visitors pass the Tanjung Bidara Beach Resort, located on a pleasant stretch of beach about 20 kilometres (12 mi) from Malacca.

Kuala Linggi is at the mouth of the Linggi River, which separates the state of Malacca from that of Negri Sembilan. Here on a low hill is the tumbledown Fort Filipina, built by the Dutch. Named after a Dutch governor, the fort is nowadays nothing more than a pleasant place from which to view the river estuary and enjoy a picnic.

Some 12 kilometres (8 mi) inland from Malacca, on the road leading to the North-South Highway, is the **Air Keroh Recreational Forest**, 70 hectares (170 acres) of jungle sufficiently tamed to provide walks, deer reserves, picnicking spots and camping sites. There are several places to stay in this area including Air Keroh D'Village and the Malacca Village Park Plaza Resort and Park Villas.

Numerous "tourist attractions" spread along either side of Air Keroh Road some typical and others not so: a butterfly park, a crocodile farm, a fish world, a tennis centre, a *feng shui* garden, and **Taman Mini-Malaysia**, which features model houses representing the various styles of architecture found in Malaysia's 13 states, along with cultural and entertainment programmes. Nearby is the **Malacca Zoo**, with boating and refreshment facilities, and the 18-hole **Air Keroh Country Club**.

The road to Seremban and Kuala Lumpur goes through the district of Alor Gajah and passes **Naning**, the principality whose chieftain defied the British in the 19th century. Dato' Dol Said now rests in his tomb near the roadside.

Near Dol Said's grave and around this area are some 90 stone megaliths reminiscent of those mysterious stones in Kuala Pilah in Negri Sembilan. **Gadek Hot Springs** is located along the route to Tampin. The restorative waters are captured in pools and are surrounded with handicraft shops, refreshment stalls and a children's playground.

Friendly faces.

188

TAMAN NEGARA: THE GREEN HEART

Boating through swirling rapids, fishing for giant carp, shooting game with a camera, climbing mountains, watching birds, exploring caves, swimming placid river waters, going on safari through jungles 130 million years old, visiting Orang Asli settlements – and getting away from 20th-century traffic and pollution. Malaysia has what few countries in the world have – a great, undisturbed outdoors waiting for discovery. With two thirds of the country under jungle, where lush greenery begins at the edge of the sea and climbs up to the highest mountains, there is certain to be adventure for everyone who dares.

Topping all accessible jungle haunts in the peninsula is the **Taman Negara** (National Park), which spreads over the northern interior of the Malay peninsula in the state of **Pahang**. Within this area, around the central massif of Gunung Tahan, the highest peak in peninsular Malaysia, there are countless limestone hills thickly covered with forests, fast-running streams and an abundance of delightful wildlife.

Travel within the park is chiefly by water, although visitors can make land trips from any of the posts on the **Tembeling River**. Equipment, guides and porters are supplied by the park service. Around the headquarters at Kuala Tahan, the many trails and walks are well-marked and laid out for pleasant strolls into the green interior.

A jungle trip through Taman Negara is the closest anyone can come to the green heart of Malaysia, and conveniently it is flexible enough to range from a leisurely two days' fishing to a two-week tropical safari. Entrance to the park is usually by river, although you can also fly there, but the river trip itself is the best introduction to the park, as with the miles covered, you feel civilisation ebbing away.

Outboard motors of the park service carry visitors the 60 kilometres (40 mi)

Falls at Sungai Tahan.

from Kuala Tembeling Halt on the Malaysian Railway System to the park headquarters, at Kuala Tahan on the Tembeling River.

Although the trains do not usually stop at Tembeling Halt, they will do so if prior notice is given, or you can alight at Jerantut and take a taxi to the jetty, which is only 30 minutes away. There are also several tours to the park that operate from major cities, and transport to and from the park is arranged.

Boating down Sungai Tembeling: The boat journey to Kuala Tahan takes 3 to 4 hours depending on the level of the river. If the water is low, passengers are asked to disembark and walk along the banks of the river, while the boatmen negotiate the shallow waters.

After travelling 35 kilometres (20 mi), you reach the boundaries of the park on your left. On the right riverbank is more cultivated land, scattered with Malay *kampung*.

On arrival at **Kuala Tahan**, visitors can book accommodation, arrange trips and seek information at the reception.

An excellent travel guide to the park is also available at the reception and gives details of trails and river trips, as well as suggestions for fishing, and information about flora and fauna. It also contains maps of the area.

Visitors can stay at the **Headquarters** at Kuala Tahan in a variety of accommodation, ranging from the rest house and chalet facilities to the hostel and camping sites. At the hostel there are cooking facilities, or you can eat at one of the two restaurants. A small shop sells basic supplies (vegetables, fruit, canned food), and limited types of film are sold at the reception.

Outside the headquarters area, there are lodges at Kuala Trenggen and Kuala Kangsem, and several fishing lodges further up the rivers. You can even spend the night in the thick of the jungle in one of the five jungle hides, with basic sleeping facilities, or in several camping sites spread out around the park.

The headquarters have some camping, fishing and trekking equipment, but you would do well to check beforehand

Arrivals at Park Headquarters.

if it is available when you need it. The telephone number, address and booking arrangements are supplied at the back of this book in the Travel Tips section, and there is also a suggested list of the most necessary items to bring to the park.

The park service has a nightly slide show and film giving background information about the park, and explaining some of the wildlife you will see in the forest. Knowledgeable guides are also available from the reception, should you wish for a conducted tour of the plant and animal life.

To the jungle canopy: One hundred and thirty million years of evolution has produced some extraordinary plants and animals. Many plants have become highly specialised and are interlinked with other species in both parasitic and symbiotic ways. The *rattan* plant is a thick vine with huge spines, the smaller, younger rattan tendrils often taking you by surprise along the jungle trails.

Other plants that "hitch a ride" include the orchid family, with its several hundred varieties.

Another, more ominous "hitchhiker" is the strangling vine, which is dropped as a seed onto an unsuspecting tree, then grows into a small appendage on the host tree. The parasite eventually twists and twines itself around until the larger tree can hardly be seen. It takes 100 years for a strangling vine to kill off the host tree, after which the tree's strange hollow structure stands until the weight of other epiphytes bring it crashing to the jungle soil. Fruit and flowering trees abound here as well.

The jungle is not a quiet place as one might suppose – it is as noisy as any big city downtown with the cacophony of insect noises, bird calls and animal cries.

Bird-watching is a delight in the jungle, and a simple pair of binoculars will enable you to catch sight of the bird that arrested you with the hum of its wings. Several kinds of kingfishers, precious hornbills, fishing eagles and osprey abound in the forest.

Noisy but shy long-tailed macaques are heard but rarely seen; more visible animals are monitor lizards, otters and the domestic buffalo, bathing in the rivers near Malay villages.

Larger wildlife is also present in the jungle, but their secretive lives make them hard to spot.

Night in the jungle: An absolute must is at least one night in a jungle hide, small huts on stilts, usually near a stream and a salt-lick, that enable you to sit quietly in the dark and observe nocturnal animals. It is best to arrive at the jungle hides early, say around 5pm; bring a packed supper and a flashlight, and settle down to wait. Binoculars are also handy. As night falls, the forest becomes alive, and your eyes gradually adjust to the dark – moonlit nights are especially magical.

You will think your eyes are deceiving you when you see what seem to be ghostly spirits flitting in between the trees. These are fireflies and beetles with fluorescent wings and tails. On the ground, dead leaves glisten brightly in the jungle gloom, covered with luminescent lichen.

Deer are the most commonly seen animals from the hides, but if visiting **Malayan tapir.**

one of the hides farthest away from the headquarters, you may be lucky to see a tapir, and very lucky indeed to see an elephant, the quietest creature in the jungle, or a Malaysian tiger. Don't count too much on seeing these magnificent animals though; sightings of elephants and tigers, or even deer and tapir, are to be counted as a bonus to the already thrilling experience of being out in the forest. You will, however, see your fair share of spiders, frogs, toads and snakes amongst the undergrowth. Most visitors take turns to "watch", shining the torch every 10 minutes or so.

After a night out in the jungle, you will find that a new respect emerges for the inhabitants of the forest, animals and people alike. The Negrito hunters move amongst the trees as stealthily as the animals, armed with only a blowpipe.

Negrito communities are a common sight around the Headquarters, and it is said that the forest service provides food for them so that they will stay in the area. All around Kuala Tahan, you'll see their makeshift huts, which they return to from time to time, and they may even be in residence. The Negrito peoples have a natural dignity; don't be too quick to turn them into a tourist spectacle with the click of a camera.

Mountain hikes or river fishing: Trails around Park Headquarters range from a 10-minute stroll to a bathing place on the small **Tahan River**, to a nine-day jungle trek to the **Gunung Tahan**, highest mountain on the peninsula.

The trek up to the peak, at 2,187 metres (7,175 ft), is not difficult since the ascent is not steep, but climbing through jungle can be arduous and takes time. For this trip, it is important to be well organised, and to take with you only what is absolutely necessary. You should also take a guide, as it is easy to get lost on your own, with other secret jungle paths branching off from the main one. The trek is an exhilarating experience, and one that should be attempted if you are fit and healthy.

For those who prefer fishing, boats are for hire from the headquarters for access to the fishing grounds; the fur-

A nature lover's delight.

ther you go from there, the less people and the better chance of landing a giant.

February and March, and June to August, are generally considered best for fishing. The best time of day for fishing is during the middle of the day or in the late evening. Spinning is the most popular form of fishing. You can either bring your own tackle or arrange to hire some from the headquarters.

Tackle recommended is a 2-metre (6.5-ft) rod – any longer is cumbersome in the forest – line from 6 kilograms (13 lbs) as a start, moving on to finer line (3.5 kilograms/8 lbs) if the catch gets too big to handle! Line length should be a minimum of 30 metres (100 ft).

Fixed spool reels are generally used, although a multiplying reel is also operable. Since most fishing here is in pursuit of predatory fish, artificial lures such as spoons, spinners, wobblers and plugs are most commonly applied. Agreement is rare on which lure is best, but many locals swear only an "Abu Killer" will attract the big ones.

In season, local fishermen use riverside fruits for bait, cast to simulate its fall from the tree. Finally, a net or a gaff is required, the latter for its ease of transport through riverside scrub.

Riding the rapids: If fishing is not for you, then maybe just boating up the magical rivers in a narrow boat will appeal to you. Experienced boatmen, both Malay and Negrito, know the rivers like the backs of their hands, but not with their eyes closed. As you sit back and relax, they will be standing alert, poles in hand, watching for jagged rocks and sandbanks.

Although outboard motors are mostly used, the trickier waters will require progress by pole power, and if the river is high, you can enjoy floating down the river with just the current on your return trip. The boatmen will point out basking snakes, woodpeckers, kingfishers and deer to you, so be ready with binoculars. Further up the Tembeling from the headquarters are seven sets of rapids, which provide an exciting ride when the river is in full flood, but you must be prepared to get wet. On the smaller Tahan, a waterfall or bank of rapids provides a worthwhile trip: below the rapids is a natural swimming pool, the water tepid but refreshing. Or else climb up the rapids and find yourself in a natural jungle jacuzzi.

Bat caves: Further down the Tembeling River, a 15-minute walk inland, is the **Goa Telinga** (literally, Ear Cave) where fruit- and insect-eating bats cluster on the low roofs of the cave ceilings. Entry to the caves is by a tiny crevice in the rock – wear some old clothes for this adventure, as you're going to have to slide through mud and bat droppings, centimetres thick on the cave floors.

Crawling along a narrow passageway, you emerge at last into a cave where you can stand up, and with the help of a flashlight, can pick out the two different types of bats. The fruit bats congregate near the crevices that let in a little sunlight, while the insect-eating ones gather below in darker corners.

Huge toads, bigger than the size of a large fist, survey the scene, and the cave racer, a long white snake that feeds exclusively on bats in the cave, can be seen, suspended from the ceiling, from where it disengages its jaws and entwines its long tail around the struggling bat. Large spiders and cockroaches scuttle around on the floors, as if in a scene taken out of an Indiana Jones movie. Although they may be unnerving to many people, all the animals in the cave are harmless to humans. A rope runs through all the caves to guide you to the narrow exit on the other side.

Two days is the minimum for a visit to the Taman Negara, and a longer stay with more extensive exploration brings rich rewards. For the more adventurous, trips can be arranged to plunge into less-known parts of the jungle (including the areas in the north of the park reached from the state of Kelantan), preferably with Orang Asli guides. The main hindrance to such an expedition is the high cost. You will be told that you will need more than just a backpack – several guides, porters, various equipment and a boat are required. If you have unlimited amounts of time and money, this would be the most rewarding and thrilling adventure you will ever embark upon.

Ethereal light shines through jungle foliage.

JOHOR:
SOUTHERN COMFORT

The state of Johor occupies the entire southern tip of the Malay peninsula. Its west coast, facing the Straits of Malacca, is well developed with a large population, but in the centre and in the southeast of the state, the population is sparse and vast stretches of jungle separate one settlement from another. The jungle is not visible for the visitor travelling by road, however. Along the good network of roads in the state, the landscape is dominated by oil palm and rubber plantations (sometimes pineapple), which stretch across the undulating hills to the horizon.

Johor is reputed to be the home of classical Malay culture; its people are known to speak the best Malay in the peninsula and the women wear the *baju kurong*, the national dress, nearly everyday. Many of the Malays here are of Javanese descent, and Johor is the only state in Malaysia where you can see the *kuda kepang*, a dance of Javanese origin, in which the dancer stands astride a "hobby horse" and is said to possess magical and visionary powers while dancing in a trance.

Johor only evolved its own identity after the fall of the Malacca sultanate to the Portuguese in the 16th century. Malacca's last ruler, Sultan Mahmud, refused to capitulate but fled to Johor. The present royal family of Johor is related to him by a collateral line. Despite this pedigree, Johor's rulers never attained the pinnacle of power, prestige and influence which the sultans of Malacca had enjoyed.

Johor was basically a trading empire that had its moments of power and prosperity interspersed with the darker days of disaster. Not only did it have to contend with the Portuguese of Malacca, and then with the Dutch, but also with the new power of Aceh in north Sumatra. When Aceh weakened, the marauding Menangkabau and Bugis began to flex their muscles. At first the rulers of Johor had their capitals along the protected reaches of the Johor River, but later had to settle in the Riau archipelago, which was more accessible to trade – and further attacks. Twice a sultan of Johor was taken captive to Aceh, and his royal capital was reduced to ashes. By the beginning of the 18th century, Johor sultans had become the puppets of the Bugis chiefs, who held all the real power.

A turning point: The 19th century saw a decisive change in Johor's fate. At that time, Johor was the fief of a *temenggung*, an official of the sultan. Abu Bakar, who became temenggung in 1862, elevated himself to *maharaja* in 1868, and in 1885 he was acknowledged by Great Britain as Sultan of Johor, thereby discounting the former sultan's lineage. The present royal family of Johor are his direct descendants.

Sultan Abu Bakar was educated in Singapore by English clergy. He spoke fluent English and came to know influential Europeans in the business world. Under his rule, the foundations of modern Johor were laid; locals today still regard him as the father of modern Johor.

In 1866, he moved his capital to Johor Bahru and within a few years had transformed a humble fishing village into a thriving new town. He was also responsible for founding the modern towns of Muar and Batu Pahat; he introduced a modern bureaucracy and gave Johor the first constitution ever to be written for a Malay state.

The sultan used western methods of policy-making and administration in conducting Johor's internal affairs. (Britain still had control over Johor's foreign matters.) This enabled him to convince the British that his government was good and stable, and so deferred the appointment of a British "advisor" to help him rule his state. He maintained close ties with Englishmen in Singapore and in London, being the first Malay ruler to visit England and becoming a personal friend of Queen Victoria.

After his death in 1895, British pressure became too strong, and his heir reluctantly accepted the "assistance" of a British General Advisor in 1914. Hence, Johor was the last Malay state in the peninsula to come under direct British control.

Sulphur springs and tombs: A pretty town called **Muar** lies just under the Johor/Malacca border. It is considered, along with its surroundings, as a cultural centre, and Johor *ghazal* music concerts and the kuda kepang trance dances can be seen here.

En route to Muar, approaching Malacca, a detour on the road to Segamat leads to **Gunung Ledang** (Mount Ophir), popular with hikers and naturalists. Sagil Falls tumbles off the 1,276-metre (4,186-ft) peak into clear pools below. Closer to Muar are the **Sungai Kesang** hot sulphur springs, 5 kilometres (3 mi) off the main road. Simple changing rooms are provided.

At **Pagoh**, 26 kilometres (16 mi) from Muar, there is an old fort containing the tombs of two Malacca sultans. Situated atop a small rise, it was constructed to protect the sultans from attacks by pirates. Nearby in the graveyard at **Kampung Parit Pecah** stand 99 tombstones, marking the graves of an entire

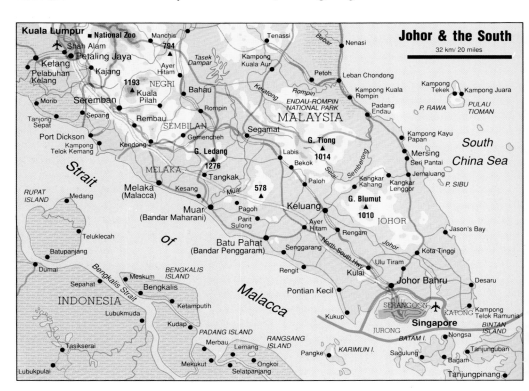

village which was wiped out by a single spear about 500 years ago. According to legend, this happened at a wedding party. The spear was tossed by a jealous lover into the chest of a bridegroom, removed and tossed again, eventually killing the bride and all the wedding guests.

Batu Pahat, notorious for its floods at high tides, is a conference centre, and Chinese food is considered to be good here. There is a small beach and a legendary well nearby at **Minyak Beku**. Nineteen kilometres (12 mi) south of Pontian Kechil, the road finally ends at famous Kukup on the southernmost tip of the Malay Peninsula.

Chili crabs and lobster pots: Raised on stilts above the water, houses in the Chinese village of **Kukup** are linked to one another by plank walks, looking as though they might topple into the sea. Late afternoon is the ideal time to arrive, when the sun is low over the sea and the evening breezes begin. However, it is not to watch the sunset that the hoards of visitors, especially from nearby Singapore, come to Kukup. It is to eat chilli crabs, for which Kukup is rightly famous. The restaurants do not have fancy decor – and some do not even have walls – but they do have atmosphere and great food. Since Kukup has become popular with Singaporeans, the seafood is not as cheap as it used to be, and the drinks especially are very expensive.

For years, a huge net along a railing facing the sea in one restaurant was lowered and raised by an ancient, wooden crank. Boys wound the net up from the sea and scooped out the daily menu – eels, fish, crabs, lobsters. Today, however, this sight has become increasingly rare.

Street shopping: Astride the old trunk road that runs south to Johor Bahru – and not far off the new North-South Highway – is a small crossroads town called **Ayer Hitam**, about 30 kilometres (20 mi) from Batu Pahat and 90 kilometres (50 mi) from the state capital. Ayer Hitam is a popular stopover for tourists on their way between Kuala Lumpur and Singapore. Dark coffee shops and rows of heavily laden street

Malaysia is a land of gentle smiles – this one is in Muar.

stalls become "a drinking hole and a shopping centre" for weary travellers, who descend on the stalls to hunt down last-minute souvenirs or snap up preserved fruits, durian cakes, peanut nougat and other local produce. So are fruits like bananas, chempedak and rambutans, which hang down in luxurious bunches.

Travellers familiar with Ayer Hitam head for Claycraft Coffee House, which is an unusual air-conditioned restaurant doubling up as a pottery shop. The place is half hidden by the street stalls but on entering, it is a different experience altogether. Patrons sit on stoneware stools and drink out of dainty ceramic tea cups. The room is taken up by tables, half of which are filled with arty relics.

Further south, in a village called **Machap**, is a famous craft factory called Aw Potteries, proclaimed by two colossal earthenware genies. The Menangkabau-style showroom displays all sorts of pottery in the distinctive Aw glazes. Behind the showroom is the studio itself, where you can watch craftsmen at work throughout the process.

Causeway connection: Johor Bahru is connected to Singapore by a causeway carrying vehicular traffic and a railroad. Its proximity to Singapore makes it a gateway for urban vacationers at weekends. Then, traffic slows down to a snail's pace. Timber lorries, tourist buses, outstation taxis, motor scooters and Singaporeans escaping city life in their Hondas and Mercedes vie for positions at the immigration gates. Whether it's to buy X-rated videos banned in Singapore, find a beach, or try the roulette wheels at Genting Highlands, the crowds flocking from Singapore to Malaysia create traffic jams. A second crossing between the two countries – between Tanjung Kupang and Tuas, at Singapore's western side – opened in the late 1990s. The RM2.2-billion bridge stretches 2 kilometres (1.5 mi) across the Johor Strait.

Downtown "JB" changes by the day as new high-rise buildings take shape. The place has a real boom-town feel – muddy streets, platoons of sweaty workers and a constant din of jackhammers

Temple on wheels, Kukup.

and pile drivers. The city's more recent landmarks are the luxury Puteri Pan Pacific Hotel and the adjacent Plaza Kota Raya shopping mall, which features the same modern air-conditioned ambience and eclectic shopping as Singapore's Orchard Road – but much cheaper prices.

Remnants of old Johor are found amid the hustle and bustle of the downtown district. The area behind **Jalan Ibrahim** harbours many old shophouses where Chinese and Indian traders flog everything from spices and joss sticks to tailored suits and the latest colour TVs. Mixed in among the shops are cheap Chinese restaurants and Indian cafes, where "banana leaf" curry and *roti* are the specialties.

Nearby are an elaborate Hindu temple called **Rajamariamman Kovil** (Tokong Hindu in Malay) and a Chinese **Taoist shrine** (Tokong Cina), both along Jalan Terus. Crowning the crest of the nearby hill is the gleaming white spire of **St Joseph's Catholic Church**. The old colonial train station is in this same neighbourhood.

Bangunan Sultan Ibrahim crowns the top of Bukit Timbalan, a huge Saracen-style building with arches, columns and enclosed stone balconies faintly reminiscent of the Moorish architecture of southern Spain. A silver crescent and star crowns the central tower, while a gold seal of the State of Johor marks the massive front doors. Inside the building are the State Council Chamber and Secretariat, and the local office of the Malaysian Tourist Promotion Board (MTPB). Unfortunately, the open-air gallery at the top of the tower is no longer open to the public.

The **Istana Besar** (or Grand Palace) and its sweeping lawns are located a bit further down the waterfront, overlooking the Johor Strait. The stark-white structure was commissioned by Sultan Abu Bakar in 1864 as the primary royal residence. Over the last century it has hosted royalty from around the globe, including the Duke of Edinburgh (Queen Victoria's son), Archduke Franz Ferdinand of Austria (whose assassination sparked World War I) and the future King Edward VIII of England (who abdicated to marry Wallis Simpson).

While the Istana Besar remains in royal hands, it was opened to the public in 1991 as a dazzling museum dedicated to the golden age of Johor. There is no other museum in Southeast Asia like it, reminiscent of visiting the aristocratic homes of rural England.

The first stop on the palace tour is the **Dewan** (audience hall), now a gallery detailing the history of the Johor sultanate. Next comes the **Grand Palace**, crammed with antiques and strange knickknacks. The four-poster beds in the State Bedrooms are made from teak with Corinthian-style columns fashioned in England during the 1860s by a master craftsman. The bedrooms are still used for the lying-in-state of deceased members of the royal family. Further down the hall is the opulent Reception Room, with a Baccarat crystal table and chairs. The nearby Throne Room, with its matching guilt thrones, is used each year for investiture ceremonies on the sultan's birthday. The crowning glory

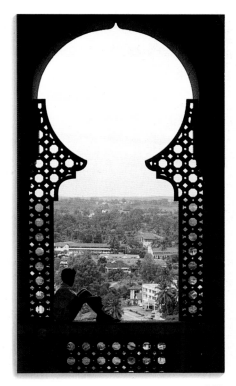

of the palace is the Banqueting Room, where the opulence can be compared to almost anything found in Europe. The last part of the tour takes you through the extensive royal collections, including Malay hand arms (*kris, badik* and *sundang*), and the splendid state regalia and gold collections.

Surrounding the palace are the **Istana Gardens**, with rolling park land, immaculate lawns and several flower gardens. Just uphill from the Dewan are a Japanese garden and tea house presented by Crown Prince Hirohito on the occasion of his state visit to Malaysia in 1936. The western part of the gardens is taken up by the small but interesting **Johor Zoo**, once the sultan's private menagerie.

The next landmark along the waterfront is **Sultan Abu Bakar Mosque**. Abu Bakar laid the foundation stone in 1892 but died before the mosque was finished eight years later. The architecture is a bizarre blend of Italian rococo, classical Greek and traditional Muslim styles, painted beige with blue trim.

Non-Muslims are barred from entering the mosque, but you may be able to sneak a peak through one of the doorways. Be sure to remove your shoes if you are invited to venture inside. The interior is decorated with Corinthian columns, crystal chandeliers and Oriental carpets. At the front of the main hall are a fabulously ornate gilt *minbar* (pulpit) and an ancient grandfather clock. Hawkers frequent the mosque grounds selling prayer rugs, velour wall hangings and other souvenirs.

Further along the waterfront is **Istana Bukit Serene**, home of the present ruler. The huge complex is off-limits to the general public, but you can get a good view of the palace from Jalan Skudai (which runs along the waterfront) or Straits View Road. The building is a good example of the rustic Art Deco style – thick stone walls surmounted by a green-tiled roof and a 350-metre-high (1,150-ft) stone tower. The expansive grounds contain a private air strip, a huge satellite dish, an orchid garden and a menagerie.

Modern mosque has a fairytale look.

Johor Bahru has several good handicraft centres. **JARP (Johor Area Rehabilitation Organization)** has a showroom and workshop on Jalan Sungai Chat where handicapped people produce cane furniture, soft toys, rattan baskets and customized book binding. Across the street is **Perbadanan Handicraft Centre**, where *songet* cloth, batik and pottery are sold. Closer to downtown is the **Mawar Gift Shop**, on the grounds of Istana Besar and offering batik, pewter and woodcarving.

Local nightlife draws many customers from nearby Singapore, attracted by cheaper drinks and looser censorship, although the JB town council is starting to crack down on the more sinister aspects of nightlife. Still, the city has numerous nightclubs, discos, hostess clubs and karaoke lounges which come alive after dark.

Another thing that entices many people across the Causeway is the many golf courses in the Johor region. Among the best known are the 18-hole Royal Johor Country Club, Desaru Country Club and Palm Resort Country Club, not far from Senai Airport. Anyone interested in golf is strongly advised to book at least three days in advance.

Kota Tinggi is a small, quiet town with a loud splash. Fifteen kilometres (9 mi) northeast of the town centre are the famous **Kota Tinggi Waterfalls**, which thunder down 36 metres (118 feet) to the polished rocks below. Swimming is permitted to anyone who dares to plunge into the icy waters. Well-furnished Swiss-type chalets (with cooking facilities, utensils, a gas range and a refrigerator) face the falls, inviting visitors to spend the night. An open-front restaurant serves both Chinese and European dishes. In the evening the falls are illuminated, making a lively, dancing spectacle for the dinner guests.

On the outskirts of Kota Tinggi, at **Kampung Makam** on the road to Mersing, is the burial ground of the 17th-century sultans of Johor, and nearby, the last resting place of Johor's *bendahara* (chief ministers) during the early days. Farther down the road, near

This local youngster waits for a ride.

the turn to Kampung Makam, another junction to the right leads to Desaru, one of Malaysia's best-known beach resorts, which sits in a wide bay south of Tanjung Penawar. Before reaching Desaru – about halfway along this road – a laterite track on the right-hand side branches off through an oil palm plantation to **Johore Lama** (old Johor) on the Johor River. It was once a great trading centre and a royal capital, boasting one of the most powerful forts in the area. Until very recently, Johore Lama could only be reached by river.

Today, Johore Lama is a tranquil sleepy village, on whose fringes archaeologists have uncovered some massive ramparts of the old fort. The road is rather hard to negotiate without a four-wheel-drive vehicle. Arrival at the village is somewhat disappointing, as even the villagers seem to be deserting the area for more accessible places. The view over the Johor Straits to Johor Bahru, however, is very pretty.

Desaru Resort is much frequented by wealthy Singaporeans and Malaysians, staying at the Desaru View Hotel and the Desaru Golf Resort during the weekends. For those eager to shun big hotels, there is the delightful Desaru Garden Beach Resort with chalets near the beach. Desaru also sports a youth hostel, a camping site and basic traditional huts, all occupied during school holidays.

The hotels and the chalets provide usual beach facilities of water sports, pony trekking and golf and tennis, and the Desaru Golf Hotel runs a scuba diving centre.

One final note if planning to go: Desaru can also be reached by a new auto ferry service that runs between Changi Point in Singapore and Tanjung Pengelih in Malaysia; the driving distance from the ferry terminal to the resort is 57 kilometres (35 mi).

The main road northwards from Kota Tinggi pursues a lonely, undulating course. At the 14th kilometre, a sign points the way to **Jason's Bay**, or Teluk Mahkota, which was once the most popular of Johor beaches. But now the

There is a fair sprinkling of tropical isles offshore.

long beach has silted up and there are mud flats at low tide. There are no facilities at the beach but those who wish to get away from it all will find their solitude interrupted only by the sound of sea birds, the pricks of sand flies, and an occasional visitor.

Mersing, situated on the right bank of the river of the same name, is a peaceful and pleasant town, except at the river mouth. Here is a large, bustling fishing fleet bringing all the excitement one associates with a fishing port. Around the first of May comes the annual festival of Kayu Papan in Mersing, where you may be lucky to see the kuda kepang, a trance dance seldom seen outside Johor.

Inland from Mersing along Route 50 is a giant knot of jungle that clusters around the twin peaks of **Gunung Belumut** and **Gunung Lambak**. Forest parks provide shady hiking trails, campsites and picnic grounds. Mersing is also the jumping off spot for visits to numerous small islands in the clear-blue South China Sea.

Islands in the sun: Mersing is the setting off point for a group of 64 idyllic volcanic islands in the South China Sea. One of these, **Pulau Tioman**, was mentioned 2,000 years ago in what was perhaps the first guide to Malaysia. Arab traders then made note in their "sailing directions" that Tioman, lying about 55 kilometres (35 mi) off the east coast of the Malay peninsula, offered good anchorage and a freshwater spring for filling their casks.

Centuries afterwards, the twin peaks called "Ass's Ears" at the southern tip of the island guided ships at sea. Ming pottery found in caves reveals that early Chinese traders also made Tioman a port-of-call.

Gone are the Arab and Chinese traders, their places now taken by lotus-eating sybarites. Today, Tioman is everybody's dream of a tropical island. When Hollywood was looking for a mythical island to film *South Pacific*, it chose Tioman to portray the legendary Bali Hai. Lovely beaches fringe the western side of the island and the waters

Tioman is on everyone's "world's best islands" list.

surrounding it are startlingly clear. But be warned: sea-urchins abound.

The more energetic may wish to trek across the island on the path that begins next to the airport and emerges on the eastern side of the island at **Kampung Juara**, taking a boat back from there to the western coast. The walk takes about three hours, and walkers report that it is easy to get lost along the path as there are often several pathways to choose from. Keep your eyes open for signs!

Snorkelling should not be missed, as the coral reefs around the island have some beautiful marine life. A small islet in the bay of the Tioman Resort holds some beautiful corals and even better is **Pulau Rengis**, an hour by fishing boat from **Kampung Tekek** jetty.

The choice of transport to Tioman, from fishing boats to 12-seater planes (from Kuala Lumpur or Singapore) to high-speed ferries (from Mersing and Singapore) is somewhat confusing. Travelling time ranges from 30 minutes to 4 hours.

The Berjaya Tioman Beach Resort, like all top-class hotels in Desaru, offers international-class hotel facilities. There are also chalets for rent along the lovely beach at Kampung Tekek (the name means Lizard Village).

Many of the chalet owners can arrange a package tour from Mersing, including transport and accommodation. Accommodation ranges from air-conditioned chalets to coconut A-frame huts and is scattered along the beaches from Tekek to **Salang Beach** in the far north. Wherever you stay, don't miss a stroll along the beach at sunset to enjoy the cooler air and the coloured skies.

Much smaller than Tioman is the pretty little island of **Rawa**, which is also accessible from Mersing, just an hour away from the port.

However, the rather overdeveloped resort can be a little crowded at weekends. Picnickers are not allowed on the island, and if you decide to spend the day here, you will have to eat at the island's one restaurant. Accommodation is in the form of chalets with shared bathrooms. The staff are very friendly at the resort and will tell you where to find the best snorkelling. The resort has its own little "zoo" with monkeys, birds and small mammals. Turn left along the beach from the resort, climb over the rocks at the end of the bay, and you will discover a sea cave with a spectacular arch.

There are many other islands in the Mersing group. **Pulau Sibu Besar** offers white sand beaches, coral reefs and plenty of budget accommodation. Uninhabited **Pulau Tengah**, a former Vietnamese refugee camp, is now a marine national park with many protected species. **Pulau Besar** and **Pulau Pemanggli** both have colourful reefs and simple beach front chalets. Secluded **Pulau Aur** has turquoise lagoons and offshore pools. **Pulau Sibu Tengah** offers a modern seaside resort with pool, tennis courts and restaurant. **Pulau Tinggi**, one of the largest islands, has a towering jungle peak and reefs.

Offices for boat services to all the islands are located around the jetty at Mersing, or wander down to the pier and try your luck at bargaining with the men on the fishing boats.

Heart of darkness: Known to few is the **Endau River**, along the border between the states of Johor and Pahang, and terminating at the sea and at the small town of Endau. From Endau you can travel the river up into the remote regions of the interior, but this is not a journey for casual tourists. Before making the journey, adventurers must have camping and trekking equipment ready, hire guides, preferably Orang Asli guides, and boats.

No river in the peninsula is so remote yet so close to civilisation as the Sungai Endau. At the lower reaches, it is bordered by mangrove swamps, but further up you are surrounded by dense jungle in which tigers prowl and rhinoceros hide. The interior is an extensive Orang Asli area, and the fierce rapids separate them from many a prying stranger, afraid to proceed beyond the frothing waters. You may visit their settlements, where you will be welcomed, but as the Orang Asli are a protected people, you must first obtain an entry permit from the State Security Council in Johor Bahru. **Teeing off on Tioman.**

206

HIGHWAYS TO THE EAST COAST

After exploring the west coast of Malaysia, with its large modern cities and countryside of rubber, oil palm and disused tin mines, most visitors to Malaysia now turn their eyes to the alluring east coast, an area specifically connected with the Malays of the country.

There are to be found exclusively Malay *kampung,* the traditional arts and sports, and a relaxed and easy-going way of life. Especially popular with tourists are the gorgeous stretches of white beach which fringe the entire coast; and the exquisite islands enclosed in teeming coral reefs which lie in easy reach off the coast.

Not too long ago, the east was almost entirely cut off from the west, with the **Main Range** of mountains dividing the two, and thick impassable jungle making progress so slow that the sea route was often preferred.

Nowadays, however, there are three good highways which reach out between the coasts, carrying news, business and tourism from west to east and from east to west.

The first highway runs from Johor Bahru in the extreme south to Mersing, a fishing port on the east coast of Johor state. The second highway, and by far the most used, runs across the middle of the country from Kuala Lumpur to Kuantan in the state of Pahang. Taking this highway, you have an option of making a small detour to the Taman Negara (National Park) before continuing on your way.

The third highway is the most recent and to date, the least used. This road connects Butterworth and Penang to Kota Bharu in the northernmost section of the East Coast, located in the state of Kelantan. The scenery here, along the Thai border is wild and exotically romantic, and one of the least populated areas on the peninsula.

There are also several more unusual and less used routes to the East Coast,

View from the East-West Highway.

for those who dislike busy roads, and who wish to take in at leisure the remote village life in the jungled and mountainous centre of the peninsula. You might just be the only foreigner to be seen along these small roads, but you will be made welcome by friendly and curious village people.

Johor Bahru–Mersing Highway: The road from **Johor Bahru** to **Mersing** cuts through extensive rubber and oil palm plantations, some of which you will be able to visit. **Kota Tinggi** (40 kilometres [25 mi] from Johor Bahru) has a waterfall and chalets nearby. After Kota Tinggi, you can either turn south for the **Desaru Resort**, or continue northwards to Mersing (135 kilometres [80 mi] from Johor Bahru). This same road will take you up the entire stretch of the East Coast, hugging the seashore almost all the way.

KL–Kuantan Highway: The second route, from **Kuala Lumpur** to **Kuantan**, cuts straight across the landmass from west to east. Drive out on the clearly marked highway from Kuala Lumpur and through the northeastern suburbs, passing the Batu Caves. You will soon cross over into the enormous state of Pahang, shortly after which is the turnoff for the **Genting Highlands**, the cool mountain resort and popular gambler's paradise.

The road now crosses the Wangsa Mountains before dropping down into the plains of Pahang. After some 150 kilometres (90 mi) from the capital, you will reach **Mentakab**, a town on the Jungle Railway (which goes up to Kota Bharu and Thailand). After Mentakab, a turnoff takes you to the small settlement of **Tembeling**, starting point for boats to the **Taman Negara**. Or you can just continue eastwards through to Temerloh.

Many small villages follow before you arrive at **Gambang**. Here a road plunges straight down to Segamat in Johor state. Along this road, you will cross the Pahang River, directly after which is a small road leading off to the right, taking you to Kampung Kuala Chini and the legendary **Lake Chini** (see the East Coast section on Kuantan for more details).

Gambang is just 20 kilometres (12

mi) from Kuantan. From Kuantan, you can either head south for Mersing and Pulau Tioman, or northwards for the turtle beaches in Kuala Terengganu and Kota Bharu.

Butterworth–Kota Bharu Highway: The third and perhaps most thrilling highway to the East Coast is in the far north of the country, at times touching the Thai border, and crossing a wild and deserted landscape. From **Butterworth**, pass Bukit Mertajam and take the north road to **Keroh** on the Thai border. The road is sprinkled with small settlements all along this road. These diminish in number on the road between Keroh and **Gerik**, 160 kilometres (100 mi) from Butterworth. This is an Orang Asli settlement area, and for those wishing to explore the surrounding wilderness, there is a government resthouse at Gerik and a few small Chinese hotels. East of Gerik is the huge Temenggor Reservoir, and the Banding Fishing Resort on its shores.

Here, there are opportunities for fishing, trekking, hiking and picnicking.

There is also a campsite and a resthouse for those who wish to experience the feeling of spending the night in one of peninsular Malaysia's least populated areas. Indeed, traffic on this highway is not yet a problem, and for many kilometres you will have the entire road almost to yourself.

After Gerik, you will pass through a very large army presence in this area, for it was here that the Communist guerillas had their last hideout in Malaysia. There are still fears that they would return to this desolate place, should they inspire an uprising in the future.

The highway between Gerik and Tanah Merah in Kelantan state is closed between 6pm and 6am for the same reason, so make sure you set out early enough to be on this section of road by late afternoon.

The landscape is at its most extravagantly wild here, and it is worth stopping to drink in the fresh cool air. The road crosses **Lake Temenggor**, a reservoir of great and mysterious beauty. One hundred and thirty kilometres (80 mi) from Gerik, the Thai border is touched for the second time near Kampung Nibong.

Twenty-nine kilometres (18 mi) later, you reach the town of **Tanah Merah** (Red Earth) on the Kelantan River, and once again you are in civilisation. It is immediately apparent that the villages and countryside are very different from those on the west coast.

From Tanah Merah, you can head south to **Kuala Krai** on the Pahang River. It is possible to take boats from here to Kota Bharu at the mouth of the river, passing picturesque Malay villages, where many of the state's arts and handicrafts are produced.

Travellers can also continue straight on to **Pasir Puteh**, an area blessed with numerous and wonderful waterfalls. From there, it is a short drive to the coast at Kuala Besut, the jumping-off point for the exquisite **Perhentian Islands**, equipped with its own fine beaches and rest house.

Turning north from Tanah Merah, the road ploughs through quiet little vil-

Long distance travel is the norm.

210

lages, crosses the Kelantan River and brings you to **Kota Bharu**, the capital of Kelantan and the centre for East Coast arts and crafts.

More options: These three routes are certainly the most used, and take you past many interesting sights on the way. However, if you have a penchant for out-of-the-way places and the rarely-trodden roads, there are several other possibilities, mostly optional routes leading off from the main ones.

One of these roads leads from **Batu Pahat** on the west coast of Johor, crossing the north-south highway at **Ayer Hitam** and continuing on a smaller road through **Keluang**, on the railway across a plain of little rivers and small villages to meet the Johor Bahru, to Mersing road at **Jemaluang**.

Another larger road runs from Melaka (Malacca) to **Segamat** in the north of Johor state. From Segamat, you can either turn south or head steeply north, passing into a remote village area in the south of Pahang.

A side road follows the **Rompin River** to the coast at Kampung Leban Chondong north of Kuala Rompin. Otherwise you can continue northwards, passing the turnoff to **Lake Chini** and finally joining the Kuala Lumpur to Kuantan highway.

Another route from Malacca goes towards **Gemas**. Just before Gemas, take the turnoff which leads northwards to **Temerloh**, situated at the crossroads of the Jungle Railway and the main Kuala Lumpur to Kuantan road.

Passing the town of **Bahau** in eastern Negri Sembilan, a turnoff to the right not far out of town takes you to **Tasik Dampar**, a large body of water attached to the more famous **Tasik Bera**, Malaysia's largest natural lake.

Tasik Bera is more easily reached by continuing along the Temerloh road and turning down a rough road at **Triang**.

Five Orang Asli villages nestle on the lake's shore, and at **Pos Iskandar** village, there is a government resthouse for those wishing to extend their stay in this remote countryside. Permits are required for visitors to enter the villages on Tasik Bera, and these can be obtained either by post from, or by direct application at the Temerloh police station. A passport-sized photograph must be attached to the permit, which is issued free of charge.

On the Kuantan/Kuala Lumpur highway, you can turn north at Mentakab for the **Taman Negara**. After a visit to that splendid park, you can take a small road which follows the western boundaries of the park. At **Gua Musang**, the road widens and carries local traffic northwards through the Kelantan countryside to **Kuala Krai**, and eventually to Kota Bharu.

The final option is to take the remote road that pursues its lonely course through the **Upper Perak** region, from **Kuala Kangsar** through rural Orang Asli villages to **Gerik**. From there you can join the east-west highway, which will lead you to **Kota Bharu**.

On the main highways, filling up your car with petrol is no problem, but if you are taking one of the small road options, start with a full tank, just to be on the safe side.

A kite for sore eyes: rural backroads scene.

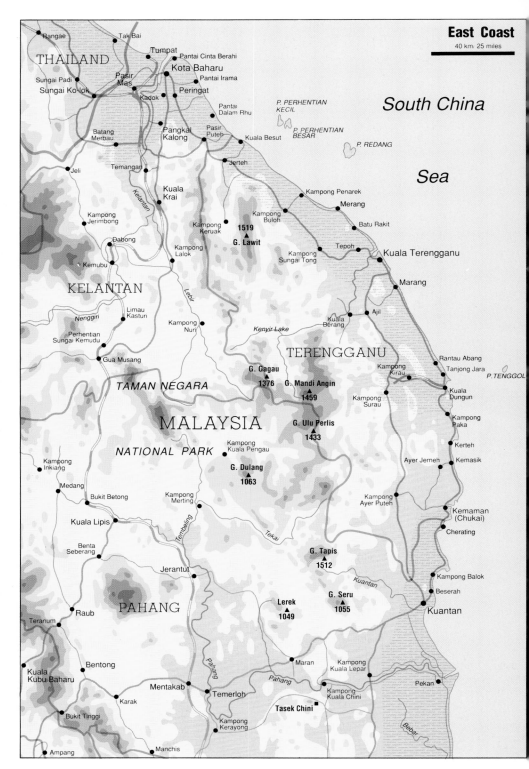

East Coast

40 km/ 25 miles

THAILAND

Rangae

Tak Bai

Tumpat

Pantai Cinta Berahi

Kota Baharu

Pasir Mas

Pantai Irama

Sungai Padi

Peringat

Sungai Ko-lok

Kadok

Pantai Dalam Rhu

Batang Merbau

Pangkal Kalong

Pasir Puteh

Kuala Besut

P. PERHENTIAN KECIL

South China

P. PERHENTIAN BESAR

Jeli

Temangan

Jerteh

P. REDANG

Sea

Kuala Krai

Kampong Penarek

Merang

Kampong Jerimbong

Kampong Buloh

Batu Rakit

Kampong Keruak

1519

Dabong

G. Lawit

Tepoh

Kuala Terengganu

Kampong Lalok

Kampong Sungai Tong

Kemubu

KELANTAN

Marang

Limau Kasturi

Kampong Nuri

Kuala Berang

Ajil

Nenggiri

Kenyir Lake

Perhentian Sungai Kemudu

TERENGGANU

Gua Musang

G. Gagau

Rantau Abang

1376

Kampong Kirau

Tanjong Jara

P. TENGGOL

TAMAN NEGARA

G. Mandi Angin

1459

Kampong Surau

Kuala Dungun

MALAYSIA

G. Ulu Perlis

1433

Kampong Paka

NATIONAL PARK

Kampong Kuala Pengau

Kerteh

Kampong Inkiang

G. Dulang

1063

Ayer Jerneh

Kemasik

Medang

Bukit Betong

Kampong Merting

Kampong Ayer Puteh

Kemaman (Chukai)

Kuala Lipis

Cherating

Benta Seberang

G. Tapis

1512

Jerantut

Kampong Balok

Kuantan

Beserah

Raub

PAHANG

G. Seru

1055

Teranum

Lerek

1049

Kuantan

Bentong

Maran

Kampong Kuala Lepar

Kuala Kubu Baharu

Mentakab

Pahang

Kampong Kuala Chini

Pekan

Karak

Temerloh

Bukit Tinggi

Tasek Chini

Kampong Kerayong

Bebar

Ampang

Manchis

214

EAST COAST: FAR FROM THE CROWDS

To discover the soul of Malaysia, one should visit the East Coast. Bordered by Thailand on the north, isolated from the west by a chain of rugged mountains and separated from the south by swamps and rivers, the East Coast has retained its own identity through the ages. Its relaxed villages and *kampung*, where leisure nurtured the arts, have survived more or less unchanged.

Whenever the Sultan of Johor has a birthday celebration, the dancers are imported from Kota Bharu. The University of Malaya puts on a cultural show and they recruit the renowned *mak yong* actors from Kelantan. Foreign dignitaries are being entertained by the *wayang kulit* shadow play – a treasured cultural favourite in Terengganu.

The East Coast's exquisite silver artisans, cloth and mat weavers, and batik makers are renowned throughout the country. And where else but on the East Coast can you see farmers competing in top-spinning and kite-flying, as well as watch 750-kilogram (1,650-lb) sea turtles lay their eggs on the same stretch of beach that has been unchanged over numerous centuries?

Peaceful, timeless fishing villages, palms bending out over a blue sea, colourfully painted fishing boats pulled up on the shore waiting for the tide to carry them to their fishing grounds, islands floating upon an unattainable horizon – these are the scenes on the quieter side of the Malay peninsula.

Oily operations: The East Coast is still unsophisticated in the most natural sense of the word, although the modern world is beginning to intrude. Offshore oil installations in the South China Sea off Terengganu have converted the state from one of the poorest in the federation into one of the richest. Over the last few years, Kuala Terengganu has transformed from a place ignored by time into a rapidly expanding modern city, while farther down the coast huge new oil refineries and depots, modern bungalows and houses are springing up where palm trees had waved in golden solitude over deserted beaches.

Malaysia's East Coast embraces the states of Kelantan, Terengganu and Pahang and the eastern half of Johor. Kelantan and Terengganu are two Malay states which have retained much of their traditional character, cut off as they are by the jungle-clad peaks of the Main Range from the rest of the peninsula. Until the end of the 19th century, these two states were the most heavily populated in the peninsula and their inhabitants remain predominantly Malay today. The practices of Islam in these two states, however, have changed very little despite the country's economic success and modernization.

Annalistic rubdown: Kelantan has a long story of independent existence going back to the dawn of history. Important traces of New Stone Age people have been found at various places in the state, which emerged as an important kingdom in the days of the Malaccan sultanate and was ruled by the legendary

beauty, Puteri Sa'adong, in the 17th century. In more modern times Kelantan was under the shadow of Thailand, and Thai influence did not come to an end until a treaty, signed in 1909 between the Thais and the British, placed Kelantan under British protection. However, Thai influence can still be seen in the Kelantan architecture, dialect and art forms of today.

The sultans of Terengganu are direct descendants of the Johor and Malacca royal families, and the state itself was once a fief of Malacca and then Johor before it came under Thai suzerainty. Although it sent "golden flowers" to Bangkok as a token of tribute, Terengganu was largely left to its own devices until 1909, when it was transferred along with Kelantan to British overlordship.

Pahang's past does not differ much from its northern neighbouring states. It was part of the kingdom of Malacca and later came under the control of Johor. Its rulers, called the *bendahara*, maintained a precarious independence for centuries; as late as the 1880s, one of them finally shook off the Johor connection and converted his state into a sultanate. But the new sultan was not able to enjoy his new status for long before the British took over.

Until this century, the East Coast states possessed no roads. Travel along the coast was by boat, and inland transportation was made on rivers or jungle tracks. During the monsoon season from November to January, the states were entirely cut off from the rest of the world as the northwest monsoon flooded the countryside and closed the beaches. Even today the monsoon season is not the time to visit the East Coast.

The East Coast is a place to explore. Do not hesitate to travel off the beaten track to a small fishing village. A friendly gesture will be the return of a smile, or perhaps an invitation to tour the village where the soothing rhythms of Malay life have endured for centuries. Only then, does one really come to know the soul of Malaysia.

River mouths of Pahang: Numerous rivers spill their bubbling waters into the

On the way to school.

sea along the coast of the state of Pahang. Coming from Johor, the state boundary is marked by the **Endau River**, which curls its way into Orang Asli country. Only a few kilometres northwards are several more rivers: the **Anak Endau** (child of the Endau), the **Pontian River** opening out into the sea at Kuala Pontian, and the end of the **Rompin River** at Kuala Rompin. Nearby is a comfortable government resthouse. In the town of **Kuala Rompin**, you can rent a four-wheel-drive vehicle and drive inland to **Iban** (10 kilometres/6 mi) and **Kampung Aur** (25 kilometres/15 mi), where you will find Orang Asli settlements of the Jakun tribes.

Other interesting rivers moving northwards include the **Merchong** and **Bebar**. There are no roads here: you must rent a boat if you wish to explore further.

Islam, royalty and polo: At the southern end of the Pahang River is a pleasant town called **Pekan**. The river is gentle and sylvan at this point, and with its tidy little houseboats reminds one of the Thames at Henley. Pekan was the former capital of Pahang and is still a royal town, being the residence of the sultan. It is a small and unremarkable town, but on the way to the **Istana Abu Bakar** (Abu Bakar Palace), visitors pass a mausoleum and two handsome, white-marble mosques with a riot of golden domes. One of the mosques is newly built and attests to the vitality of Islam in this part of the country – as well as to the population boom. The sultan's palace, further on, has an enormous polo ground which, when not in use for that sport, provides what must be the flattest golf course in the world.

The town houses the **State Museum** of Pahang, which displays many items of historical interest; the most recent acquisitions are the treasures recovered from a Chinese junk lying at the bottom of the South China Sea. Pekan also boasts a silk-weaving centre, situated at **Kampung Pulau Keladi**, 5 kilometres (3 mi) from Pekan.

Forty-four kilometres (27 mi) north of Pekan is **Kuantan**, the capital of Pahang and its commercial centre. There

is not much here to detain the visitor except for the handsome stadium, a pleasant children's playground alongside the Kuantan River, or the 1-kilometre-long (0.5-mi) river esplanade where there are some good eating stalls. Several shops sell regional handicrafts along Jalan Besar. However, there is a great deal to see and do around Kuantan.

Accommodation is available in Kuantan, but most visitors will prefer to stay at the beach. Drive through town for 3 kilometres (2 mi) and reach a crossroad where, at the corner, is a small villa belonging to the sultan. Drive straight on for 1 kilometre (0.5 mi) to reach **Teluk Chempedak Beach**, once pleasant but now rather overcrowded with hotels and tourist development. Here are the deluxe Hyatt and Merlin hotels, as well as a good selection of cheaper accommodation.

The local tourist office will make arrangements – although it may take two or three days – for performances of *silat* and wayang kulit, as well as the local dances – *olek mayang* and *rodat*.

The latter is a traditional fishermen's dance in which hand movements feature prominently. Olek mayang is a remarkable trance dance in which one of the villagers clutches a bunch of betel nut flowers and is lulled into a trance by his fellow dancers chanting a song, inviting the spirits of seven princesses to cast a spell upon the dancer. This forces him to dance the steps and movements of their choice. At the conclusion of the chanting, the dancer collapses, and so tightly does he clutch his bouquet that it takes several men to pull it from him.

Naturally, the best time to see these happenings is during a festival. The alternative is to have the tourist bureau hire an entire village to stage a festival. The charges are moderate if divided among several patrons.

Kuantan and its surroundings are noted for authentic craftsmanship – wood carving, brocade, batik and weaving. Places where handicrafts are made or the arts performed are marked by a board with green, yellow and red circles and a ten-point red star. However, most

The Hyatt Kuantan.

218

of the signs are dilapidated and should not be taken too seriously. The **Brocade Weaving Centre** at Selamat village (part of Kuantan town), where silk sarong are handwoven with intricate designs in gold and silver, and where one of the block printing shops on Jalan Selamat still use primitive methods in preparing designs, can readily be visited. There is also a **Batik Centre** at Beserah, a pretty little fishing village just north of Kuantan. Kite-flying and top-spinning can also be seen here.

Lake monsters and crocodiles: Some excellent side trips can be made from Kuantan. One unusual journey is to **Lake Chini**, actually a conglomerate of 12 connecting lakes. The lake is large and, from June to September, is covered by a brilliant carpet of red and white lotuses, which contrast sharply with the surrounding green hills.

The Jakun tribes live along the shores of this lake. The Jakun use blowpipes to catch monkeys and other jungle animals; to supplement their diet, they collect lotus seeds when the flowers on the lake wilt. When ripe, the cream-coloured seeds, slightly smaller than quails' eggs, taste distinctly nutty and are a good source of protein.

The Jakun people have long lived by this lake, and their narrative traditions are alive with the legends abounding in the area. Of the origin of the lake, the headman will relate the experiences of his ancestors, who while clearing a section of forest one day, met an old woman with a stick. She claimed that the area was hers, and to make her point clear, stuck her stick firmly into the ground there before vanishing.

Hunters, distracted by a barking dog and running to where the dog was, found a large black log. Overcome with curiosity, one man plunged his spear into it. Others followed suit and blood began to spurt out of the log, the sky grew dark, and thunder and lightning added to their panic. In the pandemonium that followed, the old woman's stick was uprooted and from the hole, water poured forth, flooding the whole area and thus creating Lake Chini.

Kite flying.

Other tales tell of *naga* – dragons or monsters – living in the lake. Two of these mythical creatures are said to have become the islands of Tioman and Daik. British officials, possibly recalling the famous Loch Ness Monster, claimed many years ago to have seen mysterious beasts swimming in the lake. Crocodiles have certainly been spotted here, and on the shores of the lake lived an old woman who was legendary for her friendship with these reptiles. It is said that she saved them from being hunted and they saved her from being drowned, by pushing her to the shore with their noses. Living to over a hundred years old, her memory may have been a little confused about events, but she remembered her friends with fondness.

Another tale tells of a lost city beneath Chini's waters, and archaeological examination of the site has proved that there are remains of civilisation to be found 12 metres (40 ft) below the lake's surface, possibly the ruins of a Khmer settlement, verified by historical descriptions of one in the vicinity.

Tasik Chini lies on a rough road off the Kuantan to Segamat road. There you can hire a boatman and a guide for a tour which takes you down the Pahang River and out into the lake. The entire trip can be done in one day, but if you wish to linger in this myth-filled place, there are camping grounds and chalets.

Cliffs, caves and caverns: Another interesting side trip is northwest along the road to **Sungai Lembing**. Near the 24-kilometre mark, a turn to the right leads through dusky rubber estates and lush green oil-palm plantations until suddenly, without warning, travellers find themselves under the lee of a towering limestone cliff, known as the Charah Caves. At its foot are a couple of small shops, and when you look upwards there seems to be no top. Far above are a ledge and a railing, and right in front is a steep and rickety stairway. You are at the foot of **Gua Panching**.

Until about 25 years ago, the fact that this huge limestone outcrop contains great deep caverns was unknown, except to a few locals. Then a Thai Buddhist

Mat weaver.

220

monk chanced by and made the caves his home. In the deepest of them, he laboriously built a massive reclining Buddha, carrying the building material up the rugged rock face by himself with the aid of a handful of acolytes. He devoted the rest of his life to this project, and by the time he died a few years ago, the task of devotion was completed.

The climb up to the ledge is taxing, the view exhilarating. The path leads up further into the main cave. A guide will take you through the entrance and into its recesses to the innermost cavern where the Buddha lies. The path which leads downward is slippery and it takes a while for your eyes to adjust to the darkness. Suddenly the guide stops and points upward. Unbelievable! What you see is not a cave but a cathedral. Thin shafts of light filter down through cracks hundreds of metres above. In the half-light distances are deceptive. Bats flutter away. The guide starts a generator for lights and leads you to a second cave, almost as big as the first. Here is the work of a lifetime, a giant statue of the sleeping Buddha, measuring 9 metres (30 ft) long. There are more caves, and more exploring to do. If you wish to venture deeper, arrangements can be made with the guide.

If you continue driving on the same road to Sungai Lembing, and if you have made prior arrangements with the manager of Pahang Consolidated Ltd, you can tour the world's second-largest and deepest tin mine. Tin mines, however, can be dangerous and most supervisors are hesitant about allowing visitors on the premises and will certainly not allow them underground. Travellers must obtain special permission in advance before they are allowed a close-up view of one of West Malaysia's most valuable exports.

About 16 kilometres (10 mi) away inland from Sungai Lembing is the **Gunung Tapis** mountain and nature park. A conservation area, the park offers exciting activities such as shooting rapids in nearby rivers, fishing for the delicious *ikan kelah*, going on wildlife walks, or simply bathing in the various

Rural bus station.

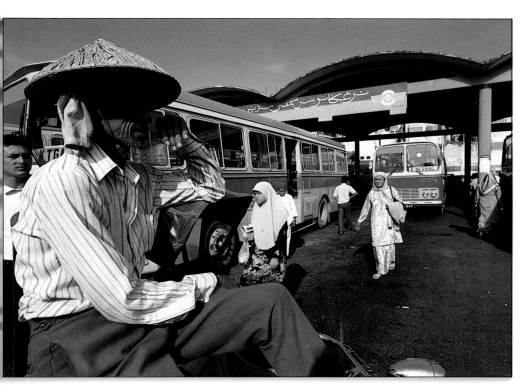

hot springs scattered around the park. Arrangements to visit and stay in the park can be made at the tourist information centre in Kuantan, or through the local outwardbound society.

Chalets by the coast: Moving northwards out of Kuantan, the road follows the coast. Chalets are scattered on these delightful palm-fringed beaches, beginning at the 15-kilometre marker and continuing into the state of Terengganu. At the 45-kilometre marker you will arrive at the friendly and relaxed village of **Cherating**. If you haven't tried staying in simple beach accommodation in Malaysia yet, this is definitely the best place to start.

Nowhere could be more relaxed than the homely Coconut Inn, with its meticulously clean huts and chalets. The beach is close by, and the huts and chalets are cooled by coconut palms. In the evenings, the kitchen will cook you a slap-up dinner on the barbecue, while travellers sit waiting at the tables, exchanging travel news. The inn will also arrange river trips for you, or a tour taking you to **Pulau Ular**, a small island 1 kilometre (0.5 mi) offshore, which is an ideal place for a day trip and picnic.

At the other end of the accommodation scale is Asia's first Club Med, situated between Kemaman (called Chukai on the road signs) and Cherating village. The club only caters for members but membership can be immediate. Viewed from the sea, the club appears to be walled off from the outside world, and within are the reddish brown buildings with their peaked roofs, surrounded by olive casuarina trees. Excellent French and local food, free wine with lunch and dinner, as well as the usual fun and games are all part of this exclusive and somewhat expensive establishment. Because of its emphasis on outdoor activities, the club closes during the monsoon.

Further along the road to Kemaman is **Chendor Beach**, where sea turtles come to lay their eggs at night from May through September. These turtles are a smaller species than their protected Terengganu cousins.

Kelantan fishing boats.

Oil country: Crossing the border into Terengganu, the coast highway continues north through the heart of Malaysia's oil country. You can't see the wells because they are located offshore in the South China Sea, but there is plenty of oil-related activity along the shore. **Kemaman** (also called Chukai) is a supply base for offshore platforms, and **Kerteh** is a major refining centre with huge silver tanks and flame-spouting gasworks. Despite the industry, there are some pretty beaches to be found on either side of Kerteh, especially the deserted strand on the north side of the **Kerteh River** mouth.

There is very little traffic along this stretch of coast. Waves break along the empty beaches. Inland are rice fields, where imaginative farmers have animated the landscape with lifelike scarecrows, some dressed in regal splendour. At **Kampung Paka**, the road crosses a bridge with a striking view of a fishing village nestled along the lower reaches of the Paka River. The road turns inland, skirting a jungle-covered mountain.

Kuala Dungun, a dreamy little seaside town and port, was once an outlet for the state's great ore-mining industry at Bukit Besi. Most of the mines have closed down, and once again the town has reverted to its ancient trade of fishing. From here, you can get boats out to **Pulau Tenggol**, 29 kilometres (18 mi) offshore. Thirteen kilometres (8 mi) north of Dungun is the government-run Tanjung Jara Beach Hotel, especially attractive for its traditional Malay style of construction, which uses only timber. Most appealing are the spacious rooms on the second floor with their wide verandahs facing the sea. For the energetic, cycling, tennis, squash and water sports are offered.

From Tanjong Jara, the road follows the sea along a 65-kilometre (40-mi) stretch of exquisite shoreline. It is dotted with houses and willow casuarina trees, which the Malays say grow only near the sound of the surf. During good weather the houses are on the east side of the road near the beach, since the folk are fishermen. However, during the

Tanjung Jara Beach.

monsoon season the fishermen carry their houses further inland. Pulled high up the beach are the elegantly designed *prahu*, many of which still display bows called *bangau*, elaborately carved in the shape of mythical birds or demons, forming an art in their own right. Fishing nets hang to dry on trees. Swimming is excellent and you can stop almost anywhere along the road to take a dip.

Turtle watching: A popular entertainment on the East Coast is turtle watching. On a stretch of beach 35 kilometres (22 mi) north of Kuantan, all seven known species of turtles struggle ashore, lay their eggs in the sand and then depart, never to see their young. If the eggs survive the attacks of predators, they will hatch after six to eight weeks, depending on the species.

There can be no doubt that the star of this attraction is the giant leatherback turtle and, like any great performer – it may be the largest reptile in the world – it is determined not to be upstaged. Although on occasion they do put in an appearance at Chendor Beach, leatherbacks are best seen at a turtle-watching area called **Rantau Abang**, 160 kilometres (100 mi) north of Kuantan and 55 kilometres (35 mi) south of Kuala Terengganu. Here, you can witness the miraculous spectacle of the arrival of the giant leatherback turtles coming ashore. Once a year, they lay their eggs at the very same beach where they themselves were born, and to which their offspring will return when they are fully mature and laden with eggs. Seldom do other species use Rantau Abang for their accouchement. There is a visitors centre at Rantau Abang, where you can rent self-contained wooden chalets and visit the turtle museum.

The leatherback grows to a length of 2.5 metres (8 ft) and may weigh up to 750 kilograms (1,650 lbs). Like the other species, it lays eggs from May through September, the last two weeks of August being the peak of the laying season. During these months, visitors come from the world over to await the turtles. The best time to see them is at night, especially at high tide. All that is needed is a **Lobster fisherman.**

light and patience. Industrious village folk at Rantau Abang have built shelters along the beach in which travellers can pass the night dozing on a simple bed or drinking coffee. Youngsters with lamps scan the sands and at the first sighting of a turtle, they give the signal.

The subject of turtle watching is controversial. Observers are often appalled by the way local people gather up the eggs, ride on the backs of the turtles, flash lights in their eyes and even molest them. It might appear that the magnificent leatherbacks are on the road to extinction, since turtle eggs bring good prices at the marketplace. However, a short walk down the beach during daylight would prove otherwise. Here, members of the Department of Fisheries keep close tabs on turtles and record their habits and migrations across the seas. Even more important is their systematic collection of eggs.

A great leatherback usually lays about a hundred eggs in a large hole it digs in the sand with its rear flippers. Threats to eggs come not so much from people as from certain predators, such as crabs and various insects. Even more critical is the period after the eggs are hatched, when young turtles must make their way to the sea, usually across several hundred metres of open, hostile beach. Many fall prey to the flocks of birds circling overhead. When the young turtles hatch, they crawl to the surface. Each morning before dawn inspectors collect and release them in the sea. Only after about 40,000 young have returned to the sea each year are people allowed to collect the eggs.

Leatherbacks have been sighted in waters as far from Malaysia as the Atlantic Ocean, yet the huge turtles return to lay their eggs only on this one stretch of beach. To watch their laborious and brief sojourn on land is reason enough to visit the East Coast. In spite of local efforts to protect the turtles, their numbers are fast diminishing, and fewer and fewer of them return. Alarmed scientists are at work to determine the cause of this, and sea pollution and the changing of sea currents are two reasons cited.

Turtle watching, and mending the fish nets.

River mouths and islands: The picturesque fishing village of **Marang** lies just south of Kuala Terengganu and is well worth a visit, if only to hire boats from there to the islands of **Pulau Kapas** and **Pulau Raja**. Both are a delight for coral lovers and sun worshippers. The Beach House in Marang has seafront chalets and boats which can zip you out to Kapas in 45 minutes. Pulau Raja is about the same distance, and you can either hire your own boat or take the one from the Beach House. Pulau Raja has been designated a marine park because of its beautiful waters alive with multicoloured corals and fish.

Setting its own pace: Over the last four or five years, **Kuala Terengganu** has developed from a timeless fishing port and a marketplace of yesteryear into a bustling modern town that owes its growing affluence to Terengganu's offshore oil. But enough of the old charms remain to set it apart from the contemporary worries of an urban town. Terengganu (and its neighbouring state Kelantan) is also set apart from other states by its weekends, which occur, not on Saturday and Sunday, but on Thursday (half-day) and Friday.

The pulse of Kuala Terengganu is felt in the **Central Market** alongside the river in the early morning, when fishermen bring in their catch. They come directly to the market with their boats and soon the scene is alive with heated haggling over prices. The market is a modern concrete building, with fresh food stalls downstairs in the courtyard and numerous general merchandise shops on the first floor.

This early morning hustle and bustle spills out into the neighbouring streets; in **Jalan Sultan Ismail**, batik and handicraft stores open their doors early to Malay housewife and tourist alike. The activity spreads to **Kampung Dalam Kota**, a place whose name means Village Inside the City, and that is just exactly what it is.

Just beyond the market in the direction of the river mouth is a broad esplanade which faces the **Istana Maziah**, the official residence of the Sultan of

Harbour at Marang.

Terengganu, who actually lives in another palace a few miles away. The Istana resembles a French country house and was built at the beginning of the century to replace an older palace destroyed by fire some years before. The Istana is located at the foot of a small hill called Bukit Puteri, or literally, The Hill of the Princess. Behind the Istana is the new **Zainal Abidin Mosque**, built on the site of a much older mosque constructed in wood during the reign of Sultan Zainal Abidin.

The road from the market runs on into what was, until only recently, Kuala Terengganu's main thoroughfare, **Jalan Bandar** (Main Street), a narrow and congested crescent-shaped street lined with Chinese shophouses. The architecture here dates back several generations to when Terengganu was still an independent sultanate. Stroll down this street (or take a trishaw, still the most popular means of transport in downtown Kuala Terengganu) and peek into the narrow doorways: the houses seem to stretch back forever, through dark rooms, and at the back Granny can be seen sipping tea. Better shopping, however, can be found in the modern premises beyond Jalan Bandar.

The small jetty at the end of Jalan Bandar is the place to hire a boat to cruise along the island-studded estuary of the Terengganu River and get a close look at typical Malay villages by the shore. **Pulau Duyung**, the largest of the islands, is immediately opposite the jetty and is renowned as a shipbuilding centre. Once upon a time, its master craftsmen were responsible for building the unique junks with fore- and main-masts, and bowsprits called *bedor*. These fine boats were used to fish off Terengganu's shores. Today, only a couple of shipyards survive by building yachts for Australian, American and other foreign boating enthusiasts, who know that a Terengganu shipbuilder is without peer in the region. Fishing further up-river is excellent and 10-kilogram (20-lb) bites are not uncommon.

Fine examples of local artistry and craftsmanship are displayed at the **State**

Pulau Kapas.

Museum, off Jalan Air Jerneh. The museum, tucked away in a couple of rooms in a corner of the State Assembly Building, also houses a wealth of exhibits relevant to Terengganu's past.

On the way to Marang, about 7 kilometres (4 mi) out of town, you will notice a fine Malay house on the right. This is the **Istana Tengku Nik**, a traditional timber house in which the aristocracy of Kelantan and Terengganu once lived. This palace used to stand near the Istana Maziah at the foot of Bukit Puteri and was originally built in the 1880s as a temporary palace for the sultan. It was moved at the expense of a foreign mining company to its present site to make way for an extension to the Istana Maziah, and to save it from destruction. Each wooden panel adorning the Istana has entwining patterns which form Koranic inscriptions.

The **MARA Centre** in town will assist travellers who want to see any of the cottage industries at work. Good buys of batik from the Terengganu area can be found at the centre, which displays many of the state's arts and crafts. Kuala Terengganu offers the usual Chinese town hotels as accommodation as well as the international class hotel, the Primula Beach Resort. Situated close to the town centre, this hotel has fine views of the sea, and full programmes of water sports are available to guests staying at the hotel.

Merang is 28 kilometres (17 mi) north of Kuala Terengganu, the jumping off spot for trips to **Pulau Redang**. The coral reefs at Redang island offer excellent scuba and snorkelling, but there is no accommodation, only camping. Boats can be hired at Merang jetty.

The adventurous traveller may also want to visit the picturesque **Sekayu Waterfall** near Kuala Brang, 56 kilometres (35 mi) west of Terengganu. Getting to the falls entails a 3-kilometre (2-mi) hike from the end of the road at Kampung Ipoh. A refreshing swim is the reward. **Kuala Brang** is famous as the place where a 14th-century Muslim inscription, the oldest in the whole of Malaysia, was found. The stone is now **Sekayu Waterfall.**

preserved in the National Museum in Kuala Lumpur.

Fifteen kilometres (9 mi) west of Kuala Brang is a huge artificial lake called **Tasik Kenyir**, which backs up behind the largest dam in Southeast Asia. There is a new visitor's centre which gives facts and figures on the hydroelectric project: the main dam is 155 metres (500 ft) high and the lake covers an area of 36,900 hectares (91,180 acres). Finished in 1987, the project took 15 years to complete. Boats can be hired at a landing near the dam.

Fishing is said to be good with numerous freshwater species including the carnivorous *toman*. There are 14 waterfalls around the edge of the lake and about 300 tiny islands. The only accommodation (besides houseboats) is the Primula Kenyir Lake Resort, with 50 chalets along the shore.

Though village life in Terengganu and Kelantan has changed, many of the traditional arts it fostered are as lively as ever. Seasonal fishing and farming brought village folk leisure and from leisure came time to devote to their arts. Folk dances, shadow plays and traditional games such as kite-flying and top-spinning were celebrated during festivals after a harvest. Many processions and rituals were related to the spirit of the rice, a carry-over from ancient animistic beliefs. Today, village festivals are rarer occasions, since farmers are busy planting rice twice a year instead of once, and the Islamic doctrine discourages customs connected with spirit worship. Yet the fun-loving Terengganu Malays have not forgotten the good old times and all the song and laughter that went with them. This is a legacy that lives on.

Handicrafts have also flourished in Terengganu; once for sale in the town market and for local use, handicrafts are nowadays also patronised by the tourist trade. At **Kampung Tanjung** almost every house has a loom which engages the time of mother and daughters in weaving the richly coloured cloth known as *kain songket*.

At **Rusila** there is a handicraft centre for visitors to look around, or to wander around the village to watch mat and basket weaving taking place. These are woven from *pandanus* or *nipa* palm leaves, with two or three colours combined. Typical handicrafts include mats, multi-shaped boxes and containers, fans, hats, dish covers, and baskets of all shapes and sizes. Other handicrafts to be found in and around Kuala Terengganu are traditional brasswork and handmade batik.

Remote and unspoiled: From Kuala Terengganu the road runs north for a distance of 170 kilometres (110 mi) to Kota Bharu and soon loses sight of the sea. About midway at Pasir Puteh, a turnoff leads to **Kuala Besut**, a remote and unspoiled fishing village on the coast. Twice daily, at dawn and at dusk, fishing boats make a dramatic show as they arrive from across the sea and unload their catches at the jetty, where some tough bargaining takes place between fishermen and merchants. Visitors go about completely unnoticed, and photographers can snap away without anyone paying attention. For those who

East Coast mosque.

want to stay over, there is a resthouse, situated on the south side of the river. Kuala Besut is also a jumping-off place for the idyllic **Perhentian Islands**, only 20 kilometres (13 mi) offshore.

Weather permitting, fishermen will willingly ferry visitors across to these lovely, unspoiled islands. Perhentian consists of two islands, **Perhentian Kecil** and **Perhentian Besar**.

Although some villagers will take visitors into their homes for a small fee at Pulau Perhentian Kecil, most travellers head for the larger island. The only village is at the smaller island, which you can visit should you wish to buy foodstuffs to do your own cooking. Just grab a boat to take you across the narrow channel. The villagers sometimes have traditional dance and music festivals which you may be invited to watch.

On the large island is the Perhentian Island Resort, situated in an exquisite little bay with amazingly clear waters. Accommodation is in the form of chalets, some on the beach and some half-hidden in the wooded slopes be-

hind. There is also a dormitory. A simple restaurant serves up good local food and western-style breakfasts.

On the bay facing the smaller island are several simple huts and chalets, owned by the villagers from the other island. Life is slow and relaxed here. You can walk over several beaches and, with the help of a guide, penetrate some of the dense jungle that covers the whole island right down to the beaches. A bath involves drawing water from a well; a shower can be had by pouring the contents of the bucket over your head.

Basic cooking facilities are positioned outside each chalet, or you can walk to the next bay and eat at a small cafe, where you can sample some of the day's fresh catch.

During the day, you may be able to stop an old man and his wife, who wander the beaches with their tame monkey, trained to climb up palm trees and bring down young coconuts for visitors to drink their delicious milk. The government resthouse is no longer open to the public, but the choice of

Kota Bharu's Central Market.

230

places to stay is wide enough to suit most tastes. The island, however, is still unspoilt, and it can be hard to leave this South China Sea paradise.

South of the Thai border: The northern-most city on the East Coast is bustling **Kota Bharu**, the capital of Kelantan state and only a few kilometres from the Thai border. It is the residence of the Sultan of Kelantan. Kota Bharu has one of the best-known markets in Malaysia, where in the early morning, fishing folk arrive with their produce from the countryside. The market is also a good shopping place for East Coast crafts, particularly the batik and silverwork for which the state is famous. Intricately designed beach mats are a good bargain and craftsmen can work up your own design in a day or two.

Another early morning pastime is the training of the *merbok*, a jungle bird greatly prized for its sweet song (*burong ketitir*). The merbok enthusiast takes immense pains to train his birds for the dawn competitions. The highlight of the year is the great bird-singing competition held in Kota Bharu in June. Contending merboks are hoisted aloft on 9 metre (30 ft) poles whilst an entourage of judges determines the champion on the basis of loudness, pitch and the melody of its song.

Near the **Central Market** and the taxi rank is a vacant lot, which at night is transformed into a fascinating array of food stalls. The food here is almost exclusively Malay, with a few stalls selling food with Thai overtones. Walk around the stalls and choose your food; then take a table near the drinks stalls, where the servers will provide you with tea, coffee, cold drinks and cutlery. Improvised shows of medicinal wares or magic tricks sometimes spring up here. Music and chatter is all around, and listening to the latter, you will find that the Kelantan Malays have a dialect all of their own, barely comprehensible to Kuala Lumpurans.

Just beyond the market is **Padang Merdeka** (Liberty Square) flanked by a mosque and an old palace. The **State Mosque** exhibits a syncretism of architectural styles and looks, at first glance when approached from certain directions, more like a house of Christian worship than one of Muslim prayer. Few people in Kelantan are not Muslim and even many Chinese have accepted the word of the Prophet.

The old palace, which stands within a large compound, is called **Istana Balai Besar** (Palace with the Large Audience Hall). It was built in 1884 by order of Sultan Mohamed II and has recently been restored. At the first ceremony ever held there, the sultan received a letter from the King of Thailand, recognising him as ruler. The building, which can be viewed with permission, contains the Throne Room, the State Legislative Assembly Hall and the enormous, multi-columned Hall of Audience.

On another side of the square, next to the Istana Balai Besar, stands another smaller palace, the **Istana Jahar**, which has now been converted into the state museum. Though quite small, the museum is well worth a visit, for it gives an introduction to Kelantan's life and culture. Outside the front entrance is a

Communal pounding of grain.

wakaf, one of the wooden platforms with tiled roofs, which not only serve as resting places but also adorn the otherwise plain Kelantan countryside.

Kota Bharu is the centre for Malaysian arts, sports and pastimes, and regular cultural shows are held at **Gelanggang Seni** (Court of Arts) on Jalan Mahmood. Patrons can also arrange festivals from here, or even better, you may chance upon such a festival in Kota Bharu or in its surrounding villages.

Here, in the afternoons and evenings, you can watch a variety of art forms, sports and games. *Wau* or kites of Kelantan float above you in the sky. In a small wakaf or rest hut outside the main hall of the Court of Arts, old men tune up their instruments while drowned by the sound of the *rebana*. These huge drums are fashioned out of logs and require a great deal of energy and enthusiasm to play. On the green, the *gasing* (spinning top) experts are twisting themselves round, ready to spin down their prized tops onto a concrete square. From here, they are removed with a wooden palette onto dowels sheltered by a hut. Hundreds of tops are spinning, and their owners watch anxiously to see how theirs are competing with the others in length of spinning time.

Other arts to be seen here include *wayang kulit* (shadow puppet plays), *kertok* (wooden drums), *silat* (the Malaysian form of self-defence) and *mak yong*, which combines theatre, dance, opera, drama and comedy. The Court of Arts produces a leaflet giving details of the times and locations of its performances. This brochure can be picked up at most major hotels or at the **Tourist Information Centre** on Jalan Sultan Ibrahim.

Ten kilometres (6 mi) south of Kota Bharu, on the road to Kuala Krai, is **Kampung Nilam Puri**, the home of an Islamic college.

Opposite the college is a regular four-square building of timber with a pyramidal two-tiered tiled roof, typical of a Javanese mosque. Known as the **Old Kampung Laut Mosque**, it is reputed to be the oldest surviving mosque

Museum at Istana Jahar.

in Malaysia (although the Malaccans might dispute that). It indeed dates back to the 18th century and is built of stout *chengal* wood.

The mosque used to be located at Kampung Laut River on the banks of the Kelantan River, opposite Kota Bharu, but, threatened by the encroaching river, it was removed to its present site with funds raised by the Malaysian Historical Society.

Intriguing itineraries: Kota Bharu has many other delights to offer. Being the most "Malay" town in the whole of the peninsula, it is a thrill to simply wander along the streets, or to be wheeled around in a hired trishaw. Hunt out an antique shop – there are three or four in town – and get lost amongst traditional Malay games, wonderfully graceful bird traps, handmade Chinese lanterns, wavy Malay daggers, musical instruments, mythical birds, masks and puppets and exotic coins of a bygone age. The prices quoted are outrageous. Or are they? It depends on your purse, your mood and your scale of values.

Kota Bharu is surrounded by a patchwork of little villages set between rice fields and orchards and linked to one another by little roads akin to twisting English country lanes. Explore them and you will come across all sorts of surprises; a Thai *wat* (temple) – for the Thai border is not far away – is one of them, hidden by thick laurels and tall palms back from the road.

Kuala Besar fishing village is another, where you can watch the boats go down to the sea in the cool of the morning and see them return in the afternoon, laden with the catch.

If you are keen to see more of the Thai Buddhist temples, venture off the road to **Tumpat**, Kota Bharu's port. Between Cabang Empat and Kampung Jambu, you will find the **Wat Photivihan**, with a huge reclining Buddha draped in pink robes. Further along this same rural road is another Thai shrine called **Wat Uttamaram**, which is just outside the village of Repek.

The traditional centre of the silversmiths' craft in Kelantan is at **Kampung**

Reclining Buddha, Wat Photivihan.

Sireh (at Jalan Sultanah Zainab). It may be possible to see some of the smiths at work, fashioning a filigree butterfly brooch or an embossed cosmetic case. Designs show both Thai and Indonesian influence, as well as the motif of the Indian lotus blossom. These items are sold throughout Malaysia and also in Singapore.

Kota Bharu also has a 20th-century claim to fame: **Pantai Dasar Sabak**, 13 kilometres (8 mi) north of the town, is a pleasant, wide, casuarina-shaded beach which is popular with the locals. It was here, on 8 December 1941, that the Japanese began their brutal march southward to Singapore. (The attack on Pearl Harbour was not to take place until 95 minutes later, 7 December on the other side of the dateline.)

There are many other beautiful beaches in Kelantan – **Pantai Dalam Rhu** (also known as Pantai Bisikan Bayu, the Beach of the Whispering Breeze) near the fishing village of Semerak, to the south of Kota Bharu; **Pantai Irama** (Beach of Melody), 25 kilometres (16 mi) south of Kota Bharu near Bachok; and **Pantai Kuda** (Horse Beach), 25 kilometres (16 mi) north of the city near Tumpat.

Those who take the time to venture inland will find beautiful waterfalls near **Pasir Puteh**, feeding natural swimming pools in the midst of the tropical jungle. The pools at **Jeram Pasu** are frequented by many local students during the weekend (remember this is Thursday and Friday in Kelantan, as it is in Terengganu, and not Saturday and Sunday) and school holidays. It can be reached by an 8-kilometre (5-mi) hike along a jungle path from Kampung Padang Pak Amat. There are more waterfalls to be found at **Jeram Tapah**, **Jeram Lenang** and **Cherang Tuli**.

Back on the seashore, Kota Bharu's most famous beach, **Pantai Cinta Berahi** – The Beach of Passionate Love – attracts Kota Bharu's citizens at weekends. In spite of the fact that the setting is marvellous, with yellow sands, warm sea and coconut palms, the vision with its romantic name is rather marred by untidy development and litter. And, needless to say, since this is a Muslim country, passionate love is definitely not to be seen here.

On the way to this beach are a number of small *songket* weaving "factories" which are open to the public. These are usually simple rooms with a few girls sitting behind huge looms, turning fine balls of silk and cotton into finished fabric. There are also several handmade batik shops.

Despite its historical contact with the Thais and the Japanese, life in Kota Bharu follows the gentle rhythms of the Malay countryside, with the muezzin's call to prayer from the mosque's minaret from morning to evening.

Kota Bharu is a place of the past, but since the building of the highway between here and Butterworth, it has become a crossroads for travellers and news. Kota Bharu is also the terminus for the eastern railway line, also known as the Jungle Railway. A few kilometres away, across the border in Thailand, begins the line that whisks travellers all the way to Bangkok.

Left, sitting on the dock by the bay. **Right**, Kelantan fishing boat's colourful motif.

SABAH:
BELOW THE WIND

Glittering with those uncertainties on which all rumours thrive, the mysteries of Borneo have long spun a golden thread of intrigue throughout the world. For centuries, no one knew its shape or size, other than that Borneo was a seemingly boundless island. Buckles of "golden jade" adorned the imperial belts of the Son of Heaven, yet none of the audacious Chinese merchants who bartered Sung porcelain for golden jade had ever actually seen the sacred hornbill from which it came. The merchants resigned that privilege to the jungle dwellers, who always disappeared again into sunless forests they knew so well.

At the turn of the century, the world was still mystified. Western outsiders had populated the coasts in scattered settlements, claiming to govern vast tracts of land they had never seen. Impressionable British officials wrote strange stories in which the hero was held captive by head-hunting savages and published them in leading magazines back home. Their tales were half-truths and half-fiction, just as Borneo had always been.

Out of this eerie heritage emerged the state of Sabah in 1963, the year British control ended and north and northwest **Preceding pages: Mount Kinabalu.**

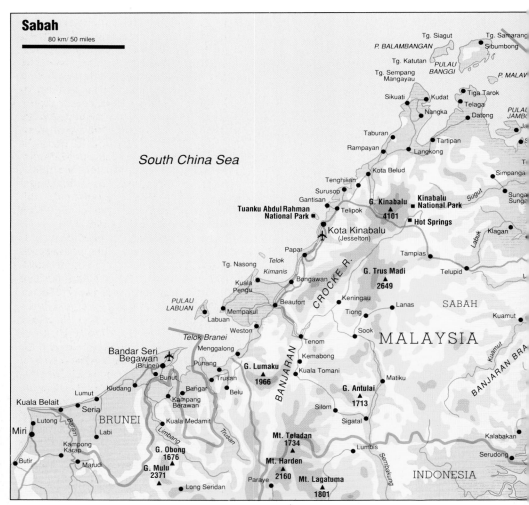

Sabah

80 km/ 50 miles

South China Sea

Tg. Siagut
Tg. Samarang
P. BALAMBANGAN
Sibumbong
Tg. Katutan
PULAU BANGGI
Tg. Sempang Mangayau
P. MALAV
PULAU JAMB(
Sikuati
Kudat
Tiga Tarok
Telaga
Nangka
Datong
Ja
Taburan
Tartipan
Rampayan
Langkong
T
Kota Belud
Simpanga
Tenghilian
Surusop
Sungai
Gantisan
Sugut
Sunga
G. Kinabalu
Kinabalu National Park
Tuanku Abdul Rahman National Park
Telipok
4101
Hot Springs
Labuk
Klagan
Kota Kinabalu (Jesselton)
Papar
Tampias
Telok
Tg. Nasong
Kimanis
Bongawan
G. Trus Madi
Telupid
Kuala Pengu
Beaufort
2649
Keningau
Lanas
SABAH
PULAU LABUAN
Tiong
Kuamut
Mempakul
Labuan
Weston
Sook
MALAYSIA
Telok Branei
Menggalong
Tenom
Bandar Seri Begawan
Kemabong
(Brunei)
Puhang
G. Lumaku
Kuala Tomani
BANJARAN BRA
Bunut
Trusan
1966
Matiku
Kludang
Bangar
Belu
G. Antulai
Lumut
Kampang Berawan
1713
Kuala Belait
Seria
Kuala Medamit
Silom
Sigatal
Miri
Lutong
BRUNEI
Labi
Kalabakan
Kampong Karap
G. Obong
Lumbis
Serudong
Butir
1676
Mt. Teladan
Marudi
1734
G. Mulu
Mt. Harden
INDONESIA
2371
Paraye
2160
Mt. Lagatuma
Long Seridan
1801
CROCKER R.
BANJARAN
Kuamut
Sembakung
Trusan
Limbang
Belait
Baram

Borneo became part of the Federation of Malaysia. Sabah covers the northern tip of the world's third-largest island. The state of Sarawak lies to the south. Together they bridge 1,000 kilometres (600 mi) of sea to join the Malay peninsula as a nation. Though Sabah and Sarawak occupy only the north and northwest coast of Borneo, together they are larger than peninsular Malaysia and, on an island with footprints dating from the Ice Age, their nationhood is newer.

Kota Kinabalu, the state capital on the northwest coast, is changing rapidly from stilt villages perched over the sea and a sprawl of 1950s shophouses, into an increasingly modern city.

Ever since it was chosen as the site for the British North Borneo's west coast base, the town has continued to encroach on the sea. Reclamation was the answer to the shortage of flat land, a process that continues today for the construction of modern shopping complexes. Even the "new" coastal highway is being pushed inland by the reclamation of a huge area of shallow sea.

Although many areas outside the city still require a 4-wheel-drive vehicle, the trunk road linking Kota Kinabalu with the east coast was finally paved in 1993.

The native people of Sabah have ancestors who practised the most diverse trades. The Kadazans were farmers, the Muruts were blowpipe hunters, the Bajaus were sea gypsies and the Illanuns were freebooters. Sabah's Brunei Malays belonged to a sultanate that once ruled all Borneo and then sold most of it piecemeal to ambitious and adventurous Europeans. The Chinese people have ancestors who sailed to Borneo before the days of Kublai Khan in quest of kingfisher feathers and bezoar stones (stones with supposed medicinal value extracted from the stomachs of monkeys). Now the offspring of these diverse peoples are citizens of Malaysia. In daily life, they toil the rice fields, build the roads, man the factories and control the trade – timber, palm oil, copra, prawns and cocoa – on which Sabah's economy depends.

To visitors, Sabah's people are congenial, informal and polite, treating each foreigner both as stranger and guest. When requested, they seldom hesitate to help a traveller by giving directions, advising one on where to stay, and sometimes even booking a room if they have access to a telephone. The word "tourist" has not yet become ingrained to the point where locals wear a dollar sign on their lapels. This is not to say Sabah is inexpensive – in fact, hotels are quite the opposite. Most merchandise is imported and prices are higher than elsewhere in Malaysia. The range of accommodation varies from five-star luxury hotels to moderately-priced Chinese establishments. Government resthouses, once a bargain, are now priced far higher than their standard justifies.

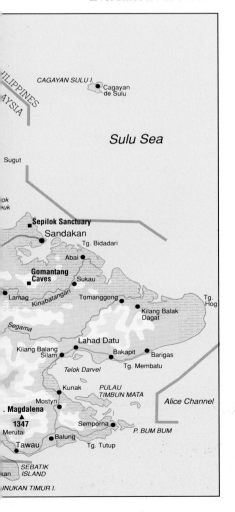

Sabah's small tourist trade works on a personal level. Exploring Sabah with a flexible itinerary leaves visitors open to unexpected "tips for travellers" that local people may volunteer in a coffee shop, a mountain retreat, a riverboat or a hotel lobby. They can take you to the glorious isolated beaches and Rungus longhouses of Kudat district, or to Suluk fishing villages on stilts over the sea at Semporna, where exquisite islands are scattered in all directions. They can lead to the virgin jungle of Danum Valley, or up the lazy Kinabatangan River past Orang Sungei villages to the haunts of the bizarre proboscis monkey. Or they go deep into the interior to the heart of Murut country, where the men still hunt with dogs, a gun now replacing the traditional blowpipe.

Where the eye lingers: The capital of Sabah, **Kota Kinabalu**, is a sprawling, relaxed town on the west coast of the state, affording a splendid view of beautiful sunsets over the offshore islands. The fiery sunsets reflect Kota Kinabalu's history, for although the state capital is now a peaceful and easy-going place, the first settlement established on nearby Pulau Gaya was burned to the ground by a local rebel, Mat Salleh. The old name for the location of Kota Kinabalu is Api Api (literally, fire), although this does not commemorate bygone arson but the name of a local mangrove tree in which the fireflies twinkle at night.

When the British Chartered Company arrived in Borneo, they settled on Gaya Island in the bay of the present city, following a British colonial penchant for offshore island bases. But Mat Salleh attacked and destroyed the settlement in 1897. Moving to the mainland, the Chartered Company then set up Jesselton, named after the company's vice-chairman, Sir Charles Jessel, and so it remained until 1968, when with independence came a new Malay consciousness. For a short time, the town was called Singgah Mata (Where the Eye Lingers) before becoming Kota Kinabalu, in honour of the great mountain whose craggy peaks give a magnificent backdrop to the city in the early

Sidewalk on stilts in Kampung Ayer.

morning and towards sunset. As a trading post, Jesselton grew to be important enough to be bombed to ruins in 1945, in order to prevent the Japanese from setting up a base in this strategic position. Over the following decade, Kota Kinabalu grew into a gentle, unimposing town, occupied with covering up the scars of World War II. Within the past decade, the town has mushroomed with some of the most striking buildings in all Malaysia, as befits the capital of one of the fastest growing states.

Amongst the most impressive of these buildings, to the north of the city at the end of Likas Bay, is the gleaming tower of the **Sabah Foundation**, an institution created out of the timber royalties of the state. Being one of the few "hanging" structures in the world, this 72-sided polygon rises up some 30 storeys.

The monumental **State Mosque** is also worth a visit to see its fine contemporary Islamic architecture. Nearby is the new **State Museum**, built in the longhouse style of the Rungus and Murut tribes. Along the length of the roof,

white concrete structures point upwards like modernistic hands held together in prayer. The museum has a wealth of historical and tribal treasures, as well as a good section on Sabah's fascinating flora and fauna. The complex also has a **science centre** with a large exhibition on the oil and petroleum industry, and an **art gallery**. One of the museum's most striking exhibits is a collection of life-sized traditional houses of six different ethnic groups. A restaurant, coffee house, ethno-botanical garden with an artificial lake and a souvenir shop complete the complex.

The town itself is a blend of ultramodern structures and old Chinese shophouses, with a water village called **Kampung Ayer** along the seafront. The bustling **Central Market** sits midway along the waterfront, best seen early in the morning as fishermen unload their catch directly onto market tables and Kadazan women display their fresh fruit and vegetables, brought down from the hills surrounding Mount Kinabalu.

At the other end of the day, Kota

Market day.

Kinabalu's restaurants come alive, and some of the best food in the state is served in small coffee shops dotted around the town. As with towns in peninsular Malaysia, night markets are ever present, selling clothes and curios, as well as local culinary delicacies. On Sunday mornings, there is the very popular **Jalan Gaya Fair**, where bargains in local handicrafts can be found.

For a good idea of what Kota Kinabalu looks like as a whole, visitors can climb **Signal Hill**, situated at the eastern end of the city, by car or tour bus. South of town, off the airport road, is the famous **Tanjung Aru** beach. The sea here is clear, the sand is clean and the coastal food stalls and restaurants offer delicious local seafood. The huge orange-roofed complex at the tip of the cape is the posh Tanjung Aru Beach Resort.

Offshore from Kota Kinabalu, surrounded by azure waters, are the five islands of **Tunku Abdul Rahman National Park**, one of the most picturesque marine reserves in Southeast Asia. The park headquarters is on **Pulau Gaya**,

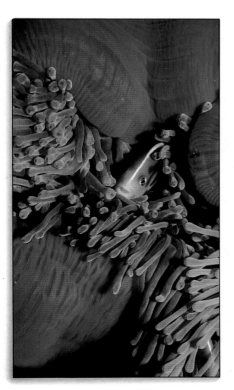

the largest and most historically significant of the islands. The British North Borneo Company established a settlement here in 1882; the post was burnt to the ground by Mat Salleh and his rebels in 1897. All the islands except Sulug have nature trails. Wildlife can be spotted on occasion: look for the macaque monkeys foraging for crabs along the beach, the *pangolin* (scaly anteaters) and the strange bearded pig. Pied hornbills, sea eagles and megapode birds can also be seen on Pulau Gaya.

The other islands that make up the park are **Manukan, Mamutik, Sapi** and **Sulug**. Snorkelling is good on all of these, especially on remote Sulug. Pulau Munukan, the most developed of the islands, has chalets, a restaurant and swimming pool; there is a resthouse on Pulau Mamutik. You can camp on any of the islands if you bring your own equipment and obtain a permit from the Sabah Parks office in town. Advance bookings for Pulau Manukan must also be made here. Boats can be chartered from the waterfront and several small jetties in front of the Hyatt Hotel.

Highest mountain: Everyone in Malaysia knows about the mysterious **Mount Kinabalu**, Southeast Asia's highest peak at 4,101 metres (13,454ft). The closer that one journeys towards its famous jagged profile, which is often wreathed in feathery clouds, the better one understands the meaning the mount has for the local Kadazan and Dusun people: *Aki Nabalu,* or Revered Place of the Dead. On the forbidding peaks were said to be the spirits of the tribe's dead ancestors, and no one dared climb to the top to disturb them.

Another origin given to the name seems less likely, and is probably more recent. Kinabalu was thought to mean Chinese Widow, *kina* being a corruption of China, and *balu* a dialectical word for widow. The story goes that a Chinese prince came to Kinabalu in search of a giant pink pearl guarded by a ferocious dragon. He married a local Dusun woman, but finding himself homesick for his native land, deserted her and left for China. For the rest of her life, the unhappy widow wandered aim- **Underwater hideout.**

lessly on the mountain until she turned into a stone. You will see her if you climb to the peak.

In spite of the taboos and myths surrounding the mountain, Hugh Low, a young British officer, was still keen to reach the top. Climbing Mount Kinabalu in 1851, Low was accompanied by a local chief and his guides. Struggling through the intense tangle of vegetation, which covers the lower slopes of the mountain, Low eventually reached the summit plateau, but owing to a faulty barometer, was unable to locate the true summit. He made a second unsuccessful attempt in 1858. The honour of reaching the small peak of the summit went to naturalist John Whitehead, who named it Low's Peak after the earlier climber.

The mountain is said to be growing still at half a centimetre a year. Relatively young, its jagged crown was sculpted by the last ice age, about 9,000 years ago. Although Kinabalu's peak is below the snow line, it grows cold enough here in August for ice to form in the rock pool at the base of the summit,

and snowflakes sometimes fall. Dropping away 1,800 metres (5,900 ft) straight downwards is the terrifying **Low's Gully**, its name being a typical piece of British understatement.

To get to the top, one does not have to spend days cutting through tropical rain forest before reaching the granite slopes, unlike Low's first ascent. Well-laid trails with steps and rails made of wood help today's climber ascend and descend the mountain in just two days.

Accommodation is available both at the park headquarters and on the mountain slopes. The latter are mostly basic huts with sleeping bags for hire and cooking facilities, with the exception of Laban Rata, which has a restaurant and centrally-heated rooms. At the headquarters, accommodation ranges from hotel to chalet to dormitory-style sleeping. There are also two restaurants, and a shop selling basic food supplies for climbers. In the main administration building, there is an exhibit on mountain flora and fauna; in the basement is a film about the park.

Granite slabs are much in evidence near the peak.

The easiest way to reach Kinabalu Park from Kota Kinabalu is by mini-bus, leaving frequently from 7am onwards from near the town Padang. The trip takes a little under 2 hours and the driver will turn off the main road to drop travellers at the park entrance. A large bus leaves for Ranau at 8am daily, but is slower and drops passengers off about 50 metres from the entrance of the park. It is also possible to book a package tour through any tour operator.

Before leaving the city you should book accommodation at the **Sabah Parks Office**. Also stock up on food if you want to do your own cooking, as the shop at headquarters is limited mainly to noodles and chocolate. Other useful equipment includes a hat and gloves, as it can be extremely cold on the summit, and some kind of waterproof garment to protect from the frequent rainfall. If possible, leave most luggage at a hotel and take a light pack only, or use the luggage storage area at the headquarters. The air is thinner up on the mountain, and even the lightest pack can feel

heavy after a while. A torch is also useful for the final ascent, which starts long before dawn.

On the way to Kinabalu Park, you will pass through **Tamparuli**, 50 kilo-metres (30 mi) north of Kota Kinabalu. Less than a kilometre past this town, say goodbye to the level ground as the road begins to ascend the foothills. Although the landscape is often swathed in cloud, the mountain can't be far away because ears begin to pop.

On arrival at the reception, park rang-ers will confirm bookings, including the huts on the mountain. Maps, books, souvenirs and films are available at the souvenir store. You might choose not to climb the same day you arrive, so make yourself comfortable in your accommo-dation, acclimatise to the cool air, check out the exhibition centre with displays on the park and the mountain, and ex-plore the fascinating **Mountain Gar-den** near the administration building.

Although Kinabalu is one of the easi-est mountains to climb, it is foolish to hop straight from the office and onto a

Looking down at the world from Low's Peak.

plane, and then run up the trail. Some regular exercise is recommended before climbing, so that you don't come off the mountain a wreck of cramps, headaches and fatigue.

Just before the trail begins, there is a rather forbidding notice placed by the park authorities, listing ailments not recommended for those intending to climb the mountain: hypertension, diabetes, obesity, chronic asthma, heart disease, arthritis, anaemia, ulcers, hepatitis, muscular cramps and epilepsy.

Climbing 1,500 metres (4,950 ft) in one day – from the power station above the headquarters to Panar Laban hut – does take inordinate reserves of strength and zest for those who lead a sedentary life. Although experienced and intrepid climbers have climbed the mountain in a day, most people have an interest not just in getting to the top, but in fully experiencing the views, and the area's flora and fauna.

Attached to the headquarters, but not directly employed by them, are a team of local guides, who for a fee will accompany visitors up the mountain. If interested in the mountain flora, you should be sure that your guide is knowledgeable and also speaks passable English (which is not often the case).

One of the personalities of Kinabalu is Awok, a Dusun woman barely 1.5 metres (5 ft) tall, who chews betel nut, rolls her own cigarettes and presides over no less than 15 grandchildren. She is one of the mountain's porters, her size belying her strength. Into her *wakid* basket slung on her back, she stuffs a heavy knapsack, camera equipment and cans of food, and strides up the mountain trail, leaving unburdened climbers straggling and huffing far behind.

Porters like Awok are hired at the park headquarters and will carry luggage as far as Panar Laban hut. Here they stop and await for your exhilarated but exhausted faces to appear the following morning before beginning the descent. Fees depend on how heavy your luggage is; anything over 10 kilograms (22 lbs) will cost more.

From the hut, climbing begins at 7am;

Sure-footed Kadazan women porters.

make sure you have a bar or two of chocolate in your pocket, not a luxury but a necessity here, giving instant energy for the climb and the cold. You should also bring some headache tablets; as you will be climbing to a great height very quickly, you may suffer from headaches because of the altitude.

Passing the welcoming gate at the power station (with the slogan *Selamat Mendaki* – Happy Climbing! written over the arch), the first steps lead downward into a small, lush valley with a waterfall. After the waterfall, the climb begins, at first gently, later steeply through tropical rain forest.

All around are some of the park's 1,500 species of orchids, clinging to mossy tree trunks and surrounded by swinging vines. Steep and arduous stairs leading ever upwards are happily spaced out between gentler paths. Small rest huts and viewpoints are positioned all the way up the trail to give the out-of-breath climber an excuse to stop and admire the view. Don't bother to bring water, as there is pure mountain

water available at all rest stops. At 1,300 metres (4,200 ft), the vegetation on either side of the trail begins to change from lowland rain forest into oak and chestnut forests of more temperate plants, like ferns and flowering plants.

Proceeding up to the next level of vegetation, one has the feeling of growing larger the higher one climbs. The trail began with huge trees towering above; now the trees have shrunk and you are almost the tallest thing in the landscape. At 2,600 metres (8,500 ft), the biggest plant is but a small gnarled tree, twisted and bent and wrinkled by the mountain air. Although small, some are believed to be more than 100 years old. The soil is poor here, and lichens cling desperately to the little trees.

The soil disappears altogether at 3,300 metres (10,800 ft) and the granite body of the mountain reveals itself. Only sedges, grasses and tiny alpine-looking flowers cling to the rocky crevices where a bit of soil might remain.

Just when you thought you'd left all civilisation far below on the trail – now a hazy ribbon in the afternoon mist – you arrive at a series of huts and the resthouse where you will spend the night.

A leisurely climb should get you here by around 2pm. At **Panar Laban**, you can retreat into the cosy Laban Rata resthouse. There is a simple restaurant, as well as warm rooms and hot water. A little further up the slope is Gunting Lagadan Hostel, which has dormitory rooms, sleeping bags for hire, and a basic kitchen equipped with cooking utensils and electricity.

Once you've stopped climbing, you will begin to feel the cold, so even if you don't feel like it, have some hot soup and filling food. You will now be able to rest and think about your achievement so far – but alas! – the path you so strenuously climbed has been lost in the mountain mists.

If it isn't raining, some climbers rest here briefly and then climb for another one and a half hours to Sayat-Sayat Hut, which allows for a later rising time the following morning.

Many climbers find it hard to sleep on the mountain because of the thin air and

Trail to summit of Kinabalu.

the headaches caused by the altitude. Yet, you will need to go to sleep extra early to be able to struggle out of bed at 2am (your guide will wake you). Take a hot drink before starting the climb around 3am. If you have a thermos flask, heat some water and fill the flask with sweet tea for a reviving drink at the summit. Don't forget to stuff some more chocolate into your pocket and bring your raincoat. Other than cameras, everything else can be left at the hut for retrieval on the way down.

Soon you will be climbing rock faces of granite in the pitch black as you hold onto the rope systems that guide the way. The steepness of the incline is difficult to gauge in the dark, though, and the granite slopes can be slippery after a night rain. With an early start, you will be labouring up the slabs of granite with the peak in sight just as the skies begin to lighten. Here the granite rock, bared to the winds, is crumbling and broken, but at last Low's Peak arises.

The sun rises over the horizon like a brilliant apricot, the landscape absorb-ing the morning light. On a clear day, the lights of Kota Kinabalu and the coast and then the outlines of the Tunku Abdul Rahman islands are visible.

Venturing a look down into the depths of Low's Gully, the view is awe-inspiring. This does indeed seem a place for spirits, for few mortals could long endure the harsh weather that sweeps away the offerings of sacrificial chickens, eggs, tobacco, betel nut, sirih leaves, limes and rice left here by the Dusun. Depending on one's guide and the strength of his beliefs, he may decide to make offerings while you are gushing over the landscape's beauty. The guide may also be carrying personal charms: special pieces of wood, human teeth and other items with protecting properties.

The descent can be more leisurely, especially by climbers still glowing with success of having reached the summit. After collecting belongings from Panar Laban, one continues down through unique vegetation, such as the pitcher plants, that may have been missed on the ascent. Many climbers find the way

Laban Rata resthouse, Panar Laban.

down harder than the climb up, for the relentless steps leading ever downwards soon turn firm legs into jelly!

On arrival at the park headquarters, you can rightfully claim your badge commemorating your ascent, only for sale to those who have made it to the top (your guide can act as witness).

World's largest flower: Many climbers leave the park the same day or the day after they have made the climb. But if time permits, you should stay in the area a couple of days more, both to rest and to explore the jungle around the headquarters, which is neatly laid out in trails for nature lovers. A guide can introduce you to Kinabalu's magnificent flora and fauna, some of it unique not only in the region, but on the planet.

Amongst the rare plants found here are the famous *Rafflesia*, the largest flower in the world, measuring up to over one metre (3 ft) across, and nine species of pitcher plants. In 1858, the explorer Spencer St John chanced upon a huge specimen of the latter that contained approximately one gallon (four litres) of rain water, as well as a dead rat.

The park's 750 square kilometres (300 sq mi) are unique in the world of flora, containing plants from almost every area on earth: the Himalayas, China, Australia, New Zealand, alpine Europe and even America. There are 1,500 species of orchids (from the world's largest to the world's tiniest), 26 kinds of rhododendron and 60 types of oak and chestnut, as well as 80 species of fig trees.

Animals found here include the famous orang-utan, gibbons, leaf monkeys, tarsiers, pangolin (scaly anteaters), wild pig and deer, and a whole host of "flying" animals, some of them very rare indeed in other parts of Malaysia. These latter include flying squirrels, lemurs, snakes and lizards. Reported to be found here but seldom seen is the very rare clouded leopard.

The 518 species of birds include several kinds of hornbills, the scarlet sunbird, the mountain bush warbler, the pale-faced bulbul, the mountain blackeye, and the mountain's own Kinabalu friendly warbler. Around the **The mountain forest takes on a dream-like quality.**

area's waterfalls, look for the lovely butterflies, some as large as birds, and the less easy-to-see stick insects, well camouflaged to the human eye. You may also catch sight of squirrels, lizards, tree-shrews and bats.

Ranau and hot springs: Although the park holds all these fascinating sights and more besides, many ex-climbers will be too tired to appreciate the beauty of a pleasant stroll through the forest. After perhaps taking a quick look at the exhibition hall and the Mountain Garden, head for Poring, 45 kilometres (30 mi) to the east beyond Ranau. The motive? Natural hot sulphur springs to soothe those aching muscles, plus a canopy walkway and butterfly park.

The area around **Ranau** is Dusun country and also the market garden of Sabah, situated on Kinabalu's cool foothills. At the weekly *tamu* (market) in Ranau, one sometimes sees rural peoples dressed in a mix of traditional dress (black *sarung* and long earrings) and western attire (fake Rolex watch and Coca Cola T-shirt).

At **Poring** there are pleasant chalets, with cooking facilities, and a couple of hostels, but few visitors rest long before making straight for the baths – the outdoor ones that is. To get there, descend some steps (climbers of Kinabalu groan!) and cross a wire-and-wood suspension bridge over the river. The baths themselves are set in pretty grounds with hibiscus bushes and frangipani trees, with the untamed jungle above and beyond. They were originally built during World War II by the Japanese, with their love of communal bathing giving them the impetus to tame the jungle, and provide both hot and cold water, the latter to temper the furious heat of the volcanic water. Nothing could be nicer than to bathe here at night, with the jungle sounds all around.

Despite aching muscles (if you've climbed the mountain), it is well worth checking out Poring's 140-metre-long **canopy walkway** strung high above the ground between giant dipterocarp trees, literally offering a bird's-eye view of the forest. There is also a **butterfly**

Whitewater.

park near the baths, filled with local beauties and some remarkable insects.

Tamus and whitewater: Twenty kilometres (12 mi) south of Kota Kinabalu is **Papar**, situated on the mouth of the Papar River. Padi fields surround the town and on the coast is a pleasant stretch of sand called **Pantai Manis**, or Sweet Beach. The Sunday tamu (market) is a lively scene, as Kadazan traders bring their wares from the surrounding hills. Rice wine (*tapai*) is also made here, and if you're lucky enough to get invited to a private home, you will no doubt be offered this potent liquid.

Travelling beyond Papar, there are two choices. Just south of town is the turnoff to a seldom-travelled highway cutting through the towering Crocker Range to Keningau and Sapulut, and then along the Kalimantan border to Tawau and Sandakan on the east coast of Sabah. The coastal highway continues to **Beaufort**, a busy highway-and-railway junction and the staging point for whitewater rafting trips on through the **Padas Gorge**.

Southwest of Beaufort is a swampy peninsula with isolated fishing villages. Just offshore is **Labuan**, a burgeoning international banking centre and island that hopes to give Bermuda, Cayman and the Channel Islands a run for their money. A British naval station was established on the island in the 1870s and the Japanese forces in Borneo surrendered here in 1945, but other than those two events, little of significance has transpired on the island. After independence, Labuan was part of Sabah state until 1984, when it was ceded to the federal government for development. Tax-free status came into effect in 1991.

The Malaysian government is keen to attract banks, insurance companies and fund management brokers to Labuan, in addition to offshore holding companies and corporate headquarters. A number of steps have been taken to attract business, including preferential tax laws.

Between Beaufort and Tenom, a small and wonderfully romantic funicular railway – the only one in Borneo – winds along the river through the Padas Gorge. Built by the British North Borneo Company to service the interior rubber plantations, it now runs a commuter train for local people. As well as the rail-car service (the rail car consisting of a single carriage with passengers seats and driver's compartment), there is a regular service using full-sized trains.

A group of related hill tribes, the Muruts or "Men of the Hills", have always lived in this region. Although many young people of the tribe have adopted the fast-encroaching western civilisation creeping inland from the capital, some of them still prefer the life in the jungle, hunting with a dog, a *parang* (large sharp knife) and a shotgun. Others have turned to cultivating the countryside and growing crops.

Tenom is at the centre of the Murut community, and this small hilly town is surrounded by Murut longhouses, where young warriors still take their blowpipes and hunting dogs out for a "stroll" in the jungle to catch supper. A popular pastime in the longhouse is the *lansaran*, a huge trampoline-like structure supported by a wooden platform. The largest can **Pitcher plants.**

hold 40 people – perhaps the entire population of the longhouse.

South of Tenom, close to the village of **Tomani**, are Sabah's only rock paintings. Strange distorted faces and enigmatic figures are painted on massive boulders; they are thought not to be more than a thousand years old, but they are impressive all the same. Tenom is also known for the **Agricultural Research Station**, complete with orchid garden and resthouse, and with a full-scale educational and recreational agricultural park planned. Tenom's one classy hotel, the Perkasa, sits on the hill overlooking the town.

From Tenom, travel north through Keningau and Tambunan, completing a round trip to Kota Kinabalu. **Keningau** is the centre of the interior timber industry of West Sabah, possessing many sawmills and log-holding depots. The town has prospered from its timber industry, and has several hotels and a sports complex for the managing directors visiting their logging sites.

At **Tambunan**, an old stone on a grassy plain marks the site of Mat Salleh's last fort. Here, Sabah's most renowned hero built an underground fort in the middle of the jungle, with a sophisticated bamboo aqueduct that carried water from a river 6 kilometres (4 mi) away. He might have survived longer than 1900, had not a villager betrayed his location to British North Borneo Company forces, who promptly severed his water supply, and surrounded the fort. Mat Salleh and his followers were massacred when they emerged, ending the rebellion of a native lord who refused to pay tax to foreigners.

The route back to Kota Kinabalu from Tambunan passes over the Crocker Range, with the **Rafflesia Reserve** located not far from the summit at Sinsuron Pass. The attractive information centre has displays on this extraordinary parasitic flower and rangers can advise visitors if any are blooming in the twenty-odd identified plots within the reserve.

St Michael's Church in Penampang, heartland of the Kadazan people, is the oldest church in Sabah. Memories of a

Mists in the rain forest.

previous religion can be found in the Kadazan graveyards, where there are still some ancient burial jars. The road now heads for the capital and the coast.

Limestone outcrops: Visitors intending to explore southern Sabah should equip themselves with a four-wheel-drive vehicle, food supplies and gifts for the inhabitants of the longhouses who provide accommodation along the way.

Driving southeast of Keningau, you come first to **Nabawan**, the last outpost of the government administration, and then to the settlement at **Sapulut**. From here, you can take a rough track to **Agis**, or if preferred, hire a local canoe along the **Sapulut River**, with rapids along the way. **Tetaluan**, which has a longhouse, is the settlement furthest up this river.

A ten-minute boat journey away is **Batu Punggul**, a large limestone outcrop soaring 150 metres (500 ft) upwards from the encircling jungle. A recreated Murut longhouse and a simple resthouse have been constructed opposite Batu Punggul, with trails leading to the rock through the forest. Local guides will show you the way to the top of Batu Punggul, but climb only if you have a good head for heights.

Another half hour's walk through the forest leads to **Batu Tinahas**, almost entirely obscured by the forest. This limestone massif was only recently discovered by a Sabah Museum team. Although not as high as Punggul, its cave and tunnel system is enormous and rivals the Gomantong Caves in east Sabah.

The river flows southwards past Agis and eventually into northern Kalimantan. There is an immigration checkpoint at **Pegalungan**, but it is doubtful that you will be allowed to cross the border, unless you have already obtained an Indonesian visa. Even then you might be turned down.

At this point, the Sapulut joins the **Tagal River**. Down the Tagal is **Pensiangan**, the former centre of district administration, transferred to Nabawan over three decades ago because it was far more accessible. Pensiangan has a rest house and several shops where eve- **Wild orchids.**

rything is twice the price as in the city. Just four hours travel takes you on a most adventurous trip from Pegalungan to Kalimantan. Traditional longhouses sit along the riverbanks, where boats are built and the women engage in weaving, making intricate rattan mats and elaborate beadwork.

Travellers are most welcome to stay the night, and the Muruts are renowned for their hospitality. Remember that it is polite to accept a drink when offered, as it is a host's duty to please guests with a cup of tapai. If you do not drink alcohol, simply touch the cup with your lips or the tips of your fingers and get the guide to explain that you don't wish to partake of the fiery liquid.

Gifts of food for the adults and toys for the children are customary, and items from your own country will be even more welcome than a product available in Kota Kinabalu.

Cocoa and timber: Flights from Kota Kinabalu and Sandakan arrive at **Tawau** on the southeast coast of Sabah, an important area for timber and cocoa.

Being the present timber capital of the state, Tawau is also the home of a reforestation programme situated at **Kalabakan**, where 30,000 hectares (70,000 acres) are planted with fast-growing trees such as *Albizia facalaria*, the fastest growing of which is said to have soared 30 metres (100 ft) in just five years.

However, Tawau's real pride is the cocoa plant, which thrives in the region's volcanically rich soils, making Sabah the largest cocoa-producing state in Malaysia; oil palm is grown, too. Tawau also boasts an international-standard hotel, a recreation park, hot springs and waterfalls.

The Tawau district can be reached from Keningau, via Sapulut in the interior, travelling along logging tracks. Four-wheel-drive vehicles, which have obtained permission to carry passengers through the logging concessions, make the trip daily. The drive from Keningau to Tawau takes approximately eight to ten hours, depending upon the condition of the tracks.

Family life is simple in the more remote regions.

Malaysia's only oceanic island: The road from Tawau now travels up the coast towards Lahad Datu and Sandakan, arriving first at **Semporna**, a small settlement of Bajau and Suluk tribespeople, and Chinese shopkeepers.

Semporna is best known as the departure point for **Pulau Sipadan**, Malaysia's only true oceanic island rising up 600 metres (2,000 ft) from the seabed. The marine life of Sipadan has been hailed by both Worldwide Fund for Nature and Jacques Cousteau as among the best in the world. A local company, Borneo Divers, built simple huts to accommodate scuba divers in 1990, and other operators have followed suit. Efforts are being made to protect the reefs and island, as over-exploitation of this tiny island could threaten its near-pristine condition.

Closer to Semporan, Pulau Bohey Dulang (once the site of a Japanese pearl farm) and the surrounding islands have been designated a marine park, but development of facilities is not expected for some time to come.

The rich marine life around Semporna yields delicious seafood, which can be bought (often live) at Dragon Inn, part of the Semporna Ocean Tourism Centre on the waterfront. They will cook it for you in any style and serve it with locally grown vegetables. Attached is a motel that, like the restaurant, is perched on stilts over the sea.

Birds' nests for Chinese cuisine: An hour's drive northwest of the town leads to **Madai**, where there is a limestone outcrop with large caves. The outcrop lies just two kilometres (1.5 mi) off the main road. Outside the caves is a village that may be deserted except for one or two people, but will be packed twice a year when birds come to build nests in the caves. The nests are much coveted by the villagers, who climb the rickety network of ladders and bamboo platforms to collect them.

Both the black and the white nests are edible, with the latter fetching up to US$1,000 per kilogram (2.2 lbs) in Hong Kong's markets. They are used as the main ingredient in bird's nest soup, con- **Orang-utans.**

254

sidered a delicacy in Chinese cuisine. A flashlight is necessary for exploring the caves; although sunlight filters down through crevices in the limestone roof of some caves, many of the deeper caves are pitch black. Remains found at Madai prove that people have been in the area for over 15,000 years.

Eighteen kilometres (11 mi) west of Madai is **Baturong**. This limestone structure is situated in the middle of an area that was once a lake called Tingkayu, which drained away 16,000 years ago. There is evidence that the region was settled some 20,000 years ago. With a guide from Lahad Datu or Kunak, you can visit this fascinating massif. The journey involves an hour's drive through cocoa and oil palm plantations to a mud volcano.

The road northwards from Semporna ends up in **Lahad Datu**, often called Sabah's "cowboy town" for its lawlessness, as it is close to Sulu islands of the Philippines and subject to pirate attacks. South of the town is the **Danum Valley Conservation Area**, a 440-square-kilometre (170-sq-mi) forest reserve established by the Sabah Foundation for recreation and research. The area is totally unlogged and has numerous walking trails. Among the animals calling this valley home are the rare Sumatran rhino, orang-utans, gibbons, mousedeer, bearded pigs, giant flying squirrels and more than 270 species of bird.

The valley houses a highly regarded field research centre, and also the first "eco-resort" in the region, the **Borneo Rainforest Lodge**, with restaurant, bar and comfortable chalets overlooking the Danum River.

The lodge's design derives from traditional Kadazan and Dusun dwellings. Among the activities offered here are guided nature walks, jungle treks, night drives in an open jeep, river swimming, bird-watching, nature videos and slide shows, visits to the **Danum Valley Field Centre**, and excursions to local logging sites and timber mills.

One-time Hong Kong: In **Sandakan**, the busy boom town of northeast Sabah, people call the logs bobbing in the Sulu Sea "floating money". Logs are floated down the Segama River from timber forests near and far into the hands of Chinese entrepreneurs, who ship them via massive freighters to Japan. So prosperous was Sandakan that at one time many investors thought the town would become another Hong Kong, but the speed of deforestation of the Sandakan region has quenched that dream.

The capital of North Borneo from 1883, Sandakan was completely razed to the ground during the bombings of World War II; the modern town was built on these ruins. The original town began as a gunrunning settlement under the Spanish.

The gunrunners were mostly Germans, remembered by older local people, who still refer to all white foreigners as *orang Jerman* (German man) rather than using the usual *orang putih* (white man).

The town was at one time a highly cosmopolitan place of traders from all over the world: Europeans, Arabs, Japanese, Dusun, Javanese, Bugis, Chinese and even Africans. The Chartered Company also had its main settlement here, as the harbour was one of the finest in Borneo and the town was protected by hills from behind.

Pulau Selingan is the largest of three islands within the confines of **Turtle Islands National Park**, off the coast at Sandakan. The other two islands are **Pulau Bakingan** and **Pulau Gulisan**. Green and hawksbill turtles come here to lay eggs nearly every night of the year, but the best time to watch is between July and September. Rangers will take you out to the beaches where you can observe female turtles lay their eggs. Later, the eggs are scooped into plastic buckets and reburied at a nearby turtle hatchery, where they are safe from predators. Later that same night, previous batches of eggs hatch, and you can enjoy the sight of the little critters running down the beach in search of their ocean home.

Besides wildlife, Pulau Selingan has everything needed in a desert island: coconut palms, sandy beach, protective coral reef, a limited supply of fresh water and chalets near the beach. Accommodation on Selingan is limited and must be booked in advance either through a tour operator or at the Sabah Parks' Sandakan office, 9th floor, Wisma Khoo Saik Choo, Jalan Buli Sim Sim, or P.O. Box 768, Sandakan. The Park's office can put you in touch with private operators who run regular boat services for the 1.5-hour trip to the island.

Across the harbour from Sandakan are the **Gomantong Caves**, some of the largest in Borneo. Thirty kilometres (20 mi) south of Sandakan, they are home to one million swiftlets, whose nests are collected to furnish the tables of the many Cantonese restaurants in town. Collectors scale the bamboo ladders up to heights of 90 metres (300 ft) to collect these treasures in the vast caves. Bats are also in evidence, and their huge, odorous guano pile is gradually raising the cave floor level. If visiting these caves, bring a flashlight.

A 20-minute drive westwards from Sandakan brings you to the **Sepilok Sanctuary**, an orang-utan rehabilitation centre. In 1964, 4,000 hectares (9,880 acres) were designated as a reserve for these magnificent and intelligent primates. The centre helps orang-utans, who have lived in captivity, to adjust gradually for a return to the wild. Instruction to the animals includes encouraging them to climb, build nests in trees (something wild orang-utans do naturally) and forage for food in the jungle. They are gradually weaned from provided food and taught to fend for themselves.

One can also explore the nature trails set around the park, see elephants and a rare rhinoceros, visit the nature centre and watch a video show on orang-utans in the wild.

Another excursion that can be undertaken from Sandakan is a cruise up the **Kinabatangan River**. After crossing **Sandakan Bay**, the first stage of the journey is dominated by mangrove swamps and twisting waterways. The Kinabatangan and its tributaries are famed as the home of the long-nosed, pot-bellied proboscis monkey, found only in Borneo.

Wreathed hornbill.

Sukau in particular, a village accessible by road as well as by boat, has several tourist lodges located along the river bank.

Kota Belud: On the road from Kota Kinabalu to Kota Belud and the north, visitors will pass through Tuaran and its famous pottery factories. **Mengkabong Water Village** can be reached by a side road just before Tuaran. Mengkabong is a Bajau village built on stilts over the water of an estuary. Transport around the village is by canoe, although many houses are connected to one another by precarious-looking plank walks. Handicrafts can be purchased here as well as in Kota Belud.

Kota Belud is a couple hours' drive north from Kota Kinabalu and has two claims to fame. First, it is renowned for the Bajau "cowboys", famed for their rearing and handling of horses. Second, it is the scene of one of Sabah's most colourful tamu. Bajau and Dusun market women, their faces crinkled by the harsh sun and hours of laughter, squat beside tobacco wrappers and sugary doughnuts for hours on end, perpetually chewing the omnipresent betel nut, which stains their gums and teeth with a macabre red. There is always more on sale at the tamu than mundane necessities, even if those necessities include such remarkable things as buffalo and ponies. A Pakistani medicine man, complete with white moustache, strikes up his one-man band accompanied by a histrionic sales chatter in four languages, while his assistant busies himself with the products – pink bottles filled with a mysterious sticky liquid.

Of course, an entire row of market displays is devoted to the art of betel nut chewing, which every saleswoman unconsciously and continually demonstrates. These women use the tamu, not just to sell their wares, but also for a chance to catch up on what's what.

Ever since the days of the Chartered Company, which encouraged country people to get together at the main settlements, tamu have been popular with old and young, the favourite day being Sunday. The word *tamu* actually means

Fishing boats find gold.

"meeting place", and even today it is as much a picnic as a marketplace. Visitors will find many of Sabah's tribal handicrafts here, muddled up with betel nut stalls and electrical items from Taiwan. And as anywhere in Malaysia, the taste treats are also to be found here.

Longhouses and beaches: At the northern tip of Sabah is **Kudat**, the state's first capital (for a brief two years), and once an important port in the trade between China and Europe. The East India Company took advantage of this position and set up a trading post on Balembangan Island in 1773. However, they were much deterred by lack of water and continual pirate raids. Enraged by the Company's meagre payment to them, local chiefs sacked the post and the area was abandoned for less troubled waters.

Today, Kudat has become the peaceful centre for the northwestern administrative district, and is also an active fishing port. The indigenous tribe of the region are the Rungu, who are traditional agriculturalists and a subgroup of

the Kadazan and Dusun tribes. Many of the Rungu still live in their traditional longhouses around Kudat. They have retained traditional spiritualistic and animist beliefs, much longer than have the other tribes of Sabah. Their architectural style of building (with outwardly leaning walls) is mirrored in the state's museum in Kota Kinabalu.

The Rungu are also famous for the long brass coils, used by the women to decorate their necks, arms and legs. Nowadays, this practice has been discontinued, although forearm coils may still be seen. The women still work on their distinctive mat weaving and beadwork, much prized items in Sabah's Sunday tamus.

There is also a large Hakka Chinese community living in Kudat, the first area to be inhabited by Chinese in the 1880s; many of them are Christians and farmers by tradition. On the island of **Banggi** lives a small tribe long thought to be of Dusun extraction, but their dialect contradicts this ancestry. They remain apart, living much as they have done for the last several hundred years.

Although the Kudat region has escaped the attention of tourists in the past, it seems likely that more visitors will discover the interesting culture, handicrafts and longhouses of the Rungu, as well as the district's beautiful beaches. Already there are several traditional longhouses built especially to accommodate visitors at **Kampung Bavanggazao**, with more planned for eventual construction.

The ideal way to explore the region is in a 4-wheel-drive vehicle, as many of the roads are little more than dirt tracks. If you don't fancy staying overnight in a longhouse, then modest yet modern, air-conditioned hotels are available in both Kudat and Kota Marudu.

If you are looking for the beach while visiting Kudat, you're likely to be directed to the local favourite, Bak Bak, which is equipped with toilets and picnic tables. However, glorious virginal beaches, some with tiny lagoons, can be found all along the west coast, particularly near the village of Sikuati, at Indarasan Laut and at Teringkai.

Left, ceremonial costumes. Right, Canopy Walkway, Poring.

SARAWAK: IN THE LONGHOUSE

The name of Sarawak still evokes romance rather than reality. White Rajahs and Borneo headhunters ring more bells than 125,000 square kilometres (48,260 sq mi) of hills, jungle and swampland just north of the Equator. In this land of abundant rainfall, innumerable rivers weave their way over the state's boundaries into Indonesian Kalimantan and provide routes into remote jungle areas.

Borneo is also a Kelabit agricultural centre, a Malay fishing village, an Iban longhouse, a Punan jungle camp, a Melanau sago factory and a Bidayuh rice field all at once.

The days of the reign of the White Rajahs and head-hunting have now passed. Since 1963, Sarawak has been a member of the Federation of Malaysia, and traces of colonialism soon began to disappear under the struggle to form a modern state. With colonialism's end, some of the old serenity went too, accelerated by the advent of the oil industry, Kuala Lumpur's interest in developing the state, and the logging disputes in recent years. Without a doubt, Sarawak is undergoing great changes.

Sarawak's long tradition of open hospitality is what makes city or jungle travel so genuine. A traveller can find

Preceding pages: "The Pinnacles" Mulu National Park.

himself made welcome in a Kuching market where Chinese women offer free samples of their wares, and also at an Iban longhouse, where he may sit with the chief over a glass of the heady, home-brewed *tuak*, the ubiquitous rice wine of Sarawak.

Tourism has begun to grow up in a somewhat disorganised and unpredictable fashion. While some tour operators offer a genuine experience, taking you inland to visit caves, longhouses and national parks in small intimate groups, others with little understanding of tribal pride and dignity will take you to commercialised longhouses close to the capital, where the inhabitants will perform dances and "exhibit" their way of life.

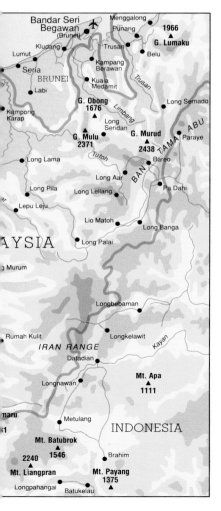

The experience seems demoralising, and smacks of the clumsy explorations of tourism in the 1950s and 1960s.

It is far better to strike out on your own, or to visit some of the reputable tour operators recommended at the back of this book. The real challenge of Sarawak is a trip up-river to visit the "real" longhouses and settlements of the Kayan, Kenyah, Murut, Iban, Kelabit and Punan people.

Two weeks is a minimum for a trip up-river to areas far from the commercial and touristic world. You can start first at the **Tourist Information Centre** in Kuching, but probably the best sources of information will be people you meet on the river or at small river towns such as Kapit and Belaga. Most likely they will be from the Iban or other tribes, many of whom have a tradition of going *berjalai* or walkabout and may decide to join you. You'll need a guide to take you to the smallest and most interesting little streams, as well as food stocks and gifts for your longhouse hosts. Food items and things for the children are most acceptable.

This kind of trip can become rather expensive, with many people wishing to tag along as paid "guides", so be prepared for some bargaining. All those who have done it with good preparation claim that there is nothing like weaving your way through the jungle on Sarawak's highway – the river.

Although there is a fairly good network of roads in and around Kuching, these are minimal at best as you head inland. A road has been cut between Sibu and Kuching, but it is much faster to travel by express boat or by plane. Most travel around the state will be by boat, canoe and small aircraft. Malaysian Airlines has an extensive network around Sarawak (see Travel Tips section at the back) including a Rural Air Service which flies to remote destinations. Travelling to a place in Sarawak is certainly more than half the fun!

It seems extraordinary that a white man once ruled in this land of jungles and tribal traditions, yet this came about, unusually for colonial history, not by force but by invitation.

The young debonair James Brooke, whose admiration for Sir Stamford Raffles lured him to the East, forsook the cocktail parties and fashionably dressed women of Singapore for a trip to Borneo.

Aside from a brief stint in the Indian Army, James held no titles among the British foreign legion, but his charisma embodied the romance of a cultured Englishman in search of adventure, and what he lacked in rank, he made up for in personality. He was also a diplomat and a strategist, assets which, aside from his awe-inspiring appearance, earned him almost by accident the sole rule of all of Sarawak.

When James Brooke's ship *The Royalist* wound its way up-river to Kuching in 1839, Sarawak was suffering. Rebellions against the brutal extortions demanded by the Brunei overlords, as well as struggles between Malays and Land Dayaks, were increasing everywhere. Returning a year later, Brooke was asked by the Sultan of Brunei to help settle these disputes.

To the amazement of all, Brooke managed to talk both sides into agreeing upon a truce, but even more incredible to the Brunei overlords was his insistence that the lives of the rebels be spared and that they be allowed to return to their villages. Thus, Brooke gained the friendship of the Dayak, the Malays and the Chinese.

In return, the Sultan offered him the title of Governor and Rajah of the Sarawak region, thus initiating the "rule of the White Rajahs." The novelty of Brooke's rule became its essence: justice without favouritism.

If it was the peculiar genius of James Brooke that conceived Sarawak as a state where a handful of Europeans should guide numerous Eastern races to a life of harmonious peace, then it was his nephew, Charles Brooke, who succeeded him, and sealed its reality.

Unlike James, who lived in a nimbus of international glamour, Charles was reserved in manner and difficult to approach. He had accustomed himself to months of loneliness as a district officer in the jungle where he lived among Dayak friends. Throughout his reign, he cultivated a betel-nut plantation at the back of the Astana (palace) which provided gifts for his Dayak chief guests. He was in fact more relaxed in their presence than at a stiffly formal gathering of European officials.

Typical of his taciturn nature, Charles Brooke proposed marriage to the young Margaret de Windt by handing her a note while she was playing the piano. It read:

"With a humble demean
If the King were to pray
That you'd be his Queen,
Would you *not* say nay?"

To her parents' horror, Margaret agreed to become Ranee of Sarawak. Margaret wrote several books about her life there and accompanied her husband on journeys up-river where her gentle kindness to her native hosts did much to create goodwill. Living with Charles Brooke can't have been easy, but he held great respect for Margaret, and when a fort was built in Kuching, he named it after her.

Charles Brooke was a benevolent despot who insisted on having his hand in every affair, right down to choosing the marble slabs which were to be used for the fish stalls in Kuching Market.

He commissioned the design of all public buildings, supervised the construction of the Astana, chose the paint colour for Fort Margherita and was involved in choosing the uniforms for the Sarawak Rangers. He even sailed all the way to the Philippines to select a suitable conductor for the municipal band and personally determined all of its music. Missives were directed by him to his district officers in the outback, insisting among many other things that they should never be caught sitting in a comfortable easy chair.

Until his last years, Rajah Charles Brooke would rise with the five o'clock gun, dress in white trousers and a blue serge coat, with a sprig of honeysuckle in his buttonhole, and proceed ceremoniously to the court house across the river, where he had the last word. He also spent some time in the Treasury, and though the accountants quivered beneath his sharp eye, Sarawak had never been so prosperous. Nor was it ever peaceful for so long. During his reign, too, the first oil was found at Miri in 1895, and the Sarawak Oil company set about exploiting it in 1910. Rubber was also introduced as Sarawak's first real cash crop.

At 86, Rajah Charles Brooke still oversaw national affairs in the morning and took a 3-kilometre walk in the afternoon. When he died in 1917, a significant era of white rule ended.

Several years later, his eldest son Charles Vyner Brooke, some European officials, Malay aristocrats, Dayak chieftains and Chinese merchants congregated outside the old Court House to honour the man who had devoted 65 years of his life to the rule and care of Sarawak, 49 of them as Rajah. As the Iban chief Penghulu unveiled the obelisk memorial, the first aeroplane ever sighted in Sarawak appeared. Several of the guests were sure that the spirit of the old Rajah had returned.

Fort Margherita. Charles Vyner Brooke's rule was to be short-lived, as the state of Sarawak was handed over to the British Crown in 1945. With the formation of the Federated States of Malaysia in 1963, Sarawak discarded the epoch of the White Rajahs, save for the stories which are still retold at night in the longhouse.

Midtown sampan: Sarawak's capital city, **Kuching**, is suffused with memories, especially the many colonial buildings that have withstood the march of 20th-century progress. Amid the noisy traffic and the bustling markets, which are typical of every Malaysian town, the old buildings give the capital an elegant and dignified air.

Charles Brooke's **Astana**, built in 1870 for the newly married Rajah, still stands, although it has undergone several renovations since. It consists of three bungalows, supported by square brick pillars, with the low, spreading roof giving shade to the interior. The Astana is now the official residence of Sarawak's head of state.

Fort Margherita still commands a position on the long stretch of the Sarawak River next to the town. How-

ever, by the time it was built in 1879, Sarawak was enjoying a period of calm and peace without attacks from outside powers, and the fort was never used for its intended purpose. The only time that the fort came under fire was after the Brooke era, when the Japanese took Kuching in an air raid. No severe damage was caused to the fort. Since the war, the fort has been used mainly by the police force, and today it houses the Police Museum.

Kuching's **Courthouse** is a rather plain colonial building; Brooke obviously had functionalism in mind here. Built in 1874, the building later had the addition of a clock tower in 1883. The **Charles Brooke Memorial** stands facing the courthouse, erected there in 1924.

The **General Post Office**, with its Corinthian columns, is more decorative and was built in 1931. An imaginative building is the **Square Tower**, built in 1879, the same year as the fort. Its architecture harks back to the Victorian era's fascination with medieval culture. Although equipped with a real dungeon for prisoners, the tower later came to be used as a popular dancing hall.

In 1886, the odd-looking **Round Tower** was built in Carpenter Street to house the town dispensary. Brooke seems to have had a predilection for fort structures, as the Round Tower was also meant to double up as a fort in times of attack. Nowadays, the building has yet another use – as offices attached to the Judiciary Department.

Other buildings of interest abound in Kuching. One of the oldest is the **Bishop's House** of 1849, built by James Brooke for Rev. Thomas Francis McDougall and his wife. With his typical astuteness, Brooke selected McDougall for the position of Bishop of Kuching because he had previously been a surgeon. **The Pavilion**, close to the Round Tower and the Courthouse, is of an uncertain date and its elaborate frontage is very different from other colonial buildings in Kuching. It was built as Kuching's medical headquarters, but is now being used as offices for the Ministry of Education.

Tua Pek Kong.

The Sarawak River has always been a focal point of Kuching. Shops are built along the road on its northern bank and are referred to as **Main Bazaar**. The bazaar and the riverside were greatly transformed in 1993 by the opening of the **Kuching Waterfront Park**, almost 1 kilometre of recreational areas, gardens, walkways, stalls and restaurants. The park is extremely popular with locals, who can be seen enjoying themselves here at all hours of day. The Main Bazaar is now firmly established as a shopping mecca for tourists, with many of the old Chinese shophouses taken over by souvenir and antique stores specialising in primitive art.

At the down-river end of the Waterfront Park is the old Chinese Chamber of Commerce Building, now transformed into an interesting little **Chinese Museum**. Immediately opposite is the shrine devoted to **Tua Pek Kong**, its construction in 1912 confirming the strong presence of the Chinese community in Sarawak. Now they are ubiquitous; rising from the handful that James Brooke found in 1839, they trade not only in the main towns and cities, but also up-river, attached to remote longhouses as suppliers of goods from down-river and building up a network of trade and news wherever they go.

Indian traders, following the Chinese example in the last century, headed for Sarawak to set up cloth shops and moneylending facilities. The **Indian Mosque**, hidden in between India Street and Gambier Road and dating back to 1876, is a mark of their success here. The streets around the mosque are a labyrinth of small Indian shops and curry-filled restaurants.

Images charged with intensity: Perhaps the most important and enthralling building for the visitor is the marvellous **Sarawak Museum**, set in its grounds between Jalan McDougall and Jalan Tun Haji Openg. Naturalist and co-founder of the theory of evolution along with Charles Darwin, Alfred Russell Wallace spent many years in Borneo, and became a particular friend of Rajah Charles Brooke. With Wallace's encourage-

Sarawak Museum.

ment, Brooke built the museum to house a permanent exhibition of native arts and crafts, as well as specimens from Wallace's extensive collection, many of which Wallace shot and preserved himself while exploring the jungle.

The facade of the building, however, betrays another influence. Its architecture was inspired by the Rajah's French valet, after a house in Normandy. The interior of the building is dedicated to the soul of Borneo, and its exhibits take one far beyond the paved streets of Kuching into the land's heart.

The Brookes were steadfast in their sense of justice. They suppressed crime and established peace in the state. But they wisely refrained from imposing any "civilised" versus "primitive" comparisons upon the native cultures. The Rajahs insisted upon capable curators, whose Western expertise was to serve only to illuminate the ethnological richness of Borneo and the vivid expressions of the societies it nourished.

One display case in the museum is devoted to the bead-conscious Kelabit people, who have names for 60 varieties of ancient glass beads, each one with a special price. Another case houses figurines carved 2,000 years ago by the now-extinct Sru Dayaks. An entire corner of the museum has been transformed into a walk-in replica of an Iban longhouse, with simulated fires burning, genuine human skulls hanging from the rafters, as well as a warrior's elaborate headdress and finely shaped weaponry resting near his bedside. It is set up to make one almost expect the warrior to walk in and sound the battle cry. Smaller models of other styles of longhouses are also found here.

The Sarawak tribespeople's great love of adornment is reflected in the high walls of the interior, painted with flowing designs. A museum employee found one end of a Kenyah longhouse at Long Nawang completely covered with a majestic mural celebrating "The Tree of Life" and he returned to Kuching and commissioned painters to reproduce it inside the Museum. Past rituals that lent a somewhat brutal aspect to tribal soci-

Art on display at the museum.

268

eties remain here on record. Giant hand-carved burial poles with the ashes of the dead enshrined in lofty niches were carried from up-river graveyards and placed impressively on the front lawn of the new Museum Annexe. In days gone by, slaves were sometimes crushed to death at the foot of these poles, if the family was in dire need of a human sacrifice to appease the deceased.

The old part of the museum has an eclectic character that recalls a succession of spirited curators, as well as the great diversity of Sarawak. There is a human dental plate on display that was found in the stomach of a 6-metre crocodile. A rhinoceros horn cup that can detect poison is another item. If the drink was contaminated, the liquid bubbled up to the top, and since princes were always trying to poison one another, rhinoceros horn was in high demand during the days of the dynasties.

Over in the Invertebrate Gallery, visitors can discover that the Damsel fly has been on earth for 300 million years, that the long-horned beetle was Wallace's favourite insect, and that the flea is the world's strongest jumper, leaping as much as 200 times the length of its body, which is roughly equivalent to a child jumping 300 metres (1,000 ft).

If the museum is the storage of a wealthy heritage, it is also a living museum. The old museum is joined by a footbridge over the road to the new **Museum Annex** completed in 1983. Here, besides more galleries devoted to the ways of life and industries of the various tribes, Chinese porcelain, and a reconstruction of the Niah caves where people lived 40,000 years ago, there are contemporary exhibitions and films, videos and slide-shows in various rooms.

These are on such Sarawak topics as the great golden hornbill (Sarawak is often known as the land of hornbills), the orang-utan, life in the jungle, and popular tribal dances. Schoolchildren are driven round in well-ordered droves and at weekends, many families come here for cultural fun.

Outside the museum is a pleasant garden with an outdoor aquarium and a

Waterfront Kuching.

small tea-shop run by two elderly Chinese ladies. The annex also has a good shop which is non-profitmaking and aims to help encourage local craftsmen. Although some of the exhibits you fell in love with back in the Iban or Kenyah sections might not be for sale here, there is still a good selection of handicrafts produced far away on the verandah of a longhouse.

Other treasures: Some of the local handicrafts you might have admired in the museum are for sale in small shops along **Wayang Street** – for a price. Outrageously fanciful and symbolistic renditions of the sacred hornbill are carved on a large scale and painted with vivid reds and greens. Behind in a case is a human skull, which makes you catch your breath – but the proprietor grins, and explains it is a plastic replica. If you are disappointed, he will lead you to his display of charms, bundles of human and animal teeth, Chinese coins and special pieces of wood, wound together to protect the owner from evil and malicious spirits.

Like many other Malaysian towns, Kuching has its share of ornate temples. Apart from the Tua Pek Kong, there is the **Kuek Seng Ong Temple** on Lebuh Wayang, built in 1895. Henghua fishermen pray here for good catches and a safe return from the sea. The temple is dedicated to the god Kuek Seng Ong, whose figure is placed on a sedan chair on the 22nd day of the second moon, and carried through the town's main thoroughfare.

The popular **Sunday Market**, which attracts Dayak tradesmen from the surrounding countryside, is situated on the outskirts of town at Jalan Satok. The stall holders arrive and set up market on Saturday night and continue till Sunday morning. All manner of strange foodstuffs – wild boar, bats, lizards, monkeys and turtles – are for sale here, alongside fruits, vegetables and fish.

Relatively modern additions to the Kuching cityscape include the golden domed **State Mosque** (Masjid Negara), which rises on the western side of downtown. Built in 1968, the mosque is sur-

Fruit stall, Kuching.

rounded by a large Muslim graveyard. The city also has several interesting **food markets**, including a large fruit and vegetable market across the street from the State Mosque and a fish market on Jalan Gambier.

Sarawak's beaches: Sun worshippers, beach lovers and golfers head for **Damai Beach**, near Santubong, just 30 minutes by road from downtown Kuching. The pioneer resort here, Holiday Inn Damai Beach, has been joined by the Santubong Resort and Damai Lagoon Resort. As well as the various water sports offered by the resorts, an 18-hole golf course and jungle walks on Mount Santubong increase the recreational options.

The fishing village of **Santubong** is also worth a visit. For those interested in history, the village's past dates back to the Tang and Sung dynasties between the 9th and 13th centuries, when it was an important trading centre. Ancient rock carvings of Hindu and Buddhist influence have been discovered around the river delta. Nearby is the state's popular tourist attraction, the **Sarawak Cultural Village**, which spreads across 6 hectares (15 acres) of jungle at the foot of Santubong Mountain. The village offers demonstrations of traditional arts and crafts, as well as dance and music demonstrations by Iban, Kayan, Kenyah and Bidayah people. Traditional longhouse dwellings offer a fascinating insight into traditional Sarawak cultures and lifestyles.

Other beach resorts further south along the coast include the Santin Resort, hidden among mangroves 30 kilometres (20 mi) west of Kuching. Tour buses leave the capital and take you to the jetty, where a boat zips you to the resort, which is inaccessible by land. There are boats to take you snorkelling and a fine beach lined with casaurina trees. With prior permission, you may be allowed to visit the **Pulau Satang Turtle Sanctuary**, where turtle eggs are carefully guarded.

If you have a four-wheel-drive vehicle, you can get to **Sematan** in the far west of the state. In this relaxed little fishing village, accommodation is in the form of self-contained chalets. Book

first from Kuching. From there you can visit several turtle sanctuaries situated on the nearby islands or visit the Silkworm project. The forest reserve at **Samunsan** is accessible only by boat and, at this stage, lacks visitor facilities.

Tours from Kuching: Tour companies arrange many trips from the capital to many of the surrounding points of interest. Choose your tour operator carefully; the Tourist Information Office may be able to help you select one to suit your interests (see Travel Tips).

Semmongok is Sarawak's orang-utan sanctuary, 22 kilometres (14 mi) from Kuching. Rehabilitation is organised there, not just for the orang-utans but also for hornbills, monkeys and honey-bears. **Serian**, a town just southeast of the capital, is popular with the locals for its waterfalls.

Other trips take you up the **Skrang River**, where your tour may include a visit to a longhouse. The experience may not be very genuine, as the inhabitants are used to seeing the tour buses roll in. Some tour companies even offer

Temple joss sticks.

wedding tours for those who wish to tie the knot in a Sarawak longhouse. Needless to say, if you want to see "real" longhouses, you'll have to venture further up the river and independent of tour companies. **Segu Benuk**, just 35 kilometres (22 mi) from Kuching and accessible by road, is one of the most frequently visited.

Sarawak's newest nature experience is Batang Ai Longhouse Resort, situated about 275 kilometres (170 mi) north of Kuching, near the headwaters of the **Lupar River**. Opened in 1994, the resort features "longhouse living with all the modern conveniences" including air conditioning, hot water and a modern restaurant. The primary reason for coming here is the jungle: Batang Ai is surrounded by virgin rain forest and within a short boat ride of **Batang Ai National Park**. Among the wildlife found in this region are several hundred species of bird – including the majestic hornbill – plus noisy gibbons, tiny barking deer, leaf monkeys and wild boar. The Hilton-run resort offers nature walks, jungle treks and boat trips, as well as excursions to nearby Iban communities and the open-air market at **Bandar Sri Aman**.

Rugged coastal jungle: A bus ride and a boat trip away from Kuching brings you to **Bako National Park**, situated on a peninsula at the mouth of the Sarawak River. Bako's relatively small area of 30 square kilometres (10 sq mi), has primary rain forest bounded on one side by a picturesque coastline of sandy bays and steep cliffs, and is uniquely rich in both flora and fauna.

The rain forest is home to beautiful insect-eating flowers and plants, and also to small animals such as the long-nosed monkey, the long-tailed macaque, pigs and sambar deer, some of which find their way down to the beaches. Within the park is a good system of well-marked paths, and on arrival you will be handed a guide map. One of these trails will take you to the Lintang salt lick, and a small observation hide allows you, if enormously patient, to see animals come here to drink.

Shopping in Kuching can be an adventure.

NATIVE ARTS

Another path takes you across several trails, first along the Lintang path through thick jungle, then up to **Bukit Tambi** to get a view of the park. A side-trail from here takes you across a plateau landscape, where the vegetation and geological formations look distinctly Australian. Then, after this hot and vigorous walk, what could be better than to stumble across two perfect little bays called **Teluk Pandan Besar** and **Teluk Pandan Kecil**, where you can refresh yourself by diving into the sea.

Bako National Park is an easy day trip from Kuching. Should you wish to stay in the park, accommodation is available at the resthouse, dormitories and chalets at the headquarters at **Teluk Assam**. There is a small shop where you can buy provisions, or visit the market before you leave Kuching. A canteen offers a very limited menu. Beware of the overfriendly long-tailed macaques who will try their best to find their way into your chalet kitchen! To book accommodation, apply at the National Parks office in Kuching.

Journey up the Rejang River: Beyond Kuching, cosmopolitan city life fades away and the innumerable rivers that mark Sarawak's green interior become the highways to the centre of inland settlements. **Sibu,** capital of Sarawak's third and largest division, is an easy-going and predominantly Chinese town, where trishaws are still in service and where fish markets overflow with gigantic freshwater fish such as carp and the much-prized *kolong,* which finds its way to the elegant dining tables of Hong Kong.

Although it is possible to take a bus from Kuching to Sibu, you will have your bones considerably rattled by the time you arrive. A more pleasant way is by express boat via Sarikei, or by small plane, the latter giving you a wonderful view of the never-ending jungle with its silver rivers snaking their way through the landscape. The flight takes only forty minutes. Flights also go further up the Rejang River to Kapit and Belaga, so you have the choice of taking the boat one way and flying the other.

Dayak woman.

From Sibu, the express boats, long and narrow and with interesting names, depart regularly. They can take you up to Kapit, and also to Belaga if the river level is high enough. You will be tumbling aboard with an assortment of other passengers: Chinese merchants taking their wares to distant longhouses, river and inland officials (usually Iban) off to attend a longhouse festival, and schoolchildren who learn their lessons in Sibu but return for holidays to their family longhouses.

Although express boat prices are fixed, hire of longboats depends (even for locals) on the water level, weather, time of day, river currents and how willing the boatman is to hurry the journey to fit your schedule. For foreigners, prices will naturally be much higher and bargaining is in order.

Along the way, the express boat stops at **Kanowit** and **Song** and even smaller settlements. On the river, boats and canoes struggle up or fly down-river, and suddenly a huge floating raft comes into view. Sarawak's longest river is also the

natural conveyor belt for the massive timber industry, and huge logs are stacked on rafts to float downstream. Should one of these hazards become waterlogged, they present considerable danger to outboard motors; with that very danger in mind, the express boats have their bellies lined with steel.

To those who live far up the Rejang River, the bustling market town of **Kapit** is the local equivalent of London. Kapit has electricity 24 hours a day, shops selling goods at considerably higher prices than back down the river at Sibu, a market and several small hotels.

Kapit lies in the heart of Iban country, Sarawak's largest indigenous population. Ibans were once the headhunters who gave Borneo its romantic and primitive reputation. Some understanding of their culture will help the visitor to see that they were not merely bloodthirsty in an anarchic way.

To bring good fortune to the longhouse and fame and a bride for themselves, young Iban warriors would (and some still do) set out from home to travel "the world". Heads of a few enemies were brought home to imbue the longhouse with protective spirits. Only warriors of equal strength, and never women, the old or sick, were killed. Sadly, these traditions were much misunderstood by the 19th-century writers who revelled in writing lurid stories about the Iban tribes.

Ibans are in truth a proud and democratic people, sharing a communal way of life in their longhouses, honouring the supernatural forces recognised by their religion, and remaining loyal to their heritage and to their heroes.

If they have been converted to Christianity, as many have, they take up hymn-singing in the evenings with as much gusto as in the days of tribal chanting and sacrificial ceremonies, and there is still much overlap between the old and the new faiths.

One early leader of the Iban was the warrior Rentap, whose name in Iban means "one who makes the world shake". Tribal wars were common in Rentap's days, when neighbouring tribes competed for favourable soils in which to plant their rice. Sarawak is an infertile

Nomadic Punans help to transport goods.

land once the jungle vegetation has been removed, and the thin topsoil quickly erodes after a monsoon season or two. For many years, longhouse dwellers were forced to resettle, even if it meant destroying another community's chances to do so.

Rentap, being a powerful and dauntless Iban chief, did not want James Brooke or any other foreigner to rule over his people. He fought so fiercely against the Rajah's foot soldiers that it took five years and a 4.5-kilogram (10-lb) cannon to defeat the chief. Rentap eventually surrendered, but not before letting the Rajah know that Ibans could not be pushed around.

The Iban gradually grew to respect the Brookes, even if their ideas conflicted with the traditions of head-hunting and piracy. The second Iban to rise to fame was Penghulu Koh, reputedly tattooed from head to toe. Tattoos are given to warriors for their great deeds, and Penghulu Koh had obviously done quite a few. However, he reformed to become one of the Rajah's staunchest supporters, and was later conferred the title of Master of Peace Ceremonies, and paramount chief of all Ibans.

The spirit of Penghulu Koh still lingers in many Iban longhouses. Faded photographs of the Rajah Brookes and Queen Elizabeth in her twenties reverently hang alongside those of the great Iban chief.

Nowadays, life is slowly changing in the longhouse. Along with these photographs may be found newspaper clippings of Asian beauty queen competitions, racing cars and Mr and Mrs Elvis Presley cutting their wedding cake. The "secluded daughter" tradition has lapsed. Many longhouse heirlooms – beautiful antique swords and silver belts – have been sold to Chinese jewellers from the big towns. Children who once enjoyed carefree days frolicking in the longhouse and the rice fields are now in school studying *bahasa Malaysia* and physics.

Tourism has a mixed effect on the longhouses. On the one hand, the virile and difficult dance of the warrior, and the chants and gongs accompanying it,

Iban social hour.

are being revived because of touristic interest. On the other, the traditional handicrafts made by the women in the olden days with such loving care are now being churned out at a fantastic rate to meet the demands of the tourist shops in Kuching, casting aside much of the quality on the way. Without a doubt, further changes are on the way.

On the optimistic side, many young Ibans, even though they may have ignored the tradition of tattooing, are becoming more and more interested in their heritage, and in protecting their traditional homes from the onslaught of modernism and from the threat of logging. Of all the tribes the Ibans have been one of the most vociferous opposers of the latter problem, mainly because many of them have had foreign education and greater contact with the modern world than such tribes as the nomadic Penan and Punan.

To get an idea of what is afoot in the way of changes in longhouse communities, make the effort to spend at least one night in a longhouse. Remember to bring the customary gifts, which, you may find after your stay there, are hardly sufficient recompense for the warm hospitality offered to you.

Boom towns and inland rivers: Bintulu and Miri lie on the northwest coast of Sarawak and are the towns that mushroomed with the oil industry. **Bintulu** is an increasingly modern town with luxurious hotels, restaurants and bars which cater to the new-found wealth of the town's inhabitants.

On top of **Canada Hill** overlooking **Miri** is Sarawak's first oil well. Constructed by the Shell oil company in 1910, the well was the forerunner of a further 623 oil wells drilled in the area known as the Miri Land Field. It also survived longer than most of the other 623. After over 6 decades of an estimated extraction of 600,000 barrels, its productivity and that of the wells around it ceased in the early 1970s.

Oil drilling has now moved southwards to Bintulu, where the oil industry is still producing a steady output.

From Miri, several exciting and adventurous trips can be made inland up the rivers. Longhouses are scattered from the coast all the way into the Kelabit district and into Kalimantan. By road you can get as far as **Kuala Baram**, from where boats depart down the Baram river for Marudi. You can also enter the sultanate of **Brunei** from that point. **Marudi** is the starting point for the long river trips that take you down the large and then increasingly smaller rivers. From here, you can also take off by plane for the vast Gunung Mulu National Park or for Bareo, in the cooler Kelabit highlands.

Bareo is the "capital" of Kelabit country. You can travel here by four-wheel-drive vehicle from Lawas (either a muddy or very dusty ride) or fly there from Marudi, Miri and Long Lallang in one of Malaysian Airlines' Twin Otters (which seat 12).

The Kelabit community is split in two by the border between Sarawak and Kalimantan, but such formalities seem not to trouble the Kelabit people, who travel over it frequently without ever seeing an immigration point. Unfortunately for visitors, it is not nearly so easy to do this trip, as one must first hunt around for someone to stamp his passport on the Malaysian end, and then do the same thing all over again in Kalimantan.

From Bareo, and with the help of Punan guides, it is possible to climb **Gunung Murud**. At 2,400 metres (8,000 ft), this is the highest peak in Sarawak, and you need five clear days to ascend and descend the mountain – a memorable experience. Punan guides and porters will also take you on a six-day walk back to **Long Lallang**, from where you can fly back to civilisation. For those who are adventurous and fit, one of these expeditions is definitely worth experiencing.

Stone-age secrets: Back in Miri, there are a couple of side-trips which are what attracts most travellers to Sarawak. The **Lambir Hills National Park** just south of Miri makes a pleasant day trip. The park's highlights are waterfalls with natural swimming pools and a climb up **Bukit Lambir**.

Much more famous, and perhaps with

more to offer, is the **Niah Caves National Park**. The limestone caves and their past inhabitants are the attraction here. In the 1870s, animal collector and adventurer A. Hart Everett came across the caves already well-known and protected by the local people – only to dismiss them as "rather dull".

It was not until the 1950s that the Sarawak Museum heard of the caves being an archaeologist's gold mine. Sure enough, when the curator dug down 5 metres (16 ft) he found the skull of a young *Homo sapiens* who had lived here possibly up to 40,000 years ago. The Deep Skull, as it was known, was what remained of the earliest known community of modern people in the East. It contradicted the haughty theories which insisted that humanity's true ancestor originated on the west side of the Middle East and only later "wandered" over to this part of the world.

As the archaeologists probed deeper, they found haematite paintings, featuring stick figures with strange little boat-like objects. Other discoveries revealed that people living here worked with instruments made from bone and shell, made pottery, cut stone adzes and carved wooden coffins or burial boats. Many agreed that these discoveries were as significant as the unearthing of Java Man. More recent objects, canoe-shaped coffins and paintings found in the cave known as the Painted Cave, date from only 1,000 years ago.

When the Iron Age reached Borneo in AD 700, the Niahans were trading hornbill ivory and edible birds' nests for Chinese porcelain and beads. They decorated enormous earthenware urns and placed them beside the graves of special men. Then in AD 1400, they seem to have entered a tropical Dark Age, which forced them to desert the caves. They then vanished from history.

The Niahans may have been the forefathers of the nomadic Penan, whose elders still maintain beliefs and rituals that allude to those in the prehistoric graveyards of the Great Caves. The Penan rediscovered the caves in the 19th century and found them to be unbe-

Sarawak River.

lievably rich in edible birds' nests. Millions of swiftlets inhabit the bowels of the Niah Caves. Their glutinous saliva with which they build their nests is believed to be medicinal and is the most expensive delicacy in Borneo.

The cost of these nests must have much to do with the markets they attract – China, Hong Kong and Singapore – but perhaps most of all because of the way they are collected. A typical day's work entails scurrying up 60 metres (200 ft) on a slender bamboo pole, scraping nests off rock ceilings and from deep crevices, and keeping balance where any fall could be fatal. You could say that the high cost of nests takes a man's life insurance into consideration.

Naturally, nest collectors guard their trade jealously, and pass their inherited territory on only to their sons. The hundreds of chambers, chimneys and sub-caves where the tiny swiftlets nest are divided into sectors, each privately owned. Some yield but a few hundred nests, others several thousand. The cave owners live in villages and longhouses situated in the park area, and during birds' nest season – normally two or three times a year, sometimes more – they bring the entire family along to help gather up the riches.

To get there, you must drive or take a bus or a taxi from either Miri or Bintulu, the former being much closer. From **Batu Niah** village, a short trip across the river brings you to the **Niah Caves Visitor Centre** at Pangkalan Lubang.

There are a few hotels at Batu Niah, but you'll have to backtrack 13 kilometres (8 mi) down the river. It is much more pleasant to stay right in the park, at the government-run hostel. The hostel is a friendly and relaxed place, providing cooking facilities, bedding, toilets and showers, and electricity till 10pm. There is a basic canteen here, as well as two twin-room chalets for hire. You can shop at the little store just across the river from the visitor centre.

The plank-walk to the caves begins from Pangkalan Lubang, just next to the visitor centre. The 3-kilometre (2-mi) path is built of the mighty *belian* wood,

The Niah Caves were inhabited by people 40,000 years ago.

278

a wood that is reputedly so dense that it will not float. Forty-five minutes should get you to the caves if the planks are dry. Sensible shoes are preferable to sandals both for the plank-walk and the caves. Other necessities include a strong torch with spare batteries and some water-proof clothing.

It is well worth stopping during the walk to absorb the atmosphere of the forest and listen to the jungle chorus. Down one of the forks in the plank-walk, you can visit a collectors' long-house, although they may charge you to have a look around their home.

At the end of the plank-walk you will arrive at the caves. The **Great Cave** is the main area for birds' nest collection – and also for another interesting sub-stance. Besides the three species of swiftlets of which there are said to be around 4 million, there are 12 species of bats, also countable in the millions. Their slimy, strong-smelling guano lines the cave floor and is collected almost as avidly as the birds' nests – for it is a rich fertiliser. In fact, you may have given way to some of the guano collectors on the plank-walk up to the caves. The guano is carried manually to Pangkalan Lubang, where it is weighed and then sent down-river to Batu Niah and to the markets beyond.

With a strong torch, you will be able to pick out the creatures that inhabit the caves. Only two of the caves are open to visitors without a guide, and the second, the **Painted Cave**, can only be entered with a permit issued by the National Park Office in Kuching.

The most spectacular sight of all at Niah makes it worth taking camping equipment along. At 6pm, the swiftlets return into the caves to sleep in their nests, while the bats, being nocturnal animals, sweep past them out of the entrance of the cave into the night. This great flurry of activity is a wonderful sight, and in spite of their numbers, the bats and birds never collide. The reverse "shift" takes place at daybreak. It is a sight that humans must have watched and wondered at even 40,000 years ago.

World-class cave: A trip to **Gunung Mulu National Park**, together with a visit to a longhouse, must be the crown-ing glory of a visitor's stay in Sarawak. Getting to the park once involved a bus ride from Miri to the mouth of the Baram River, followed by a series of boat rides. Some visitors still prefer to spend an entire day travelling in this fashion, although the wise visitor takes the plane from Miri for the roughly 20-minute trip to the landing strip just outside the park boundary.

Flying over part of the park gives you a good idea of its vastness and of the variety of the terrain, another bonus is that if the weather is good, the pilot will fly near to the spectacular Pinnacles. If you want to experience the trip along the Baram, do it on your return as the down-river voyage is always faster.

A number of tour operators in Miri offer package tours which include trans-port as well as accommodation and meals in their simple lodges located just out-side the Park boundaries. There is also a range of accommodation within the park, as well as the luxurious Royal Mulu Resort, complete with swimming pool.

Travelling in Mulu National Park.

Be aware that within the park, you are obliged to pay for compulsory guides and, if not on a package tour, must pay high prices for boats to get to a couple of the show caves. A trip to Mulu is not necessarily cheap, but it is the experience of a lifetime.

The park is Sarawak's largest, covering 53,000 hectares (130,600 acres) and was reopened in 1985. It is home to many interesting flowers, fungi, mosses and ferns, as well as eight species of the fabulous hornbill. Pitcher plants of ten kinds also flourish here.

The centre of attraction for all are the magnificent caves. One hundred and fifty kilometres (100 mi) of caves have already been surveyed, but specialists feel they may have only scraped the surface of this giant cave system.

Sarawak Chamber is reputed to be the largest cave in the world. Its size is not readily described in metres, but only in fascinating comparisons that set the imagination working – the chamber is allegedly big enough to hold 16 football fields or 40 jumbo jets.

The other cave with a claim to fame is the **Clearwater Cave**, definitely the longest cave passage in the world stretching 50 kilometres (30 mi). Comparisons for this passage suggest that "it could hold St Paul's Cathedral five times over". Visitors can get an idea of how true the boasts are about the Clearwater Cave, but unfortunately, the Sarawak Chamber is at present only accessible to scientists and museum experts, much of it being extremely dangerous.

The Clearwater Cave is an experience indeed and visitors wishing to enter it require a good torch. The 355-metre (1,165-ft) deep cave is very dark inside, but with a strong torch, you'll be able to see the marvellous limestone formations and the cave's inhabitants, which include scorpions, frogs and centipedes. An exquisitely clear river flows out of the cave from under a sheer rock face, providing a popular bathing spot for visitors, who generally enjoy a refreshing swim followed by a picnic lunch in the shelters built nearby.

A seepage of water near the toilet block at this location is a superb place to spot butterflies, including the dramatic iridescent green and black Rajah Brooke's Birdwing.

Another cave the explorer has access to is the **Gua Payau** or Deer Cave. This underground hall is 2,160 metres (7,090 ft) long and 220 metres (720 ft) deep. Thirty minutes is all it takes to walk from one end to the exit at the other, where the bats are pouring in. With some illumination as well as your own torch and crevices in the ceiling, you should be able to get a good view of the magnificent stalagmites and stalactites, still growing, as water cascades down through the roof crevices. It is possible to camp here, the best way to watch the abundant nightlife that clusters around the cave entrance.

The other attractions, apart from pleasant walks along jungle trails, are the two peaks **Gunung Mulu** and **Gunung Api**. Gunung Api is of special interest, being the highest limestone mountain in Malaysia, and possessing **The Pinnacles**, strange limestone spikes, like figures watching the park below, with some standing 45 metres (150 ft) high. The steep ascent to these marvels involves a 2-day trip, camping out overnight at a simple hut near the Melinau River.

Gunung Mulu is a much harder and longer trip. Expert mountain climbers have "done it" in one and a half days, but the average modest climber should aim at doing it in a leisurely five. You have to take all your goods and chattels with you: cooking utensils, food, water, a sleeping bag, a raincoat, good walking shoes and a strong torch.

There are camps all the way up, but these are simply glorified shelters, and your pleasure must derive from travelling in this wild landscape, far away from cities, deep in an ancient jungle.

At the peak, stop and survey the landscape, folding away into a green carpet below, split only by limestone outcrops. You have seen Sarawak, you have seen the changes taking place in the city and longhouses alike. Yet this final experience in some of the world's most spectacular and complex geology confirms what you have believed all along: Borneo is still Borneo.

Bats take flight in Mulu.

INSIGHT GUIDES
Travel Tips

Your vacation.

Your vacation after losing your wallet in the ocean.

Lose your cash and it's lost forever. Lose American Express®
Travelers Cheques and get them replaced. They can mean
the difference between the vacation of your dreams and
your worst nightmare. And, they are accepted like cash
worldwide. Available at participating banks, credit unions, AAA offices
and American Express Travel locations. *Don't take chances. Take American Express
Travelers Cheques.*

do more

Travelers Cheques

Getting Acquainted

Time Zones

Malaysia's standard time is 8 hours ahead of Greenwich Mean Time.

Climate

A tropical sun and clouds laden with the makings of a sudden downpour compete for the skies of Malaysia, with the odds on the sun. Malaysia's seasons follow the monsoon winds, which splash rains inland from September to December on the west coast of the peninsula, only to be overtaken by sunshine within the hour. Rains arrive later, between October and February, on the east coast of peninsular Malaysia and in Sabah and Sarawak. Malaysia's weather, however, is generally warm, humid and sunny all year round, with temperatures wavering between 32°C during the day and 22°C at night. The highlands, both during the day and at night, and the lowlands in the evening, are comfortably cooler, which is why Malaysia's nightlife is liveliest outdoors.

The People

The population of 18.2 million comprising Malays, Chinese, Indians, Pakistanis and other indigenous, is spread over 13 states. The capital city of Kuala Lumpur alone has a population of approximately 1.5 million.

Culture & Customs

The customs, religions and language of many nations converge in Malaysia. With everyday etiquette relaxed, visitors behaving courteously stand little chance of unintentionally giving offence. It is beneficial, however, to learn something of how Malaysians behave towards one another so that you truly experience the culture.

Seniority is much respected. The oldest male member of a family is greeted first, often sits in the best and highest seat, and is consulted first on any matter. Pointing with the finger is considered very rude and a whole hand is best used to indicate a direction (but not a person).

All Malays, Indians and Chinese remove their shoes at the door to keep the house free from dirt. No host would insist his visitors do so, but it is the polite way to enter a home. One can always tell if there is some kind of get-together at someone's house – by the number of shoes and sandals scattered around the front door.

For those interested in learning more about Malaysian customs, a good source is the Times Editions guidebook *Culture shock! Malaysia and Singapore.*

The Economy

Petroleum, natural gas, electronic goods, computer parts, automobiles, timber, palm oil, cocoa and rubber are the main exports. Its main trading partners are Japan, Singapore and the United States.

The Government

Malaysia is the official name of the former British protectorates of Malaya, British North Borneo and Sarawak. Independent since 1957, the Malaysian government is regulated by the Parliament comprising the Yang di-Pertuan Agong, King or Supreme Sovereign, and two Houses: the House of Representatives and the Senate. The executive functions of the government are carried out by the Cabinet, led by Dato' Seri Mahathir Mohamad who became Prime Minister in 1981.

Planning The Trip

What To Bring

There is very little need to worry about leaving something important behind when you visit Malaysia. Toiletries, medicines, clothes, photographic film, suntan lotion and straw hats are all readily available in most towns, and definitely in the large cities. In fact, the best advice is to take as little as possible so that you can travel lightly.

Electrical supply is on a 220 volts, 50 Hz system. Most hotels can supply an adaptor for 110 – 120 volt, 60 Hz appliances.

If you are planning to visit the hill stations, a light sweater would be a good idea for the cooler evenings. If you're embarking upon the Mount Kinabalu climb, a lightweight plastic raincoat is a must, as are a warm hat and gloves, but all these items can be found in Kuala Lumpur, Singapore, or Kota Kinabalu. Camping gear is often available for hire in national parks, but it is also under heavy demand; so it may be best to bring a lightweight tent with you. If you intend to go jungle trekking, the Taman Negara National Park issues a list of contents for the average backpack: rucksack (lightweight and waterproof), sleeping bag (if climbing), cooking pots/utensils, Swiss Army knife or similar, plates/cutlery, can opener, *parang* (local knife for cutting wood etc.), notebook and pens, camera and film, 1 litre water container (minimum), spare set of clothes, soap, toothbrush, etc., repair kit, food – rice, noodles, canned foods, packet soups, dried fish, fresh vegetables, sweets/chocolate, fat, tea/coffee, powdered milk, sugar, rolled oats, fruits and nuts.

In more remote areas, you will not have the luxury of a shaving point, but disposable razors are sold widely in towns and cities, or you can buy a battery-operated razor at reasonable prices. Sanitary protection for women is also available in larger centres. Cheap clothes are everywhere – batik shirts are colourful and cool, and tee-shirts with interesting slogans are also a good buy. You may even decide to adopt the multi-purpose sarung as skirt, towel or sheet! So... just bring your camera.

What To Wear

In Malaysia's tropical climate, informal wear is most suitable and comfortable. However, since this is a predominantly Muslim and conservative country, observance of local customs is important. Men may wear tee-shirts or cotton shirts with short sleeves, and open sandals. Women should not wear dresses, skirts or shorts that are too short and should always wear a bra. Topless sunbathing is frowned upon. In cities, towns and villages, shorts are not a good idea – save them for the beach. Check the required attire before entering any house of religious worship.

For businessmen, a white shirt and tie are adequate for office calls – jackets are seldom required. For women a tailored dress or business suit is most appropriate. In the evenings, only a few exclusive nightclubs and restaurants favour the traditional jacket and tie. Most hotels, restaurants, coffeehouses and discos except casually elegant attire. However jeans and sneakers are taboo at some restaurants and discos. To avoid embarrassment, it is best to call in advance and check the dress code of better establishments.

Entry Regulations
Visas & Passports

Valid passports and a health certificate of vaccination against yellow fever are required if travelling from an infected area. Citizens of Commonwealth countries (except India), Ireland, Switzerland, the Netherlands, San Marino and Liechtenstein do not need a visa to visit. The following countries do not need a visa for a visit not exceeding three months: Austria, Italy, Japan, South Korea, Tunisia, the United States, Germany, France, Norway, Sweden, Denmark, Belgium, Finland, Luxembourg and Iceland.

Immigration requests that your passport be valid for at least 6 months. Bear in mind that Sabah and Sarawak are treated like other countries, and you will have to go through customs again there, both from peninsular Malaysia and between the two states in Borneo.

On arrival, the most common visa will be for 30 days. If you wish to extend your stay, and are from one of the countries enjoying diplomatic relations with Malaysia, then you may do so at any of the following immigration offices in each state:

Federal Territory, Blok 1, Tingkat 2-3, Pusat Bandar, Damansara, Bukit Damansara, 50490 Kuala Lumpur, Tel: 03-255 5077.

Kuala Lumpur, Headquarters Office, Blok 1, Tingkat 4-7, Pusat Bandar Damansara, 50490 Kuala Lumpur, Tel: 03-255 5077.
Johor, Wisma Persekutuan Johor, Blok B, Tingkat 1, Jalan Air Molek, 80550 Johor Bahru, Tel: 07-224 4253.
Kedah, Tingkat 2, Wisma Persekutuan, 0500 Alor Setar, Kedah, Tel: 04-733 3302.
Kelantan, Tingkat 2, Wisma Persekutuan, Jalan Bayam, 15550 Kota Bharu, Kelantan, Tel: 09-748 2120/ 748 2644.
Melaka (Malacca), Tingkat 2, Wisma Persekutuan, Jalan Hang Tuah, 75300 Malacca, Tel: 06-282 4955.
Negri Sembilan, Tingkat 2, Wisma Persekutuan, Jalan Datuk Abdul Kadir, 70675 Seremban, Negri Sembilan, Tel: 06-762 0000.
Pahang, Tingkat 1, Wisma Persekutuan, Jalan Gambut, 25000 Kuantan, Pahang, Tel: 09-514 2155.
Perak, Bangunan Persekutuan, Jalan Dato' Panglima, Bukit Gantang, 30000 Ipoh, Perak, Tel: 05-241 5233/254 9316.
Perlis, Tingkat 1, Menara Kemajuan pknp, Jalan Bukit Lagi, 01000 Kangar, Perlis, Tel: 04-976 2636.
Pulau Pinang (Penang), Jalan Leboh Pantai, 10550 Pulau Pinang, Tel: 04-261 5122.
Sabah, Tingkat 4 & 5, Bangunan Penerangan, 88550 Kota Kinabalu, Sabah, Tel: 088-216 711.
Sarawak, Peti Surat 639, 93908 Kuching, Sarawak, Tel: 082-245 661.
Selangor, Kompleks pkns, 40550 Shah Alam, Selangor, Tel: 03-559 0653.
Terengganu, Tingkat 1, Wisma Persekutuan, Jalan Paya Bunya, 20200 Kuala Terengganu, Terengganu, Tel: 09-622 1424.

Customs

Import duties seldom affect the average traveller, who may bring in 225 grams (½ lb) of tobacco or cigars, or 200 cigarettes, and a one-quart bottle of liquor duty-free as well as personal cameras, watches, cassette players, cosmetics etc. On rare occasions, visitors may be asked to pay a deposit for temporary importation of dutiable goods (up to 50 percent of the value) which is refundable upon departure. Be sure to get an official receipt for any tax or deposit paid. Pornography,

weapons and walkie-talkies are strictly prohibited. Possession of narcotics and other illegal drugs carries the death sentence, and firearms are subject to licensing.

The above duty-free items are not available to you if you are travelling on a domestic flight, or from Singapore.

Health

Travellers have little to worry about in a country where the health standards are ranked amongst the highest in Asia.

Water in cities is generally safe for drinking, but it is safest to drink it boiled. Bottled drinks are also widely available. Avoid drinking iced water from roadside stalls. It is important to drink sufficiently to avoid dehydration; drink more than you would normally if you're coming from a cold country.

The sun is deceptively strong here: one hour of sunbathing a day for the first few days will get you a lasting tan without giving you sunstroke.

If you are visiting remote jungle areas, it is advisable to take malaria tablets; your doctor will know which type is suitable for the region. To help keep mosquitoes at bay, use insect repellents, mosquito coils and nets at night. If you intend to travel to Borneo, ask your doctor about outbreaks of cholera. These are rare, but should there be any, you would be wise to have a vaccination before leaving home.

Treat open cuts and scratches immediately as infection in humid climates can delay healing, and at worst, cause tropical ulcers. If you are swimming in the sea near coral reefs, do not touch any of the shells, snakes and other creatures you find there. Many of them are poisonous, so keep your distance and get medical attention if you are bitten. To avoid getting sea urchin prickles in your feet, it is a good idea to wear plastic shoes or flippers while exploring the coral reefs.

Medical supplies are widely and readily available in Malaysia, and all large towns have government polyclinics as well as private clinics. French and German-speaking doctors can be found by contacting the relevant embassies. Travel and health insurance, as well as documents concerning allergies to certain drugs should also be carried.

In an emergency, the charge-free number to call is 999 for ambulance, fire or police services. Below are also some hospitals in the Kuala Lumpur area that have 24-hour outpatient emergency services:

Assunta Hospital, Jalan Templer, Petaling Jaya, Tel: 03-792 3433.
Subang Medical Centre, 1 Jalan SS12/1A, Subang Jaya, KL, Tel: 03-734 1212.
Tawakal Hospital, 202A, Jalan Pahang, KL, Tel: 03-423 3500.
City Medical Centre, 415-427, Jalan Pudu, KL, Tel: 03-222 0413.

Currency

The Malaysian currency note is the ringgit or Malaysian Dollar, which is divided into 100 sen. The amount of Malaysian dollars you are allowed to bring in or take out of Malaysia is unlimited. At the current exchange, US$1 will give you approximately RM2.50, A$1 – RM1.90, and £1 – RM4 (at press time). Singapore and Brunei dollars are worth about 70 percent more than the Malaysian ringgit, and no longer circulate freely in Malaysia. You may be able to use Singapore dollars in the state of Johor, but they are counted as having the same value as the ringgit.

Banks and licensed money changers offer better rates than do hotels and shops, where a service charge may be levied (usually 2–4 percent). Make sure that you have enough cash before you leave for smaller towns or remote areas.

Banking

The nationwide network of about 40 commercial banks has all the facilities to cope with simple as well as more complex transactions. The various banks operate more than 550 offices throughout the country and have connections with the major financial centres of the world. Some main bank branches are:

Public Bank, Bangunan Public Bank, 6 Jalan Sultan Sulaiman, KL, Tel: 03-274 1788.
Malayan Banking, Menara Maybank, KL, Tel: 03-230 8833.
Bank Bumiputra, Menara Bumiputra, Jalan Melaka, KL, Tel: 03-291 9199.
Standard Chartered, 2, Jalan Ampang, KL, Tel: 03-232 6555.

Banking hours in most states are Monday through Friday 10am to 3pm, and Saturday 9.30 to 11.30am. However, in Kedah, Perlis, Kelantan and Terengganu banking hours are Saturday through Wednesday 10am to 3pm and 9.30 to 11.30am on Thursday.

Travellers' Cheques & Credit Cards

In the more flashy quarters of the larger towns, in department stores, shops, first-class restaurants and hotels, travellers' cheques change hands easily. Have your passport ready when changing cheques. Off the beaten track, you may find it harder to change travellers' cheques. Established credit cards – Diners Club, American Express, Visa, MasterCard and JCB – are honoured in the major cities but off the beaten track, make sure you have local cash on hand.

Public Holidays

January
Jan 1 – New Year's Day (except Johor, Kelantan, Terengganu, Kedah and Perlis)
Jan 21 – Birthday of the Sultan of Kedah (Kedah only)

February
Feb 1 – Federal Territory Day (Federal Territories of Kuala Lumpur and Labuan only)
Feb 12 – Hari Hol Almarhum Sultan Ismail (Johor only)

March
Mar 5 – Ishak and Mikraj (Kedah and Negri Sembilan only)
Mar 8 – Birthday of the Sultan of Selangor (Selangor only)
Mar 10 – Birthday of the Sultan of Terengganu (Terengganu only)
Mar 11 – Official Opening of the State Mosque, Shah Alam (Selangor only)

April
Apr 8 – Birthday of the Sultan of Johor (Johor only)
Apr 13 – Good Friday
Apr 19 – Birthday of the Sultan of Perak (Perak only)

May
May 1 – Labour Day
May 7 – Hari Hol Pahang (Pahang only)
May 29 – Dayak Day (Hari Gawai) (Sarawak only)

May 30 & 31 – Harvest Festival (Federal Territory of Labuan and Sabah only)

June
June 5 – Birthday of Yang di-Pertuan Agong (King)
June 14 – Birthday of the Yang di-Pertua Negri Melaka (Malacca only)

July
July 16 – Birthday of the Yang di-Pertua Negri Pulau Pinang (Penang only)
July 16 – Birthday of the Yang di-Pertuan Besar of Negri Sembilan (Negri Sembilan only)
July 31 – Birthday of the Sultan of Kelantan (Kelantan only)

August
Aug 23 – Birthday of the Rajah of Perlis (Perlis only)
Aug 31 – National Day

September
Sept 16 – Birthday of the Yang di-Pertua Negri Sabah (Sabah only)
Sept 16 – Birthday of the Yang di-Pertua Negri Sarawak (Sarawak only)

October
Oct 26 – Birthday of the Sultan of Pahang (Pahang only)

December
Dec 25 – Christmas Day

Getting There

By Air

Malaysia is well connected by airlines to all continents, and if coming from Europe or North America, you will enter the country at the **Kuala Lumpur International Airport**, opened in 1998 as one of the most advanced airports in the world, situated 70 kilometres (43.5 mi) south of Kuala Lumpur. A high-speed rail passes through the so-called Multimedia Super Corridor to connect with KL's city centre.

If you are arriving from a nearby Asian country (Hong Kong, Thailand, Indonesia or Singapore), it is possible to fly to some other Malaysian cities either directly or by connecting flights through Kuala Lumpur. Penang, Langkawi and Tioman can be reached directly from Singapore. For details of flights, contact your airline or travel office. For reconfirmation of flights, below is a list of some international airlines:

Air New Zealand, Tel: 03-242 5577
Air Lanka, Tel: 03-274 0211
Air Nippon, Tel: 03-244 1331
British Airways, Tel: 03-232 5797
Cathay Pacific, Tel: 03-238 3377
China Airlines, Tel: 03-242 7344
Emirates Air, Tel: 03-244 3288
Eva Air, Tel: 03-262 2981
Garuda, Tel: 03-262 2811
Gulf Air, Tel: 03-242 4311
Japan Air, Tel: 03-261 1722
KLM, Tel: 03-242 7011
Korean Airlines, Tel: 03-242 8311
Lufthansa, Tel: 03-261 4666
Philippine Airlines,Tel: 03-242 9040
Qantas, Tel: 03-238 9133
Royal Brunei Air, Tel: 03-230 7166
SAS, Tel: 03-242 6044
Saudi Airlines, Tel: 03-201 7788
Singapore Airlines,Tel: 03-292 3122
Sempati Air, Tel: 03-263 1612
South African Air, Tel: 03-241 7456
Thai International, Tel: 03-293 7100
Northwest Airlines, Tel: 03-336 3371
United Air, Tel: 03-261 1433

For details on domestic flights within Malaysia, contact your nearest Malaysian Airline office (see *Getting Around* section).

By Rail

An extensive railway network runs through Malaysia (for information on trains, see *Getting Around* section) from Singapore, with connections to Bangkok. The Thai-owned International Express leaves daily from Bangkok for Butterworth and trains from Haadyai in the south of Thailand connect to trains on the Eastern Malaysian railway. The trip from Bangkok takes about two days, and you can travel in a first-class air-conditioned sleeper, a second-class non-air-conditioned sleeper, or in upright seats in third class. For reservations, contact the railway station in Bangkok (Hualamphong) or a local travel agent. Trains from Singapore to Kuala Lumpur and Kota Bahru run several times daily and take from 7 to 10 hours (Kuala Lumpur) or 12 to 15 hours (Kota Bahru) respectively.

By Road

From Thailand, it is possible to get buses from Bangkok or Haadyai that cross the border at Padang Besar and travel to Penang or Kuala Lumpur, or at Sungai Golok on the East Coast. From Singapore, there are buses which travel to peninsular Malaysia from the Ban San Street terminal, Singapore. For more information call: (65) 292 8151. Long-distance taxis also run from Queen Street in Singapore, although you will get a better bargain by taking the bus to Johor Bahru across the Malaysian causeway and taking a taxi from there.

Alternately, you can rent a car in either Thailand or Singapore and have complete freedom during your stay in Malaysia. The new North-South highway makes traveling along Peninsula Malaysia's west coast a breeze – with trips from the Thai border to Singapore possible in about 10–12 hours. However, try and avoid border crossing on Friday afternoons or during public holidays as there can be bad congestion.

Practical Tips

Most transactions in Malaysia are carried out in metric. Road distances are always given in kilometres, but if you ask a kampung dweller for directions, he may give distances in either miles or kilometres.

Business Hours

In an Islamic nation with a British colonial past, weekly holidays vary. In the former Federated States which were united under the British – Selangor, Malacca, Penang, Perak, Pahang, Negri Sembilan, Federal Territory, Sabah and Sarawak – there is a half-day holiday on Saturday and a full-day holiday on Sunday. The former unfederated states, which remained semi-autonomous under British rule – Johor, Kedah, Perlis, Terengganu and Kelantan – retain the traditional half-day on Thursday and full-day holiday on Friday; Saturday and Sunday are treated as weekdays. The workday begins at 8am and ends at 4.30pm with time off on Friday from noon until 2.30pm for communal Friday prayers at the mosque. Most private businesses stick to the nine-to-five routine. Shops start to close at 6pm, but large supermarkets and department stores are open 10am–10pm.

Tipping

Tipping is not common in Malaysia, especially in more rural areas. In most hotels and large restaurants, a 10 percent service charge is added to the bill along with 5 percent government tax. In large hotels, bellboys and porters usually receive tips from RM2 to RM5 depending on the service rendered. Outside these international establishments, however, simply a thank you (*terima kasih*) and a smile will do.

Religious Services

Minarets, spires, domes and steeples adorning the skyline of Kuala Lumpur reflect a rich diversity of faiths in Malaysia. Below is a small selection of places of worship in the Kuala Lumpur area. Hotels and travel agents provide the times of services and can help arrange transportation.

Kuala Lumpur Baptist Church, 70 Cangkat Raja Chulan, KL, Tel: 03-241 9154.
Mar Thoma Church (Syrian), Jalan Ipoh, KL, Tel: 03-626 0015.
National Mosque (Masjid Negara), Jalan Sultan Hishamuddin, KL.
Seventh Day Adventist Mission, 166 Jalan Bukit Bintang, KL Tel: 03-242 7795.
Sikh Temple Maindaub, 75 Jalan Pudu Lama, KL, Tel: 03-238 7435.
Sri Maha Mariamman Temple (Hindu), 163 Jalan Bandar, KL, Tel: 03-238 3467.
St Andrew's Presbyterian Church, 31 Jalan Raja Chulan, KL, Tel: 03-232 5687.
St Francis Xavier Church (Roman Catholic), Jalan Gasing, Petaling Jaya, Tel: 03-757 7136.
St John's Cathedral (Roman Catholic), Bukit Nanas, KL, Tel: 03-238 5089.
St Mary's Church (Anglican), Jalan Raja, KL, Tel: 03-292 8672.
Wesley Methodist Church, off Jalan Hang Jebat, KL, Tel: 03-232 9982.
Zion Church, 21 Jalan Abdul Samad, KL, Tel: 03-274 1033.

Etiquette

Removing one's shoes before entering a mosque or an Indian temple has been an unspoken tradition for centuries. Within, devotees do not smoke. Neither of these customs generally apply to Chinese temples where more informal styles prevail. Visitors are welcome to look around at their leisure; but ask permission before taking photographs – a gesture that is appreciated and seldom refused. Moderate clothing, rather than short skirts, shorts or sleeveless tops, should be worn. Most temples and mosques have a donation box for funds to help maintain the building. Contributing a few coins before leaving is customary.

Media

Newspapers & Magazines

Malaysia's newspapers come in a variety of languages, from *Bahasa Malaysia* (Malay, the national language), English and Chinese, to Tamil, Punjabi and Malayali. *The New Straits Times* and the *Star*, masters of the English press, arrive every morning with national and world news and views. The two other English papers are *The Sun*, a liberal, lifestyle-focussed daily, and *The Edge*, a business-oriented paper. *The Malay Mail*, an afternoon paper, is less formal and more chatty, and entertains its readers by focussing more on local news and entertainment. *The Sabah Times, Sabah Daily News, Daily Express, People's Mirror, Sarawak Tribune* and *Borneo Post* hail from East Malaysia with international news appearing next to events from the remote jungle. Foreign newspapers and magazines can also be purchased in large cities.

Radio & Television

Radios can also be heard everywhere, blaring out a wild assortment of different sounds; a flick of the dial will tune you into Indonesian pop, Malay rock and heavy metal, Indian pop or classical music, Chinese theatrical or the number one sound in Britain or America. Soap operas and programmes of daily events around the country will also familiarise you with the Malay culture. The three English radio stations are: Time Highway Radio on 99.3 FM; Radio Music on 95.3 FM and Radio Four on 100.4 FM. Check the local newspaper for more detailed programming information.

Television is the most popular medium in Malaysia, watched in international hotel rooms and longhouses with the same enthusiasm. Programmes are cosmopolitan and British and American sit-coms and documentaries are shown alongside Indonesia's hottest film and Koran reading competitions from Kuala Lumpur. Sports in general have a generous slot of transmission time. The news in English is broadcast at 8pm on RTM Channel 2 (also known as TV2), 10.30pm and midnight on TV3, and at 11.30pm on Metrovision. RTM Channel 1 broadcasts the least in English programming. TV 1 and TV 2 are government-run, while the other two are private. Most hotels also offer in-house video and satellite channels.

Postal Services

Malaysia postal services are quick and reliable. There are post offices in all state capitals and in most cities and towns. Except for the General Post Office in Kuala Lumpur, which opens from 8am–6pm (Monday–Saturday), most post offices are open from 8am–5pm.

Most large hotels provide postal services; and stamps and aerogrammes are often sold at the small Indian sweet and tobacco stalls on street corners.

Telecoms

Local calls in Malaysia cost 10 sen, and public phones can be found in most towns, often located in front of restaurants. Many now accept credit cards and/or telephone cards which are sold at many small shops. Long-distance and international calls can be made from the post office, hotels and some public phones.

Inter-state calls require the following prefix codes:

Johor	07
Kelantan	09
Kuala Lumpur	03
Langkawi	04
Melaka	06
Negri Sembilan	06
Perak	05
Perlis	04
Pulau Pinang	04
Sabah	088
Selangor	03
Sarawak	082
Terengganu	09

Other useful numbers include:

IDD	007
Fault reporting	100
Trunk calls assistance	101
Connection difficulties	102
Directory enquiries	103
Telegram	104
International operator	108
Time signal	1051
Weather report	1052
(Office hours)	
Emergency	999
(Police/Fire/Ambulance)	

Tourist police:

Kuala Lumpur	03-241 5522
Malacca	06-222 222
Johor Bahru	07-232 222
Penang	04-615 522

A 24-hour Kedai Telekom, located at the Central Telegraph Office, Bukit Mahkamah, is available in the town centre of Kuala Lumpur. For further enquiries, call 102, Telekom's 24-hour enquiry line.

Tourist Information

Malaysian Tourist Promotion Board (MTPB) has various offices throughout Malaysia (see the following list). Offices vary in the amount of literature available, but there are usually brochures on local places of interest. The regional offices can also be contacted for information on reputed tour operators and travel companies, most of which are registered with the MTPB.

MTPB Offices in Malaysia:

Head Office, 24-27th & 30th Floor, Menara Dato' Onn, Putra World Trade Centre, 45 Jalan Tun Ismail, 50480 KL, Tel: 03-293 5188.

East Coast Region, 2243, Ground Floor, Wisma MCIS, Jalan Sultan Zainal Abidin, 20000 Kuala Terengganu, Terengganu, Tel: 09-622 1433.

Northern Region, No. 10, Jalan Tun Syed Sheh Barakbah, Penang, 10200 Pulau Pinang. Tel: 04-261 9067.

Southern Region, 1, Fourth Floor, Tun Abdul Razak Complex, Jalan Wong Ah Fook, 80000 Johore Bahru, Johor, Tel: 07-222 3591.

Sabah, Ground Floor, Wisma Wing Onn Life, 1, Jalan Sagunting, 38000 Kota Kinabalu, Tel: 088-248 698.

Sarawak, 2nd Floor, Rugayah Building, Jalan Song Thian Cheok, 93100 Kuching, Sarawak, Tel: 082-246 575.

For more tourist information, contact:

Malaysia Tourist Information Complex (MATIC), 109 Jalan Ampang, 50450 KL, Tel: 03-264 3929.

Embassies & Consulates

Australia, 3 Jalan Semantan 2, Damansara Heights, 50490 KL, Tel: 03-255 0176.

Canada, 7th Floor, MBF Plaza, 172 Jalan Ampang, 50450 KL, Tel: 03-261 2000.

China, 229 Jalan Ampang, 50450 KL, Tel: 03-242 8495.

Denmark, 22nd Floor, Bangunan Angkasa Raya, 123 Jalan Ampang, 50450 KL, Tel: 03-241 6088.

France, 192-196 Jalan Ampang, 50450 KL, Tel: 03-248 4122.

Germany, 3, Jalan U Thant, 55000 KL, Tel: 03-242 9666.

India, Jalan Taman Duta, off Jalan Duta, 50480, KL, Tel: 03-353 3510.

Indonesia, 233, Jalan Tun Razak, 50400 KL, Tel: 03-984 2011.

Iran, 1 Lorong U Thant 1, 55000 KL, Tel: 03-451 4824.

Iraq, 2, Jalan Langgak Golf, off Jalan Tun Razak, 55000 KL, Tel: 03-248 0555.

Italy, 99 Jalan U Thant, 55000, KL, Tel: 03-456 5122.

Japan, Wisma AIA, 47 Jalan Tun Razak, 50400, KL, Tel: 03-242 7044.

Kuwait, 229 Jalan Tun Razak, 50400, KL, Tel: 03-984 6033.

Libya, 6 Jalan Madge, off Jalan U Thant, 55000 KL, Tel: 03-248 2122.

Myanmar, 5, Taman U Thant I, 55000 KL, Tel: 03-242 3863.

Netherlands, 4 Jalan Mesra, off Jalan Damai, 55000 KL, Tel: 03-248 5151.

New Zealand, 193, Tun Razak, 50400 KL, Tel: 03-248 6422.

Norway, 11th Floor, Bangunan Angkasa Raya, Jalan Ampang, 50450 KL, Tel: 03-243 0144.

Oman, 24 Lingkunan U Thant, off Jalan Ru, 55000 KL, Tel: 03-475 011.

Pakistan, 132, Jalan Ampang, 50450 KL, Tel: 03-241 8877.

Papua New Guinea, 1 Lorong Ru Kedua, off Jalan Ampang, 55000 KL, Tel: 03-457 4202.

Philippines, 1 Changkat Kia Peng, 40450 KL, Tel: 03-248 4233.

Saudi Arabia, 7 Jalan Kedondong, off Jalan Ampang Hilir, 55000 KL, Tel: 03-457 9433.

Singapore, 209, Jalan Tun Razak, 50400 KL, Tel: 03-261 6277.

South Korea, 422 Jalan Tun Razak, 50400 KL, Tel: 03-984 2177.

Sri Lanka, 2A, Jalan Ampang Hilir, 55000 KL, Tel: 03-456 0917.

Sweden, 6th Floor, Wisma Angkasa Raya, Jalan Ampang, 50450 KL, Tel: 03-245 5981.

Switzerland, 16 Persiaran Madge, 55000, KL, Tel: 03-248 0622.

Thailand, 206 Jalan Ampang, 50450 KL, Tel: 03-248 8222.

United Kingdom, 186 Jalan Ampang, 50450 KL, Tel: 03-248 2122.

United States of America, 376 Jalan Tun Razak, 50400 KL, Tel: 03-248 9011.

Vietnam, 4 Persiaran Stonor, 50450 KL, Tel: 03-248 4036.

Photography

Professionals working in the tropics have one big suggestion for good results in colour: beware of the heat. Exposure of film or camera equipment to hot sun causes changes in the chemical emulsions of the film, which detract from natural colour. Whenever possible, store your camera and film in a cool place; if not in an air-conditioned room, at least in the shade. Experienced photographers also recommend buying film in the cities rather than in the countryside where proper storage facilities for colour films are not guaranteed. Also, get your films processed as soon as possible, either in Malaysia or in Singapore.

Humidity can be another tropical hazard, particularly with jungle photography. The solution here is to carry equipment and film in a closed camera bag containing silica gel, a chemical that absorbs moisture. For suitable tones and rich colour, the best times to photograph are before 10.30am or after 3pm. Few films take noon time sunlight well. Pictures often lose subtle gradations in colour because the light is too strong. In the early morning or late afternoon, sidelights give softer contrasts and deeper colour density. You perspire less as well!

Most Malaysians are more than amiable about having their pictures taken. It usually takes a gang of schoolchildren about 15 seconds before they merrily begin jabbing peace signs in front of your 20 mm lens. Mosques and temples are rightly more reserved about photographers posing their subjects in front of altars. Whatever the situation, you should always ask first for permission, especially with tribal people, who may have an aversion to having their photo taken. Keep a respectful distance from religious ceremonies. If you can bear to carry one, a zoom lens will enable you to photograph interesting groups of people without interfering with them.

Film processing is offered everywhere in Malaysia in almost all good-sized towns and in every city. All outlets will process colour print film (regardless of brand), sometimes in as little as half an hour. Processing of black and white and transparency stocks are undertaken by the more reputable firms, with a turn around of approximately 48 hours.

Getting Around

Malaysia is one of the easiest Asian countries to travel around in. Transportation ranges from an Orang Asli dugout canoe up remote rivers, to a trishaw in Kuala Terengganu, to funicular railways and fast modern jets. There are almost always several alternatives to travelling to a place. Travelling in Malaysia can be as exciting and as adventurous as you want to make it. To get a feel of the country, you should try several of the different modes of transport.

On Arrival

Buses, public and private, taxis and even limousine services operate from major airports in Malaysia. Many airports have a taxi desk, where taxis can be booked and paid for and where the price is fixed. Where there is no such service, inquire at the information desk about how far the town is from the airport, and how much you should pay a taxi driver. Taxi fares from airports are in general much higher than around the town and if you are in a hurry to get to the airport, you may have to pay the taxi driver more to persuade him to take the expressways, because of the tolls.

Domestic Travel
By Air

Malaysia Airlines (MAS) runs an extensive network of airways over the entire nation. In remote jungle areas, the Fokker 50s and Twin Otters operate services linking out-of-the-way places to national centres. Singapore Airlines, Royal Brunei, Cathay Pacific and Thai International have regular flights to Malaysian destinations other than Kuala Lumpur. Inquire at the appropriate offices. Below is a list of MAS offices in Malaysia for bookings and confirmations   (T=ticketing, R=reservations):

Alor Setar, Lot 180, Kompleks Alor Setar, Lebuhraya Darulaman, 05100 Alor Setar, Kedah, Tel: 04-731 1106 (T), 04-731 1186 (R).

Bintulu, 129 Taman Sri Dagang, Jalan Masjid, 97000 Bintulu, Sarawak, Tel: 086-332 898 (T), 086-331 554 (R).

Ipoh, Lot-08, Bangunan Seri Kinta, Jalan Sultan Idris Shah, 30000 Ipoh, Perak, Tel: 05-241 4155.

Johor Bahru, Suite 1.1, Level 1, Menara Pelangi, Jalan Kuning, Taman Pelangi, 80400 Johor Bahru, Johor, Tel: 07-331 0035 (T), 07-334 1001 (R).

Keningau, H/A-Pan Fui Liong, Lot 13, 1st floor, Bangunan Persatuan Hakka 98007 Keningau, Sabah, Tel: 087-31553.

Kota Bharu, Ground Floor, Komplek Yakin, Jalan Gajah Mati, 15050 Kota Bharu, Kelantan, Tel: 09-748 3477 (T), 09-744 7000 (R),

Kota Kinabalu, 10th floor, Blk C, Kompleks Karamunsing, P.O. Box 10194, 88802 Kota Kinabalu, Sabah, Tel: 088-239 310 (T), 088-213 555 (R).

Kuala Lumpur, 33rd floor, Bangunan MAS, Jalan Sultan Ismail, 50250 KL, Tel: 03-261 0555; Lot 157, 1st floor, Complex Dayabumi, Jalan Sultan Hishamuddin, 50050 KL, Tel: 03-274 8734; Shop Lot No. 15/16 Menara Majlis Perbandaran Petaling Jaya, Jalan Tengah, 46200 Petaling Jaya,

Selangor, Tel: 03-755 0770; Reservations (24 hours) Tel: 03-746 3000.

Kuala Terengganu, No. 13, Jalan Sultan Omar, 20300 Kuala Terengganu, Terengganu, Tel: 09-622 2266.

Kuantan, No. 7, Ground floor, Wisma Bolasepak Pahang, Jalan Gambut, 25000 Kuantan, Pahang, Tel: 09-515 7055.

Kuching, Lot 215, Jalan Song Thian Cheok, 93100 Kuching, Malaysia, Tel: 082-244 144 (T), 082-216 622 (R).

Labuan, Lot No. 1, Wisma Kee Chia Jalan Bunga Kesuma, 87008 Wilayah Persekutuan Labuan, Tel: 087-412 263.

Langkawi, Lot 1598, Bangunan Tabung Haji, 07000 Pokok Asam, Pulau Langkawi, Kedah, Tel: 04-966 6622 (T), 04-966 7822 (R).

Malacca, 1st floor, Hotel Shopping Arcade, City Bayview Hotel, Jalan Bendehara, 75100 Malacca, Tel: 06-283 5722 (T), 06-283 5723 (R).

Miri, Lot 239, Beautiful Jade Centre, P.O. Box 180, 98007 Miri, Sarawak, Malaysia, Tel: 085-414 144, 414 155.

Penang, Third floor, Tun Abdul Razak Complex, Penang Road, 10000 Penang, Tel: 04-262 1403 (T), 04-262 0011 (R).

Ranau, H/A Ranau Travel Service, Lot D, No 1, P.O. Box 11, 89307 Ranau, Sabah, Tel: 088-876 152.

Sandakan, Mezzanine floor, Sabah Bldg., Jalan Pelabuhan, 90007 Sandakan, Sabah, Tel: 089-273 966, 273 962.

Sibu, No. 61, Jalan Tuanku Osman, 96000 Sibu, Sarawak, Tel: 084-321 055 (T), 084-326 166 (R).

Tawau, Lot 1A, First and Ground floor, Wisma Sasco, Jalan Perbandaran, P.O. Box 547, 91008 Tawau, Sabah, Malaysia, Tel: 089-765 533.

By Rail

Malaysian Railways or Keretapi Tanah Melayu (KTM), runs right from the heart of Singapore's business centre, through the Malay peninsula and on into Thailand in the north, calling at major cities and towns including Kuala Lumpur. Another line, the East Coast line, branches off the main one at Gemas, plunges through the central forests and emerges eventually at Tumpat, near the border to Thailand. Malaysian trains are generally comfortable, many equipped with televisions screening movie videos. Passengers

can choose from air-conditioned first-class coaches or, on the night trains, first class twin berth cabins. In second class are fan-cooled sleepers and sleeperettes are in the third-class coaches. The passenger has also the choice of travelling on a normal train which stops at most stations, or the express train, which stops only at major towns.

For foreign tourists, KTM offers a railpass which entitles the holder to unlimited travel in any class and to any destination for a period of 10 or 30 days. The Railpass costs approximately RM130 for adults for 10 days, and RM300 for 30 days. The cost of the pass does not include sleeping berth charges, and for these you would be wise to book in advance. For more information, call the KTM Central information line, Tel: 03-274 9422.

Water Transport

Traditionally, transport in Malaysia, particularly in the west, was by water. In Pahang, on the Endau River, and of course, in Sarawak, water transport still has some importance, but in general, roads have taken over as the main means of transport.

On rivers in peninsular Malaysia, you may find boats for hire, but often the best way is to find out which boats are going where and hitch a ride. Boat rental can sometimes be expensive, especially, for example, if you want a ride downriver. The boatman will be reluctant, because he has to motor all the way upriver again afterwards. He might prefer to sell the boat to you!

In Sarawak, there is a lot of traffic on the rivers inland throughout most of the year as roads are still few and far between and mostly in poor condition. On the Rejang River, regular boats run between Sibu and Kapit, and if the waters are high enough, all the way to Belaga. Boats to smaller rivers and to remote longhouses can be fearfully expensive, and it is best to go down to the jetty and see where all those women with baskets are heading for and change your plans accordingly.

Other regular ferry and boat services include boats to the islands of Pangkor, Penang and Langkawi. Boats to Pangkor stop running at 7pm, but ferries to Penang run 24 hours, and boats to Langkawi till 6pm.

Boats out to islands on the east coast are slightly less regular, especially in the monsoon season when several services may stop altogether. There are services to the Perhentian Islands, Kepas, Redang and Tenggol in the north, and many boats run out to the islands off Mersing. Mersing boats can be a little confusing as there is a wide choice. Boats to Tioman range from fishing boats that charge RM25 per person one way, or catamarans and ferries that cost RM30 and take 2½ hours, to the hydrofoil which takes 75 minutes and costs around RM25. Some of the other islands also have ferries (e.g. Rawa and Sibu) or you can hire a fishing boat to get there. The price of the boat is the same whether you are one person or 12 (maximum).

Public Transport

Taxi

Taxis remain one of the most popular and cheap means of transport. You can hail them by the roadside, hire them from authorised taxi stands, or book them by phone, in which case, mileage is calculated from the stand or garage from which the vehicle is hired.

Although most taxis are fitted with meters, not all drivers use them. Make sure that your driver is willing to use his meter, or negotiate a charge at the beginning of the journey.

Flagfall is RM1.50 for the first 2 kilometres (1.2 mi) and the meter then turns over in 10 sen lots every 20 metres (22 yds). There is a RM1 charge for a telephone booking, trips between midnight and 6am will have a 50 percent surcharge and there could be a small additional charge for more than two passengers.

From most airports and railway stations, taxi fares are fixed and you should prepay at the taxi counter. For 24-hour taxi service in Kuala Lumpur, call Saujana Taxi, Tel: 03-241 5193; Comfort Taxi, Tel: 03-733 0507; or Public Cab, Tel: 03-718 1718. For taxi complaints, call 03-255 4444.

Bus

There are three types of buses that operate in Malaysia: the non-air-conditioned buses plying between the states, the non-air-conditioned buses that provide services within each state, and the air-conditioned express buses connecting major towns in Malaysia. Buses seldom adhere to the schedule but are frequent between 9am to 6pm. Buses plying within towns and cities usually charge fares according to distance covered, with the exception of the mini buses in Kuala Lumpur, which charge a standard fare of 60 sen.

Travelling by bus within Kuala Lumpur and to the surrounding areas of Petaling Jaya, Subang Jaya and Klang is definitely not for the faint-hearted. Published or posted timetables are a mystery to most, and listings of the stops or final destinations of each route are equally elusive, save for the signs carried on the front of each individual vehicle. However, for those determined to savour this fascinating grass-roots mode of transport within the Capital and its environs, the experience is likened to an exhilirating roller coaster ride, thanks to the driver's daredevil attempts to meet their quotas, irrespective of traffic laws and other road users.

Kuala Lumpur bus terminals:
Eastcoast Express: Putra Bus Station (opposite the World Trade Centre), Tel: 03-442 9530.
Eastcoast: Pekeliling Bus Station, Tel: 03-442 1256.
North and Southbound: Pudu Raya Bus Station, Tel: 03-230 0145.

Trishaw

If you want to see the city at your own pace, you can still find trishaws. These are very popular in cities such as Malacca, Kota Bahru, Kuala Terengganu and Georgetown, Penang. For short trips, they are better than taxis as their slow pace allows you to see points of interest along the way, and provide more photographic opportunities.

Except in Penang, where passengers sit in a sun-hooded carriage in front of the cyclist, a trishaw is a bicycle with a side carriage. In Penang, trishaw drivers will warn you to hold on to your bags firmly for fear of snatch-thieves on motorcycles. Incidences of this kind, however, are rare nowadays.

It's important that you fix the price before proceeding in a trishaw. A little bargaining is necessary, and you should inform the peddler if you wish to stop somewhere along the way, as stopping time also has to be calculated. In some places, especially in Penang, you can rent trishaws by the hour, which can be economical should you wish to see several places. A trishaw ride should cost approximately RM25 for half a day of sightseeing.

Private Transport

Car Rental

Having your own transport gives you the freedom to explore places off the beaten track at your leisure. The principal car rental firms are listed here. Most have branches in the main towns throughout Malaysia including those in Sabah and Sarawak.

Cars are usually for rent on an unlimited mileage basis. The daily rates vary from RM148 for economy cars per day to RM428 for cars in the super luxury class. Weekly rates are also available. Four-wheel drive is advisable in Sabah, Sarawak, and the central regions of the Malay peninsula. 24-hour breakdown service is not available.

Avis Rent A Car, 40, Jalan Sultan Ismail, Kuala Lumpur, Tel: 03-242 3500, (Toll free: 800 3500) Fax: 03-244 3813, airport: 03-746 3950.
Budget Rent A Car, 29 Jalan Yap Kwan Seng, Tel: 03-242 5116 (Toll free: 800 3191), Fax: 03-242 9362, airport: 03-746 3139 (Terminal 1), 03-746 2667 (Terminal 2).
Hertz Rent A Car, Lot 214A, Kompleks Antarabangsa, Jalan Sultan Ismail, Tel: 03-248 6433, airport: 03-746 2091, 746 2333.
National Car Rental, Shop 9, Ground floor, President House, Jalan Sultan Ismail, KL, Tel: 03-248 0522, airport: 03-746 2025.

Motoring in Malaysia

An international driving licence is required by visitors who wish to drive in Malaysia. National driving licences are only acceptable upon endorsement by the Registrar of Motor Vehicles. Travel insurance must also be taken.

From the causeway connecting Singapore and peninsular Malaysia, the main trunk road runs up the west coast to the Thai border. The North-South Highway linking Johor Bahru with Padang Besar, in the Thai Border, opened in 1993. Two main highways cross the peninsula to the east coast. In the north, the East-West Highway connects Butterworth with Kota Bahru, while in the central part of the peninsula, the Kuala Lumpur-Karak Highway cuts through the Main Range and joins a road leading to Kuantan on the east coast. In Sabah and Sarawak, motorways run along the coast connecting major towns. Roads leading to more remote areas inland are often unpaved or rough, and a four-wheel drive is advisable for these routes.

Driving is on the left-hand side of the road. International traffic signs are used, along with a few local ones such as *Awas* meaning caution, *ikut kiri* meaning "Keep left", *kurangkan laju* meaning "slow down", and *jalan sehala* meaning "one-way street" in the direction of the arrow. Where compass points are given, *Utara* is north, *Selatan* south, *Timur* east, and *Barat* west.

The speed limit in towns is 50 km/h. Outside towns, the speed limit is 80 km/h. On highways it is 110 km/h. The wearing of seat belts by drivers and front seat passengers is compulsory. Monsoon rains can cause hazards for motorists. Drive slowly and be prepared for delays on smaller roads as whole roads are sometimes washed away entirely.

For safety, local drivers have developed a few signals of their own. There are individual variations on these, so watch to see what the other motorists do. If the driver in front flashes his right indicator, he is signalling to you not to overtake. This is usually because of an oncoming vehicle or a bend in the road, or he himself might be about to overtake the vehicle in front of him. If he flashes the left indicator, this means to overtake with caution. A driver flashing his headlamps at you is claiming the right of way. At roundabouts or traffic circles, the driver on the right has the right of way.

Petrol is inexpensive and petrol stations are to be found in or on the fringes of towns. Many operate 24 hours (24 jam).

The Automobile Association of Malaysia (AAM) is the national motoring organisation and has offices in most states. The head office is located at: 25 Jalan Yap Kwan Seng, KL, Tel: 03-242 5777.

Touring

Eastern & Oriental Express: Introduced in 1993 the Orient Express is the ultimate $30 million recreation of a bygone age of elegant Asian rail travel. Decked out in the E & O livery of cream and racing green, and carrying a maximum of 132 passengers on the two-night trip from Singapore to KL and through the Cameron Highlands, southern Thailand to Bangkok (or vice versa). The 2,030-kilometre (1,262-mile) route was planned to enable its passengers to enjoy the best of Malaysia and Thailand's scenery during daylight hours. Side trips include Penang and Kanchanaburi.

If the sleeper compartments, corridors, restaurant car, rear observation platform seem familiar. If the uniformed stewards serving breakfast of fresh fruit, croissants and coffee in your state-room evoke a pre-war era of rubber planters in tropical suits and Panama hats sipping Singapore Slings and G & T, it is completely intentional. The interiors of the 22 carriages where completely refitted in mahogany marquetry and Burmese rosewood were inspired by the 1932 Marlene Dietrich film Shanghai Express, with added air-conditioning, of course. Not surprising the sales brochure's recommended clothing list includes tropical evening wear!

This luxury does not come cheap; a one-way trip per person costs from US$1,460 inclusive of meals, accommodation and service. For reservations, you may call:

Singapore	(65) 323 4390
Malaysia	(03) 781 1337
Thailand	(662) 216 5939

On Departure

Airport tax is collected at all airports. For domestic flights, the tax is RM5; for flights to Brunei and Singapore and all other international flights, the departure tax is RM20.

Where To Stay

Accommodation in Malaysia encompasses many different styles. You can choose anything, from youth hostel and crash pads to top-class international hotels with saunas, jacuzzis and tennis courts. To sample all of Malaysia, it is worth to try out accommodation from several different categories. The smaller and more homely establishments will be more likely to bring you closer to the Malaysians.

Most small Malaysian towns, in any case, do not offer the cosmopolitan facilities of a worldwide hotel chain; instead, they provide the personal touch, simplicity and cleanliness of a wayside inn. A typical urban street is dotted with small budget hotels renting simply furnished rooms for between RM10 and RM40 (depending on whether the room has air-conditioning or a simple ceiling fan). If you intend to visit one of Malaysia's national parks, it is necessary to go to the national park's office in the nearest town in order to book accommodation. In some cases, a deposit must be paid towards the accommodation and permit.

The following list of hotels is by no means exhaustive, but will give the visitor some idea of what is available. The hotel room rates are divided into three approximate price ranges: $$$$ for regular room rates above RM400, $$$ for rates between RM200-400, $$ for rates between RM100-200, and $ for rates below RM100.

Hotels
Kuala Lumpur

Agora Hotel, 106-110 Jalan Bukit Bintang, Tel: 03-242 8133, Fax: 03-242 7815. 39 air-conditioned rooms. $$

Carcosa Seri Negara, Taman Tasek Perdana, Tel: 03-282 1888, Fax: 03-282 7888. 13 extravagant suites, full room facilities and service, butlers, restaurant, bar, meeting rooms, business centre. $$$$

City Hotel, 366 Jalan Raja Laut, Tel: 03-441 4466, Fax: 03-441 5379. 101 air-conditioned rooms, centre of town, 30 mins from rail terminal, room service, telephone. $$

Concorde Hotel, Jalan Sultan Ismail, Tel: 03-244 2200, Fax: 03-244 1628. 673 air-conditioned rooms, full room facilities and service, Asian specialty restaurant, coffeeshop, swimming pool, business centre, shopping arcade. $$$

Crown Princess, City Square Complex, Jalan Tun Razak, Tel: 03-262 5522, Fax: 03-262 4422. 528 rooms, full room facilities and service, restaurants, 24-hour coffeehouse, lounges, convention facilities, health centre, swimming pool, shopping arcade. $$$

Federal Hotel, 35 Jalan Bukit Bintang, Tel: 03-248 9166, Fax: 03-248 2877. 450 rooms, fully air-conditioned, a revolving lounge, Western and Chinese restaurants, bars, banquet halls, supperclubs with international shows nightly, 24-hour coffeehouse, swimming pool, bowling alley (18 lane), shops, air-conditioned limousine service. $$$

Grand Pacific Hotel, Jalan Tun Ismail/ Jalan Ipoh, Tel: 03-442 2177, Fax: 03-442 6078. 110 rooms, telephone, coffeehouse, nightclub, health centre, colour TV available on request. $$

Holiday Inn City Centre, 12 Jalan Raja Laut, Tel: 03-293 9233, Fax: 03-293 9634. 250 rooms, air-conditioned. Chinese restaurant, coffeeshop, business centre, swimming pool. $$$

Holiday Inn on the Park, Jalan Pinang, Tel: 03-248 1066, Fax: 03-248 1930. 200 rooms, restaurants, beauty shops, car rental. $$$

Istana, 73 Jalan Raja Chulan, Tel: 03-244 1445, Fax: 03-244 1245. 461 rooms, full room facilities and service, restaurants, coffeeshop, lounges, discotheque, health centre, swimming pool. $$$$

International Youth Hostel, Jalan Kampong Asap, Tel: 03-230 6780. $

KL Hilton, Jalan Sultan Ismail, Tel: 03-242 2222, Fax: 03-244 2157 581 rooms, full room facilities and services, restaurants, grill, coffeehouse, lounge, swimming pool, tennis, squash, health centre, disco, night club, shops, business centre, car rental. $$$$

KL Mandarin, 2-8 Jalan Sultan, Tel: 03-230 3000, Fax: 03-230 4363. 126 rooms, 24-hour room service, TV, coffeehouse, Chinese restaurant, bar lounge, beauty and barber shops, health centre, travel service. $$

Lodge Hotel, 2 Jalan Tengah, off Jalan Sultan Ismail, Tel: 03-242 0122, Fax: 03-241 6819. 50 rooms, full room facilities and service, restaurant. $$

Pan Pacific Kuala Lumpur, Jalan Putra, Tel: 03-442 5555, Fax: 03-441 7236. 571 rooms, full room facilities and service, restaurants, grill, 24-hour coffeehouse, cocktail lounge, bar, swimming pool, gymnasium, tennis, squash, health centre, water sports, disco, barber shops, business centre, car rental. $$$

Puduraya Hotel, 4th Floor, Puduraya Station, Jalan Pudu, Tel: 03-232 1000, Fax: 03-230 5567. 200 rooms, restaurants, coffeehouse, health centre. $$

Regent of Kuala Lumpur, 160 Jalan Bukit Bintang, Tel: 03-241 8000, Fax: 03-242 1441. 469 rooms, full room service and facilities, restaurants, coffeeshop, swimming pool, health club, business centre, shops; banquet and meeting rooms. $$$$

Shangri-La Hotel, Jalan Sultan Ismail, Tel: 03-232 2388, Fax: 03-230 1514. 721 rooms, full room facilities and service, restaurants, grill, coffeehouse, bar, cocktail lounge, swimming pool, tennis, squash, health centre, disco, beauty salon, business centre, car rental. $$$$

YMCA of Kuala Lumpur, Jalan Padang Belia, Tel: 03-274 1439. 60 dormitories and rooms, cafeteria, sports facilities. $

Selangor

Hyatt Saujana Hotel and Country Club, off Subang International Airport Highway, Tel: 03-746 1234, Fax: 03-733 1299. 386 rooms with full five-star facilities. $$$$

Holiday Villa, 9 Jalan SS12/1, Subang Jaya, Tel: 03-733 8788, Fax: 03-733 7448. $$$

Merlin Subang, Jalan 12/1 Subang Jaya, Tel: 03-733 5211. 162 rooms. $$$

Subang Airport Hotel, Kompleks Airtel Fima, Tel: 03-774 6122, Fax: 03-746 1097. 157 rooms, coffeehouse, piano bar, swimming pool, and conference facilities. $$$

Petaling Jaya Hilton, Jalan Barat, Tel: 03-755 9122, Fax: 03-755 3909. 398 rooms with full services. $$$

Negeri Sembilan

SEREMBAN

Allson Klana Resort, Jalan Penghulu Chantek, Taman Tasek, 70100 Seremban, Tel: 06-762 9600, Fax: 06-763 9218. 223 rooms, full room facilities and service, restaurants, coffeehouse, bars, business centre, fitness centre, swimming pool. $$$

Carlton Hotel, 47 Jalan Dato' Sheikh Ahmad, Tel: 06-762 5336. 34 rooms, air-conditioned, Chinese restaurant, coffeehouse, bar, fitness centre. $$

Majestic Hotel, 1 Jalan Dato' Sheikh Ahmad, 7000 Seremban, Tel: 06-762 2506. $

PORT DICKSON

Ming Court Beach Hotel, Batu 7, Jalan Pantai, Tel: 06-662 5244, Fax: 06-662 5899. 165 rooms, restaurant, swimming pool, water sports, conference facilities. $$$

Pantai Dickson Resort, Batu 12, Jalan Pantai, Tel: 06-662 5473. 200 Bungalows. $$$

Regency Hotel & Resort, Batu 5, Jalan Pantai, Tel: 06-647 4090, Fax: 06-647 4792. 217 rooms, 3 restaurants, 24-hour coffeehouse, sea sports and recreational centre. $$$

Sea View Hotel, 841 Batu 1, Jalan Pantai, Tel: 06-647 1811. 20 rooms. $

Malacca

City Bayview Hotel, Jalan Bendahara, Tel: 06-283 9888, Fax: 06-283 6699. 182 rooms, swimming pool. $$$

Emperor Hotel, 123 Jalan Munshi Abdullah, Tel: 06-284 0777, Fax: 06-283 8989. 240 rooms. $$

Malacca Renaissance, Jalan Bendahara, Tel: 06-248 8888, Fax: 06-284 9269. 295 rooms, air-conditioned, Chinese restaurant, coffeehouse, Renaissance Club, fitness centre and conference facilities. $$$$

Regal Hotel, 66 Jalan Munshi Abdullah, Tel: 06-284 5500. 30 rooms, air-conditioned, restaurant, bar. $

Tanjung Bidara Resort, Tanjung Bidara Masjid Tanah, Tel: 06-542 990, Fax: 06-542 995. 85 rooms, restaurant, lounge, swimming pool, banquet and conference facilities. $$

293

Tapa-Nyai Island Resort, Pulau Besar, Malacca, Tel: 06-236 733, Fax: 06-243 588. 140 rooms, restaurant, coffeehouse, bars, water sports, health centre, disco, banquet and conference facilities. $$$

AYER KEROH

Air Keroh Country Resort, Air Keroh, Tel: 06-325 211. Chalet resort. $$
Air Keroh d'Village Melaka, Air Keroh, Tel: 06-327 542, Fax: 06-327 541. 274 chalets, seafood restaurant, coffeehouse, pool terrace, sports facilities, banquet hall. $$
Malacca Village Park Plaza Resort, Air Keroh, Tel: 06-323 600, Fax: 06-325 955. 147 rooms, swimming pool, restaurant. $$$

Penang

City Bayview Hotel, 25A Lebuh Farquhar, 10200 Penang, Tel: 04-263 3161, Fax: 04-263 4124. 160 rooms, full room facilities, Malay, Chinese and Japanese restaurants, coffeehouse, lounge bar, business centre, swimming pool, tennis, squash. $$$
Eastern and Oriental Hotel, 10 Lebuh Farquhar, 10200 Penang, Tel: 04-263 0630, Fax: 04-263 4833. 100 rooms, swimming pool, waterfront views, one of Somerset Maugham's favourite hotels. $$$
Equatorial Penang, 1 Jalan Bukit Jambul, Bayan Lepas, Tel: 04-643 8111, Fax: 04-644 8000. 460 rooms, restaurants, coffeehouse and terrace bar, 18-hole golf course, tennis, squash, gymnasium and jogging tracks. $$$$
Hotel Continental, 5 Penang Road, 10000 Penang, Tel: 04-263 6388, Fax: 04-263 4495. 116 rooms, bar, restauarant, nightclub. $$
Hotel Embassy, 12 Jalan Burmah, Tel: 04-377 515. 27 rooms, air-conditioned, 24-hour room service, telephone, bath/shower, coffeehouse. $
Hotel Fortuna, 406 Penang Road, 11600 Penang, Tel: 04-229 8159. 32 rooms, air-conditioned, telephone, piped-in music, bath/shower, health centre. $
Ming Court Hotel, 202A MacAlister Road, Tel: 04-229 8588, Fax: 04-229 7257. 110 rooms, full room facilities, restaurant, coffeehouse, bar. $$
Shangri-La Inn Penang, Jalan Magazine, 10300 Penang, Tel: 04-262 2622, Fax: 04-262 6526. 442 rooms, full room facilities, coffeehouse, Chinese restaurant, lobby lounge, poolside bar, disco, business centre, health club, swimming pool, beauty salon, travel office, tours, car rental. $$$$
Sheraton Penang, 126 Jalan Burmah, 10050 Penang, Tel: 04-376 788, Fax: 04-376 788. 295 rooms, fully air-conditioned, restaurant, grill, coffeehouse, bars, swimming pool, health centre, indoor games, disco, shops, beauty salon, business centre. $$$

BEACH HOTELS IN PENANG

Bayview Pacific Resort, Batu Ferringhi, 11100 Penang, Tel: 04-881 2123, Fax: 04-881 2140. 426 rooms, three restaurants, coffeehouse, swimming pool, three bars, tennis. $$$$
Crown Prince, Tanjung Bungah, Tel: 04-890 4111, Fax: 04-890 4890. 295 sea-facing rooms, 2 executive floors, Sichuan and Cantonese restaurant, coffeehouse, bar, swimming pool, water sports, fitness centre, business centre. $$$
Ferringhi Beach Hotel, Batu Ferringhi Road, Tel: 04-890 5999, Fax: 04-890 5100. 350 rooms, full room facilities and service, restaurant, grill, coffeehouse, bar, swimming pool, disco, shops, beauty salon. $$$
Golden Sands Hotel, Batu Ferringhi Beach, Tel: 04-881 1911, Fax: 04-881 1880. 395 rooms, full room facilities, sea views, restaurants, barbecues, swimming pool, sea sports, trekking, tennis. $$$
Holiday Inn Penang, Batu Ferringhi Beach, Tel: 04-881 1611, Fax: 04-881 1601. 352 rooms, full room facilities and services, 24-hour coffeehouse, Baron's Table Steakhouse, bar, rock garden, swimming pool, water sports, shops, travel service. $$$
Lone Pine Hotel, 97 Batu Ferringhi, Tel: 04-881 1511. 54 rooms, air-conditioned, cocktail lounge, fishing, tennis. $$
Mar Vista Resort, 1 Jalan Batu Ferrenghi, Tel: 04-890 3388, Fax: 04-890 3886. 1,000 studio apartments and flats, 4 restaurants, bars, swimming pool, recreation centre, business centre. $$$
Motel Sri Pantai, 516G Jalan Hashim, Tanjong Bungah, Tel: 04-890 5566. 21 rooms, water-skiing. $
Mutiara Beach Resort, 1 Jalan Teluk Bahang, Tel: 04-885 2828, Fax: 04-885 2829. 440 rooms, full room facilities and service, restaurants, bars, fitness centre, water sports, squash, tennis, volleyball, badminton. $$$$
Palm Beach Hotel, 105A Batu Ferringhi, Tel: 04-881 1621, Fax: 04-881 1051. 145 rooms, full room facilities and services, two restaurants, swimming pool, water sports, tennis, meeting and banquet facilities. $$$
Penang Parkroyal, Batu Ferringhi Beach, Tel: 04-881 1133, Fax: 04-881 2233. 333 rooms, full room facilities and services, restaurant, delicatessen, water sports. $$$
Rasa Sayang Hotel, Batu Ferringhi Beach, Tel: 04-881 1611, Fax: 04-881 1180. 536 rooms, full room facilities and service, Western, Chinese and Japanese restaurants, swimming pools, squash, croquet, putting green, water sports, health centre, shops. $$$$

BUTTERWORTH

Butterworth Travel Lodge, 1 Lorong Bagan Luar, Tel: 04-333 3399, Fax: 04-332 3599. 50 rooms. $$
Hotel Kuala Lumpur, 4488 Lorong Bagan Luar, Tel: 04-332 6199, Fax: 04-332 6021. 45 rooms. $

Perak

IPOH

Casuarina Hotel, 24 Jalan Gopeng, 30250 Ipoh, Tel: 05-255 5555, Fax: 05-255 8177. 217 rooms, full room facilities, Italian restaurant, coffeehouse, cocktail lounge, disco, beauty shop, health centre, swimming pool, shopping arcade. $$$
Excelsior Hotel, Clarke Street, 30300, Ipoh, Tel: 05-253 6666, Fax: 05-253 6908. 133 rooms, mini-bar, TV/video, restaurant, coffeehouse, bar, disco, travel service, car rental. $$$
Hotel Eastern, 118 Jalan Sultan Idris Shah, Tel: 05-254 3936, Fax: 05-255 1468. 30 rooms, coffeehouse, Chinese restaurant. $
Tambun Inn, 91 Tambun Road, 30350 Ipoh, Tel: 05-57 7211, Fax: 05-567 887. 100 rooms, full room facilities, restaurant, coffeehouse, bar, health centre, disco, travel services, car rental. $$$

LUMUT

Orient Star, Lot 203 & 366, Jalan Iskandar Shah, Tel: 05-683 4199, Fax: 05-683 4223. 150 rooms sea-facing rooms, restaurants, lounge, swimming pool, gymnasium, games room, banquet and convention facilities. $$$
Government Rest House, Lumut, Tel: 05-683 5494. 9 rooms, museum. $
Lumut Country Resort, 331 Jalan Titi Panjang, 32200 Lumut, Tel: 05-683 5109, Fax: 05-683 5396. 44 rooms, room service, restaurants, bars, swimming pool, disco, shops. $$

PANGKOR ISLAND

Pangkor Laut Resort, Pulau Pangkor Laut, Tel: 05-699 1100, Fax: 05-699 1200. 123 rooms offering a choice of hillside or beachfront villas as well as suites set on stilts over the sea, swimming pools, water sports, conference facilities. $$$$
Pan Pacific Pangkor, Teluk Belanga, Tel: 05-685 1399, Fax: 05-685 1095. 161 traditional style rooms and chalets, full room facilities and service, water sports, boat trips, restaurants, bars, barbecue on beach, disco, private beach. $$$
Sea View Hotel, Pasir Bogak, Tel: 05-685 1605, Fax: 05-685 1705. 37 rooms, some air-conditioned, chalets, bar, lounge, restaurant, water sports, boat trips. $$
Pangkor Anchor, Pasir Bogak, Tel: 05-685 1363. Coconut huts, garden, breakfast, restaurant next door. $

Kedah

Holiday Inn Pedu Lake Resort, KB1, 06300, Kuala Nerang, Kedah, Tel: 04-730 4888, Fax: 04-730 4488. (KL reservations, 03-348 1242) 200 chalets, restaurant, coffee house. $$$

ALOR SETAR

Grand Continental Hotel, 134, Jalan Sultan Badlishah, Tel: 04-733 5917. Fax: 04-733 5161. 130 rooms, full room facilities and services, restaurant, coffeehouse, bar, disco, business centre, car rental. $$

SUNGAI PETANI

JW Palace Hotel, Jalan Pahlawan, Sungai Petani, Tel: 04-422 0420, Fax: 04-423 3423. $$$
Pantai Merdeka Resort, Kota Kuala Muda, Sungai Petani, Tel: 04-437 5588, Fax: 04-43 75599. $$

PULAU LANGKAWI

Burau Bay Resort, Pantai Kok, Tel: 04-955 1061, Fax: 04-955 1001. 150 rooms in tent-style cabins, air-conditioned, full room facilities and services, restaurant, coffeeshop, lounge, swimming pool, water sports. $$$
Datai Langkawi Resort, Jalan Teluk Datai, Tel: 04-959 2500, Fax: 04-959 2600. A choice of villas or rooms; 3 restaurants, lounges and bars, private beach, swimming pools, tennis, adjacent 18-hole golf course, health club, water sports. $$$$
Delima Resort, Kuala Muda, Tel: 04-955 1801, Fax: 04-955 1811. 1,400 rooms in longhouse-style chalets, full room facilities and services, restaurants, bars, water sports, fitness centre, swimming pool, shopping mall. $$
Langkawi Island Resort, Pantai Dato'Syed Omar, Kuah, Tel: 04-966 6209, Fax: 04-966 5301. 100 rooms, water sports. $$$
Pelangi Beach Resort, Pantai Cenang, Tel: 04-955 1011, Fax: 955 1122. 350 traditional style bungalows and chalets, full room facilities, restaurants, swimming pools, games room, health centre, conference facilities (Queen Elizabeth stayed here in 1989), disco, water sports, tours, jeeps for hire. $$$$
Sheraton Langkawi, Teluk Nibung, Tel: 04-955 1901, Fax: 04-955 1968. 155 chalet rooms, full room facilities and service, restaurants, bars, swimming pool. $$$$

Kelantan

KOTA BAHRU

Perdana Hotel, Jalan Mahmud, Tel: 09-748 5000, Fax: 09-744 7621. 136 rooms, full room facilities, restaurants, coffeehouse, bars, swimming pool, tennis, squash, water sports, golf course, beauty salon, car rental. $$$
Perdana Resort, Jalan Kuala Pa'amat, Pantai Cinta Berahi, Tel: 09-773 3000, Fax: 09-773 9980. Sea sports. $$
Temenggong Hotel, Jalan Tok Hakim, Tel: 09-748 3844, Fax: 09-744 1481. 36 rooms, air-conditioned, restaurant, disco, coffeehouse, bath/shower. $$

Terengganu

KUALA TERENGGANU

Motel Desa, Bukit Pak Apil, Tel: 09-622 3438, Fax: 09-622 3443. 20

rooms, air-conditioned, room service, hot water, swimming pool, restaurant, bar. $$
Primula Beach Resort, Jalan Persinggahan, Tel: 09-622 2100, Fax: 09-623 3360. 264 rooms, full room facilities, 4 restaurants, coffeehouse, ballroom, disco (top floor), bars, swimming pool, tennis, horse-riding, watersports, island trips, turtle watching, fishing, handicraft shop, trips to Sekayu Waterfalls, shops, business centre. $$$$
Bunga Raya Hotel, 105-11 Jalan Banggol, Tel: 09-622 0527. 39 rooms, some air-conditioned, hot water, coffeehouse. $

KENYIR LAKE

Kenyir Boating Holidays, 895 Jalan Dato Jaya Batu Buruk, Kuala Terrenganu, Tel: 09-630 170, Fax: 09-630 272. Houseboats for hire on Kenyir Lake. $$$
Primula Kenyir Lake Resort, P.O. Box 43, Jalan Persinggahan, 20904 Kuala Terengganu, Tel: 09-622 2100, Fax: 09-622 3360. Standard and superior chalets, restaurant, conference and meeting halls, camping site, water sports, fishing, trekking. $$$

DUNGUN

Tanjong Jara Beach Hotel, 8th Mile off Jalan Dungun, Tel: 09-844 1801, Fax: 09-844 2653. 100 rooms, air-conditioned, full room facilities, tennis, golf park, squash, swimming pool, sauna, restaurants, bars.$$$

PULAU REDANG

Berjaya Redang Beach Resort, Tel: 03-242 9611. Fax: 03-248 8249. 152 rooms, restaurants, 200-seater function hall, sea sports, and recreational facilities. $$$

RANTAU ABANG

Rantau Abang Visitor's Centre, Batu 13, Jalan Dungun, Tel: 09-844 1533. Huts and chalets, turtle watching. $

MARANG

Hotel Sri Malaysia, Kampung paya, Marang. Tel: 09-618 2889, Fax: 09-618 1285. $$

Pahang

KUANTAN

Coral Beach Resort, Tel: 09-544 7544, Fax: 09-544 7543. 162 rooms, full room facilities, restaurants, bars, shops, watersports, travel service, car rental, swimming pool. $$$

Le Village Beach Resort, Lot 1260 Sungai Karang, Beserah, Kuantan, Tel: 09-544 7900, Fax: 09-544 7999. Beachside chalets and rooms, four restaurants, bar, water sports. $$

Gloria Maris Resort, Mastura, 1/1402, Kampung Baru Beserah, Kuantan, Tel: 09-544 7788. 17 chalets in beachside compound. $

TELUK CHEMPEDAK BEACH

Hyatt Kuantan, Teluk Chempedak, Tel: 09-513 1234, Fax: 09-513 7577. 353 rooms, full room facilities and service, squash, tennis, health centre, business centre, swimming pool, restaurant, bar, coffeehouse, disco. $$$$

Merlin Inn Resort, Teluk Chempedak, Tel: 09-513 3001, Fax: 09-513 3523. 106 rooms, full room facilities and services, swimming pool, golf club, restaurant, disco. $$

CHERATING

Cherating Holiday Villa, Lot 1303, Mukim Sungai Karang, Tel: 09-581 9500, Fax: 09-581 9178. 94 rooms with full facilities, restaurant, bar, tennis, squash, sauna, gymnasium, swimming pool, island excursions, horse-riding, golf, fishing, water sports; from RM175 to RM280.

Club Med. For reservations and membership, apply at Bangunan MAS 1st floor, Suite 1, 1 Jalan Sultan Ismail, 50250 Kuala Lumpur, Tel: 03-261 4599; Pantai Cherating, Tel: 09-859 1131, Fax: 09-850 4141. The usual Club Med facilities, fun and games. Membership fee RM80; weekly package including flight from KL. $$$

Impiana Resort Cherating, Jalan Kuantan-Kemaman, Tel: 09-581 9000, Fax: 09-581 9090. 250 rooms, full room facilities and service, restaurants, bars, water sports, swimming pool. $$$

Legend Resort, Lot 1290, Sungai Karang, Cherating, Tel: 09-581 9439, Fax: 09-581 9400. 152 rooms, full room facilities and service, restaurants, 24-hour coffeeshop, bars, discotheque, tennis, squash, water sports, swimming pool. $$$

For budget travellers, there are a multitude of cheap and cheerful chalets for rent along the entire stretch of Cherating beach. The price varies with the duration of the stay and bargaining is expected and advised.

CAMERON HIGHLANDS

(accessible from Perak State)

The Lakehouse, 30th Mile Ringlet, Tel: 05-495 6152, Fax: 05-495 6123. 16 rooms, Tudor architecture, antique furnishings, restaurant, fishing, jungle walks, waterfalls and lakes. $$$

Merlin Inn Resort, Tanah Rata, Tel: 05-491 1211, Fax: 05-491 2718. 64 rooms, telephone, full room facilities, restaurant and bar, tennis, adjacent golf course, disco, shops. $$

Strawberry Park Resort, P.O. Box 81, Tanah Rata, Tel: 05-491 1166, Fax: 05-491 1944. 127 rooms, full room facilities, restaurant, coffeehouse, grill, bar, tennis, squash, health centre, golf course, horse-riding, disco, shops, travel service. $$$

Ye Olde Smokehouse, Brinchang/Tanah Rata, Tel/Fax: 05-491 1214. Tudor architecture with English country garden, log fires, 20 family suites, dining and tea rooms, bars, 18-hole golf course, jungle walks, cream teas. $$$

Golf Course Inn, Tanah Rata, Tel: 05-491 1214. 30 rooms, restaurant, golf and badminton. $$

GENTING HIGHLANDS

(accessible from Kuala Lumpur)

Genting Highlands Resort, 51 km (32 mi) from KL, Tel: 03-211 1118 (Central Resort), 03-262 3555/800 8228 (Enquiries/reservations), Fax: 03-261 6611. Comprises of sister hotels: **Genting Hotel**, **Highlands Hotel**, and **Resort Hotel**. Full room facilities, restaurants, Malaysia's only casino, coffeehouse, bars, health centre with jacuzzi and sauna, beauty salon, flower nursery, amusement park, video arcade, cable car, nightclub, bowling alley, golf course, shops, lake and boating, swimming pool, squash, revolving disco, car rental/limousine service. $$$

Awana Golf and Country Resort, comprising Awana Hotel, Awana Condominium, Ria and Kayangan Apartments. Tel: 03-262 3555/800 8228, Fax: 03-261 6611. Tower block hotels rooms, full room facilities, condominium suites, golf course, specialty restaurants, horse ranch. $$$

FRASER'S HILL

(accessible from Kuala Lumpur)

Fraser's Hill Bungalows/Chalets, c/o Fraser's Hill Development Corporation, Fraser's Hill, Tel: 09-382 201. 69 rooms, dining room, tennis, 18-hole golf course, barber shop, skating rink, swimming pool. $$

Merlin Hotel Fraser's Hill, Jalan Lady Guillemard, Tel: 09-382 300, Fax: 09-382 284. 109 rooms, full room facilities, restaurant, horse-riding, 9-hole golf course, tennis. $$$

TIOMAN ISLAND

(in Pahang state but accessible from Johor at Mersing)

Berjaya Tioman Beach Resort, 185 Seaview, Tel: 09-445 445, Fax: 09-445 718. Hillview, chalet and standard rooms, air-conditioned, full room facilities and service, restaurants, cocktail lounge, picnic packs, all water sport including scuba diving, boat trips, glass-bottom boats, jungle treks. $$$

Tioman Paya Resort, Kampung Paya Tioman, Tel: 07-799 2602, Fax: 07-799 2603. Chalets, air conditioned, restaurant, 50 metres (55 yds) to beach, jungle treks. $$$

Taman Negara

Department of Wildlife and National Parks, Taman Negara, Kuala Tahan, Tel: 09-296 1267. KL Office: 10th kilometre Jalan Cheras, 56100 KL, Tel: 03-905 2872. Information and bookings for Taman Negara can also be obtained at the Malaysian Tourist Information Centre (MATIC), 109 Jalan Ampang, KL, Tel: 03-242 3929.

Entry Permit: RM1; Camera Licence: RM5; Fishing Licence: RM10; Return boat fare to Park Headquarters: RM30; Park Deposit: RM30. Gunung Tahan Climb: RM400 per guide per week, and RM50 for every subsequent day. Camping and fishing equipment for hire, 2 restaurants at headquarters, cooking facilities at hostel; cash payment only at the park.

Accommodation: Camping: RM1 per person per night; Fishing Lodge: RM8 per person per night; Jungle Hides: RM5 per person per night.

Taman Negara Resort, Park Headquarters, Kuala Tahan, Jeranjut, 27000 Pahang, Tel: 09-263 5000, Fax: 09-263 1500. Book through KL office: 2nd Floor, Istana Hotel, Jalan Raja Chulan, 50250 Kuala Lumpur. Tel: 03-

245 5585, Fax: 03-261 0615. Malaysian-styled wooden chalets with balconies which open onto the park, 110 rooms, dormitories, camping, restaurant and cafeteria, bar, library, meeting facilities, jungle trekking, guides available, equipment for hire. Boat transfer: Per person: RM36; Per boat: RM480. Accomodation $ to $$$$.

Johor

JOHOR BAHRU

Hyatt Regency Johor Bharu, Jalan Sungai Chat, P.O. Box 222, Tel: 07-222 1234, Fax: 07-222 0159. 406 rooms and suites, restaurants. $$$$
Holiday Inn Crown Plaza Johor Bahru, Jalan Dato Sulaiman, Tel: 07-332 3800, Fax: 07-331 8884. 200 rooms, full room facilities and services, swimming pool, health centre, disco, shops, travel service. $$$
Puteri Pan Pacific, Jalan Salim, Tel: 07-223 3333, Fax: 07-223 6622. 500 rooms, full room facilities and service, restaurants, bars, fitness centre, business centre. $$$
Merlin Inn, Lot 5435 Jalan Bukit Meldrum, Tel: 07-223 7400, Fax: 07-224 8919. 104 rooms, air-conditioned, full room facilities. $$
Regent Elite Hotel, 1 Jalan Siew Nam, Tel: 07-224 3811. 76 air-con rooms, restaurant, nightclub. $

DESARU

Desaru Garden Beach Resort, Tanjung Penawar, Kota Tinggi, Tel: 07-822 1240, Fax: 07-822 1221. 35 chalets on beach, from simple 3-bed chalets with sitting room and verandah (TV on request), to family chalets with cooking facilities, all chalets with airconditioning; restaurant, water sports, golf by arrangement, cycling. $$
Desaru Golf Hotel, Tanjung Penawar, Kota Tinggi, Tel: 07-822 1479, Fax: 07-822 1455. 100 rooms, full room facilities, swimming pool, restaurant, billiards, video games, boardgames, horse-riding, cycling, jogging, jungle treks, scuba diving, tennis, table tennis, volleyball, 18-hole golf course. $$$
Desaru View Hotel, Tanjung Penawar, Kota Tinggi, Tel: 07-822 1221, Fax: 07-822 1101. 134 rooms, full room facilities and services, restaurant, grill, bar lounge, disco, shops, swimming pool. $$$

MERSING

Mersing Merlin Inn, 1st Mile Endau Road, Tel: 07-799 1312, Fax: 07-799 3177. 34 air-conditioned rooms, TV, bath/shower, restaurant, swimming pool, room service. $$

Johor Islands
(accessible from Mersing; for Tioman, see Pahang section)

PULAU BESAR

Radin Island Resort. Bookings from office near jetty, or write to Jalan Abu Bakar Mersing, Tel: 07-799 4152. Coconut-framed huts, bungalows, sea sports, jungle treks, restaurant, barbecues on request; family-run business.$$ for two people.

PULAU RAWA

Rawa Safaris Island Resort. Bookings and boats from Mersing, Tel: 07-799 1204. Wooden chalets and bungalows (some with air conditioning), some with attached bathroom, electricity till midnight, lanterns provided, restaurant, seafood, barbecues, windsurfing, canoeing, scuba diving, snorkelling, fishing, equipment for hire, aqua and other shops. $$

PULAU SIBU

Sibu Island Cabanas, Tel: 07-331 7216. Chalets, fan-cooled, private bathroom, soap and towels, restaurant, sea sports, indoor games, fishing. $$$ (including ferry service, all meals)

Perlis

KANGAR

Federal Hotel, 104 Jalan Kangar, Tel: 04-976 6288. 35 rooms, air-conditioned, bath, room-service, restaurant. $
Sri Perlis Inn, Jalan Kangar, Tel: 04-976 7266. 50 rooms, full room facilities, restaurant, coffeehouse, shops.$

Sabah

KOTA KINABALU

Berjaya Palace Hotel, 1 Jalan Tangki Karamunsing, Tel: 088-211 911. 160 rooms, castle architecture, full room facilities, coffeehouse, Chinese restaurant, bar lounge, business and travel centre, swimming pool. $$$

Hotel Capital, 23 Jalan Haji Saman, P.O. Box 11223, Tel: 088-231 999, 102 rooms, IDD telephone, coffee shop and restaurant. $$
Hotel Jesselton, 69 Jalan Gaya, P.O. Box 10401, Tel: 088-223 333, Fax: 088-240 401. 24 rooms, air-conditioned, hot and cold water, cable TV, bar and 2 restaurants. $$
Hyatt Kota Kinabalu, Jalan Datuk Salleh, Tel: 088-221 234. 315 rooms, full room facilities, 24-hour coffeehouse, restaurant, swimming pool, cruises, business centre, travel service, car rental, beauty salon, health centre, golf course arrangements. $$$$
Tanjung Aru Beach Resort, Tanjung Aru Beach, Tel: 088-58711. 504 rooms, full room facilities, swimming pool, restaurants, bars, fitness centre, water sports, boats to islands, business centre, travel service, shops. $$$$

KUNDASANG

Perkasa Hotel, wdt 11, 89309 Ranau, Tel: 088-889 511. 74 rooms, full facilities and services, restaurants, bar, tennis, fitness room, indoor games, golf course nearby, climbing tours of Mt Kinabalu. $$

SANDAKAN

Hotel Hsiang Garden, Leila Road (behind Capital Theatre), P.O. Box 82, Tel: 089-273 122, Fax: 089-273 127. 45 rooms, air-conditioned, 24 hour room service, cable TV, bar and restaurant. $$
Sabah Hotel, Jalan Utara, P.O. Box 275, Tel: 089-213 299. 28 rooms, air-conditioned. $$$
Renaissance Hotel Sandakan, Jalan Utara, Sandakan, Tel: 089-213 299, Fax: 089-271 271. 116 rooms, air-conditioned, full room facilities and service, restaurant, coffeehouse, lounge, tennis, squash, gymnasium, swimming pool. $$$

DANUM VALLEY

Borneo Rainforest Lodge, Danum Valley Conservation Area. Book through P.O. Box 11622, 88817 Kota Kinabalu, Tel: 088-243 245, Fax: 088-243 244. 10 rooms, private baths, solar-heated water, restaurant. Full board. $$$

TAWAU

Belmont Marco Polo Hotel, P.O. Box 1003, Tel: 089-777 988, Fax: 089-763 739. 150 rooms, full room facilities, restaurants, coffeehouse, bar. $$$

KINABALU PARK

Sabah Park. Head Office, Jalan Tun Fuad Stephens, P.O. Box 10626, Kota Kinabalu, Tel: 08-821 1585. Entry Permit: RM1; Climbers' Permit: RM10.
Accommodation in Park Headquarters: Lodges: sleeps 8, kitchen, dining room, fridge, lounge, fireplace, hot water. $$$
Double Storey Cabin: sleeps 7, 3 bedrooms, kitchen, sitting room, fridge, hot water. $$
Single Storey Cabin: sleeps 5, 2 bedrooms, kitchen, sitting room, fridge, hot water. $$
Duplex Chalets: sleeps 6, kitchen, sitting room, fridge, fireplace, hot water. $$. Annex Rooms: sleeps 4, 2 bedrooms, no cooking facilities. $
Twin-bed Cabins and Basement Rooms: sleeps 2, attached bathroom, hot water. $

Accommodation on Mount Kinabalu
Waras Hut: (3,300 metres/11,000 ft) bunk beds, cooking facilities and gas, sleeping bags for hire, no electricity; from RM1 to RM4.
Laban Rata Rest House: electricity, hot water, room heater, bedding provided, restaurant. $
Sayat Sayat Hut: (3,811 metres/ 12,500 ft) same as Waras Hut.

Accommodation at Poring Hot Springs
Old Cabin: sleeps 6, 3 bedrooms, sitting room, kitchen, bathroom. $
New Cabin: same as Old Cabin, but sleeps 4. $
Poring Hostel: dormitories, cooking facilities, from RM2 to RM8.
Camping Ground: cooking facilities, bathrooms, from RM1 to RM2.

TUANKU ABDUL RAHMAN NATIONAL PARK

Sabah Parks, Head Office, Jalan Tun Fuad Stephens, P.O. Box 10626, Kota Kinabalu, Tel: 088-211 585.

Accommodation
Rest House Pulau Mamutik: sleeps 12, kitchen, dining/sitting room, bathrooms. $$
Camping: Only with prior permission.

Sarawak

KUCHING

Borneo Hotel, 30C-F Jalan Tabuan, P.O. Box 1498, Tel: 082-244 121. 37 rooms, air-conditioned. $$
Damai Lagoon Resort, P.O. Box 3159, Kuching, Tel: 082-234 900, Fax: 082-234 901. 250 fully serviced rooms and suites, with 15 beach-side chalets. Restaurants, swimming pool, tennis, squash, fitness centre with steam bath, jacuzzi and massage, access to 18-hole course, wide variety of non-motorised watersports, jungle trekking, bicycles, indoor games room, banquet facilities. $$
Holiday Inn Damai Beach Hotel, P.O. Box 2870, Tel: 082-411 777. 302 rooms, full room facilities, restaurants, bars, disco, business centre, fitness centre, indoor games, tennis, squash, mini-golf, swimming pool with whirlpool, water sports, mini zoo, 18-hole golf course, convention facilities, car rental. $$$
Holiday Inn Kuching, Jalan Tuanku Abdul Rahman, P.O. Box 2362, Tel: 082-423 111. 320 rooms, full room facilities, restaurant, bar, swimming pool. $$$
Kuching Hilton, Jalan Tuanku Abdul Rahman, Tel: 082-248 200. 322 rooms, full room facilities and service, restaurants, bar, grill, beauty salon, health centre, swimming pool, shops. $$$
Riverside Majestic, Jalan Tuanku Abdul Rahman, Tel: 082-247 777, Fax: 082-425 858. City centre, beside river, 250 rooms, full room facilities and services, restaurants, lounge, business centre. $$$$

BATANG AI

Batang Ai Longhouse Resort, Batang Ai. Book c/o the Kuching Hilton, Jalan Tuanku Abdul Rahman, Kuching, Tel: 082-248 200, Fax: 082-428 984. $$

SIBU

Premier Hotel, Jalan Kampung Nyabor, P.O. Box 1064, Tel: 084-323 222. 120 rooms, full room facilities and service, restaurants, bars, health centre, golf course, disco, nightclub, shops, travel centre. $$$
Rex Hotel, 32 Jalan Cross, P.O. Box 1031, Tel: 084-330 625/330 933. 30 rooms. $

BINTULU

Aurora Beach Hotel, Jalan Tanjong Batu, Tel: 082-240 281. 108 rooms, nightclub. $$
Li Hua Hotel, 2.5 Mile, Miri-Bintulu Road, P.O. Box 191, Tel: 086-335 000, Fax: 086-335 222. 90 rooms, air-conditioned. $$

MIRI

Dynasty Hotel, Lot 683, Block 9, Jalan Pujut-Lutong, Tel: 085-421 111, Fax: 085-422 222. 132 rooms, air-conditioned, coffee shop, restaurants, bar, shopping mall next door. $$
Holiday Inn Miri, Jalan Temenggong Dato' Oyong Lawai, Tel: 085-418 888, Fax: 085-419 999. 168 rooms, full room facilities and service, meeting facilities, restaurants, business centre. $$$
Park Hotel, Jalan Raja, P.O. Box 443, Tel: 085-414 555, Fax: 085-414 488. 95 rooms, air conditioned, hot water, cable TV, restaurant and bar. $$
Rihga Royal Hotel, Jalan Temengong Datuk Oyong Lawai, Tel: 085-421 121, Fax: 085-421 099.

GUNUNG MULU NATIONAL PARK

Royal Mulu Resort, (Lot 154156, 2nd floor, Jalan Sungai, Padungan, Kuching) Mulu Caves, Mulu National Park, Tel: 082-421 121, 082-413 877, 010-887 5858. 44 guestrooms, air-conditioned, full room facilities and services. $$$

LAWAS

Country Park Hotel, Lot 235 & 236, Jalan Trusan, P.O. Box 99, Tel: 084-85522. 36 rooms. $$

BAKO NATIONAL PARK

Park Headquarters, Jalan Gartak, off Jalan Mosque, Tel: 085-248 088. Payment for accommodation in Kuching. Local buses for Bako jetty leave from bus stop just outside parks office.

Accommodation:
Rest Houses: sleeps 6, kitchen, verandah, bathroom. $
Hostel Cabins: sleeps 5 to a room, bedding, cooking facilities provided; from RM1 per person.
Permanent Tents: sleeps 3, no bedding provided, fireplace for cooking; from RM1 per person.
Canteen sells foodstuffs and simple meals (restaurant planned).

NIAH NATIONAL PARK

National Parks Head Office, Jalan Gartak Kuching, Tel: 085-246 6477, 248 988. Permits must be obtained at one of these offices, and a deposit of RM20 towards accommodation paid, unless you are taking a tour. Dormitories, cooking facilities, no bedding. Small canteen selling tinned and dried foodstuffs. Hostels are RM5 per person per night.

Eating Out

What To Eat

The different people that comprise Malaysia's multiracial population provide the country with a vast variety in food and dining environments.

During your stay in the country, you should eat at the roadside stalls or hawker centre at least once, for it is there that some of the country's most famous and tastiest foods are cooked. And very often, you will find the stall holders as attentive as the waiters of the hotels.

The most popular cuisines are those of the Malays, the Chinese and the Indians. Thai food is also well represented, especially in the north-east Malaysian states. Western food is now ubiquitous, and American fast food outlets are springing up in most towns.

Fruits of the Land

The tropical fruits of Malaysia may be exotica to many, but to Malaysians, they are a year-round, indispensable part of everyday life. Seasons for each fruit overlap perfectly throughout the year, providing Malaysia with one luscious fruit after another, till the delicious cycle starts all over again. Fresh from the tree in a *kampung* compound or private garden, or bought from a *pasar tani* (farmer's market), *pasar malam* (night market) or modern supermarket, local fruits feed the addiction of Malaysians, and exhilarate (or rudely bombard) the senses of every visitor who dares to experience them.

Durian – the football sized durian is easily recognized by its spiked green casing, and even from a distance, by its distinct but indescribeable smell. Proudly dubbed the "king of the fruits" by locals, one durian can cost a week's salary. Although now available year round, the prime season is June to August, when the dry weather allows more concentrated flavours in the fruit. Durians are never harvested; they fall from their extremely tall, straight trees, when, and only when it is time. The durian industry is constantly churning out new, improved species, with names like D29, D99, Sultan and so on, each trying to produce the sweetest, and creamiest yellow flesh, with the smallest, smooth beige seed. Beyond the overpowering smell, and the treacherous shell (tackled only by the experienced), the taste is sweet and unique.

Mangosteens are a traditional accompaniment when eating durian, as the seasons of both fruits coincide. The mangosteen is the size of a small orange, and has a thick, dark purple skin. This pliable rind is squeezed open, revealing five to eight snowy-white, segments, each containing a small, bitter seed. The mangosteen's flesh is perfectly astringent and sweet, but be careful of the rind's purple juice – it stains your clothes yellow. Malaysians believe that the mangosteen should be eaten after eating durian, to neutralize the potent, "heaty" properties of the prickly fruit.

Rambutan means "hairy" in Malay, an apt name as the bright red fruit is covered by many dark thin hairs. The fruit grows in bunches, with each egg-shaped fruit approximately 5 centimetres (2 in) long. Open the rambutan by inserting a thumbnail into the thin rind, and prying it apart like a rubbery egg. A close relative of the lychee. the rambutan's translucent, white flesh is extremely succulent and sugary sweet, and encloses a long, flat grey stone.

Pomelo – The pomelo looks like a larger, sweeter grapefruit and is popular among the Chinese. Beneath the green rind a thick layer of spongey pith, are the large segments which are gently pryed apart. Go to Ipoh, Perak for the undisputedly sweetest and juiciest pomelos in Malaysia.

Papayas, The papaya was introduced into Southeast Asia in the 16th century, and today, local varieties abound. Hailed for its digestion-aiding properties, the papaya is available everyday of the year and is a staple in any market or on any fruit menu. These fruits vary greatly in size, colour and taste, but most local ones are about a foot long with a thin yellow skin. In the fruit's hollow centre lies a mass of slippery, round, balck seeds. The orange flesh is smooth and slightly sweet. A sqeeze of lime for contrast is the common practice.

Starfruit – This pale yellow fruit looks like a three-dimensional, elongated, star, thanks to wings running from its base to the apex. The waxy edible skin covers a translucent, watery flesh, often juiced for a acidic, slightly sweet thirstquencher.

Jackfruit – Locally known as *nangka*, this long and large fruit grows all year round, and is often seen on trees covered with sacks or plastic bags to protect them from the hungry birds and insects. Averaging 50 by 25 centimetres (18 by 9 in), its thick rind is bumpy and greenish yellow. Cut it in half to expose the 20 to 30 oval meats, each encasing a large, brown seed. The jackfruit's meat is sweet and fragrant, with a firm, plasticky texture. A close relation to the jackfruit is the **chempedak**, which is smaller, with sweeter, creamier-textured, and stronger-smelling flesh. Jackfruit and chempedak are often battered and deep-fried for a delicious snack, and even the nutty seed inside is edible.

Pineapples, a familiar favourite, are grown in the southern state of Johor, while a sugary sweet variety comes from the East Malaysian state of Sarawak. Don't be surprised to see locals sprinkling salt onto slices of the fruit – fresh pineapples are said to "cut the tongue", probably an enzymatic process, and salt supposedly counteracts this painful effect.

Ciku – This Malaysian fruit (pronounced *chickoo*) looks deceptively like a hairless kiwifruit. Its flesh, however, is unmistakeable: light brown, painfully sweet and smooth, with an ocassional pear-like, gritty texture. Flat, black seeds are found in the centre of each fruit.

Guava – Called *jambu* in Malay, this local fruit comes in different sizes. It's flesh is either pink or white, with an edible green skin. The fruits's tiny white seeds are edible but are usually avoided. Generally, the pink types are sweeter and juicier, while the large ones, originally imported from Thailand but are now grown in Malaysia, are crisp and milder tasting. Irregularly-shaped and seedless varieties are now found, but they are somewhat lacking in flavour. For an added punch, locals commonly eat guavas sprinkled with a sweet-sour plum powder. For the best guavas, most Malaysians head for Bidor or Ipoh in the state of Perak.

Duku – This seasonal Malaysian fruit is about the size of a golf ball, and is available from August to September. Its leathery light-brown rind is peeled off to reach the small segments of transparent tangy-sweet flesh. Care must be taken not to bite on the small green seed in each segment. Langsat is a related species of fruit, but with a much thinner, lighter-coloured skin. Also available is duku langsat, a hybrid of the two fruits.

Buah susu, literally translated "milk fruit", is better known as passion fruit. There are many different varieties, all equally delicious. Crisp-skinned and orange from Indonesia, purple from Australia, New Zealand and California, but the local ones have soft, velvety yellow skins. The translucent seeds inside are sweet and juicy.

Custard Apple – Not an apple at all, but its sweet, flesh is custardy smooth and sweet. About the size of a person's fist, the knobby green skin is easily peeled off to expose the delicate flesh dotted with flat, black seeds.

Sour sop – This fruit looks like a close cousin of the custard apple, and despite its dour name, the sour sop's flesh is fragrantly sweet and tangy, with a succulent, fibrous texture. The Malays call it buah durian blanda. which means "Dutch durian", but the similarity with the odorous spiked fruit ends at the name.

Mangoes are well-known world-wide, conjuring up images of exotic, lush tropical islands, or the fruit-laden trees of Eden. The sweet, perfumed, juicy flesh of the mango is a local and foreign favourite. Many varieties of mango are enjoyed in Malaysia – there are small, hard and pungent jungle types, usually eaten with salt or a spicy soy sauce dip to cut the sap; sweet, bright orange varieties dripping with juice; and pale yellow, milder flavoured ones of Thai origin.

Where To Eat

The list of restaurants below are just to get you started on your taste journey in Malaysia. Restaurants in hotels have generally not been listed, as most large major hotels carry Chinese and Western restaurants. Venture out of the hotels and explore. There are delicious treats ahead. And don't forget the local foodstalls, where you can eat Malay, Chinese and Indian foods all at one meal.

Kuala Lumpur

MALAY

East West Kopitiam, Level 2, Sungai Wang Plaza, Jalan Sultan Ismail, Tel: 03-248 4289.
Rasa Utara, Bukit Bintang Plaza, Jalan Bukit Bintang, Tel: 03-248 8639.
Satay Anika, Bukit Bintang Plaza, Jalan Bukit Bintang, Tel: 03-248 3113.
Selera, Pan Pacific Hotel, Jalan Putra, Tel: 03-442 5555.
Spices, Concorde Hotel, Tel: 03-244 2200.
Sri Melayu, 1 Jalan Conlay, Tel: 03-245 1833.
Yazmin, Ampang Park complex, 6 Jalan Kia Peng, Tel: 03-241 5655.

CHINESE

Chef Rasa Sayang Sharksfin, 104-106 Jalan Imbi, Tel: 03-242 8592.
Esquire Kitchen (budget dumplings and pork dishes), Level 1, Sungai Wang Plaza, Jalan Sultan Ismail, Tel: 248 5006.
Golden Phoenix (Cantonese with exotic game and seafood), Hotel Equatorial, Jalan Sultan Ismail, Tel: 03-261 7777.
Hunan Garden, Crown Princess Hotel, City Square Complex, Jalan Tun Razak, Tel: 03-262 5522.
Marco Polo (Cantonese), 1st floor, Wisma Lim Foo Yong, Jalan Raja Chulan, Tel: 03-242 5595.
Maxim Sharksfin & Seafood, 112 Jalan Bukit Bintang, Tel: 03-244 8081.
Meisan Szechuan, Holiday Inn City Centre, Jalan Raja Laut, Tel: 03-293 9233.
Shang Palace (Cantonese), Shangri-La Hotel, 11 Jalan Sultan Ismail, Tel: 03-232 2388.
Szechuan, 42-3 Jalan Sultan Ismail, Tel: 03-248 2806.
Tsui Hang Village (Cantonese), Shahzan Prudential Tower, 30 Jalan Sultan Ismail, Tel: 03-244 2922.

INDIAN

Annalakshmi (Vegetarian), 40 Jalan Maarof, Bangsar, Tel: 03-282 3799.
Bangles (North Indian), 60 Jalan Tuanku Abdul Rahman, Tel: 03-298 3780.
Betelnuttier (banana leaf), Jalan Pinang.
Bilal (Indian-Muslim), 33 Jalan Ampang, Tel: 03-238 0804.
Devi Annapoorna, 94 Lorong Maarof, Bangsar, Tel: 03-255 6443.
Mitra Kanchana Curry and Tandoor (Northern and Southern), 237G Jalan Tun Sambathan, Tel: 03-273 4153.
Omar Khayam, 5 Jalan Medan Tuanku, Tel: 03-298 8850.
Taj (North Indian), Crown Princess Hotel, Jalan Tun Razak, Tel: 03-262 5522.

JAPANESE

Chikuyo-Tei, Basement Plaza See Hoy Chan, Jalan Raja Chulan, Tel: 03-230 0729.
Edi Kirin, Regent Kuala Lumpur Hotel, Jalan Bukit Bintang, Tel: 03-241 8000.
Hatsuhana, 1 Jalan Yap Kwan Seng, Tel: 03-242 0882.
Keyaki, Pan Pacific Hotel, Jalan Putra, Tel: 03-442 5555.
Kyoka, Hotel Istana, 73 Jalan Raja Chulan, Tel: 03-241 9988.
Nadaman, Shangri-La Hotel, 11 Jalan Sultan Ismail, Tel: 03-232 2388.

KOREAN

Koryo Won, Komplek Antarabangsa, Jalan Sultan Ismail, Tel: 03-242 7655.
Seoul Garden, 37 Jalan Sultan Ismail, Tel: 03-242 0425.

THAI

Barn Thai, 370B Jalan Tun Razak, Tel: 03-244 9966.
Chili Padi, level 2, The Mall, Tel: 03-442 4319.
Coca Thai Suki, Level 1, Lot 15, KL Plaza, Jalan Bukit Bintang, Tel: 03-245 9600.
Restoran Sri Thai, 16-18 Jalan Telawi 3, Bangsar Batu, Tel: 03-283 1136.
Sawasdee, Holiday Inn on the Park, Jalan Pinang, Tel: 03-481 066.

WESTERN

Bon Ton (mixed), 7 Jalan Kia Peng, Tel: 03-241 3614.
Carcosa Seri Negara, (Italian), Taman Tasik Perdana, Tel: 03-282 1888.
Ciao (Italian), Jalan Tun Razak, Tel: 03-986 2617.

El Palma (Mediterranean), 18 Jalan Telawi, 2, Bangsar Baru, Tel: 03-282 4492.
Hard Rock Cafe (Tex-Mex), Concorde Hotel, Jalan Sultan Ismail.
L'Amigo (Italian), Level 2, Shahzan Prudential Tower, 30 Jalan Sultan Ismail, Tel: 03-244 4112.
La Terasse (French/Mediterranean), 388 Jalan Tun Razak, Tel: 03-248 4243.
Le Coq d'Or (mixed menu), 121 Jalan Ampang, Tel: 03-242 9732.
L'Escargot (French), Lot 2-53, The Mall, 100 Jalan Putra, Tel: 03-443 1988.
T.G.I. Friday's (Tex-Mex), Ground floor, Life Centre, Jalan Sultan Ismail, Tel: 263 7761.
The Ship (steaks and seafood), Jalan Bukit Bintang and Jalan Bukit Ismail, Tel: 03-241 8805.
Victoria Station (steaks and salads), Jalan Ampang, Tel: 03-457 3388.

SEAFOOD

Bangsar Seafood, Lot 43873, Jalan Telawi 4, Bangsar Baru, Tel: 03-255 7252.
Eden, Jalan Raja Chulan, Tel: 03-241 4027.
Subang View, 229 Airport Road, Tel: 03-746 1401.

Selangor

Kelana Seafood Centre, Lot 1122, Section 7, Jalan Perbandara, Tel: 03-703 8118.
Lakeview Floating Restaurant (Chinese, seafood), Tasik Tengah, Taman Tasik, Shah Alam, Tel: 03-550 5995.
Mutiara Kelana (Malaysian), Kelana Jaya, PJ, Tel: 03-703 3339.
Sri Melaka (Nonya, Thai, Chinese, Western), 7 Jalan 52/8 Merdeka Square, PJ, Tel: 03-756 3497.
Sri Thai (Thai), Wisma Selangor, Jalan University, PJ, Tel: 03-756 3535.
The Ship (seafood and steak), Jalan SS21/56B, Damansara Utama, PJ, Tel: 03-7188 020.

Negri Sembilan

Bilal Restaurant (Indian-Muslim), 100 Jalan Dato' Bandar Tunggal, Seremban, Tel: 06-712 521.
Happy Restaurant (Chinese), 1 Jalan Dato' Bandar Tunggal, Seremban, Tel: 06-729 063.
Negeri Restaurant (Malay), Jalan Tuanku Munawir, Seremban, Tel: 06-730 101.

Malacca

Anda (Malay), Jalan Hang Tuah, Tel: 06-283 1984.
De Nolasco (Portugese), Portugese Settlement's Square, Tel: 06-283 4792.
Keng Dom (Chinese), 148 Taman Melaka Raya, Tel: 06-283 9759.
Kiraku (Japanese), Park Plaza Resort, Air Keroh, Tel: 06-283 3600.
Lim Tian Puan (Chinese), 251 Jalan Tun Sri Lanang, Tel: 06-283 2737.
Moti Mahal (Northern Indian), 543 Taman Melaka Raya, Tel: 06-283 7823.
Nona Sayang (Chinese), Malacca's Tourist Market, Jalan Tun Sri Lanang, Tel: 06-283 7869.
Nyonya Makko (Nyonya), 123 Taman Melaka Jaya, Tel: 06-283 0737.
Sang Kancil Satay (Malay), 627 Taman Melaka Raya, Tel: 06-283 2123.
Seribu Rasa (Malay), 158 Komplex Munshi Abdullah, Jalan Munshi Abdullah, Tel: 06-283 6182.
Tandoori House (Northern Indian), Level 1, First Elite Hotel, Jalan Taming Sari, Tel: 06-283 7488.
Tay Sing (Vegetarian), 311 Jalan Gajah Berang, Tel: 06-283 8508.

Penang

Chikuyo-Tei (Japanese), The City Bayview Hotel, Farquhar, Tel: 04-263 5175.
Dawood (Muslim), 63 Lebuh Queen, Tel: 04-261 1633.
Eden Seafood Village (Chinese seafood), 69A Jalan Batu Ferringhi, Tel: 04-263 2427.
House of Kampung Malay Food (Malay), 387 Jalan Batu Ferringhi, Tel: 04-881 2745, 04-881 1273.
Mistral (Mediterranean), Bayview Beach Resort, Tel: 04-881 2123.
Moghul Arch (North Indian), 195-0-4 Jalan Batu Ferringhi, Tel: 04-881 2891.
Nyonya Corner, 15 Jalan Pahang, Tel: 04-228 1412.
Pearl Garden, 34C Batu Ferringhi, Tel: 04-881 1589.
Peppino's (Italian), Golden Sands Hotel, Batu Ferringhi, Tel: 04-881 1911.
Shang Palace (Cantonese), Shangri-La Hotel, George Town, Tel: 04-262 6526.
Ship (steak), 46 Sri Bahari Road, Tel: 263 3551.
Tandoori House, 34-36 Lorong Hutton, Tel: 04-261 9105.

Tower Palace (Cantonese), Level 59 Komtar, Tel: 04-262 2222.
Wunderbar (German), 37 F, Jalan Cantonment, Tel: 04-228 1080.
Yosenabe (Japanese steamboat), 763 Jalan Sultan Azlan Shah, Sungai Nibong, Tel: 04-884 1196.

Perak

Chao Phraya (Thai and Chinese), 2 Jalan Green, Ipoh, Tel: 05-254 2872.
Fook Heng, (Chinese Seafood), 6 Main Road, Pangkor, Tel: 05-685 1319.
Kok Kee (Chinese), 272 Jalan Sultan Iskandar, Ipoh, Tel: 05-543 991.
Ocean, 115 Jalan Titi Panjang, Lumut, Tel: 05-683 5494.
Pakeeza (Indian-Muslim), 15-17 Jalan Dato' Seri Ahmad Said, Ipoh, Tel: 05-255 1057.
Restoran Choong Wah (Chinese herbal), 52 Jalan Theatre, Ipoh, Tel: 05-313 2251.
Restoran Samudera Raya (Indian and Malay), 39 Jalan Sultan Idris Shah, Lumut, Tel: 05-683 5948.
Ye Lin Seafood Garden (Chinese seafood), 200 Jalan Pasir Bogak, Pangkor, Tel: 05-685 1881.

Kedah

Air Hangat Village (cultural dinner show), Km16, Jalan Air Hangat, Langkawi, Tel: 04-959 1358.
Barn Thai, Kampung Belanga Pechah, Mukim Kisap, Langkawi, Tel: 04-966 6699.
Pantai Cenang (East/West), Langkawi, Kedah, Tel: 04-966 2355.
Restoran Selera (Malay), 64 Jalan Teluk Wanjah, Alor Setar, Tel: 04-726 738.
Sari Seafood, Pusat Pelancongan Langkawi, Komplek Market Lama, Langkawi, Tel: 04-966 7193.
Spice Market (mixed), Pelangi Beach Resort, Pantai Cenang, Langkawi, Tel: 04-966 1001.

Perlis

Chahaya Bintang Restoran, 314 Jalan Mutiara, Kangar, Tel: 04-976 3984.
Embassy, 53 Jalan Jubli Parak Kangar, Tel: 04-976 5301.
Fortune Palace (Chinese), Level 1, Pens Travel Lodge, Tel: 04-976 7755.

Kelantan

Budaya Restaurant (Malay, Thai), 367 Jalan Temenggong, Kota Bahru, Tel: 09-748 1185.

Lak Kau Hok Restaurant (Chinese), 2959 Jalan Kebun Sultan, Kota Bahru, Tel: 09-748 3762.

Puspa Restaurant (Chinese, Malay and Western), Hotel Kesina Baru, Jalan Padang Garong, Kota Bahru, Tel: 09-748 1455.

Terengganu

Awana Restaurant (Chinese, seafood), Jalan Kelab Kerajaan, Kuala Terengganu, Tel: 09-623 3309.

Cascase Grill (Western), Primula Beach Resort, Jalan Persingganan, Kuala Terengganu, Tel: 09-622 2100.

Nara Restoran (Malay), 1 Jalan Kamaruddin, Kuala Terengganu, Tel: 09-622 4669.

Nil Restoran (Malay, seafood), 906 Pantai Batu Burok, Kuala Terengganu, Tel: 09-622 3381.

Pahang

Apollo Restaurant (Chinese, Western), 23 Telok Chempedak, Kuantan, Tel: 09-544 4452.

Gloria Maris Resort Restaurant (mixed menu), Mastura 1/1402, Kampung Bahru Beserah, Kuantan, Tel: 09-513 7788.

Ye Olde Smokehouse (Western), Tanah Rata, Cameron Highlands, Tel: 05-491 1214.

Hugo's, Hyatt Kuantan, Teluk Chempedak, Tel: 09-513 1234.

Johor

Eastern Dragon (Chinese), 49-51 Jalan Serigala, Century Garden, JB, Tel: 07-331 9600.

Jaws 5, 1-D Jalan Skudai, JB, Tel: 07-223 6062.

Kobe Teppan Yaki, 164A Jalan Ngee Heng, JB, Tel: 07-222 1185.

Korean Garden, Level 3, K1-407 Jalan Ibrahim Sultan, JB, Tel: 07-224 4677.

Manhattan Grill, Kotaraya Shopping Complex, JB, Tel: 07-224 7946.

Marina Seafood Villa, 1-D Jalan Scudai, JB, Tel: 07-224 1400.

Sedap Corner (Malay), 11 Jalan Abdul Samad, JB, Tel: 07-224 6566.

Selasih Restaurant, Puteri Pan Pacific Hotel, Kotaraya, JB, Tel: 07-223 6662.

Tajmahal, 8 Jalan Mawai Kota Tinggi, Tel: 07-883 3250.

Sabah

100% Seafood Restaurant, Jalan Aru, Tanjung Aru Beach, Tel: 088-238 313. Wide range of market-style seafood

cooked to your specifications.

Sri Kapitol Restaurant, Hotel Capital, Jalan Haji Saman, Tel: 088-231 999. Selection of Chinese and Malaysian favourites.

Sedco Square, Kampung Air. Open-air food stalls operating after 5pm, satay and seafood are the specialities.

Kedal Makan Mars, Sinsuron Shopping Complex, Southern Indian favourites including vegetarian dishes. Lunch or early evening.

Sarawak

Chinese food centre, opposite Chinese temple in Carpenter Street. Food stalls selling Kuching laksa and Chinesse specialities.

Golden Dragon, Central Road, Tel: 082-425 236. Chinese specialities.

Fook Hoi, Jalan Tun Haji Openg, opposite Post Office. Popular home-style Chinese cooking.

Permata Food Stalls behind Standard Chartered Bank. Open-air food stalls offering all kinds of local as well as Western food after dark.

Drinking Notes

In general, alcohol is expensive in Malaysia. A glass of wine may cost as much as a tot of brandy, and the heat of the tropics does not always guarantee a good flavour. Alcohol is forbidden to Muslims, so if you want to indulge in alcoholic beverages, head for the hotels and Chinese eating establishments or liquor stores. Tiger and Anchor beers and abc and Guiness Stout are the most popular. Don't be surprised if a bucket of ice is served with your beer – tthis is the way many locals enjoy their brews – ice cold to battle the heat.

Far more refreshing in the steamy atmosphere of the tropics are the fruit juices, to be found at small stalls, coffee shops and night markets. Choose your combination: pineapple and orange, starfruit and water melon. If you don't want sugar, ask them not to add the sugar syrup; in Kelantan, salt is often added to cut fruits and juices, which may not be to your taste - ask them for plain fruit or juice. There are a variety of very sweet coconut and soya bean drinks for sale at small stalls, with alarmingly bright colours added to them. Young coconuts produce a refreshing clear juice which can

be drunk straight from the coconut with ice added and a straw stuck into a hole made in the top. Mineral water is sold in grocery stores and supermarkets.

Attractions

Culture

Museums

Malaysia has a host of museums. Most intriguing and most talked about is the Sarawak Museum in Kuching, founded in 1888 by the second white Rajah, Sir Charles Brooke, and the great evolutionist, Alfred Russell Wallace. Their foresight resulted in the finest collection of Borneo artistry, and the museum is visited annually by more than 10,000 people.

Other museums that must be visited include Kuala Lumpur's Musium Negara (National Museum), with its life-size displays of court and *kampung* life, the Malacca Museum, crowded with Menangkabau treasures and colonial mementos, the Perak State Museum in Taiping and the Abu Bakar Museum at the Grand Palace in Johor Bahru. All museums in Malaysia are documented in Exploring Malaysia in the appropriate sections. Most museums are open from 9am-6pm daily, except for Fridays when they are closed between noon and 2.30pm. Admission to museums is free. Permission to view archives not on display can be obtained by consulting the curator of the museum. For more information, call the Museum Information Office, Tel: 03-282 6255.

Art Galleries

Paintings on Malaysian art gallery walls mirror the essence of the traditional way of life, and the conflict of the new. Much can be gleaned about how young Malaysian artists envision the future. Current exhibitions are well worth a visit. Batik painting is much favoured, combining an old art with contemporary scenes – a youth and his girl-friend on a motorbike. But other media are equally popular, and range from water colours of *kampung* scenes to abstract oil paintings to performance art.

The National Art Gallery is located at Jalan Sultan Hishamuddin (opposite the Kuala Lumpur Railway Station). The Gallery is housed in the former Majestic Hotel built in 1932, and is now conserved under the National Heritage Trust. A permanent collection of works by local and foreign artists are displayed. The gallery is open daily from 10am to 6pm (closed on Fridays from 12.45 to 2.45pm), and admission is free. Tel: 03-293 7111.

Besides the main public art galleries, there are many small galleries in towns, cities and artists' villages, where you can buy a painting from the artist himself. For more information, call the Ministry of Culture, Arts and Tourism, Tel: 03-293 1515.

Handicrafts

Of all Malaysia's traditional handicraft, decorated textiles provide the appeal of variety and usability. **Kain songket** is Malaysia's most highly-prized woven cloth Deep blue, forest green, maroon or purple silks embroidered with silver and gold thread, the material was orginally only worn by royalty. Today, Malays of all backgrounds wear the *kain songket* for weddings and other special occasions. Although imitation gold and silver threads are now used, weaving the cloth still requires great old-world skill. One piece of cloth may require the talents of five different weavers, each specialized in a certain pattern interwoven into the overall design. Malay women cultivate a hierarchy of weavers, the most experienced arranging the warp threads on the loom and the least experienced flicking the shuttle. The body of the cloth is usually plain with an ornate border of stylised floral and geometric motifs. In former times, the entire *kain* was a medley of silver thread on silk and the finest were sent for inspection at the sultan's palace.

Somewhat related to the *kain songket* is **tekat**, an ancient craft of gold embroidery on rich, dark velvet. This luxurious material is popular among Malays for home furnishings, wall hangings, cushions and even bedroom slippers.

A less ornate cloth is **batik**, a cloth decorated by patterns produced by the use of dyes and wax. It was a method practised by the Javanese at least 2,000 years ago, but evidence also shows that it was also known to the ancient Egyptians. Although much of the batik available today is produced in batik factories, prized pieces are still created by hand. The best Malaysian batik comes from the East Coast, Kelantan in particular, where artisans use metal stencils (*cap*), to stamp cotton with molten wax designs. The cloth is then dipped into a vat of dye. The waxed areas resist the dye, and after drying, the process is repeated several times for different colours. A soft, cracked effect is achieved by crumpling the waxed cloth, allowing dyes to seep into the cracks. Recently, hand-painted batiks (*batik tulis*), especially on silk, have regained popularity, and new dyes and techniques have also enabled batik to be printed on poplin, lawn, shirting, cambric, swiss voile, cheesecloth and satin.

Malaysians favour more modern motifs than their Indonesian neighbours, although even these modern designs are interspersed with stylized birds, flowers and plants that were found on batik centuries ago. With the onset of tourism, batik is no longer confined to beachwear or the graceful *sarung*. Batik tablecloths, purses and bags, and even batik wallpaper fill shops in the states of Kelantan, Kuala Terengganu and Kuala Lumpur.

The East Coast is also the traditional centre of the **silverwork** cottage industry. Kelantan in particular, is full of small workshops where silversmiths hammer out designs onto silver plates. The filigreed work is fine and delicate, reflecting cosmopolitan inspiration. Patterned bowls, boxes, tableware, and ornate filigreed jewellery are some of the silverwork available. Some patterns of the hibiscus flower – Malaysia's *bunga raya* (national flower), were found on Majapahit jewellery 600 years ago. Other pieces are inspired by shadow play figures with Siamese influence, while the conventional lotus blossom is Indian in origin. The Iban of Sarawak also use silver for ceremonial headdresses and girdles, often sold on the peninsula.

Weaving mats from *nipah* or *pandanus* leaves is a more down-to-earth craft, though still requiring great skill.

It is practised from Mauritius in the Indian Ocean down to East Timor in Indonesia. In Malaysia, mat weaving is a trademark of the East Coast. Throughout the country though, woven mats are an essential part of daily life, used on the floor in *kampung* houses, on beds, on the beach, in mosques, for drying food under the sun, and anywhere else a convenient, light covering is needed. Weaving begins at the centre of the mat and moves outwards, using dyes to produce simple crisscross patterns. More professional weavers (mostly women) fashion hexangonal boxes of *nipah* plam leaves. These women often set up shop in markets, on the beach, or even right in their own living rooms. In Sabah and Sarawak, floral and even pictorial stories are part of the woven mat's design. Breathtaking as these pieces may be to visitors, weaving is not undertaken simply as a neccessary craft, not an art.

A relatively recent but now highly profitable industry is **pewterware**. Pewter-making was introduced from China in the mid-19th century. The alloy, which is 95 percent tin with small amounts of antimony and copper, was the perfect alloy for Malaysia, which was, until recently, the world's largest tin producer. The fineness of the surface imparted by the high tin content allows beautiful items to be made: vases, goblets, tankards, trays, picture frames, and jewellery are just some of the gift possiblities available in pewter. Malaysia's best pewter is made by Royal Selangor, the world's biggest pewter manufacturer, which has a large factory in Kuala Lumpur. Royal Selangor was started by Chinese immigrant Yong Koon in 1885, and is still run by the Yong family.

Cinema

Subtle drama never stays on the action-packed billboards long. Most Asians buy tickets for noisy, wild entertainment and the more action the better. Favourite topics are bloody fist fights, mass murder, dope smuggling, opium smoking, prostitution and car chases. Fans flock to see the "good guys" win in the end, in the guise of sword fighters, war heroes, gang leaders, tough detectives and sharp-shooting cowboys.

The Asian cinema, if you can take the gore, is unabashedly explosive and violent. Vampires and dinosaurs shriek across the screen nearly every week. There are, of course, soft moments that linger on young love and family comedy. Indonesian movies are very popular, and often deal with mythological characters fighting the battle of Good versus Evil.

You will be able to sample this kind of cinema if you hop on a long distance bus. Regardless of whether you want to hear and see it, the bus video with the sound at top volume is suspended from the ceiling to alleviate the boredom of the journey. American car chases and kung fu fights strike an incongruous note when viewed alongside the passing scenery.

Dances

Performances of Wayang Kulit, Mak Yong, Menora and Ronggeng are most likely to be found on the east coast of the peninsula, unless there is an official occasion such as National Day. Details of these dances and shows are usually documented in the region's Calendar of Events released by the Malaysia Tourism Promotion Board (MTPB) and can be picked up from their offices. In remoter places, a friendly local may well tell you if there is something on in the vicinity – it's always worth asking if they don't.

MALAYSIAN CULTURAL SHOWS

Central Market, Central Market, Jalan Hang Kasturi, KL, Tel: 03-274 9966.
Yazmin Restaurant, 6 Jalan Kia Peng, KL, Tel: 03-241 5655.
Sarawak Cultural Village, Kuching, Tel: 082-428 988.

Nightlife

Kuala Lumpur has a thriving nightlife but many of the more popular places do not start to fill up until after 11pm or even midnight. Live bands are popular, and almost all the larger hotels have bars featuring live music. This is usually broad-appeal, middle-of-the-road music, so hotel bars are not listed here unless they have established a reputation for something out of the easy-listening bracket. Discotheques draw large crowds of youngsters and the karaoke craze has swept Kuala Lumpur, too.

Kuala Lumpur

ARR KTV Lounge, Lower Ground floor, Plaza Imbi, 28 Jalan Imbi, KL, Tel: 03-244 3233. Karaoke with private rooms.
Aviary, Kuala Lumpur Hilton, Jalan Sultan Ismail, KL, Tel: 03-242 2122. Easy-listening jazz.
Barn Thai, 370B Jalan Tun Razak, KL, Tel: 03-244 6699. Live jazz in attractive Thai wooden house.
Betelnut, 16 Jalan Pinang, KL, Tel: 03-241 6455. Disco and bar.
Blue Moon, Hotel Equatorial, Jalan Sultan Ismail, KL, Tel: 03-261 7777. Live pop and evergreen nightly.
Blues Cafe, Lot R1, Street Level, Annexe Block, Lot 10 Shopping Centre, 50 Jalan Sultan Ismail, KL, Tel: 03-244 4517.
Boom-Boom Room, 11 Leboh Ampang, KL, Tel: 03-232 6907. Bastion of Kuala Lumpur's alternative nightlife, highly popular with both gay and straight crowd. Entertaining nightly drag show.
Brannigans, Off Jalan P. Ramlee, KL. Tel: 03-230 3567. Popular meeting place for the younger yuppie set.
Bull's Head, Central Market, Jalan Hang Kasturi, KL, Tel: 03-274 6428. Smoky, English pub.
Cathy's Place, Wisma Stephens, Jalan Raja Chulan, KL, Tel: 03-248 1724. Tiny bar with friendly crowd.
Cee Jay's, Menara SMI, 6 Lorong P Ramlee, KL, Tel: 03-232 4437. Live pop and rock nightly.
Cheers, 8-4 Jalan Batai, KL, Tel: 03-255 3391. Pub and grill.
Club Fukiko, Menara Promet, Jalan Sultan Ismail, KL, Tel: 03-241 7835. Expensive Japanese lounge with hostesses.
Club Oz, Shangri-La Hotel, 11 Jalan Sultan Ismail, KL, Tel: 03-232 2388. Upmarket disco for the smart set.
Fire, Basement Menara Sabre, 8 Lorong P Ramlee, KL, Tel: 03-230 0880. Hot, multi-level disco, young crowd.
Hard Rock Cafe, Wisma Concorde, 2 Jalan Sultan Ismail, KL, Tel: 03-244 4152. Live band plays pop after 11pm.
Hook D'Hoop, Basement, Wisma Central, Jalan Ampang, KL, Tel: 03-262 2097. World music crowd.
Karumba, Basement level, Park Royal Hotel, Jalan Sultan Ismail, KL. Tel: 03-242 5588. Live World music venue in sumptuous settings.

Lounge Avenue, 148 Jalan Bukit Bintang, KL, Tel: 03-242 8043. Karaoke in many languages.
Machine One, Life Centre, Jalan Sultan Ismail, KL, Tel: 03-263 1482. Live rap and pop.
Modesto's, Off Jalan P. Ramlee, KL. Tel: 03-985 0385. Popular among smart set and latin music lovers.
Musictheque, Hotel Istana, 73 Jalan Raja Chulan, Tel: 03-241 9988. Upmarket disco.
Pertama Cabaret Niteclub, Pertama Complex, Jalan Tuanku Abdul Rahman, KL, Tel: 03-298 2533. Entertainment by Hong Kong and Taiwanese starlets.
Pyramid, Lot 345, PT47054, Pusat Bandar Damansara, Tel: 03-253 3616. Large bar with live entertainment.
Rainbow, Imperial Hotel, 76-80 Cangkat Raja Chulan, KL, Tel: 244 8263. Big-screen video in this karaoke lounge and bar.
Rasta Pub, 55 Jalan SS21/56B, Damansara Utama, PJ, Tel: 03-719 7466. Live rock and Caribbean music.
Renaissance, Level 3, Plaza Yow Chuan, Jalan Tun Razak, KL, Tel: 03-242 0540. Disco with private karaoke rooms.
Riverbank, Central Market, Jalan Hang Kasturi, Tel: 03-274 6651. Live jazz nightly.
Seventh Avenue, Level 1, Menara Aetna, Jalan Raja Chulan, KL, Tel: 03-261 5448. Smart karaoke bar.
The Jump, Wisma Inai, Jalan Tun Razak, KL, Tel: 03-245 0046. Very popular American-styled eatery and watering hole.
Tin Mine, Kuala Lumpur Hilton, Jalan Sultan Ismail, KL, Tel: 03-242 2222. Disco popular with a more mature crowd.
Tsim Sha Shui, 1 Jalan Kia Peng, KL, Tel: 03-241 4929. *The* Cantopop disco in the country.
Uncle Chilie's Fun Pub, PJ Hilton, Jalan Barat, Petaling Jaya. Tel: 03-755 9122. Suburban dance spot with American-style food, drink and decor.

Johor

BBQ, 2 Jalan Laut Klung, Tel: 07-732 5211. Karaoke.
Caesar's, Holiday Plaza, Tel: 07-333 6100. Disco.
Christine's Place, 2 Jalan Tebrau, Tel: 07-248 891. Japanese night club, lounge and karaoke.

Kalab Malam Dallas, Wisma Daiman, Tel: 07-332 8162. Night club.
Millennium, Holiday Inn Crowne Plaza, Tel: 07-332 3800. Disco.
Wind Surfing, 18A Jalan Sutera 2 Tmn Sentosa, Tel: 07-333 8124. Karaoke.

Festivals

General

It's difficult to say which is the most exciting spectacle – a blowpipe's bull's eye in the Borneo interior; a top that spins for 50 minutes under a make-shift canopy on peninsular Malaysia's east coast; an imperial howl at Penang's Chinese opera; or an Indian dancer with bells on her toes. In Malaysia, not only do all these occur, but several may be going on at the same time. The country has a public holiday nearly every month, not counting the market feasts, regal birthdays and re-ligious processions that sprinkle calendar pages like confetti. The only problem is distance. Malaysia spreads out over 5,000 kilometres (3,107 mi) and so do its festivals.

The Muslim calendar consists of 354 days in a year. The Chinese and Hindu calendars, unlike the Gregorian calendar, use the lunar month as their basic unit of calculation. Hence dates vary widely from year to year. These festivals and celebrations with variable dates probably include some of Malaysia's more exciting events. For immediate events, read the daily newspapers and Kuala Lumpur This Month, distributed free at leading hotels.

Holidays That Are Not Fixed

The following holidays are moveable feasts depending on the Christian, Muslim, Buddhist or Hindu calendar:
Chinese New Year (2 days; 1 day in Kelantan and Terengganu)
Hari Raya Puasa (2 days)
Hari Raya Haji (1 day; 2 days in

Kedah, Kelantan, Pahang, Perlis)
Deepavali (except Sabah, Sarawak and the Federal Territory of Labuan)
Prophet Mohammed's Birthday
Awal Ramadan
Birthday of the Sultan of Terengganu (Terengganu only)
Vesak Day
Thaipusam (Negri Sembilan, Penang, Perak and Selangor only)

If a holiday falls on a weekend or a Friday, the following day becomes a holiday.

Shopping

Where & What To Buy
Kuala Lumpur

SHOPPING CENTRES

Ampang Park Shopping Centre, Jalan Ampang, KL, Tel: 03-261 7006.
Bukit Bintang Plaza, Jalan Bukit Bintang, KL, Tel: 03-248 7653.
Central Market, Jalan Hang Kasturi, KL, Tel: 03-274 6542.
Chinatown, Jalan Petaling, KL.
City Square Complex, Jalan Tun Razak, KL. Tel: 03-262 1566.
Goldsmith's Row, Along Lebuh Pudu and Jalan Bandar.
Hankyu Jaya Shopping Centre, 452 Jalan Tuanku Abdul Rahman, KL, Tel: 03-442 4866 and Ampng Park, Jalan Ampang, KL, Tel: 03-261 4133.
Indian Shopping Area, Jalan Masjid India and Jalan Melayu, KL.
Kota Raya Complex, Jalan Tun Cheng Lock, KL, Tel: 03-232 2562.
Kuala Lumpur Plaza, Jalan Bukit Bintang, Tel: 03-241 7288.
Lot 10, Jalan Sultan Ismail, KL, Tel: 03-241 0500.
Malaysian Emporium, 38 Jalan Tuanku Abdul Rahman, KL, Tel: 03-298 3850.

Pertama Complex, Jalan Tuanku Abdul Rahman, KL, Tel: 03-292 7457.
Plaza Yow Chuan, Jalan Tun Razak, KL, Tel: 03-242 1566.
Sogo, Wisma Pernas Sogo, Jalan Tuanku Abdul Rahman, KL, Tel: 03-298 2111.
Sungei Wang Plaza, Jalan Sultan Ismail, KL, Tel: 03-243 0311.
The Mall, Jalan Putra, KL, Tel: 03-442 7122.
The Weld Shopping Centre, Jalan Raja Chulan, KL, Tel: 03-261 8422.

ANTIQUES

Artiquarium, 273A Jalan Mdn Tuanku, Tel: 03-292 1222; 54 Jalan Bandar 3 HKlang, Tel: 03-408 8593.
Asia Arts & Crafts, Kuala Lumpur Hilton, Tel: 03-242 3631.
China Arts Co., 219, Jalan Tuanku Abdul Rahman, KL, Tel: 03-292 9250.
Eastern Stamps, Coins & Antiques, Sungai Wang Plaza, Tel: 03-248 7217.
H Raby Antiques, 4 Jalan Pinggiran 2, Tel: 03-457 3698.
K C Yat Antique Gallery, S5A level 2, Plaza Yow Chuan, Jalan Tun Razak, Tel: 03-241 8286.
K L Goh Crafts, 137 Jalan SS2/24, PJ, Tel: 03-774 3650.
King's Art, Lot 23, 1st Floor, Shangri-la Hotel, KL, Tel: 03-230 6180.
Peiping Lace, 223 Jalan Tuanku Abdul Rahman, Tel: 03-292 9282.
Peking Art Co., Sungai Wang Plaza, Tel: 03-248 7781.
Peking Crafts & Furniture, 61 Jalan SS2/55, PJ, Tel: 03-776 1350.
Warisan Syarikat (Heritage), Central Market, Jalan Hang Kasturi, Tel: 03-274 0180.

HANDICRAFTS & SOUVENIRS

Asianika Beauty Crafts, Central Market, KL, Tel: 03-274 6743.
Batek Malaysia (batik), Wisma Batik, Jalan Tun Perak, Tel: 291-8608 and 114 Jalan Bukit Bintang, Tel: 03-242 4825.
Cottage Patch (patchworks and quilts), 447 Jalan Ampang, Tel: 03-456 3106.
Dayang Ceramica, M31 Central Market, Tel: 03-274 6593.
Eaton House (batik), 7 Jalan Eaton, Tel: 03-248 0949; Hilton Hotel Shopping Arcade, Tel: 03-245 2050.
Gallery Cocoon (batik and artifacts), 7 Jalan Kia Peng, Tel: 03-245 0626.
Global Silk Store (batik and other fabric), Jalan Tuanku Abdul Rahman.

J Hill (Jutia jewellery), Mezzanine floor, Plaza Yow Chuan, Tel: 03-248 7137.

Karyaneka (government handicraft centre), 186-188 Jalan Raja Chulan, Tel: 243 1686.

Phoenix Syarikat, 16 Jalan Yong Shook Lin, PJ, Tel: 03-756 9195.

Royal Selangor, 4 Jalan Usahawan Enam, Setapak Jaya, Tel: 03-422 1000; The Mall, Tel: 03-442 2617; Yaohan, Tel: 03-441 2839; Plaza Ampang, Tel: 03-248 2744; Kuala Lumpur Plaza, Tel: 03-241 6844; Sogo Department Store, Tel: 03-299 6173; Isetan, Tel: 03-244 1527; Hilton Hotel, Tel: 03-248 5104; Shangri-la Hotel, Tel: 03-230 3070; Malaysia Tourist Information Complex (MATIC), Tel: 03-262 1531; Emporium Bebas Cukai, Tel: 03-282 2705; Starhill, Tel: 03-242 1495; Renaissance Hotel, Tel: 03-262 0524; Nikko Hotel, Tel: 03-261 5801; Kompleks Budaya Kraf, Tel: 03-264 7607; 54 Jalan SS2/67, Tel: 03-774 7290; Subang Parade, Tel: 03-736 2763.

Silver Presentation, 41A Jalan SS22/ 19, Damansara Jaya, PJ, Tel: 03-719 6744.

The Linen Shop (Malaysian designed Irish linen), Qualityworks, 134-1 Jalan 1/50A Taman Sri Setapak, Peti Surat, Tel: 03-421 7682.

Tumasek Pewter, Lot 16, Jalan Kanan, Taman Kepong, Tel: 03-634 1225.

Wilayah Batik, 68 Jalan 2/10B Spring Crest Industrial Park, Batu Caves, Tel: 03-687 3585.

Wisma Kraftangan (batik fabric), Jalan Tun Perak.

ART GALLERIES

Art Case Galleries, Level 3, City Square Complex, Tel: 03-263 5160.

Art House, Wisma Stephens, Jalan Raja Chulan, Tel: 03-248 2283.

Artfolio, Level 2, City Square Complex, Tel: 03-262 3339.

Artichoke, 10 Jalan Kia Peng, Tel: 03-242 4269.

BOOKSHOPS

Berita, Bukit Bintang Plaza, Tel: 03-241 6071.

Golden Books, Ground floor, Ampang Park Shopping Centre, Tel: 03-261 0910.

MPH, Bukit Bintang Plaza, Tel: 03-242 8231.

Parry's Book Centre, 60 Jalan Negara Taman Melawati, Tel: 03-407 9176.

University Cooperative Bookshop, University of Malaysia, Bangi.

NIGHT MARKETS

An integral part of shopping in KL is the pasar malam (night market). Caravan-like traders move from one spot to another selling their wares, and for those who like good bargains, jostling and pushing, it's all good fun. Always try to bargain. Here is an indication of where the markets will set up on given days of the week. However, as these locations are subject to change it is advisable to check the daily newspaper or enquire at your hotel before setting out.

Sunday: Pasar Malam Taman Tun Dr Ismail, along Jalan Tun Mohd. Fuad; Pasar Malam Taman Maluri, along Jalan Pria.

Monday: Pasar Malam Jalan Kangsar, Jalan Ipoh, along service roads and empty spaces; Pasar Malam Jalan Wira, Taman Maluri, along Jalan Wira.

Tuesday: Pasar Malam Kawasan Rumah Pangsa, 3.5th mile, Jalan Cheras, along blocks 4, 5 and 6; Pasar Malam Jalan Cemor, off Jalan Tun Razak, along Jalan Cemor; Pasar Malam Sri Petaling, along Jalan Perlak 1, Jalan Pasar 5 and 4, and Jalan Pasai.

Wednesday: Pasar Malam Bandar Baru Tun Razak, Jalan Bangsawan, along the stretch between Jalan Makmurand Jalan Ikhlas; Pasar Malam Kawasan Bukit Bangsar, along the stretch between Sri Pahang flat area and Railway Quarters; Pasar Malam Setapak Garden, along the stretch between the Surau (place of worship) and Jalan Serjak; Pasar Malam Taman Kok Lian; Jalan Ipoh, 5th Mile, on the vacant area directly opposite the shophouses.

Thursday: Pasar Malam Rumah Pangsa pkns, Jalan Kuching, the surrounding area of the departments; Pasar Malam Rumah Pangsa Sri Terengganu Sentul; Pasar Malam Taman Cheras, along the stretch between Jalan Kaskas and Jalan Chengkeh; Pasar Malam Overseas Union Garden.

Friday: Pasar Malam Kampung Cheras Baru Sentul, along Jalan Sentul; Pasar Malam Taman Desa, along Jalan Desa Utama/Jalan Desa Permai.

Saturday: Pasar Malam Bandar Tun Razak (Jalan Jujur), along Jalan Jujur Empat; Pasar Malam Kampung Pasir,

Petaling, Jalan Kelang Lama, along Jalan Kampung Pasir; Pasar Malam Setapak Jaya, along Jalan Rejang 4/ 6/7; Pasar Malam Jalan Tuanku Abdul Rahman, along Jalan Tuanku Abdul Rahman.

Note: There is a nightmarket every night (unless it rains) in Petaling Street, KL's Chinatown, and along Chow Kit Road (further up Jalan Tuanku Abdul Rahman).

Malacca

ANTIQUES

Abdul Company (furniture), 79 Jalan Hang Jebat (Jonkers Street), Tel: 06-229 099; 93 Jalan Tun Tan Cheng Lock, Tel: 06-246 676.

Chop Hin Yan (clocks), Jalan Hang Jebat (two doors from bridge intersection).

Gold Moon Coins and Curios, 76 Jalan Hang Jebat, Tel: 06-232 718.

K & S Antiques House, 22 Jalan Hang Jebat, Tel: 06-236 113.

Tay Sen Kee (furniture, jewellery, coins, porcelain etc), 105 Jalan Tun Tan Cheng Lock, Tel: 06-230 759.

Wah Aik (bound feet shoes and paintings), 92 Jalan Hang Jebat.

Yan Keng Antique Furniture, 77 Jalan Hang Jebat, Tel: 06-224 720.

SOUVENIRS & HANDICRAFTS

Ban Onn (goldsmith), 52 Jalan Hang Jebat.

Batik Mestika, (batik and handicraft), 116 Jalan Bendahara, Tel: 06-221 008.

Dragon Ho (puppets, postcards, t-shirts etc), 65 Jalan Hang Jebat .

Jonkers (artifacts and textiles), 17 Jalan Hang Jebat, Tel: 06-235 578.

Kim Lan Hiong (incense), 94 Jalan Hang Jebat.

Ong Kian Kok (incense), 30 Jalan Tunkang Emas, Tel: 06-239 287; 20 Jalan Tokong, Tel: 06-225 798.

Pusat Cendera Mata Yoon (souvenirs), 98 Jalan Hang Jebat.

Penang

Street bazaars: jewellery, general goods, antiques, handicraft, pottery, rattan etc. can be found along Jalan Penang, Lebuh Campbell, Jalan Mesjid Kapian Keling, Lebuh Chulia, Tanjung Bungah, Lebuh Pantai, Lebuh Queen, as well as Pasa Chowrasta and Kek Lok Si in Little India.

Art Gallery, 7 Gottlieb Road, Tel: 04-368 219.

City Chemist (pharmacy), Sub basement, Sunshine Square, Jalan Mahsuri, Tel: 04-838 663.

Eastern Curios (antiques), 35 Lbn Bishop, Tel: 04-615 625.

Guardian (pharmacy), ground floor, Penang Plaza, 126 Jalan Burmah, Tel: 04-288 2805.

Kim How (jewellery), 9-11 Campbell Street, Tel: 04-617 551.

Komtar (shopping complex), Jalan Penang, Georgetown.

Pinang Cultural Centre Bazaar (handicraft and souvenirs), 1 Jalan Teluk Bahang, 11050 Teluk Bahang, Tel: 04-811 175 (closed Fridays).

Royal Selangor (pewter), E&O Hotel Arcade, Lbh Farquhar, Tel: 04-636 742; Park Royal Hotel, Batu Ferringhi, Tel: 04-811 133.

Silver Crown (coin dealer), 3h Jalan Penang, Tel: 04-620 510.

Sim's Arts & Souvenir, 391 Batu Ferringhi, Tel: 04-811 697.

The Tower, (shopping complex), Georgetown. The Tower Tourist Centre on level 58 has handicraft, souvenirs and a viewing gallery.

Johor Bahru

Amran Batek Emporium (batik), Kompleks Tuanku Abdul Razak, Tel: 07-441 4421.

Apex (pharmacy), F120 Holiday Plaza, Century Garden, Jalan Dato Sulaiman, Tel: 07-331 0531.

Beta Sykt (batik), Bangmara, Tel: 07-222 4341.

Craftown (handicrafts), Jalan Scudai, Tel: 07-336 7346.

Guardian (pharmacy), Level 1 (lot 1.16) Plaza Pelan-gi, 2 Jalan Kuning, Taman Pelangi, Tel: 07-331 7721.

Hwa Ee (art gallery), 8 Jalan Sutera 2, Tel: 07-331 4281.

Fancy Bits (souvenirs), Holiday Plaza, Jalan Dato Sulaiman, Tel: 07-331 1503.

JARO (handicrafts, leather book binding to order), Jalan Sungai Chat, Tel: 07-224 5632.

Johore Central Bookstore, Level 1, Kotaraya shopping complex, Jalan Abdullah Ibrahim.

Koleksi Tok Sheikh (antiques), 57 Jalan Waspada Taman Selat Tebrau, Tel: 07-223 2624.

Kotaraya (shopping centre), Jalan Abdullah Ibrahim.

Pelangi Plaza (shopping centre), Jalan Kuning, Taman Pelangi, Tel: 07-331 5929.

Pusat Kraftangan (handicrafts), Taman Mini Malaysia, Air Keroh.

Royal Selangor (pewter), Pelangi Plaza, 2 Jalan Kuning Tmn Pelangi, Tel: 07-334 458.

Seni Pusaka (handicrafts), Corner Jalan Khalid Abdullah.

Kota Kinabalu

At the Filipino market on the waterfront you can buy from sea chandeliers to dried fish and on Sundays Gaya Street becomes an open market selling everything from kitchenware to antiques. The **Gaya Street Fair**, held every Sunday morning, is an excellent place for browsing. Everything from fresh fruit and orchids to live puppies and handicrafts.

Centrepoint Shopping Centre, corner Lebuh Raya Pantai and Jalan Centrepoint. Sabah's biggest shjopping complex, with wide range of shops inclding Yaohan Department Store and western fast food outlets.

Nusantara, Ground floor, No. 69, centrepoint Shopping Centre. Good selection of quality antiques from all areas of Borneo.

Borneo Craft, Ground floor, Wisma Merdeka. Selection of local handicrafts and souvenirs, and good selection of quality books on Asia.

Filipino Market, south of Central Market. All kinds Filipino handicrafts including basketware, and some Indonesian batik fabrics. Bargaining essential.

Sabah Tourism Promotion Corporation, 55 Jalan Gaya. Shop off entrance lobby has excellent selection of local handicrafts as well as books.

MARKETS IN SABAH

The tamu is a town market in Sabah that brings farmers and their wives down from the hills to sell their produce. Bajau cowboys come to the tamu to buy and sell horses, and there are also buffaloes for sale. A colourful array of fruit and vegetables are sold alongside betel nut, baskets, and household goods. Tamus were encouraged by the British colonial government, as they brought people from remote tribes together. If you are travelling in Sabah, you will be bound to come upon the weekly tamu in a town centre. It is best to go early in the morning when the most heated selling takes place.

Here is a list of the main tamu and the days which they are held:

Babaggon (Saturday), Beaufort (Saturday), Keningau (Thursday), Kinarut (Saturday), Kionsom (Sunday), Kiulu (Tuesday), Kota Belud (Sunday), Kota Merudu (Sunday), Kuala Penyu (1st Wednesday of the month), Kundasang (20th of the month), Mangis (Thursday), Mattunggon (Saturday), Membakut (Sunday), Mersapol (Friday), Papar (Sunday), Penampang (Saturday), Putatan (Sunday), Ranau (1st of the month), Sequati (Sunday), Simpangan (Thursday), Sindumin (Saturday), Sinsuran (Friday), Sipitang (Thursday), Tambunan (Thursday), Tamparuli (Wednesday), Tandek (Monday), Telipok (Thursday), Tenghilan (Thursday), Tenom (Sunday), Tinnopok (15th and 30th of the month), Toboh (Sunday), Topokom (Tuesday), Tuaran (Sunday), Weston (Friday).

Kuching

Main Bazaar, the road running alongside the river opposite the Waterfront Park, has an increasing number of souvenir and antique stores with local handicrafts and antiques. Thian Seng, 48 Main Bazaar, and Nelson's Gallery, 84 Main Bazaar, both specialise in primitive art. Fabrika has interesting fabrics and clothing. Inside the old Sarawak Steamship Company building on the Waterfront side of Main Bazaar are a number of stalls specialising in souvenirs and handicrafts.

The **Sunday Market**, held on Saturday night and not on Sunday, is lively bazaar as interesting for local colour as for the knick knacks you might pick up there.

River Majestic Shopping Complex, Jalan Tunku Abdul Rahaman. Next to Riverside Hotel, this complex is Kuching's newest and features Parkson's department store.

Sarawak Museum Shop, located inside new block of the museum, the shop sells local handicrafts, books and souvenirs.

Sarawak Plaza, located next to Holiday Inn Kuching, this complex has a department store, basement supermarket, fast food outlets, camera store and antique shop.

Sports

Participant Sports

Malaysia is a land of sports. A visitor can enjoy a game of football at an urban field or witness a top-spinning contest in a rural village. Badminton nets are erected on almost every vacant lot available, and not having the right equipment will never deter the sporty Malays from playing the game with improvised rackets and shuttlecocks. For those wishing to participate in a sport, there are abundant facilities throughout the country.

Fishing

There is good angling to be had in the numerous river tributaries which indent the country's coastline. Marine game fishes such as barracuda, shark and Spanish mackerel may be sighted off the east coast of the peninsula from May to October.

If your trip does not allow you enough time for the trial-and-error process of finding a good fishing hole, contact a local tour agent (see Useful Addresses) specialising in arranging fishing trips to the Taman Negara (National Park). For inland fishing, a licence is required. The months between March and October provide the most suitable weather conditions.

Golfing

Malaysia has over 100 golf clubs with 9 or 18-hole courses, with a further 50 courses presently under construction. Some of the more prominent ones are listed below.

KUALA LUMPUR

Kelab Golf Perkhidmatan Awam (KGPA), Bukit Kiara, Off Jalan Damansara, 60000 KL, Tel: 03-757 5310/4484.
Kelab Golf Titiwangsa Polis Diraja Malaysia, Pusat Latihan Polis, 50768 KL, Tel: 03-293 4964.

Kuala Lumpur Golf and Country Club, Jalan 10/70D. Off Jalan Bukit Kiara, 60000 KL, Tel: 03-253 1111.
Kundang Lakes Country Club, 7th floor, Wisma Datuk Dagang, Jalan Raja Alang, 50300 KL, Tel: 03-292 6026.
Palm Resort, Letter Box 18, 9th floor, rhb 1 424 Jalan Tun Razak, 50400 KL, Tel: 03-983 6833.
Royal Selangor Golf Club, P.O. Box 11051, 50734 KL, Tel: 03-984 8433. Course: 54-hole.
Sentul Golf Club KL, 84 Jalan Strachan Sentul, 51100 KL, Tel: 03-441 8991. Course: 9-hole Private.
Tropicana Golf and Country Resort, Level 115, Shahzan Prudential Tower, No 30, Jalan Sultan Ismail, 50250 KL, Tel: 03-242 2622.

SELANGOR

Carey Island Golf Club, West Estate Sport Club, 42960 Davey Island, Kuala Langat, Selangor, Tel: 03-331 8611. Course: 9-hole Private.
Club Rahman Putra Malaysia, 13.5, Jalan Kuala Selangor, 47000 Sungai Buloh, Selangor, Tel: 03-656 6870.
Glenmarie Golf and Country Club, 1, Jalan Glenmarie, Off Jalan Lapangan Terbang Antarabangsa Subang, 46740 Petaling Jaya, Tel: 03-703 9090.
Kelab Darul Ehsan Taman Tun Razak, Jalan Kerja Air Lama, Ampang Jaya, 68000 Ampang, Selangor, Tel: 03-457 2333. Course: 9-hole Proprietary. Night golf.
Kelab Golf and Country Kuala Kubu Bharu, P.O. Box 203, 44000 Kuala Kubu Bharu, Selangor, Tel: 03-804 2887.
Kelab Golf Negara Subang, P.O. Box 151, 46710 Petaling Jaya, Tel: 03-776 0388. Course: 36-hole Private.
Kelab Golf Sri Morib, 42700 Banting, Kuala Langat, Selangor, Tel: 03-858 1732.
Kelab Golf Sultan Abdul Aziz Shah, Peti Surat 7267, 40708 Shah Alam, Selangor, Tel: 03-550 5872. Course: 27-hole. Night golf.
Kuala Kubu Baru Golf and Country Club, P.O. Box 203, 44000 Kuala Kubu Baru, Selangor, Tel: 03-804 2887. Course: 9-hole Private.
Palm Garden Golf Club, Batu 7, Jalan Kajang Puchong, 43000 Kajang, Selangor, Tel: 03-948 7160.
Perangsang Templer Golf Club, No 1, Jalan Ipoh-Rawang, 20 Taman Rekreasi Templer, 48000 Rawang,

Selangor, Tel: 03-691 0022.
Saujana Golf and Country Club, Batu 3 Jalan Lapangan Terbang, 47200 Subang, Tel: 03-746 1466. Course: 36-hole Proprietory.
Serendah Golf Links, 38, Jalan Kuala Lumpur Ipoh, 48200 Serendah, Ulu Selangor, Tel: 03-601 1600.
Sri Morib Golf Club, Morib, 427000 Banting, Selangor, Tel: 03-858 1732.
Sungai Long Golf and Country Club, 11th Mile Jalan Cheras, 43200 Kajang, Selangor, Tel: 03-837 3733.
Templer Park Country Club, 21, Jalan Rawang, 4800 Selangor, Tel: 03-691 9617. Course: 18-hole. 9-hole night golf.
Tropicana Golf and Country Resort, Jalan Tropicana, Off Jalan Tropicana Utama, Bandar Tropicana, 47410 Petaling Jaya, Selangor, Tel: 03-245 0088.

NEGRI SEMBILAN

Gemas Golf Resort, Batu 2.5, Jalan Tampin, 73400 Gemas, Negeri Sembilan, Tel: 07-981 144.
Kelab Golf Diraja Sri Mananti, 71550 Sri Menanti, Kuala Pilah, NS, Tel: 06-889 600.
Port Dickson Golf and Country Club, 71050 Si Rusa, 5.5 Jalan Pantai, Port Dickson, Tel: 06-473 586/475 537. Course: 27-hole.
Royal Sri Menanti Golf and Country Club, 71550 Sri Menanti, Negeri Sembilan, Tel: 06-889 374.
Seremban International Golf Club, 37 Jalan Kuala Pilah, 70400 Seremban, Negeri Sembilan, Tel: 06-775 787, 775 277.
Seremban Golf Resort, Suite 7.03 7th floor, Bangunan Yayasan Negeri Sembilan, Jalan Yam Tuan, 70000 Seremban, Tel: 06-739 277. Course: 18-hole.
Staffield Country Resort, Batu 13, Jalan Seremban, 71700 Mantin, Tel: 03-816 6117. Course: 27-hole.
Tuanku Jaafar Golf and Country Resort, 71450 Sungai Gadut, Seremban, Negeri Sembilan, Tel: 06-771 777.

MALACCA

Ayer Keroh Country Club, Jalan Ayer Keroh, 75750 Malacca, Tel: 06-324 351/320 822. Course: 18-hole Private.
Golden Valley Golf and Country Club, 24 Air Panas, 77200 Bemban, Tel: 010-601 0333.

Jasin Golf Club, P.O. Box 2, Jasin, 77000 Malacca, Tel: 06-593 413. Course: 9-hole Private.

PENANG

Bukit Jambul Country Club, 2 Jalan Bukit Jambul Lepas, Tel: 04-842 255. Course: 9-hole Proprietory.

Bukit Jawi Golf Resort, 691, Main Road, 14200 Sg. Bakap, Seberang Prai Selatan, Tel: 04-582 2611/12. Course: 36-hole.

PERAK

Bukit Jana Golf and Country Club, Jalan Bukit Jana, 34600 Kamunting, Perak, Tel: 05-883 7500.

Idris Shah Golf Club, Teluk Intan, 28 Jalan Changkat Jong, 36000 Teluk Intan, Perak, Tel: 05-621 238. Course: 9-hole Private.

Kelab Golf Batang Padang, Perak, d/a Lapadang Terbang Bidor, Batu 43 Jalan Tapah, 35500 Bidor, Perak.

Kelab Golf Darul Ridzuan, Jalan Bukit Meru, Off Jalan Jelapang, Ipoh, 30020 Perak, Tel: 05-526 3377.

Kelab Golf Kuala Kangsar, 11 Jalan Sultan Iskandar Shah, 33000 Kuala Kangsar, Perak Darul Ridzuan, Tel: 05-776 2396.

Kelab Golf Samudera, Pangkalan tldm, 32100 Lumut, Perak Darul Ridzuan, Tel: 05-935 201.

Kelab Golf Kinta, Jalan Changkat, 31000 Batu Gajah, Perak, Tel: 05-683 520 ext 2585. Course: 9-hole Private.

The New Club, P.O. Box 42, 34007 Taiping, Perak, Tel: 05-823 935. Course: 9-hole Private.

Pan Pacific Resort, Teluk Belanga (Golden Sands) 32300 Pangkor Island, Perak, Tel: 05-685 1091/1399. Course: 9-hole.

Royal Perak Golf Club, Jalan Sultan Azlan Shah, 31400 Ipoh, Perak, Tel: 05-573 266. Course: 18-hole Private.

The New Club, P.O. Box 42, 34007 Taiping, Perak Darul Ridzwan, Tel: 05-823 935.

KEDAH

Cinta Sayang Golf and Country Club, Persiaran Cinta Sayang 08000 Sungai Petani, Kedah Darul Aman, Tel: 04-414 666.

Datai Bay Golf Club, Teluk Datai, 07000 Pulau Langkawi, Kedah, Tel: 04-959 2700/2620.

Dublin Club, Karangan, 09700 Kedah, Tel: 04-546 233. Course: 9-hole Private.

Harvard Club, 08100 Bedong, Kedah, Tel: 04-481 026. Course: 9-hole Private.

Jerai Golf and Country Club, 08100 Bedong, Kedah, Tel: 04-458 1504.

Kedah Golf Association, c/o Kelab Golf Diraja Pumpong, 05250 Alor Setar, Kedah, Fax: 04-737 979.

Kelab Golf Langkawi, Pulau Langkawi, Kedah, Tel: 04-788 195.

Langkawi Golf Club, Jalan Bukit Malut, 07000 Pulau Langkawi, Kedah, Tel: 04-966 7195. Course: 9-hole Public.

Royal Kedah Club, Pumpong, 05250 Alor Setar, Tel: 04-733 0467. Course: 9-hole Private.

Sungai Petani Golf Club, Jalan Sungai Kayar, 0800 Sungai Patani, Kedah, Tel: 04-420 960. Course: 9-hole Private.

PERLIS

Kelab Golf Putra Perlis, Kelab Peti Surat No. 6, 01700 Kangar, Perlis, Tel: 04-976 9660. Course: 9-hole Private.

KELANTAN

Kelab Golf Desa Pahlawan, d/a Wisma Perwira, Markas Staf Stesen, Kem Desa Pahlawan, 16450 Kota Bharu, Kelantan, Tel: 09-978 200.

Royal Kelantan Golf Club, 5488 Jalan Hospital, 15000 Kota Bharu, Kelantan, Tel: 09-743 8335/748 2102.

TERENGGANU

Dungun Country Golf Club, Suru Ulong, P.O. Box 679, 23007 Dungun, Tel: 09-844 1041. Course: 9-hole Private.

Kelab Desa Rantau Petronas, c/o Petronas East Coast Regional Office, 3rd floor, Petronas Office Complex, 24300 Kertih, Kemaman, Terengganu, Tel: 09-540 232.

Kelab Golf Desa Dungun, P.O. Box 679, 23000 Dungun, Terengganu, Tel: 09-844 1041.

Kerteh Golf Club, Rantau Petronas, Kerteh 24000 Kemaman, Tel: 09-671 357. Course: 9-hole Public.

Royal Terengganu Golf Club (Kelab Golf Diraja Terengganu) Jalan Sultan Mahmud, 20400 Kuala Terengganu, Tel: 09-629 393.

PAHANG

Awana Golf and Country Club, Genting Highlands, 69000 Pahang, Tel: 03-211 3222. Course: 18-hole Proprietory.

Bentong Golf Club, Batu 2 Jalan Tras, P.O. Box 24, 28707 Bentong, Tel: 09-222 585. Course: 9-hole Private.

Cameron Highlands Golf Course, 39000 Tanah Rata, Cameron Highlands, Pahang, Tel: 05-901 126. Course: 18-hole Private.

De Club At Fraser's, 49000 Bukit Fraser, Tel: 09-382 777, Course: 9-hole.

Fraser's Hill Golf Course, c/o Fraser's Hill Development Corpn., 49000 Fraser's Hill, Tel: 09-382 044. Course: 9-hole Public.

Kelab Golf Diraja Pahang, Jalan Teluk Chempedak, 25700 Kuantan, Pahang, Tel: 09-555 811. Course: 9-hole Private.

Kelab Golf Darul Makmur Diraja Pekan, Jalan Istana Abu Bakar, 26600 Pekan, Pahang, Tel: 09-421 601.

Kelab Golf Seri Mahkota, Kem Batu 3, Temerluh 28000, Pahang, Tel: 09-271 733.

Lanjut Golden Beach Golf Resort, Kampung Lanjut, 26800 Kuala Rompin, Tel: 09-414 5113. Course 27-hole.

Pulau Tioman Island Club, Pulau Tioman, 86807 Mersing, Johor, Tel: 09-445 445. Course: 9-hole Public.

Selesa Golf Course, 3 Bukit Tinggi, 69000 Genting Highlands, Pahang, Tel: 09-233 0039/42.

Raub Golf Club, Jalan Bukit Koman, P.O. Box 7, 27600 Pahang, Tel: 09-354 1066, 09-351 937. Course: 9-hole Private.

Royal Pahang Golf Club, Jalan Teluk Chempedak, 25700 Kuantan, Tel: 09-555 811.

JOHOR

Desaru Golf and Country Club, Tanjong Penawar, 81907 Kota Tinggi, Johor, Tel: 07-822 1445/1187. Course: 18-hole Proprietory.

Gagak Golf Club, Segamat, P.O. Box 22, Segamat, 85000 Johor, Tel: 07-911 442. Course: 9-hole Private.

Kelab Golf Batu Pahat, 678, Jalan Dato Mohd. Shah, 83000 Batu Pahat, Tel: 07-222 2022. Course: 9-hole Private.

Kelab Golf Tanjong Emas, Muar, No. JKR 202, Jalan Timbalan, Muar, 84000 Johor, Tel: 06-924 838, 06-922 190. Course: 9-hole Private.

Kluang Country Club, Jalan Mengkibol, 86000 Kluang, Johor, Tel: 07-718 840. Course: 9-hole Private.

Kukup Golf Resort, Pekan Penerok, 82300 Pontian, Tel: 07-696 0952/53/54. Course: 36-hole.

Mersing Hills Golf and Country Club, Jalan Mengkibol, 86000 Kluang, Johor, Tel: 07-428 6801.

Palm Resort Golf and Country Club, Jalan Persiaran Golf, 81250 Senai, Johor, Tel: 07-599 6222.

Royal Johor Country Club, Jalan Larkin, 80200 Johor Bahru, Johor, Tel: 07-223 3322/224 2090. Course: 18-hole Private.

Sagil Golf Club, Sagil Estate, Tangkak, 84900 Johor, Tel: 06-972 331/2. Course: 9-hole Private.

Starhill Golf and Country Club, 6.5 KM, Kg. Maju Jaya, Kempas Lama, 81330 Sekudai, Johor Bahru, Johor, Tel: 07-556 6325/6326.

Tanjung Puteri Golf and Country Club, Pasir Gudang, 81700 Johor Bahru, Johor, 07-251 3533. Course: 18- and 36-hole.

The Batu Pahat Golf Club, 678 Jalan Dato Mohd Shah, 83000 Batu Pahat, Johor, Tel: 07-442 220.

Tioman Island Golf Club, Pulau Tioman, P.O.Box 4, 86807 Mersing, Tel: 09-445 445.

Ulu Remis GCC, Ulu Remis Estate, P.O. Box 103, 81850 Layang-Layang, Johor. Course: 9-hole Private.

SABAH

Kelab Golf Kudat, 89050 Kudat. Course: 9-hole Private.

Keningau Golf Club, P.O. Box 94, 89000 Keningau, Tel: 088-331 113. Course: 9-hole Private.

Kinabalu Golf Club, P.O. Box 654, Kota Kinabalu, Tel: 088-55199, 088-51615. Course: 9-hole Private.

Sabah Golf & Country Club, P.O. Box 11876, Kota Kinabalu, Tel: 088-56900, 088-56533. Course: 18-hole Private.

The Sandakan Golf Club, P.O. Box 541, 90007 Sandakan, Tel: 088-660 557. Course: 9-hole Private.

SARAWAK

Kelab Golf Miri, Jalan Datuk Patinggi, 90800 Miri, Sarawak, Tel: 082-416 787, 085-417 848. Course: 18-hole Private.

Prisons Golf Club, Jalan Penrissen, 93250 Kuching, Sarawak, Tel: 082-613 544.

Sibu Golf Club, 10-Mile P.O. Box 1234, 96008 Sibu, Tel: 084-326 666.

Course: 9-hole Private.

The Sarawak Golf & Country Club, Petra Jaya, 93050 Kuching, Tel: 082-23622, 082-443 398. Course: 18-hole Private.

Hunting

Hunting is restricted in many areas and is subject to a licence from the Department of Wildlife and National Parks in Kuala Lumpur, Tel: 03-941272. There are hundreds of protected animal species in Malaysia. Obtain more information from the Parks Office.

Martial Arts

The popularity of karate with the locals has led to the growth of over 150 karate centres in Malaysia. Visitors who wish to try their hand at it can make special arrangements with the Chief Instructor at the Karate Budokun International (kbi) in Kuala Lumpur (Tel: 03-81470).

Watersports

Scuba-diving is catching on in Malaysia, and you will find scuba centres in most developed beach resorts such as Tioman, Langkawi, and Desaru, to name a few. Some centres also teach scuba-diving and you can gain an internationally recognised certificate. Equipment can be hired for scuba-diving, sailing, wind-surfing, snorkelling and water skiing. Check with a resort by phone first. Snorkelling equipment can be bought cheaply in local shops.

Horse Racing

Meetings are held on weekends and public holidays, rotating between Kuala Lumpur, Ipoh, Penang and Singapore. Betting is part of the attraction.

Silat

Silat is the Malay equivalent of kung fu. The origin of this self-defense art is accredited to the famous Hang Tuah of old Malacca, who did not hesitate to draw his sword, and even to strike to kill, for justice's sake. Youths today regard silat as a form of physical exercise in an artistic form. Demonstrations at weddings and other feasts are given to the rhythmic beat of gongs and drums. It is also part of the school curriculum for boys.

Language

General

When speaking Malay, you need a few basic rules. Adjectives always follow the noun. *Rumah* (house) and *besar* (big) together as *rumah besar* means "a big house" and so on. When constructing a sentence, the order is subject-verb-subject: *Dia* (he) *makan* (eats) *nasi* (rice) *goreng* (fried). *Dia makan nasi goreng* = He eats fried rice. The traditional greeting in Malay is not "hello!" but rather *Ke mana?* - "Where are you going?" The question is merely a token of friendliness which does not require a specific answer. One simply returns the smile by replying *Tak ada ke mana* - "Nowhere in particular" - and passes on.

Below are some general guidelines for th pronunciation of Malay, or Bahasa Malaysia as it is known here. No written descriptions of the phonetics can replace the guidance of a native speaker, but once you've tried pronouncing a few words, Malaysians are quick to understand and their responds is the best way to pick up a feeling for the language.

a is pronounced short as in *matter* or *cat*. *apa* – what; *makan* – eat

ai is pronounced like the sound in *aisle*. *kedai* – shop; *sungai* – river

au sounds like the *ow* of *how*. *pulau* – island; *jauh* – far

c is pronounced like *ch* as in *chat*. *capal* – sandal; *cinta* – love

e is very soft, hardly pronounced at all. *membeli* – to buy; *besar* – big

g is pronounced as in *go*, never as in *gem*. *pergi* – go; *guru* – teacher

gg is pronounced as *ng* plus a hard *g* sound: i.e. *sing-ging*. *ringgit* – Malaysian dollar; *tetangga* – household

h is pronounced as in *halt*. *mahal* – expensive; *murah* – cheap

i sounds like *i* in *machine* or *ee* in *feet*. *minum* – to drink; *lagi* – again

310

j sounds like the English *j* in judge. *Jalan* – Street; *juta* – million

ng a single *g* in a word is pronounced like the *ng* in *sing*, not with a hard sound. *sangat* – very; *bunga* – flower

ny is similar to *ni* in *onion* or *n* in *news*. *harganya* – price; *banyak* – a lot

o is most similar to the *o* in *hop*. *orang* – human being; *tolong* – help

u is pronounced as *oo* in *pool*. *tujuh* – seven; *minum* – to drink

y sounds like *y* in *young*, never as in *why*. *wayang* – opera; *kaya* – rich

There is no specific syllabic stress in Malay as in English (i.e. *na*-tion, not na-*tion*), nearly all syllables are given equal stress; however, the Malays add to their speech a sing-song intonation which often gives more emphasis to the final syllable of a word, especially the last word in a utterance. This has led to the widespread use of the appendage – *lah* to the important word. This can either charm or irritate the visitor! Its purpose is purely emphatic, and it is now used generally in Malaysia, whether the speaker is talking in Malay, Chinese, Tamil or even English! Perhaps the most famous example of this is the phrase "Cannot-lah!", uttered when you have asked something the speaker considers impossible!

Useful Phrases

Good morning./*Selamat pagi.*
Good afternoon./*Selamat tengah hari.*
Good evening./*Selamat petang.*
Please come in./*Sila masuk.*
Please sit down./*Sila duduk.*
Thank you./*Terima kasih.*
You're welcome./*Sama-sama.*
Where do you come from?/*Anda datang dari mana?*
I come from.../*Saya datang dari...*
What is your name?/*Siapa nama anda?*
My name is.../*Nama saya...*
Can you speak Malay?/*Boleh anda bercakap dalam Bahasa Malaysia?*
Yes./*Ya.*
No./*Tidak.*
Only a little./*Sedikit sahaja.*
I want to learn more./*Saya hendak belajar lebih lagi.*
How do you find Malaysia?/*Apakah pendapat anda mengenai Malaysia?*
I like it here./*Saya suka berada di sini.*

The weather is hot, isn't it?/*Cuaca di sini panas, bukan?*
Yes, a little?/*Ya, sedikit.*
Where are you going?/*Pergi ke mana?*
I am going to.../*Saya pergi ke...*
Turn right./*Belok ke kanan.*
Turn left./*Belok ke kiri.*
Go straight./*Jalan terus.*
Please stop here./*Sila berhenti di sini.*
How much?/*Berapa?*
Wait a minute./*Tunggu sekejap.*
I have to change money./*Saya hendak tukar duit.*
Excuse me./*Maafkan saya.*
Where is the toilet?/*Di mana tandas?*
In the back./*Di belakang.*
Where may I get something to drink?/*Di mana boleh saya minum?*
Over there./*Di sana.*
One cup of coffee./*Kopi secawan.*
One cup of tea./*Teh secawan.*
Fried noodles./*Mee goreng.*
Fried rice./*Nasi goreng.*
The food was tasty./*Makanan tadi sedap.*
How much does this cost?/*Berapakah harganya?*
Ten dollars./*Sepuluh ringgit.*
That's quite expensive./*Mahal sangat.*
Can you make it less?/*Boleh kurangkan?*
Seven dollars./*Tujuh ringgit.*
Fine./*Baiklah.*
I'll buy it./*Saya nak membelinya.*
Good-bye./*Selamat tinggal.*
I am sorry./*Saya minta maaf.*

Useful words

Mr/*Encik, Tuan, Saudara*
Mrs/*Puan*
Miss/*Puan, Cik, Saudari*
I/*Saya*
you (friendly)/*awak, anda*
you (formal)/*encik*
he, she/*dia*
we/*kami/kita*
they/*mereka*
what?/*apa?*
who?/*siapa?*
where (place)/*di mana?*
where (direction)/*ke mana?*
when?/*bila?*
how?/*bagaimana?*
why?/*mengapa?*
which?/*yang mana?*
how much?/*berapa?*
to eat/*makan*
to drink/*minum*
to sleep/*tidur*
to bathe/*mandi*

to come/*datang*
to go/*pergi*
to stop/*berhenti*
to buy/*beli (membeli)*
to sell/*jual (menjual)*
road/*jalan*
airport/*lapangan terbang*
post office/*pejabat pos*
shop/*kedai*
coffee shop/*kedai kopi*
money/*wang, duit*
dollar/*ringgit*
cent/*sen*

Numbers

1/*satu*
2/*dua*
3/*tiga*
4/*empat*
5/*lima*
6/*enam*
7/*tujuh*
8/*lapan*
9/*sembilan*
10/*sepuluh*
11/*sebelas*
12/*dua belas*
13/*tiga belas*
20/*dua puluh*
21/*dua puluh satu*
22/*dua puluh dua*
23/*dua puluh tiga*
30/*tiga puluh*
40/*empat puluh*
58/*lima puluh lapan*
100/*seratus*
263/*dua ratus eman puluh tiga*
1,000/*seribu*

Index

The Insight Approach

The book you are holding is part of the world's largest range of guidebooks. Its purpose is to help you have the most valuable travel experience possible, and we try to achieve this by providing not only information about countries, regions and cities but also genuine insight into their history, culture, institutions and people.

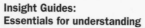

Since the first Insight Guide – to Bali – was published in 1970, the series has been dedicated to the proposition that, with insight into a country's people and culture, visitors can both enhance their own experience and be accepted more easily by their hosts. Now, in a world where ethnic hostilities and nationalist conflicts are all too common, such attempts to increase understanding between peoples are more important than ever.

Insight Guides:
Essentials for understanding
Because a nation's past holds the key to its present, each Insight Guide kicks off with lively history chapters. These are followed by magazine-style essays on culture and daily life. This essential background information gives readers the necessary context for using the main Places section, with its comprehensive run-down on things worth seeing and doing. Finally, a listings section contains all the information you'll need on travel, hotels, restaurants and opening times.

As far as possible, we rely on local writers and specialists to ensure that the information is authoritative. The pictures, for which Insight Guides have become so celebrated, are just as important. Our photojournalistic approach aims not only to illustrate a destination but also to communicate visually and directly to readers life as it is lived by the locals.

Compact Guides
The "great little guides"
As invaluable as such background information is, it isn't always fun to carry an Insight Guide through a crowded souk or up a church tower. Could we, readers asked, distil the key reference material into a slim volume for on-the-spot use?

Our response was to design Compact Guides as an entirely new series, with original text carefully cross-referenced to detailed maps and more than 200 photographs. In essence, they're miniature encyclopedias, concise and comprehensive, displaying reliable and up-to-date information in an accessible way.

Pocket Guides:
A local host in book form
However wide-ranging the information in a book, human beings still value the personal touch. Our editors are often asked the same questions. Where do *you* go to eat? What do *you* think is the best beach? What would you recommend if I have only three days? We invited our local correspondents to act as "substitute hosts" by revealing their preferred walks and trips, listing the restaurants they go to and structuring a visit into a series of timed itineraries.

The result is our Pocket Guides, complete with full-size fold-out maps. These 100-plus titles help readers plan a trip precisely, particularly if their time is short.

Exploring with Insight:
A valuable travel experience
In conjunction with co-publishers all over the world, we print in up to 10 languages, from German to Chinese, from Danish to Russian. But our aim remains simple: to enhance your travel experience by combining our expertise in guidebook publishing with the on-the-spot knowledge of our correspondents.